Home-coming of the Heart

(1932-1992)

Part-II of

The Road to Mecca

Muhammad Asad
Pola Hamida Asad

Edited and annotated: M.Ikram Chaghatai

Pakistan Writers Cooperative Society, Lahore

ISBN: 978-969-8460-41-9
978-969-9363-02-3

Third Edition 2023
Edited and Annotated M.Ikram Chaghatai
Cover Design Muhammad Javed
Price Rs. 1400.00
US $ 25.00

Publishers: **Pakistan Writers Cooperative Society**
Lahore-Pakistan

Sole Distributors: **Coopera Book Centre and Art Gallery**
70-Shahrah-e-Quaid-e-Azam, Lahore-Pakistan

Phone: 0092-042-37321161 / 37322926
e-mail: info@cooperaartgallery.com

Printers: Maktaba Jadeed Press, Lahore-Pakistan

Dedicated

To the learned ***Asadians*** of Saudi Arabia:
Saudi Arabia: The real " Home " of Muhammad Asad

ISLAM
UND ABENDLAND

BEGEGNUNG ZWEIER WELTEN

EINE VORTRAGSFOLGE
HERAUSGEGEBEN
VON MUHAMMAD ASAD UND
HANS ZBINDEN

"Islam and Occident: Meeting of two Worlds", a German book, edited by Muhammad Asad and Hans Zbinden (Switzerland, 1960), in which Muhammad Asad contributed three articles)

CONTENTS

PREFACE

Grandson of a Jewish rabbi and a Muslim convert Leopold Weiss *alias* Muhamamd Asad's (Lwów, 12.7.1900–Malaga, 20.2.1992) *The Road to Mecca*[1] (=*The Road*) appeared in 1954, and its merits and demerits were widely discussed. The reviewers and some known *Asadians* opined but differently like: essentially a "spiritual autobiography" (Pola Hamida Asad),[2] an impressive travelogue spiced with a virtuosity of literary technique (Ismā'il Ibrāhīm Nawwāb),[3] its narration is intimate and penetrating (*Times Literary Supplement*),[4] a book trenchant with adventure magnificently described (*Christian Science Monitor*),[5] a very rare and powerful book that raised completely above the ordinary by its candor and intelligence (*New York Post*),[6] a combination of memoir and travelogue (Martin Kramer),[7] intensely interesting and moving book (*The New York Herald Tribune Book Review*),[8] a book placed in the pantheon of Arabian literature (*The New York Times*),[9] a patchwork of newspaper articles or cuttings strung together for a new[s] story (H. St. John "Abdallah" Philby),[10] a famous conversion account and its charm lies in the rich and evocative description of Arabian life (Marcia K. Hermansen)[11] and an elegant admixture of fact and fiction and its scenes rather difficult to differentiate between them.[12]

Apart from these diverse comments, one can hardly deny the readability of this moving autobiography and its spontaneous flow of narration. The whole story is so gripping and interesting that the readers consider them as Asad's companions.

However, for the evaluation of this extraordinary book, one must keep in mind the romantic environment in which it was written. In 1952, Muhammad Asad resigned from the diplomatic service of Pakistan in UNO, divorced his Arabian wife, Munira bint Ḥusain ash-Shammarī (d. 1978)[13] and married Pola Hamida Kazimirska (1926-2006), a Bostonian and an American convert to Islam.[14] At the first sight (May 7, 1952), Asad fell in love with this young and beautiful woman whose appearance caused his heart to contract in a strange way. He was completely ensnared by her beauty. Finally he abandoned the diplomatic job of high rank and permanently broke the relationship with his family. After breaking all these social chains, he achieved his ultimate 'goal' and on 1st November 1952, Pola moved to his apartment in New York as his most beloved wife. Here, the married couple resided for two years. Post-marriage romantic atmosphere and the companionship of a charming young bride provided a stimulus to Asad to sit down and start writing. So, towards the end of 1954, except the final chapter, *The Road* was practically finished, and dedicated to Pola. The inimitable narrative style and its certain parts are reminiscent of this early time of their marriage.

After the publication of *The Road*, it was soon recognized as the best book on the subject and his reputation in the world reached its pinnacle. As it covers the author's life-story from his birth (1900) upto his departure from Saudi Arabia (1932), some of his close associates, intimate friends, learned persons and serious readers strongly suggested him to write down its sequel (from 1932 onwards). His wife, Pola, had been trying to persuade him to write a second volume of memoirs starting with the period when he left Saudi Arabia for India (1932).[15] One of his early reviewers expressed his hope that "some day when diplomatic discretion permits, Mr. Asad will carry his story beyond 1932."[16] After reading *The Road*, another reviewer was deeply moved by author's narrative and indirectly contacted him. In his letter [1981?], he expressed the hope that he would continue his life story from where he left off in this book. Asad replied, "I have promised my wife, who has been insisting for a long time that I should continue and complete my years in India and Pakistan……Please pray that God will allow me to accomplish this work."[17] After Asad's demise, the same reviewer wrote to Pola who informed him that the sequel of *The Road*, was partially completed –part one– and that she herself would complete the second part. It would be called *Home-coming of the Heart (=Home-coming)*, a title which Asad himself suggested.[18] Martin Kramer, a reputed Jewish historian, opined that "It is not clear whether such a return [to Saudi Arabia] was a realistic prospect, or whether the title hinted at a more spiritual homecoming. For Asad had neither completed this work nor returned to Arabia."[19] Reviewing G. Windhager's German book on Asad, Murad W. Hofmann, German Ambassador (r) and a convert to Islam, suggests that the Viennese author should "embark on a second volume, covering no longer, like here, Asad's life *towards* Islam but *in* Islam (1927-1992), this impression of life–rich, puzzling, and full of ruptures – would re-emerge. But this second period of his life was not only extremely adventurous in Saudi Arabia, Libya, India, Pakistan, the United States, Morocco and Spain."[20]

As mentioned above, Asad's wife, his friends, reviewers and correspondents constantly persuaded him to continue his life-story after 1932. In the beginning, he was hesitant to go ahead and insisted that there could not be a second *The Road.* Personally, he was convinced that he could not write another book with the same emotional energy and the stylistic intensity as *The Road*, therefore he kept postponing the writing of its sequel.

Moreover, he was deeply involved in his translation of the Qur'ān and spent about twenty years (1960-1980) in its completion. During this time, he even declined the official invitations to visit the different countries. After the publication of *The Message of the Qur'ān* (1980), his ***magnum opus***, he finally decided to fulfill the long-felt desire of his spouse, friends and readers and probably in the middle of 1980s sat down to write the second part of *The Road* under the heading *Home-coming*, a title which he himself suggested.[21] Soon he had to face severe health problems (cancer of the bladder and the fracture of the hip-bone) and the serious medical treatments. In this rapidly decaying condition of his health, he could only cover the period from his arrival in India in 1932 till 1952, when he resigned from the Pakistan Foreign Service. It was Pola who wrote the second part of the book covering the years 1952-1992. As is evident from the epistolary sources that Pola accomplished the whole script of *Home-coming*, containing two parts, after Asad's death and made proper arrangements for its publication. Unfortunately, she died in 2006 and could not see this book in the printed form. Now, for the first time this unpublished script is being published in its entirety.[22]

● ● ● ● ●

The salient points of the present book are as follows:

Asad and Afghanistan

1. Dr. 'Abd al-Ghani (1864-1943) of Jalālpur Jattan (Gujrat, Pakistan) was called "the Teacher of Afghanistan" because of his valuable services for promoting education in Afghanistan with the assistance of his two brothers, Najaf Ali and Tāj ud-Din. Before Asad was converted to Islam, he spent about six months in Afghanistan as a correspondent of *Frankfurter*

[Allgemeine] Zeitung[23] but he did not even refer the name of Dr. 'Abdul Ghani, one of the close associates of King Amānullah Khan (r. 1919-1928).

Asad first met Dr. 'Abd al-Ghani in King 'Abdul 'Aziz Ibn Sa'ūd's guest house (Mecca) during the *ḥajj* of 1927. Through him Asad was introduced to Qasūrī brothers – 'Abd al-Qādir (d. 1942) and 'Abdullah (d. 1949) who persuaded him to visit India in order to become acquainted with the large Muslim community of the subcontinent......"[24]

Asad's Reports incorporated in *The Road*

2. After Asad's arrival in India, he continued to send his reports to the Swiss newspaper, based on his personal experiences and observations, particularly an interesting reportage of his visit to Kulu.[25] In the present book, all these instalments have been included with minor alterations and additions.

Iqbal and Asad

3. The different aspects of the relationship between Iqbal and Asad have been discussed in detail in *Gift* (I: 325-330). In addition, this book (*Home-coming*) furnishes new information, such as
   a. For the first time, Asad met Iqbal in the house of Chaudhri Ilāhī Bakhsh, a retired Session Judge, in Lahore (1934). There, a heated discussion commenced on *ijtihad* and they exchanged their divergent views on the subject. Irrespective of their disagreement, they maintained cordial relations.
   b. It was Iqbal who persuaded Asad to embark on the first of his major scholarly enterprises – the English translation with explanatory notes of the *Ṣaḥiḥ al-Bukhāri* and gave up his journalistic activities. Iqbal, also took active part in getting substantial financial support from the Nizam of Hyderabad Deccan (IV=stands for chapter/vii=stands for section). Initially, it was planned to publish this translation in forty fascicules, but only five appeared and the rest destroyed.

Asad and Kashmir

4. Kashmir and its people were very close to Asad's heart. He met

some renowned Muslim scholars of Kashmir and Mir Wāʿiz Mawlawi Muhammad Yusuf Shah. He delivered lectures in the Islamia High School in Srinagar where he also established ʻArafat Press. (cf. Abroo Aman Andrabi: *Muhammad Asad. His Contribution to Islamic Learning*, New Delhi 2007, pp. 27-28).

In September and December 1948, Asad visited the military front lines of the Indo-Pak conflict in Kashmir. Major-General Ḥamīd, area commander, invited him to come and see the final military preparations to assault Poonch. As an eyewitness, Asad described in detail what he saw. Prime Minister's order for the withdrawal of the troops shocked everyone at the frontline including Asad (VII/iv).

Asad and Pakistan Movement

5. Deeply inspired by Iqbal's idea of a separate Islamic State, Asad took part in Pakistan movement with courage, honesty and enthusiasm. His struggle was primarily concerned with the ideological and intellectual domain of this newly-emerged country. For this reason, he is rightly called one of the 'intellectual co-founders of Pakistan'.

He had the privilege of having the first passport marked with the words 'Citizen of Pakistan' (VIII/vi) and he kept it until the end of his life, although he had been tempted to accept the citizenship of many other countries.

Asad and Liaquat Ali Khan's Murder

6. One day before Liaquat Ali Khan's assassination (15 Oct. 1951), he had made some notes for a public speech. These notes were found on his desk. They consisted of only a few words, all of them heavily underlined in red: "League of Muslim Nations" and "Constitution" – apparently relating to the speech that was to be delivered. Asad questioned, "Was there a connection between Liaquat Ali's death and the purport of these words? Was I, thus, indirectly responsible for his death?" (IX/vi)

Asad and Saudi Arabia

7. Soon after Partition (1947), Indian Prime Minister Jawahar Lal Nehru visited Saudi Arabia where he was warmly received. Apparently he was able to prevail upon the Saudis not to accept a Pakistan Embassy in the kingdom. So for the first four years

after Partition, Pakistan only had a small *ḥajj* mission in Jiddah, while the ambassador from Cairo was concurrently accredited to Saudi Arabia (IX/i-ii). In May 1951, Liaquat Ali Khan sent a delegation to Saudi Arabia and Asad was made its Secretary (obviously not only because of his capacity as head of the Middle East division in the Foreign Office but also because of his mastery over Arabic language and of his strong friendly relations with the Saudi royal family, especially with the Foreign Minister, Amīr Faisal). The delegation was successful in getting the required permission for a resident Pakistani mission in Jiddah. All the members of the delegation attributed this historic success to Asad.

Mawlana Mawdūdi and Asad

8. Mawlana Mawdūdi and Asad worked together and they had friendly relations based on mutual respect but later on Mawlana changed his opinion about Asad's personality and services to Islam (cf. *Gift*, I: 330-337).

During the turbulent days of Partition, Asad took three buses from Lahore and went back to Jamālpur to bring thousand of Muslim men, women and children to Lahore. With this multitude, Mawlana also reached Lahore safely, notwithstanding that he and some of his friends brought their rifles and shotguns with them which were strongly prohibited by Asad. (VI/ix)

● ● ● ● ●

A photo album contains a unique collection of photographs by Asad which is now housed in the Shah Fahad National Library (Riyadh). A few photographs have been taken from this album. I am grateful to the concerned staff-members of this Library.

I am greatly indebted to Thomas Würtz (Bern University) and Maria – Magdalena Fuch, a young German scholar, who managed to send me Asad's articles published in a Swiss newspaper (1932-1934) and helped me in their English translation.

Lahore M. Ikram Chaghatai
21 November 2011

Endnotes

1 New York: Simon & Shuster, frequently reprinted and translated in many languages including Urdu. German tr. by the author *Der Weg nach Mekka*, Berlin-Frankfurt a.M.: S. Fischer, 1955. In 1973, Asad contributed a postscript to a new edition of the book (1980)

2 See *Muhammad Asad–A Man of Desert* (in Urdu). Translated and edited by M. Iktam Chaghatai, Lahore: The Truth Society, 2009, p. 163.

3 Cf. *Muhamamd Asad: Europe's Gift to Islam* (=*Gift*). Edited, annotated and written by M. Ikram Chaghatai, 2 vols., Lahore: The Truth Society 2006, p 146.

4 Ibid., I: 154.

5 Ibid.

6 Ibid., I: 155.

7 Ibid., I: 239.

8 Ibid.

9 Ibid.

10 Ibid., I: 255.

11 Ibid., I: 283.

12 Ibid., I: ii.

13 She belonged to ash-Shammar tribe of Ha'il in Saudi Arabia. In 1930, Asad married her and their only son, Ṭalāl Asad, was born in Medina (1932), who is still living in New York. About this Arabian wife, Asad writes: "...I am no longer living with my wife and have no intention of living with her in the future. We have become estranged from one another, and there is nothing in common between us except our son."

Asad's first wife was a German painter, named Elsa ('Azīza) Schiemann (1878-1927, in Mecca), née Specht. She was twenty-two years older than him. His step-son, Heinrich Ahmad Schiemann (1916-2002) spent some years in Pakistan and corresponded with his father's colleagues and biographers, cf. Günther Windhager: *Leopold Weiss alias Muhammad Asad. Von Galizien nach Arabien, 1900-1927* (=*Windhager*) Vienna 2002, pp. 103-106.

14 Unlike Asad's first wife, Else, Pola was twenty-six years younger than her husband. She confessed that in spite of the great differences in their age and temperaments "he loved my physical attributes."

15 She also writes that "It had been difficult for me, his wife, to persuade him to undertake it at all; for years I have been pressing him to do so, and many of his friends supported me."

16 cf. Samuel C. Chew: "A Westerner finds more in Islam than in Christianity or Judaism." (in: *New York Herald Tribune Book Review*, 15 August 1953); see also Mushtaq Parker: "Death of a Muslim Mentor" (in: *The Middle East*, May 1992, p. 28)

17 cf. *Gift*, I: 305-306.

18 In a letter to G. Windhager, (February 5, 1997), Pola informed about the contents of *Home-coming* (cf. *Windhager*, p. 24, f. n. 19)

19 cf. *Gift*, I: 260.

20 Ibid., I: 603.

21 In *The Road to Mecca*, Asad clarifies "Home-coming" in these words, "My coming to this land [Saudi Arabia] was it not, in truth, a home-coming? Home-coming of the heart that has espied its old home backward over a cover of thousands of years and now recognizes this sky, my sky, with painful rejoicing?"

In its postscript (1973), he reiterates, "This, then, is the story of my road to Mecca: the story of the home-coming of my heart...... 'Home-coming of the heart': this phrase always echoes in my mind..."

According to Martin Kramer, "[This] title is said to have alluded to his contemplated return to Saudi Arabia at the invitation of Prince Salman (b. 1936), governor of Riyadh and one of Ibn Saud's sons." (cf. *Gift*, I: 260)

22 Some of my Austrian friends, particular Georg Misch (the director of the new German documentary film on Asad, released in 2008), helped me in having an access to the original script of this book. I have published its Urdu translation entitled *Muhammad Asad–Banda-i-Ṣahrā'ī* (Muhammad Asad–Man of the Desert), Lahore 2009.

The Arabic translation of the title of the book is استراحةالقلب or عودةالقلب‌الی‌وطنه.

23 See his articles, Leopold Weiss: "Die Stadt der Wilden Knaben", in: *Frankfurter Zeitung*, 21 March 1926 and "Vor den Toren Indiens. Der russisch-afghanische Freundschaftsvertrag", in: ibid, 13 Nov. 1926; cf. *Windhager*, op. cit., 157-165, esp. 163. In *The Road to Mecca* (p. 298), Asad has described in detail a warm discussion with his Afghan host who strongly believed that he was a Muslim, whereas his conversion took place in September 1926.

24 For Dr. 'Abd al-Ghani, see pp. 30-31, f. n. 4 of this book. Before going to Afghanistan, he was appointed as the Principal of Islamia College, Lahore, (16 Oct. 1904–10 Sept. 1906) (cf. Ahmad Saeed: *Hundred Years' History of Islamia College*, Lahore (in Urdu), Lahore, vol. I, 1992, pp. 55-60. See also *Dāstān-i Balākashān* (in Urdu) by Iqbal Shaidai. Edited by Abu Salman Shahjahanpuri, Karachi 2008, pp. 125-126). Iqbal Shaidai met Dr. 'Abd al-Ghani in Afghanistan and they founded "India Independence League" under the headship of Khan 'Abdul Ghaffār Khan.

25 cf. "Wer denkt an Kulu" (Who thinks about Kulu), in: *Neue Zürcher Zeitung* (Zürich), 5 Feb. 1933); "Zu den Göttern von Kulu" (The gods of Kulu), in: ibid., 12 and 19 Feb. 1933; "Die Götter tanzen" (The gods dance), in: ibid., 17 Sept. 1933; "Tempel und Gottsucher in Himalaya" (Temple and god-seeker in Himalay), in ibid., 21 Sept. 1933; "Am Grat der Welt" (Upto the edge of the world), in: ibid., 1st, 8, 15 and 22 Oct. 1933.

I
THE DUST OF INDIA
(1932-33)

I

I slept and awoke, and slept again. The sound of rushing water came to my ears, swishing through the mists of half-sleep; and with it a hardly perceptible sensation of rocking. I opened my eyes, and a shaft of sunlight struck them, slanting through a small round opening: a porthole? – a ship?

And then I became fully awake and knew that I was really on a ship: a ship ploughing through the Arabian Sea towards the coast of India — away from Arabia, away from six of the happiest years of my life. The deserts, and the dromedaries, and the black beduin tents, and the oases with their singing, creaking, soughing draw-wells, and the hospitable village houses built of mud brick resounding with the clang of brass mortars in which freshly-roasted coffee beans were being pounded; and the black coffee poured out of tall brass jugs into tiny cups and handed around by men of the King's bodyguard to his guests who sat in tight rows along the four walls of the huge *majlis* in *Riyadh*, with Ibn Saud himself ensconced in his favourite corner and rising to his great height to receive the greeting of every newcomer, patrician and ragged beduin alike; and the warmth of the King's smile and his broad, all-embracing generosity: all this lay now behind me and glided farther and farther away into the past, into the past . . .

It was the end of November 1932. The previous day I had said my farewell to the King[1] in his *qasr* in Jidda and kissed for the last time, according to Arabian custom, his nose-tip and forehead; whereupon he embraced me and said, 'Thou must come back to us soon, O my son. Do not forget that this is thy land.'

And now I was on a ship, going away from my land . . . . I felt a sudden constriction in my throat, and anger with myself: *why* was I going away?

But then a half-forgotten voice came to my mind - the voice of an old man in Kurdistan, years and years ago: 'If water stands motionless in pools, it becomes stale, muddy and foul; only when it moves and flows does it remain clear . . . ' This, then, was the reason for my restlessness and my decision to go to India - for a few months, as I then thought, and for many years, as destiny brought it about.

II

My going to India was not a sudden decision. It had slowly matured during the weeks of the recent *hajj* and my encounters with some Indian Muslims who had become my friends. Foremost among them was the tall, white-bearded Dr. Abd al-Ghani, known in his part of the world as 'the Teacher of Afghanistan'. Hailing from the Punjab, he had studied medicine in England, graduated from one of the famous teaching hospitals in London, and intended to settle down to medical practice in his native land. But just after graduation his life took an unexpected, quite different course. During one of his visits to England, the then-ruler of Afghanistan, Amir Habibullah Khan[2], met the young Abd al-Ghani and, immediately attracted by his intelligence and balanced mind, persuaded him to come to Afghanistan as his personal physician. Very soon, however, the Amir discovered new potentialities in his young protégé: he was not merely a promising doctor but also a man of wide culture, and possessed the ability to stimulate the minds of others as well; why not make use of him for the good of the country as a whole? And so the Amir gave up the idea of employing Abd al-Ghani as his personal physician and appointed him as Director of Public Instruction instead - a post that had never before existed in Afghanistan.

The young Director threw himself into his new work with enthusiasm. He called – with the consent of Amir – his elder brother Najaf Ali to his aid, and between them the two brothers laid the foundations of a network of modern schools throughout the country, starting with primary schools and gradually, over the years, established high schools in every provincial capital. Carefully selected teachers were brought in from India, each one chosen for his ability to communicate a desire for knowledge to his pupils; and in time a new type of man made its appearance in that land in which previously only warriors, tradesmen and merchants had flourished.

For some years things went well for Abd al-Ghani and his endeavours. The Amir seemed to be pleased with what he and his brother were accomplishing; and the Amir's young son and prospective successor, Amanullah Khan[3], became one of his warmest supporters.

The results of all this were spectacular - so much so that they provided an inexhaustible subject of conversation in many homes. Not only was Afghanistan gradually being provided with more and more educated young people who could be expected to fulfil, over the years, various functions in the administration of the country much more effectively than their predecessors had done, but the cultural level of the population as a whole was visibly rising. For, the new generation which came out of the new schools in Kabul and Kandahar, in Mazar Sharif and Ghazni and Herat began to appreciate not merely the practical advantages of education but, guided by Abd al-Ghani, the value of *thinking* as such. In time, many of these young people began to pose to themselves questions about various aspects of their own, individual lives and about the forms and aims of their social environment; and the answers at which they arrived did not always coincide with what their parents had taught them.

There was, of course, a lot of immaturity in the thinking of these bright young men, and much of it expressed itself in a vague, indiscriminate desire for 'change'. This brought them often into conflict with the *mullahs,* the supposedly learned religious teachers and leaders who until then had held unquestioned sway over the minds of the Afghan people as a whole; but such conflicts were almost always, and more or less easily, resolved by Abd al-Ghani, whose reputation for orthodox and Islamic learning was too firmly established to be seriously challenged. On the other hand, however, the reaction of Amir Habibullah himself to the juvenile concept of 'change' led to a sudden catastrophic reversal of Abd al-Ghani's fortunes and hopes.

Ever concerned about maintaining his prerogatives as the absolute ruler of a largely tribal and unruly country, Habibullah became apprehensive of the new, as yet inarticulated trend among the younger generation; and goaded by the whisperings of some of his advisers, who had always been jealous of the prestige and growing influence of 'the Indian doctor', began to regard him and his work as 'revolutionary' and, hence, most dangerous to his own position. The solution which presented itself to him was the traditional response of every autocratic ruler of a backward country: get rid of the troublemakers . . . . And so, one day at dawn, Abd al-Ghani and his brother were arrested and, without any trial or possibility of appeal, thrown into the darkest dungeon of the Amir's castle. For several months they languished there, fettered with heavy leg-irons and deprived of all that makes life worth living. Subsequently they were relieved of their chains and brought into a slightly more airy cell which was lighted by a small window under the ceiling. In that cell they languished for nearly ten years. . . .

They lived there as long as Amir Habibullah lived. Several people - foremost among them Amanullah Khan – repeatedly interceded in their behalf with the Amir, but to no avail. The Amir was adamant in his refusal until his death.

That death came about unexpectedly and suddenly: the Amir was murdered by one of his own officers - and it was rumoured that his son, Amanullah Khan, was behind the assassination ... But whether this was true or not, one of the first acts of Amanullah on assuming power was the release and full vindication of Abd al-Ghani[4] and Najaf Ali.

As for Abd al-Ghani, he had been put into the dungeon as a young man in his middle thirties; and when he came out at the age of forty-five, he was an old, white-bearded man with unceasingly trembling hands.

III

He was an old, white-bearded man – although only in his early fifties – when I first met him in the King's guest-house in Mecca during the *hajj* of 1927. We 'clicked' almost from the first moment. Despite his appearance of great age, his mind was lively and precise, endowed with a strong sense of humour; and he spoke a beautiful, quite un-Indian English. The ten years in the dungeons of Kabul had not affected his serenity but, rather, had deepened and enhanced it: and this, as I gradually realized, was due to the strength of his faith in God and an unflagging consciousness of His Presence. How many men could have survived such a trial with no more than whiteness of hair and unsteadiness of hands?

Through Abd al-Ghani I came to know other Indian Muslims who had come to Mecca on pilgrimage. Among them were two elderly brothers who bore the eponymic 'Kasuri' after the Punjabi town of Kasur from which they hailed. The older of them, Maulana Abd al-Qadir[5], had for many years been very prominent in the Indian independence movement – with the unavoidable consequence of several periods spent in jails – and, as I later learned, was outstanding among the *Ahl-e-Hadith* movement in his native country: and this, more than anything else, brought us close together. Ever since I had embraced

Islam in the preceding year (1926), I had been convinced that a mere reliance on the teachings of the early exponents of Islamic thought, the so-called *imams,* was not the right way to a comprehension of the message of Muhammad. What was necessary was a direct, independent approach to the Two Sources of Islam – the Qur'an and the teachings of the Prophet, forthcoming from the authentic Traditions *(ahadith)* transmitted to posterity by his Companions. This line of thought, embodied in the Indian *Ahl-e-Hadith* persuasion, appealed to me greatly and made it easy for me henceforth to describe myself as belonging to the *Ahl-e-Hadith* whenever I was asked by my Arab friends as to which *madhhab* – that is, school of thought – I followed. In addition, the idea underlying the *Ahl-e-Hadith* concept was very close to – almost identical with - the thinking of the so-called 'Wahhabis' (i.e., the followers of the eighteenth-century scholar Muhammad ibn Abd al-Wahhab[6]), a school of thought adhered to by almost all the population of Central and Eastern Arabia, including the House of Ibn Saud. As a result, I could identify myself fully with the religious thinking prevalent in what was to become, and remain, my spiritual home, as well as with my new Indian friends.[7]

It was these friends who persuaded me to visit India in order to become acquainted with the large Muslim community of the sub-continent: and thus it had come about that I now found myself- together with my Najdi wife Munira[8] and our eight-month-old son Talal[9] – on a ship sailing towards India.

I was going to India with mixed feelings. On the one side was my eager anticipation of discovering an entirely new country and of coming to know a very important segment of the Muslim *ummah* which had hitherto remained beyond my vision; and on the other, my conviction that I would not be welcomed by the British rulers of India who, because of my self-identification with the interest of Saudi Arabia and my writings in Continental newspapers, had no reason to regard me – a European convert to Islam – with friendly eyes. To them, I was bound to be and remain a 'renegade' who had been highly critical of their role in Arabia. . . . Be that as it may, my expectation of new, possibly fascinating discoveries and new links with my community outweighed the mild apprehension with which I looked forward to my Indian visit.

IV

On the third – or was it the fourth? – day the coast of India came into sight: a flat, sandy expanse, yellow-beige in colour, flat even in its buildings, with nothing high, not even trees, interrupting the monotonous landscape: the port-city of Karachi.

Our ship, coming from Jidda, was full of returning *hajjis* who now thronged the decks, eager to glimpse the first sight of their homeland, as if they had never seen it before. But this, it seems, always happens on ships – any ship – whenever they approach a port.

Loudspeakers boomed forth, informing the passengers that passport control would take place on board, and asking them not to press forward before time but, rather, to form orderly lines, so that each person could be dealt with in his or her turn. As there were several hundred passengers on board, I prepared myself for a lengthy wait before landing; but I was mistaken. Hardly had the ship touched the quay when a surprising call sounded through the loudspeakers: 'Mr. Asad! Mr. Muhammad Asad! Please advance to the bursar's cabin!' And so I made way through the throngs for myself and my wife, who carried our child in her arms, and we moved slowly, step by step, in the direction of the bursar's cabin. However, long before we reached our destination two men appeared, dressed in the conventional North-Indian fashion – baggy *shalwars,* jackets with protruding shirt-tails, and loosely-bound turbans over pointed Punjabi caps – ploughing through the masses of *hajjis* and calling out repeatedly, 'Mr. Asad! Mr. Asad!' When I called out in reply, they pushed their way through and greeted me in English in a most friendly manner. One of them said, 'We have come to facilitate your landing. . . . where is your luggage?' I asked them who they were, and they answered, 'From a ... government office, sir.' – 'What sort of office?' – 'Eh . . . eh . . . from the police. We have been told to help you, sir.' And they made way for us through the throngs, and shepherded us towards the bursar's office to the accompaniment of resentful glances from all the other *hajjis* around us, who had to await their turn. . . .

The passport officer who was sitting in the office was extremely polite. He barely glanced at my passport, stamped it and said smilingly, 'Welcome to India, sir! Where will you be staying?' I gave him the name and address of the friend with whom we were to stay for a few days in Karachi, and volunteered our future address in Lahore, namely, the house of Maulana Abd Allah Kasuri.[10] In the meantime our luggage appeared as if by magic, and we were whisked over the gangway to a waiting car. The whole procedure had taken no more than ten minutes, and I hardly had time to say a temporary good-bye to the two Kasuri brothers who had come to Karachi on the same boat.

V

My first few days in India – in Karachi – were disappointing. I was not impressed by that city, which was fairly neat, colourless and totally without character; and so I spent only two days there: the time necessary to have a couple of light-weight suits made, for I had arrived in Karachi in Arab dress, the only kind of dress that I had been wont to wear during the past six years. And all through those few days in Karachi one or the other of my two police friends was always just in sight in front of the bungalow in which we all – Munira and I and the Kasuri brothers – were staying as guests of a family who had returned from the *hajj* together with us. At first, this eternal presence of the C.I.D. irritated me; in time, however, I became accustomed to the fact of being followed wherever I went during my early days in pre-war India.[11] But more about this later. . . .

After two days of warm hospitality in the house of our Karachi friends we set out by train for Lahore. The long, long rail journey from early morning until evening, first along the broad Indus River with its green waters, then into and through an immense, dusty plain sparsely dotted with rusty, mud-coloured villages, stopping at lonely stations thronged with a confusing mass of men in loose *shalwars* and women in brightly-coloured, wide skirts and skimpy blouses, which left a strip of the body bare above the waist; and children, begging children everywhere, running up and down beside the train and raising their hands for alms towards the open carriage windows. Judging from the appearance of those children, there did not seem to be overmuch poverty here – but begging was apparently their natural reaction to the stopping of a train at their station.

And so on and on through the dusty, monotonous plain, deeper and deeper into the Punjab – the Land of Five Rivers – until at dusk we reached Lahore, which was to be our home for the next few months.

The house of our host, Maulana Abd Allah Kasuri, was situated just outside the Old City, opposite the Sheranwalah Gate[12] – the 'Gate of the Lions' – one of the few that still remained intact after the ancient city-walls had all but disappeared.

How different was the appearance of Lahore from that of Karachi! Here everything was movement and life and colour. The people were sturdier than those of Sind, the men as a rule taller, and the women far better-looking: in fact, nowhere else in the world had I seen so many beautiful women. As I learned with the passing of time, most of them were non-Muslims, for the majority of Muslim women were, unfortunately, covered from head to toe by a white over-garment called a *burqah* which made them appear like walking tents; but here and there one could see a young one who had freed herself of that abominable garb and moved about openly in the Punjabi *kurta* (tunic) and *shalwar*. And there were the Sikh women who, of course, had never worn a *burqah* – black-eyed, with long tresses hanging down over their backs; and their tall, bearded and turbaned men of very virile appearance. And there were Pathans from the frontier areas, closed of face and aloof in their bearing, dressed in long shirts and *shalwars* – strangers in this city and yet visibly at home within themselves – strolling about in small groups and congregating in one particular *chai-khanah*, a tea-house of which in time, I, too, became a frequent visitor, to drink very strong, very sweet tea with plenty of milk.

Slowly, gradually, I began to understand and haltingly to speak Urdu, the language of Muslim India which, because of its affinity with Persian (with which I was familiar since my early years in Iran and Afghanistan) was not difficult for me to 'pick up'. I began to explore the ancient, strangely attractive Old City of Lahore, entering it through the Delhi Gate[13] and wandering on through narrow lanes. On my right and on my left I saw lines of tiny shops, no more than niches about one metre above street-level, the dealers sitting cross-legged in the midst of their goods, as in so many other cities of the East. I saw and felt the bustling masses of people flowing past me in both directions, pressing, pushing, shouting; heavily-laden porters, oxcarts, two-wheeled tongas, ever-changing dresses and faces and colours, men and women and children and bicycles and donkeys, a chaos of colour, sound and form – like a multitude of most vivid paints haphazardly mixed together on a careless painter's palette, so that in the end all becomes an ungraspable mass of grey: and this, as I came to know with the passing years, was the true face of India.

Through an arched gateway which vaulted over the bazaar street I had a glimpse of the old Wazir Khan Mosque[14] which a fortunate minister, richly endowed by his king, had built some three hundred years earlier: a truly splendid monument, graced by a flowing-together of colours, of glazed tiles united in a mosaic – an entire great façade of coloured tiles brought together in perfect rhythm.

But, as happens so often in India, the next step revealed a painful contrast to that great harmony. As if with a deliberate aim to cover it up, people had erected a row of shabby booths all across the front of the mosque - booths in which sweets and milk and yoghurt were being sold, or in which cheap food was being cooked: and Wazir Khan's Mosque could display only very little of its beauty to the eye of the passerby. Although it had been erected centuries ago, this building was to me a living reality, whereas the life of India as such appeared to me like a moon which reflected the sunlight of the stranger's own imaginings and illusions, and had no light of its own. I could not discern any clear-cut 'character' in that India, which knew so little happiness in those days and was so immeasurably vast, so multiform and so full of inner contradictions, might in reality be an as-yet amorphous cosmos, pregnant with future fulfilment. . . ?

VI

After a few weeks of idleness and strolling about I became tired of the unceasing bustle of Lahore. I found it necessary, too, to concentrate for a while on the writing of some long-delayed articles for the *Neue Zürcher Zeitung*:[15] after all, I was their special correspondent in this part of the world. The open hospitality of Abd Allah Kasuri's house was not the right background for concentration: too many friends and acquaintances passed through my days, too much time flowed by in endless talk, and I was longing for a quiet interval.

And so it came about that one day I went, alone, by train to the little town of Sialkot near the border of Jammu State, and onwards by car into the foothills below Kashmir. A friend had arranged for me a pass for one of the *dak* bungalows on the road to Srinagar – the one-time post houses built in the past century and still kept up for the convenience of visiting district officers. That pass made me automatically a government guest for the days I intended to stay there, with a cook and a bearer and a set of simply but comfortably furnished rooms at my disposal. Since I was the only visitor at the time I could fully relax in the quiet of the low hills and, for a change, work undisturbed at my writing. The two servants attached to the bungalow took care of my meals and all my other requirements, and the only thing I had to do apart from my work was to tell them each day what I would like to have for lunch and dinner.

In the afternoon of the second day I went for a long walk on the hill roads. The air was pleasantly cool, tiny flowers grew in abundance on the hillsides, all was peace and quiet, and I went on and on until I began to feel hungry and thought of returning to the *dak* bungalow and a ready dinner. Suddenly, the scent of roasting meat came to my nostrils; I heard voices. Was there a village around the hill? – perhaps a tavern where one could get the delicious Punjabi *kebabs* which I liked so much and which, as the pleasant aroma promised, were now being prepared for occasional wayfarers like myself?

I went around the bend of the road and circumvented a low hill – and there it was, the source of the scent of *kebabs* – and I stood stockstill. . . .

A great pyre of burning wood sent its fiery tongues up into the afternoon air. In the midst of the flames lay a dead body, already blackened, with the bones already bared: a funeral pyre. A small group of people stood around, a priest chanted mournful incantations, and the smell of burning flesh lay heavy in the still air: a Hindu funeral. . . .

I turned around and went back as fast as I could towards my bungalow, and thought of how horrifying it must be to see one's dear ones being roasted, and to witness their being burned to ashes. But, then, I was not a Hindu, and I had a different perception of life and death – as different from theirs as day is from night.

And this was the first time that I came face to face with the Hindu religion.

VII

Almost from the very beginning of my long, long stay in India I realized that this immense country – or, rather, this continent – filled with innumerable, heterogeneous ethnic groups and social contradictions, scores of widely different languages (some of them as distant from one another as Spanish is from Russian) and a great variety of the most dissimilar religious beliefs and practices – I realized that this was truly, intrinsically, a world of unanswerable questions and insoluble conflicts.

One of its characteristics – albeit a negative one - became almost immediately apparent to me: the chasm which divided Muslims from Hindus. Like a red thread ran this chasm through one's daily life in Lahore, through all conversations, all ephemeral encounters in the bazaars: a red thread running through India's present and ominously pointing towards the future, with no coming-together of these two separate worlds of thought and feeling even distantly conceivable. On the one side there was a baroque polytheism, fading away into the most abstract speculations, with only one solid idea common to them all: the belief in a continuous series of transmigrations and re-births of the human soul; and on the other side an austere One-God faith and the principle of individual accountability in the course of *one* single life-span. On the one side – in Hinduism – a rigid caste system which splits up human society into incompatible groups, all of them more or less untouchable to one another; and on the other the conviction that the ethical purpose of religion as such is the achievement of a truly brotherly unification of all human beings who share one and the same concept of God the Creator. Never – I saw this clearly – could these two worlds meet in their perception of life and of its spiritual values unless one of them gave up its own cultural existence and merged with the other. This, however, lay beyond the bounds of possibility.

The Muslims had always been a minority - at the time of which I am speaking their numbers amounted to less than a quarter of India's total population - but their greater virility as compared with that of the Hindu majority (undoubtedly due to the more dynamic world-view of Islam) was an uncontestable fact of history. For many centuries India had been ruled by Muslim dynasties and held together by the force of Muslim arms, while the Hindus concentrated themselves on trade and the achievement of more education. In the long run this worked out to their benefit: for whereas the Muslims, lost in the contemplation of their past glories, remained largely stagnant as a community, the Hindus advanced rapidly – with the result that now by far the larger segment of India's economy lay in their hands and their role in the administration of the country, especially since the full establishment of British rule, vastly exceeded that of the Muslims. Indeed, it had come to the point that almost all the important government posts which the British rulers conceded to members of the native population were now manned by Hindus whereas the Muslims had to remain content with the lowermost clerical jobs.

Nonetheless, the Hindus did not feel entirely at ease. Since it was obvious that sooner or later, despite all temporary political reverses, India was bound to attain its independence – either in full sovereignty or as a dominion within the British Empire – they never lost sight of the fact that for many centuries they had been dominated by the Muslims:

and now they feared that one day the latter might be tempted to repeat the old experiment and – perhaps supported by other Muslim nations – make a bid to regain their erstwhile predominance. As a safeguard against such a possibility they began consciously to mobilize their incomparably larger economic resources, their much higher level of education and their greater influence in the administrative set-up of the country with an unmistakable bias against the Muslim community. Their slogan openly became 'India for the Hindus', implying that Muslims were but intruders and 'foreigners', and overlooking the historical fact that only an infinitesimal fraction of the Muslims of India descended from foreign conquerors or immigrants, whereas more than nine-tenths of their community were descendants of Hindus who had embraced Islam in the course of the centuries.

But whatever may be the facts of history, the animosity between these two segments of India's population had always been a real – albeit at the beginning more or less latent – factor of the country's socio-political life; however, since the breakdown of the Moghul Empire, it had gradually assumed the character of an almost elemental animosity, resulting in ever-recurring bloody clashes and riots all over the country. And because the Muslims were a minority, it was they, as a rule, who always suffered the greater losses in lives and property. To be sure, there were times when a common resentment of British rule seemed to weld the two mutually-averse communities into one national entity, as was the case during the great rebellion of 1857 (called by the British 'The Great Mutiny') or at the time of the independence movement in the stormy period following the world war of 1914-1918; but again and again it became obvious that the hypothetical 'unity' of the peoples of India is and always has been but an outcome of ephemeral, short-lived emotions. To the Muslims, who at first had enthusiastically embraced the idea of Muslim-Hindu unity and identity of aims, it soon became obvious that what the Hindus meant by 'national awakening' was no more and no less than an awakening of the old Hindu culture to the exclusion of all other tendencies. And since the Muslims have always been too deeply conscious of their own cultural premises to accept the prospect - however vague - of their being submerged in the concept of an 'Indian' totality, they decided to secure their own cultural existence by means of formal inter-communal agreements before joining a common political front in the struggle for independence from the British *raj.* And thus began a new phase in the history of the Indian sub-continent.

Until then, the Hindu-Muslim antithesis had been mainly

emotional and concerned with no more than socio-economic considerations; but now its basis was greatly enlarged. With the deliberate, unequivocal refusal of the Hindu leadership to grant the assurances which the Muslims demanded – and thus to recognize them as a cultural and national minority with equal rights – it became obvious that in the context of their struggle for India's independence there was no question of a community of interests between Muslims and Hindus: for, irrespective of whether it remained a dominion within the British Empire or became entirely separated from it, a fully autonomous India ruled by a statutory, sovereign Hindu majority would become the graveyard of Muslim cultural and economic existence. True, in spite of always having been a minority, the Muslims had held their own for nearly a thousand years without being absorbed by the Hindu majority. However, one must remember that during all that period, until the full establishment of British sovereignty in the middle of the nineteenth century, all governmental power had rested with the Muslims: and so they had been able to survive as a cultural and economic entity in spite of the overwhelming Hindu majority. But in the India of the future, the India of which the Hindus dreamt, the Muslims would be bound to succumb to the will of the majority.

And so, with the growth of political consciousness, it had become increasingly difficult for the Muslims to face the future in a common front with the Hindus.

This, then, was the point which the Indian independence movement had reached in those days. The 'red thread' of the Hindu-Muslim antithesis made the achievement of a definite progress in the country's political status exceedingly questionable, as had become evident in the failure of the 'civil disobedience' movement decided upon by the Indian National Congress[16] at the beginning of 1932. The goal of paralyzing the state machinery by non-violent means and thus forcing the government to give in had not been attained – for the simple reason that the Muslims had kept aloof from it. Apart from a comparatively few individuals, they had refused to follow the National Congress, and thus the latter was composed almost exclusively of Hindus. And the sequence to all this was a growing feeling of frustration and a political weariness throughout the country.

As for myself, I began to feel, vaguely, that precisely this widespread sensation of having reached a dead-end might in time force the peoples of India to come to terms with reality: that is to say, to recognize the absence of all ethnic and cultural unity among them as an organic fact of their existence, and to visualize their political future in the light of this fact. But it was only months later that this dim feeling of mine grew into articulated thought and the truth of the situation burst upon me with all its implications.

Endnotes

1 Shah 'Abdul Aziz bin 'Abd al-Rahman As-Sa'ud (1880-1953, r. 1902 till death), the founder of the present-day Saudi Arabia. For Muhammad Asad's close relationship with him see his famous book *The Road to Mecca* (s.v. Index) and also his German article in *Frankfurter Zeitung* (Berlin), 2 April 1926. For this first ruler of Saudi Arabia, see H. St. J. B. Philby: *Sa'udi Arabia*, London 1955; D. Howarth: *The Desert King: a life of Ibn Sa'ud*, London 1964; Muhammad Almana: *Arabia Unified; A Portrait of Ibn Sa'ud*, London 1980; Alexei Vassiliev: *The History of Saudi Arabia*, London 2000; *The Encyclopedia of Islam, (=EI²)* vol. XII (Supplement), Leiden 2004, pp. 3-4 (art. R. Bayly Winder).

2 On 'Abd ar-Rahman's death (1st October 1901), his son Amir Habib Allah Khan ascended the throne of Afghanistan (r. 1901-1919). He confirmed the treaty made by his father with the government of British India, securing them to the latter control of the foreign relations of Afghanistan in return for an annual subsidy of eighteen lakhs of rupees. During his reign, peace was almost wholly broken, but some advance was made in education As regards the First World War (1914-1918), he maintained a policy of neutrality.

King Aman Allah Khan (1892-1960, r. 1919-1929, assumed the royal title in 1926), a staunch supporter of modernist-nationalist thought; he introduced the first constitution of Afghanistan (1923) and announced a programme of social and educational reforms.

cf. Leon B. Poullada: *Reform and Rebellion in Afghanistan, 1919-1929: King Amanullah's Failure to modernize Tribal Society*. Ithaca, N.Y./ London, 1973.

Allama Iqbal dedicated his book entitled *Payam-i Mashriq* (in response to German poet, Goethe), (1923) to Aman Allah Khan. On his invitation, Iqbal visited Afghanistan as an official guest (1933), a few weeks before king's dethronement.

See for detail, M. Ikram Chaghatai: *Goethe, Iqbal and the Orient*, Lahore 1999; idem: *Iqbal, Afghan and Afghanistan* (English and Urdu), Lahore 2006.

Asad visited Afghanistan and King Aman Allah was his host (see *The Road to Mecca*). In one of his letters to his step-son, Ahmed Schiemann (1916-2002), Asad mentioned his stay in Herat with his first wife, Elsa, a German painter (see Asad's report sent to *Frankfurter Zeitung*, 21 March 1926)

Dr. Abdul Ghani (1864-1943) was born in Jalalpur Jattan (district Gujrat, Pakistan). He was the second son of Mawlawi 'Abdus Samad Khan. He did his graduation in Medical Science from the Government College, Lahore (1883) and was awarded Indian Government's scholarship for the higher education in U.K. He stayed in London for about seven years to complete his education.

There he vehemently pleaded the cause of Indian and Turkish Muslims. His political ideas and the true desire for the liberation from the British fascinated several Muslim countries including Afghanistan.

Amir 'Abdar-Rehman (c. 1844-1901, r. 1880-1901) of Afghanistan sent his second son Sardar Nasrullah Khan to London inviting him to Kabul and he left for Afghan capital in 1891. He started his services there as Private English Secretary to the Amir. He made incessant efforts in the field of education for the intellectual development of the young Afghan generation.

Introduction of Public Instruction on the modern lines in Afghanistan, the foundation of Habibiya School, 1903 (on the name of Habibullah Khan, afterwards upgraded to the university level), the establishment of Translation and Compilation Department, opening of Training School for teachers, launching a scheme of universal education, laying the foundation of Medical School and a Night School for the labour class are Dr. Abdul Ghani's revolutionary steps to implement the modern education in Afghanistan. Unluckily, all his such efforts were misrepresented by Mirza Muhammad Husain Mustawfi (Chief Revenue Officer). As a result Dr. Abdul Ghani was confined to prison (March 1909) with his two brothers. After eleven years' imprisonment he and his brothers were released (March 1919) by Amir Amanullah Khan who appointed him a member of the Afghan deputation for peace and sent to Rawalpindi. After the return to Kabul he and his elder brother (Mawlana Najaf Ali) were given the honour of being the members of the new legislative council (early 1921).

In 1927, Dr. Abdul Ghani went to Saudi Arabia for performing *hajj*. There, King Abdul Aziz Ibn Saud honoured him with the membership of his newly-founded Educational Council. He spent many years in Mecca (cf. article on his educational services in Hijaz, published in a journal *Tawheed* (Amritsar, 16 September, 1927). For the life and works of Dr. Abdul Ghani see Abdul Qadeer Najafi: *Dr. Abdul Ghani Jalalpuri*, Lahore, no date. See also his elder brother's autobiography. Allama Iqbal wrote a brief note on Najaf Ali's book under the title *Tuhfa-i Imaniya* (on Amanullah Khan); Zafar Hasan Aibak: *Khatirat* (autobiography) ed. Dr. Ghulam Husain Zulfiqar, Lahore 1990, pp. 87-88, 117; *A Brief Political History of Afghanistan*. By Dr. Abdul Ghani, vol. I (Lahore 1989).

5 Maulana Abdul Qadir Qasuri (d. 1942), one of the influential persons of *Ahl-i Hadith* and a prominent leader of the Khilafat movement. Cf. *Sidq* (Lucknow), 3 November 1942 and Muhammad Ishaq Bhatti: *Qasuri Khaandaan*, Mamun Kanjan 1994, pp. 46-64, and for his younger brother, Abdullah Qasuri, pp. 19-46; S. Sulaiyman Nadvi: *Yad-i Raftgan*, 1983, pp. 241-242; he is the father of Maulana Muhyiddin Ahmed Qasuri (1889-1971).

6 Muhammad ibn Abdul Wahhab (1703-1791). The religious movement known as Wahhabiyah is founded on his teachings; Saudi Arabian conservative theologian and reformer; see George S. Rentz: *The Birth of the Islamic Reform Movements in Saudi Arabia: Muhammad ibn Abd al-Wahhab and the Beginnings of the Unitarian Empire in Arabia*, London 2004; Abd Allah Salih al-'Uthaymia:

Muhammad ibn al-Wahhab: The Man and his Works. London: Tauris, 2009; cf. *The Oxford Encyclopedia of the Modern Islamic World (= OEMIW)*, Ed. John L. Esposito, vol. 2, New York/Oxford: OUP, 1995, pp. 159-160, vol. 4, pp. 307-308; Dr. Qiyamuddin Ahmad's book on Wahhabi Movement in India, Urdu tr., Karachi, 1976; "The Sa'udi Dynasty and Wahhabism" by Dr. Muhammad Said al-Shaafy. (in: *The Proceedings of the Pakistan Historical Conference* (16th session, 1968, pp. 52-57); Hamid Algar: *Wahhabism: A Critical Essay* (New York, 2002).

7 Mawlana Muhammad Ismail Ghaznawi (1895-1960), son of Mawlana Abdul Wāhid Ghaznawi Amritsari, was a staunch follower of King Abdul Aziz ibn Saud. From the Saudi Government he was officially deputed to look after the Indian *hajis*. He frequently used to go to Saudi Arabia and met the King. There, he was also acquainted with Muhammad Asad who was at that time one of the influential persons of the royal court. Ismail wrote a book on Abdul Aziz Ibn Saud (Amritsar, 1930) and also translated Sulaiman bin Sahman Nejdi's Arabic book in Urdu entitled *Tufha-i wahhabiyya* (Amritsar, no date). See for detail, *Tawheed* (Amritsar), first two volumes (1927, 1928); Abdur Rasheed Iraqi: *Ghaznawi Khaandaan*, Karachi 2003, pp. 95-97.

8 Munira bint Husain (d. 1978 in Riyadh, Saudi Arabia), third wife of Asad and the mother of his only son, Talal. She belonged to a well-known tribe of Nejd, Banu Shammar. When Asad married her (April 1930 in Ha'il), she was only 15 years of age. She accompanied Asad during his stay in the sub-continent. In New York, when Asad firmly decided to marry for the fourth time, she strongly opposed and ultimately Asad divorced her.

9 Talal Asad was born in Medina (April 1930). He spent the days of his childhood and youth in Lahore, Srinagar and Delhi. After completing his education from London he joined City University of New York from where he was retired as Professor of Social Anthropology. He permanently lives in New York. His recent book *On Suicide Bombing* was published from New York (2007).

At the end of Hayman's French book on Asad (Paris 2005), she has given some details about his father's life. In an article of David Arian entitled "Leopold of Arabia" (2001), he has produced very significant information about Asad with reference to Talal.

At the Graduate Center since 1998, Talal Asad is a socio-cultural anthropologist of international stature specializing in the anthropology of religion with a special interest in the Middle East and Islam. He earned his M.A. at Edinburgh University and B. Litt. and D. Phil. at Oxford and the universities of Khartoum, Sudan and Hull, England. He was a member of the New School graduate faculty from 1989 to 1995, and then joined the faculty at Johns Hopkins University. In the spring of 1979, he was a visiting professor at the University of California at Berkeley.

Professor Asad specializes in the studies of Sudan, Arabs and nomadic life. He is the author or contributing editor of several books including *Anthropology and Colonial Encounter* (1973, Ithaca/Humanities Press) and *Genealogies of Religion* (1993, John Hopkins Press), and has published in a wide variety of international journals; his works have been translated into many languages. Other publications include *The Sociology of Developing Societies: The Middle East*; and *The Kababish Arabs: Power, Authority, and Consent in a Nomadic Tribe*. The recipient of many awards and honors, Professor Asad has served in the Economic and Social Research Council in England and the Social Science Research Council in the United States.

10 He was the younger brother of Abdul Qadir Qasuri; died in 1949.

11 About Asad's stay in India (1932 onwards) an intelligence report was prepared by the concerned Secret Department and it is still available in the Oriental and India Office Collections of the British Library (London).

cf. *Muhammad Asad: A European Gift to Islam (= Gift)*. Edited, annotated and written by M. Ikram Chaghatai, vol. I, Lahore: The Truth Society , 2006, pp. 249-250.

12 Asad loved to be seated close to this Sheranwala Darwaza (Gate of the Lions) as his Jewish and Muslim names ('Leo' and 'Asad') also mean 'lion'. It is said that during his early years in Lahore he attended for a few months the lectures of Mawlana Ahmad Ali Lahori (1887-1962), who was a renowned religious scholar and also the founder of a *madrasah* that was inside Sheranwala Darwaza (Anjuman-e Khuddam ad-Din).

See *Puranay Chiragh*. By Sayyid Abu'l Hasan Ali Nadvi, vol. I, Karachi 1975, pp. 134-163; Khaled Ahmad's article on Asad, in: *Gift*, I: 287-291.

13 Delhi Gate (Lahore), one of the historic gates of walled city of Lahore; still exists in its original form; the big garden, attached to the gate, was a centre of social, political and literary life of the city.

cf. *The walled city of Lahore*, Lahore: LDA, 1993; Muhammad Latif: *Lahore and its architectural remains*, repr., Lahore 1953.

14 Wazir Khan Mosque, a historic mosque of Lahore, inside the Delhi Gate; built during the Shahjahan's period.

cf. Abdullah Chaghatai: *Wazir Khan Mosque*, Lahore 1975; Ghazala Misbah: *The Wazir Khan Mosque. Its Aesthetic Beauty*. Lahore 1999; Mamoona Khan: *Wazir Khan Mosque. Rediscovered*. Lahore: Co-opera, 2011.

15 Since 1927, Asad had been contributing to Swiss newspaper *Neue Zürcher Zeitung* (Zürich, Switzerland) as a correspondent for the Islamic countries of the Middle East. After his arrival in the Subcontinent, his first article "Gespräch in Indien" was published in this newspaper (11 Dec. 1932), in which he described the different aspects of "Hindustani Culture" and the worldly-known historical monuments of this city.

16 Indian National Congress, established in 1885; under the leadership of Gandhi. Congress launched the movement for the liberation of India from the British Government. After the Partition (1947), the Congress ruled India for thirty years.

✸ ✸ ✸ ✸ ✸

For people, who think.

Asad's most favourite part of a Qur'anic verse (13:3)

II
HIMALAYAN INTERLUDE
(1933)

I

One day I stood, as I had done so often, in front of Wazir Khan's Mosque in Lahore, lost in vague and somewhat sad thoughts, when a young Indian friend, a Muslim, passed by and saw me. He took me by the hand and said: 'I know a singer who lives nearby. She is not like other singing-girls; you must see and hear her.' I went with him; and ever since I would think of that strange woman whenever I felt oppressed by India's remoteness -- or so it seemed to me -- from all real life.

We found her in a carpet-covered room, in the midst of a small group of musicians with cymbals, noisy hand-drums and strangely-shaped lutes. She sang, her voice was deep and full; but this was not what struck me. She wore a most beautiful North-Indian dress: full, gold-embroidered trousers of blue brocade, a lilac tunic with wide sleeves, and over her head and shoulders a transparent Benares veil, like a cloud composed of red and golden threads; but all this, too, was of no importance as compared with the quiet reality of her movements, which appeared to be free of all convention. She was of middle age and her features did not conform to the usual concept of beauty: she had sharp, prominent cheek-bones and a somewhat broad nose. But her eyes were of that rare, perfect almond shape which can be seen only in the mountain regions of Asia. (As a matter of fact, I learned later that she belonged to the tribe of Perni, one of those nomadic tribes of mysterious origin which wander over the high table-lands of northernmost India.) Her forehead was low but broad and well-formed, and her mouth red and delicate, as if filled with deep knowledge and still greater hopes, seemingly remembering all transports of delight, all bitterness and all beauty of past and future days. But the strangest thing about her was her hands, narrow and long, filled with soft power and an inborn harmony of movement – hands that were never lax and yet never tensed, and were always beautiful.

Assisted by my friend in my as-yet very hesitant and faulty Urdu, I had a long conversation with that lady, for I had become curious about her life and outlook; and she, on her part, became impressed – however comical this might seem – by the fact of my being a *hajji* and, more than that, having resided for years in Medina, in the vicinity of the Prophet's tomb. . . . For, even though the singing-girls of India are far more than lax in their mode of life, the Muslims among them are, as a rule, strangely attracted to everything that is connected with religious faith. Usually they begin their day with a recitation from the Qur'an; they fast scrupulously during the month of Ramadhan – and yet, they are fully conscious, with a sense of melancholy resignation, of the discord between their actual life and the object of their nostalgia. But this is perhaps the reason for the fact that – although they are licentious in their behaviour – they are never really reprobate, and thus are able to preserve a certain womanly dignity in their bearing.

She sang and danced a little: it was not really dancing but, rather, a restrained striding forwards and backwards and sideways, and a slow, flowing movement of arms and wrists and fingers. Her silver bracelets and anklets clinked and jingled at every step, and her heavy almond-eyes stared out from their depths into a strange remoteness. Afterwards she sat, tired, leaning against the wall-cushions, with her shell-coloured hands flat on the dark carpet.

My friend asked her – obviously for my benefit – where she had been born, and she answered: 'My father was a musician. We used to wander through many towns and villages and all places where a fair was being held. My mother gave birth to me at the fair of Kulu, at the time when the Hindus celebrate their *Dusserah*[1] festival; and there she died because she was so weak and it was so cold. Much, much later my father told me that he buried her in a meadow while nearby the Hindus danced around their idols and drank rice-brandy; and my father wept because there was nobody who could recite some verses of the Qur'an over his dead wife.'

I asked her, 'Where is Kulu?' – but she did not know for certain. 'Somewhere in the mountains, beyond the valley of Kangra.'

And thus it happened that the name 'Kulu' entered the circle of my imaginings: I heard the pipes and the drums and the singing of throngs of men and women who moved in dance-steps around the multiform figures of deities in gold and silver and silk and brocade – in a cold mountain valley with meadows and fir trees and a hard, clear air. A desire to see Kulu took hold of me. On the same evening, on my return to the Kasuri house near the Sheranwalah Gate, I opened a map of Northern India – and there it was: a place-name and an area on the eastern edge of the Punjab, surrounded by ranges of the Himalayas and not very far from the Tibetan frontier. And there, I decided, we must go. Only a few days separated us from the *Dusserah* festival.

II

On the following afternoon my friend and I left Lahore. At night, in Pathankot, we changed trains and left the plains of the Punjab behind us. A narrow-gauge railway bore us through the dawn into the valley of Kangra with the first presentiment of the Himalayas: dark hillocks rising up against the reddening sky, cool and green under forests, sloping fields, tea plantations; here and there a mountain brook rushing over boulders. In the forenoon higher and higher rocks appeared, forcing the train into curve after curve. And then appeared the little town of Kangra, which has given its name to the valley: loosely-spread-out houses covered almost to their slate roofs in a confusion of bushes and leaves; and beyond the town, jutting upwards on a solitary hill, the ruins of the old fortress of Nagarkot. Many centuries ago it was considered invincible and in time of war had offered a secure refuge to the princes of Northern India, as well as to a host of idols covered with precious stones. However, there came a time when Mahmud of Ghazni[2] – one of the truly great warrior-kings of the Islamic Middle Ages – reached even here in order to destroy the idols and to break the power of all who worshipped them instead of the One God. He took the fortress in his first assault; and we are told that after their return from this campaign his soldiers sold jewels by the bushel in the bazaars of Ghazni, while the slaves captured in the plains and foothills of India hardly attained the price of eight silver pieces per head . . . .

Very soon we arrived at the village of Joginder Nagar, the end of the railway line. I strolled through the single narrow bazaar street bordered by small shops on either side; the houses had wooden verandahs and balconies and slate-covered roofs, which reminded me of Swiss village houses; and the smell of the tiny side-lanes was that of mountain villages in all countries of the world: the smell of freshly-cut wood and of cattle stables, of sweaty leather and milk and the cool fragrance of trees.

There were two ways from Joginder Nagar to Kulu: a footpath over the Bhabu Pass, three days long; and a roundabout-way via Mandi, one day by mail bus. I chose the mail bus.

Mandi was the capital of a semi-independent principality on the western edge of the Himalayas: a lovely little composition of mountains and foaming rivers and narrow, ascending and descending lanes, and squat houses built of stone and timber, and occasionally a beautiful woman in a colourful dress of many folds and pleats. There were, too, several tiny temples with steep narrow cupolas and half-open courtyards, each of them presided over by the figure of a strangely-shaped god or a cow cast in bronze, the head turned towards the inner sanctuary.

After the bustle and unease of Lahore, Mandi was like a blissful return to the fairy tales of one's childhood: it exuded only quietude and security, without the least false note. The houses were simple and without even any attempt at embellishment – just set down in the winding little lanes in accordance with the shapes of the hills on which the town was hanging. But what precisely constituted the beauty of Mandi was that not a single building, large or small, had any pretension to an individuality of its own, but each was simply adjusted to the demands of the terrain: that is, to reality. Similarly, the long quadrangle of the market place gently sloped downwards from the top of the town for no other reason than that only here, on the summit of the hill, could a sufficiently large and flat expanse be found; and so, too, it happened that the line of shops which bordered the market place – some of them crowned by small wooden turrets -formed, as it were, the rim of a flat bowl. Beyond that rim, on three sides, were the steep slopes which resembled a green table-cloth hanging down in many folds: and the folds were the streets and lanes, narrow, shady, twisting downwards to the still-young and noisy river Beas; and the embroidery on the table-cloth's edge consisted of many small temples, very old, oddly shaped, with conical or oval cupolas, all of them facing the river which is regarded by the Hindus as holy. In the dusky interior of each of these temples stood the usual figures of gods, seemingly contemplating the rushing river: Ganesh with his elephant head, the ten-armed Durga-Kali, and many others whose names were as yet unknown to the stranger.

III

We spent the night in a small inn and left on the following morning, cool and glass-clear. The thickly-forested slopes of the mountains displayed their green preciousness to the traveller's eye; the world had drunk its fill of the stillness of the night, and now the day spoke to us in its happy loudness. From one of the temples on the bank of the river came the shrill ding-dong of a little bell; women sang in the rice fields which descended in terraces towards the water's edge.

And then began the real Himalayas: high mountain ranges and deep valleys; the mountains were as yet softly rounded and covered with forests; brooks foamed and rushed through the valleys. After the dusty plains of India, after the desolation of an endless landscape which knows nothing of the freedom of the Central Asian steppes or of the majesty of Arabian deserts, the ascent towards the threshold of the Himalayas was like a revelation. A greenness without end – from the dark depths of the forests downwards to the rice fields swelling in the sunlight and glittering with hundreds and hundreds of tiny pools of water, down to the tender yellow-green grasses growing between the water-worn stones on the river bank: one had never known that there could be so many shades of green . . . .

We travelled for hours by car on a road high above the river, always in curves along the mountain-slopes, always climbing into a higher, wilder and more silent landscape. The rice fields disappeared. The soft mountains grew in harshness and sometimes became steep, rocky walls which held the foaming, bubbling river in their restraining grip; and all that remained for the car and us was a narrow, winding path with a mountain-wall on one side and an abyss on the other: the pass between Mandi and Kulu.

And then, gradually, hesitantly, the landscape opened up, like someone who is awaking from deep sleep and now slowly stretches his limbs before deciding to get up. The mountains began to shed their harsh inaccessibility and by degrees drew back from the river; once again they became soft, their rocky nakedness covered with humus and trees. The valley widened into an elongated plateau with meadows and woodland: and there I saw, for the first time since many years, fir forests-black-green, tall and dense, full of secrets and memories. And the years spent in the deserts and hot solitudes paled and went down, and other years came up and called out to me with long-forgotten voices; and in the startling convulsion of my heart I suddenly saw, for a second, my life hanging between two worlds, seemingly without a home here and without a home there . . . But then my mind began to work again, and I realized that the cause of such fearsome feelings was the environment in which I found myself since months and months: this strange land, this India which so completely lacked all form and meaning that it appeared almost unreal to me -- a world between worlds, without a home here and without a home there, neither eastern nor western . . . .

The first village of the Kulu valley passed us by: houses with slate-covered roofs, submerged between tea plantations; wild-eyed shepherds driving their flocks downwards from the mountains of the Tibetan borderlands towards the plains in order to avoid the Himalayan winter.

While our driver busied himself with the car, adding water to the radiator and pumping up the tyres, I strolled over to some of the shepherds who had sat down away from the road and were now eating their noon meal. I greeted them in my broken Urdu, but they did not understand me; their home was far away, in Ladakh, which is the Tibetan part of Kashmir. They wore short, shirt-like jackets made of coarse, grey-white wool and sandals tied with leather thongs. One of them offered me, without speaking, a wooden bowl full of milk. He reminded me vividly of a Kurdish boy, the first person whom I encountered in Kurdistan many years ago, and who greeted me with the same offering and the same wordless gesture; and even the eyes of this shepherd from Ladakh resembled those of the young Kurd: eyes full of a blissful, innocent dullness, warm and wondering . . . . Never can you see such eyes on the plains of India: there, the children are born old and knowing . . . .

The road was filled with colour: many men and women wandering on foot from the neighbouring villages towards Kulu for the imminent *Dusserah* festival, all of them wreathed in flowers and dressed in their best clothes. The men wore short jackets resembling those of the Ladakhi shepherds, but made of better cloth, and long, tight-fitting breeches; and on their heads round caps or black, narrow-brimmed felt hats, like those of the *gorals* in the Tatra Mountains of Poland. The dresses of the women reminded me of the Scottish highlands inasmuch as most of them consisted, in the main, of a black-and-white or multi-coloured plaid: but here it was cunningly wound around the body and tightly belted, so that it had the appearance of blouse and skirt. To be sure, these women were far less beautiful than those of the plains – heavier and stockier and, moreover, disfigured by heavy silver ear and nose rings; but all these natural and unnatural defects were overcome by their exuberant cheerfulness. They laughed a lot and seemed to enjoy the laughter of their men; and so they went rollicking along in loose groups, each adorned with yellow autumn flowers. This love of flowers was common to them all: I saw two very old men who were working on road repairs -- and even they wore flowers around their caps and stuck coquettishly behind their ears.

IV

And here was Kulu. At first one could see only a wide meadow on which a great number of people were busily doing many things: they were erecting booths and tents, dragging beams and planks from one place to another; the owner of a cook-shop was building a baking-oven of clay; traders from Chinese Turkestan were unpacking heavy bales of carpets and *kilims.* But beyond all the noise and confusion of the approaching festival there stood, like a wall of stillness, thousands of deodars, the noble fir trees of the Himalayas, outlined in indescribable grandeur against mountain and sky: wonderful and straight like the colonnades of an ancient Greek temple . . . .

A few houses stood near the meadow – a post office, a school, a *serai* for travellers, and some other small public buildings. But the real Kulu was invisible. I discovered it only in the late afternoon as I wandered between the booths of the so-called Lower Bazaar. I saw a narrow street which rose suddenly, steeply, up a mountain slope: and there began Kulu.

In old times they had built the little town on a hill-ridge and enclosed it within walls; but by now the walls had disappeared, and Kulu was hanging like a pair of saddle bags downwards on both sides of the ridge. The one single street – or, rather, lane – went up one side of the hill and down the other – a ravine between two lines of old, small houses with wooden fronts, occupied at street level by shops and carrying carved wooden balconies on the upper floor.

Great was the silence in this lane, which was so narrow that two people standing at opposite windows could greet each other by a handshake. All life seemed to have withdrawn into a shell and lost its voice. All people were silent. The traders sat wordless, cross-legged and unmoving in their shops, in which – next to the products of European factories -- dusty, strange objects from Central Asia hung and lay about. There were the white, bushy yak-tails which on festive occasions used to be held over Indian princes as symbols of their exalted status. There were embroidered felt-carpets from Khotan and Yarkand and brightly-coloured silks from Kashghar. Above an old, hand-chased incense vessel of Chinese brass hung a faded piece of cotton cloth which must have come from some place like Manchester; and next to it stood a pair of high woman's boots of red leather embroidered in yellow silk – such as are worn by wealthy Kirghiz women. In the background of one of the shops I could discern a saddle from Chitral; its copper pommel was reflected in the glass of a cheap lantern made in Czechoslovakia.

But in spite of all this, I did not sense any conflict between Yesterday and Today. The old Kulu lived on in the twilight between times, like someone whom death has overlooked; and perhaps all these traders and passers-by were so silent and taciturn in order not to remind him? However, where there is no death there can be no life . . . .

The people of Kulu had waxen faces: they were quite different from the noisy peasant women and young men in the new Lower Bazaar or over there on the meadow; they appeared to be entangled within themselves like the figures in an abandoned puppet-show. Many of the men carried on their foreheads the saffron sign of a *brahmin,* the sign of the highest caste; and the women had a quiet, proud bearing without any loud word or laughter; their faces were very fair, often of a strangely exciting, spicy beauty – so much so that I had to hold my breath whenever any of them passed me by. They walked almost always in groups, clad in rustling silks and vividly-coloured shawls, the eyes always looking unmovingly ahead, like the ladies in an abandoned puppet-show . . . .

V

A dark, arched gateway opened up for me the view of a grassy square surrounded by a few higher, more pretentious buildings. Among them stood the palace of the Rajah of Kulu – nowadays rajah in name only, without even the semblance of real power. His ancestors had once ruled not only over Kulu proper but also over the Himalayan districts of Lahool and Spiti and a great part of north-western Punjab. They had a direct diplomatic connection with the Dalai Lama of Tibet, and even the Government of the Heavenly Empire of China considered it proper to receive presents from the Lord of Kulu and occasionally to reciprocate in kind, seeing that the highways from Tibet and Chinese Tartary to India passed through Kulu. However, about the middle of the last century the British occupied Kulu and integrated it within the Indian Empire; and the man who continued to be called the Rajah of Kulu became indistinguishable from any of the other great landlords of India. Still, in the days when I visited it, the people of Kulu paid him the same veneration as their forefathers had shown to his: and therefore the Rajah felt obliged to maintain a grand palace, although the cost of its maintenance consumed almost all his revenues.

From the high, open square before the palace I could see most of the town of Kulu; and the strongest impression was the cleanliness which stood out here in vivid contrast to the smudgy villages and towns of the plains. Every house was surrounded by a small, clean-swept courtyard. On the gentle slopes of every slate roof thousands and thousands of maize-cobs were neatly spread out for drying, and many-coloured poppies and rose bushes grew before the windows.

The evening was closing in, and I thought of going back to the room that I had engaged in the *serai* when I perceived another narrow gateway leading from the palace square towards the houses crowding around the bazaar; and I took that way. But almost immediately it became clear to me that it was not a way but a very small walled courtyard with a single door in the background; and above the door were the usual bizarre figures of deities carved in stone – goddesses with many arms, gods with animal heads, and extremely detailed, almost obscene depictions of embraces between the sexes. Quite clearly this was a temple. The door was slightly ajar. I peered into the dusky interior; nobody was there. And I could not resist the temptation to enter – although I was aware that Indian temples were strictly out of bounds to non-Hindus.

Only through a narrow window below the ceiling and through the half-open door did a little light come in, and outside the sun had just set, and so it was difficult to discern the details. The ceiling was very low. A few silver and copper lamps were hanging from it on chains, but they were not lighted. In the background stood a kind of altar – a solid, pyramid-shaped block of wood on a pedestal, decorated on all four sides with masks of gods in shiny metal, probably silver; and before it a large, flat stone bowl partly filled with what appeared to be oil; and in its centre a vertical black stone -- perhaps marble -- the size of a child's arm. I knew at once that it was a *linga,*[3] the much-worshipped phallus-symbol of Hindu mythology, a symbol of fertility and re-incarnation. I was surprised to find a *linga* temple here in the Himalayas, and was about to open the door a little wider, so as to have a better look at the rooms, when suddenly I heard voices from outside. It would have been more than a scandal to be found in the temple -- an infidel, an unclean being whose mere presence would have defiled the house of the gods for many days . . . . and so I quickly withdrew into the interior and squeezed myself into a tiny alcove behind the *linga* pedestal. A huge barrel of oil -- probably holy oil for the temple lamps and the images of the gods --

offered sufficient protection from other people's eyes if I could make myself sufficiently small . . . .

An old man entered. I could see his face as he lighted one of the hanging lamps: he bore the *brahmin*-sign on his forehead and so – although his dress was not different from that of other men of Kulu – he must have been the priest of this temple. As soon as he had lighted the lamp he opened the door a little wider, and a young woman entered. She held her head low and listened to the words of the priest who spoke to her forcibly, as if in exhortation.

What should I do? I looked cautiously around and, with a breath of relief, discovered a tiny door in the rear wall of the alcove: it was locked only with a wooden bolt and led (as I could see through a crack) to the open square before the palace, with nobody in sight at this time. My way of retreat was there. I had already, gently, pushed back the bolt when I heard the squeak of the front door; and as I looked cautiously over the rim of the oil barrel, I saw the young woman standing alone in front of the divine symbol. The priest had left and closed the door behind him.

I waited. In the flickering light of the oil lamp I saw the woman's face. She looked sad and visibly depressed. For a short while she stood motionless, with folded hands; then she began slowly to unclasp the buckles which held her dress together. She threw off her shawl, and then, with hesitant movement, she took off all the remaining parts of her clothing, until she stood naked and shivering before the *linga*. Then she knelt down -- and I understood: she was a barren woman who now prayed to her own forehead and breasts and hips. And, finally, she threw herself down and struck the stone floor repeatedly with her forehead. She shivered; and I heard her suppressed weeping -- a weeping such as I had never heard before in my life: so forlorn, so helpless and filled with such despair that it made my heart stand still. For, to a Hindu woman there can be no greater misfortune than to remain without a child that would fulfil the sacred rites after her death and thus make her free for re-incarnation.

I could no longer bear this weeping. I opened the small back-door as silently as I could and slipped out into open air, and ran, as if pursued by a nameless danger, across the grassy, empty square, over which an autumnal half-moon had just begun to pour out its pale light.

VI

A drawn-out, wailing trombone-sound swept through my sleep.

awakened and sat for a while in my bed and listened. Beyond the window the night was still dark. And once again that sound, tinny and clumsy as if coming out of a gigantic child's trumpet, and at the same time deeply resounding, piercing like the cry of a helpless being in an empty street at night. Immediately afterwards big drums boomed forth in accompaniment, with their thundering echoed by the fir-clad mountain slopes. Nearer and nearer came this music; fifes chimed in, a bell tinkled, and the trombones carried their melancholy tone upwards into a shrill, breath-taking descant.

I dressed quickly and stepped out of the room. It was bitterly cold; pale stars shone over the deodar trees in the valley. Here and there small fires were burning, and even in this depth of night some people were still busy with putting up tents and booths for the festival that was to begin in the morning. And then, too, I saw the musicians drawing nearer in the light of torches across the meadow -- a long train of men and women, and in their midst, carried on poles by two men, the figure of a god wreathed in flowers: an eight-faced idol staring out of silver masks -- two and two above one another – into the four corners of the world: one of the many that were assembling at this fair of the gods in order to greet Rama-Chandra: that Rama who had been born as a son of the King of Ayodhya, destined to enter, at the end of his days, the heaven of the Indian gods as a re-incarnation of Krishna. From all sides of the valley and from all mountain paths one could now hear the fifes and the drums, the bells and trombones of the approaching processions, every village with a god of its own.

The *Dusserah* festival -- one of the highest in Hinduism -- is meant to celebrate the earthly progress of Rama-Chandra: how he was cheated by a wily step-mother of his succession to his father's kingship, and how he lived for fourteen years, together with his faithful wife Sita, as a hermit in the jungles, and how he fought against devils and demons in order to free the world from evil; and how the demon-king Rawan, who ruled over the island of Lanka, the Ceylon of our days, fell in love with Sita and abducted her through the air to his island kingdom; and how, after much toil and bitter affliction, Rama traced and freed his beloved, vanquished the kingdom of demons and burned Rawan himself to death and finally returned as a demi-god to his hereditary kingdom . . . . And this story, wreathed in many miracles and told in detail in the grand epic *Ramayana,* is to this day dearer to the Indian mind than all reality.

It is Krishna in Rama-Chandra's incarnation -- or 'Nathu Ram', as they call him in this part of the country -- who resides as the chief deity of Kulu in a temple next to the Rajah's palace; and so it is but natural that all the lesser gods of the countryside flock together these days to 'pay their respects' to their great brother. It is said that in earlier times about three hundred and sixty gods would every year assemble here for the festival; in my time the concourse was smaller, but even so, I was told, between ninety and one hundred gods would make their annual appearance. The great fair which was (and still is) held in Kulu on these occasions was quite imposing because of the fact that the trade routes from India to Tibet and Chinese Turkestan come together at this point and make Kulu a natural place of exchange of goods between India and the two Mongol countries, with traders coming from Lhasa and the Mansarovar lakes, from Kashghar and Yarkand, from Kashmir and Ladakh and Baltistan and the high Pamir regions, for ten days or so transforming the quiet valley into a noisy, exuberant mercantile centre.

VII

When I left the *serai* in the morning the broad meadow was already filled with a many-voiced throng. Everywhere one could see groups of men and women from the surrounding villages camping in the open air, each group with their festively-decorated god in the centre. The gods were not very different from one another: almost always a small wooden trestle draped with motley brocades, silken shawls and flowers, and on top of it either a bizarre figurine or simply an upright mask of chased silver or, more rarely, of gold. If the god or goddess in question had a claim to special respect, he or she was, in addition, overshadowed by a small silken canopy and one or more black yak-tails. At the times of prayer white yak-tails with silver handles were flourished over the deity; one man waved an incense bowl while another fanned the god with a fan of peacock feathers; the trombones raised their wailing voices, accompanied by the rattling of hand-drums and the booming of kettle-drums and the twittering of fifes and the jingling of bells; the priest bowed down low before the divine figure, and with him the pious men of his community; all the musical instruments would strike up to their highest pitch, wailing, fluting, jingling and thundering – until suddenly, as if by command, all noise would break off: the prayer service had come to an end.

All in all, the people who thus prayed -- men and women alike -- were far more pleasant to look at than were the gods. All of them wore flowers, and their unceremonious cheerfulness went well together with the sunny autumnal skies and the freshness of the fir forests. They laughed a lot and carolled and chased one another like children all over the meadow and around the booths in which miscellaneous wares from the plains were temptingly displayed.

And then and there two gods from two different villages 'met' for the first time; I did not know why, but apparently these two curiously-named little gods had never before come to Kulu for the *Dusserah* festival, and so they had to be introduced to one another by their respective priests.

As indicated by the mustachioed and bearded silver masks, one of these gods was of the male sex; he wore a dress of violet silk, richly embroidered with golden flowers, and his eight-faced head was overshadowed by a canopy of yak-tails and gilded tassels. His opposite was apparently a lady, less pompously got up and perhaps even of a lower degree; her dress was of pink brocade, old and well-worn, with haphazardly stuck-together fringes; and no canopy protected *her* holy figure. Each of the two deities rested on a small platform over two bamboo poles, and each was carried by two men, with its priest standing close by. In a low, monotonous sing-song the priests announced the names of their gods and (as my friend translated to me) enumerated their respective virtues and powers; and then the musicians beat their drums and jangled their bells, and the god and the goddess were made to incline towards one another seven times and thus the introduction was completed.

An old man came forward, and I was told that he was famous throughout Kulu as a seer. He stood between the two deities and touched them with his hands -- the right hand rested on the male god and the left on the goddess. For a little while he stood straight and motionless -- a small, lean figure of a man with large, deep-set eyes. All people were silent. A quiver ran over the seer's face, coming as if in waves from the inside of his body and gradually spreading by fits and starts over all his limbs -- until the whole of the little man was trembling and shaking like a dry leaf in a storm . . . . And he began to speak as people speak when they are shaken by a fever, as people speak when they are overwhelmed by utter terror, as the despairing speak when sobbing takes away their breath . . . . I could not understand his words except for 'rivers of blood' and 'death'; but he must have been speaking of extraordinary, terrifying things and happenings, as I could clearly see from the faces of the onlookers. Some of them wept: men who but a short while ago had been laughing and romping about with girls; one of them clutched at his breast, another groaned like a wounded animal; and yet another shouted a question -- and then all of them fearfully awaited the seer's answer. He began to speak again, rapidly and forcefully, as if desiring to free himself of a great burden, his face benumbed by a trance out of which he could not escape. Faster and faster came the questions and the old man's answers, pressed out of his mouth by the trembling of his body -- until his tongue failed under such an assault and his speech lost itself in a helpless stammering.

My friend -- no less upset than the others -- told me that the seer had just prophesied a great war (this was in the autumn of 1933), and added: 'In October of 1913, on a similar occasion, this same man predicted a great and bloody war . . . .'

VIII

In the afternoon most of the people assembled in groups for a dance, men and women standing in a semi-circle, with the musicians sitting in its centre: the same instrument as in the procession of the gods, and the same monotonous, melancholy music which, strangely, seemed to produce gaiety in the listeners.

A surprising metamorphosis took place: as they began their final dance in Rama-Chandra's honour, the sturdy peasants seemed to change into rococo figures. All their spontaneity disappeared, and the movements of all the men and women formed themselves into still dance-figures which would have pleased a dancing-master of the eighteenth century. They shuffled rhythmically sidewise with lightly-bent knees and tiny steps, hands placed with an exaggerated 'gracefulness' on hips or toying in too fine a manner with a silken handkerchief: too deliberate, too artificial to be genuine or even pleasing. The whole show became downright silly and -- to me -- depressing and almost tragic. Tragic, because it revealed the chaotic helplessness of the Hindu soul, with all its inner contradictions; and suddenly I knew why the trombones that had awakened me last night had sounded like the wailing of a helpless being: there was no breath in them that did not cry out in despair and the desire to find a way out of the chaos of their existence. And is anything else possible within the soul of a people whose very mythology mirrors the most extravagant flights of fancy unrestrained by the intellect, a wild, primeval chaos of imaginings and unquenchable desires? The gods of the Greeks, though dissolute, were in the last resort ruled over by the powers of Moira and Ananke -- powers which forced all arbitrariness ultimately to surrender to eternal *laws*. The gods of India, on the other hand, know nothing of such a surrender and remain arbitrary to the last. They constantly alter the direction of their will and shimmer in a myriad of changing, confusing hues. They are like the night in a tropical forest which knows no standstill of forms but is lost in the wildness of its begetting and endless procreation.

And now all the gods of Kulu danced. They had come together to pay homage to Rama-Chandra. They surrounded -- on the shoulders of the men who carried them -- the large, movable wooden scaffolding, Rama-Chandra's chariot, in which the great god had already taken his place. They danced: they rocked right and left on their elastic bamboo poles, the vivid colours of their dresses and decorations fluttered in the light of the afternoon sun, and the thousands of men and women who had come here for the feast of the gods gave their jubilation free rein and swung hand in hand in one huge round-dance around Rama-Chandra and all the minor gods. Barrels full of rice brandy stood here and there on the meadow, and from time to time one or another of the dancers interrupted his dance and scooped up the drink with the small copper bowl which was attached to every barrel. This rice brandy was as much a part of the *Dusserah* festival as were the autumnal flowers and the dancing and the wailing of trombones at night. The gaiety rose and gradually changed into lust; the dancers' singing lost all its frolicsome boisterousness and became a shriek and an orgiastic cry. But then came the merciful night.

IX

On my last day in Kulu I sat on the threshold of an ancient temple in the midst of a forest of firs, in the midst of the oldest forest not far from the end of the world. To the north-east began the highlands of Tibet; in the west the mighty massif of the Banghal Mountains, one of the least accessible regions of the world: summits wrapped in loneliness and a savage emptiness, hardly ever trod upon by man. Where I sat -- not far from the village of Manali -- there was loneliness, too, but not of a frightening kind. Thousands upon thousands of deodars, the wonderful, most noble fir trees of the Himalayas, shot up out of the dark-green twilight like masses of bushy spears against the skies. Silenced was the wind. No human being, no animal was there, only deodars and the feeling of utter remoteness; and even in the little temple before which I sat all life seemed to have died. I did not and to this day do not know what sort of gods dwelt in it, for the heavy door was locked by three wooden bolts.

It was a strange temple, the most beautiful that I had ever seen or would later see in India: a square of no more than ten paces on each side, roughly put together out of mighty deodar trunks and surmounted by a high, triple roof of pyramid shape, distantly reminding one of Mongol pagodas. The low façade was covered with the most exquisite carvings in high relief, sculptured legends of gods and their meetings with mortal men and women, dramatic shapes highly stylized and yet endowed with so much reality that I forgot, for long moments, that what I saw was a series of allegories born out of a thousand years of religious philosophy, the mythos of Vishnu: I saw only real human beings in all their convolutions of fury and carnal love, desiring, conquering, breaking down . . . . He who had built the temple and carved the reliefs – perhaps five hundred, perhaps many more centuries earlier – was an artist of high vocation, but today nobody knows his name. Much later I learned that he had to suffer most bitterly for having created this great work of art: for the people of Manali, who had entrusted him with its creation, became jealous at the thought that he might a second time, somewhere else, produce a work of equal perfection; and to prevent this, they cut off his right hand. But they deluded themselves. The man learned to use his tools with his left hand and built, some years later, a similar temple at Triloknath in the principality of Chamba, and it is said that the new building was even more beautiful than the first. But then the artist could no longer evade his destiny: for the same reason as had done the people of Manali, the Rajah of Triloknath ordered him to be maimed forever: his left hand was cut off and his eyes put out. And God alone knows whether this story is true or not . . . .

I heard a light step go over the moss and the dry fir needles. A girl was passing by. She wore a red-and-brown plaid wound around her body, a body very young and slender. I called out, and she stopped, startled, and turned her head very slowly in my direction, as do the animals of steppe or forest when they scent danger: and I saw a very fair face with dark, widely-spaced eyes and a red, trembling mouth -- and she reminded me of that strange singing-girl in Lahore who was the cause of my excursion into the Himalayas . . . . I asked, 'What is your name?' -- and she answered, 'My name is Paldassi . . . .', and so our conversation began -- a comical conversation, what with both my and Paldassi's half-knowledge of Hindustani -- and I learned that she was the daughter of the priest in charge of this very temple; her house stood somewhat deeper down in the valley. She asked, 'Would you visit our house?', and gazed at me with serious questioning eyes, neither bashful nor smiling; and once again I saw her as a young animal from the wilds, a gazelle perhaps, to be judged quite differently from other women.

A very old woman came down the forest path and rattled the temple door; and when she saw that it was locked she went away without a word. Paldassi whispered, 'This one, a saint. Lives high up the mountain, small hut, many, many years . . . . knows no *maya* any more . . . . And as she recognized me -perhaps because of the shape of my beard -- as a Muslim, she added, 'Holy man of yours, Mussalman, up there in the valley, with some other people.' It surprised me greatly to hear of a Muslim *sufi* living in these mountains, but Paldassi could not tell me anything more about him. She had only heard of him. I let her describe the way as well as she could, and started to walk.

X

For well over an hour the path led through forests up and down mountain slopes, across a brook rushing and foaming over boulders. Finally, late in the afternoon, I saw the little house: it was built of roughly-hewn stones, and the low slate roof jutted out in front to produce a verandah. On a straw mat before the door sat an old man, the 'holy man', as Paldassi had called him.

As I later came to know, he was no more and no less 'holy' than the many *sufis* who live in solitude here and there, turned away from the world and following the winding paths of mystic cognition; and yet, this man seemed to be different from any *sufi* I had met before. He was small of stature and had a face with dull, lifeless features. But his eyes: such eyes! In them there was dreaming side by side with wakefulness, and the peace of a soul that had found itself.

This man had the gift -- I could see it myself that very evening -- of bringing out the true Self in the people who accepted his spiritual guidance, and to point out to every one of them the way proper to him, and to him alone. Six or seven men lived there together as a community, all of them different from one another and (in contrast to similar congregations known to me through earlier experience) each one had a real, sharply-outlined personality. In the course of the evening the master explained to me how this had come about; since he knew Persian very well and spoke some Arabic, too, we could easily understand one another. He said (not in the words that follow but in their sense):

'As our Prophet has made clear to us, every human being is born in a perfection of his or her own -- but in the course of our lives most of us destroy that perfection, and thus our souls. Hence, the innermost purpose of religious faith is not, as so many people believe, *dynamic* in nature -- that is, a growth toward higher and higher stages of perfection -- but, rather, *static:* the preservation of one's Self, the keeping and unfolding of what has been there since our birth . . . .'

XI

In the evening, after the congregational sunset prayer, six men assembled in a semi-circle around the old man and held what is called a *dhikr* -- an Arabic word which means 'remembrance' or, more properly, calling God's Being to mind.

I had never been attracted to what may best be described as 'organized mysticism', that is to say, the pursuance of inner enlightenment in a group guided by a supposedly initiated leader, a *shaikh* (literally, 'old man'), who is presumed to have already come close to a perception of the Divine Reality and is thus able to show to his followers the 'way' (Arabic, *tariqah*) to a similar cognition. However, the very designation of such a group-endeavour as a *tariqah* brings with it, I believe, the illusion that the Ultimate Truth can be found through an organized system of 'spiritual education': in other words, through something resembling a class of students tutored by a professor and led by him, progressively, to an examination and the achievement of a final 'degree'. I had always -- from my earliest days as a Muslim -- been convinced that this method is based on self-deception on the part of those who follow it, and that inner enlightenment can be achieved only through *individual* search. The history of Islam has witnessed the rise of innumerable *tariqahs,* and none of them has resulted in anything of lasting spiritual value beyond the establishment of 'religious orders' faintly resembling the Christian ones -- both in the more or less pronounced concept of a withdrawal from the affairs of the world and in the lack of any tangible effect on the moral growth of the community as a whole.

Here, however, in this little community at the edge of the world, in the midst of mountain peaks and a forest of deodars, I saw something different from the *tariqahs* I had encountered in earlier days: I saw how one man's spiritual power brought out the innermost character of six different men to light and to reality.

The six men sat on a worn straw mat, with the uncertain light of a small oil lamp playing over their faces. Their leader sat in the shade in front of them and intoned, in a low voice, the *Fatihah* prayer in Arabic:

'In the name of God, the Most Merciful, the Dispenser of Grace . . . .' When he finished, the six men joined arms and intoned slowly, in unison, *'Huwa* . . . .' This Arabic word means 'He': it is the most simple and at the same time most powerful designation of God appearing in the Qur'an. They repeated it in an undertone, almost whispering, *'Huwa* . . .' and slowly rocked their heads in unison, their faces turned upwards, eyes closed, as if testing the sweetness of an immersion in His Presence.

They repeated again and again *'Huwa'*, and in their concentration on the breath-like sound of this Arabic word their faces seemed to reflect each man's true being -- each man quite different from the others, and each one visibly finding his Self and at the same time losing himself in Him -- so clearly, so unmistakably, that I was shaken to my depths. I had never before experienced anything like this.

XII

I spent the night as a guest of those strange men. In the early morning we breakfasted together: milk and apples -- the most wonderful apples in all the world -- large, green on one side and red on the other, of a crispness and sweet-sour juiciness never to be found elsewhere: the unforgettable apples of Kulu. And then I started on my way back.

In the valley I passed by a rice field; it was small, spread over three terraces, and covered with water. A few women waded up to their knees in this water and planted young seedlings, while a little higher up their men were digging new irrigation channels. The women laughed and sang and playfully splashed one another with water; their woollen plaid garments were raised high and bared their legs -- the strong legs of mountain women, voluptuous and abounding in young life.

At the *serai* in Kulu I rejoined my friend, and we said good-bye to Kulu. Once again we went by car to Mandi, and from there to Joginder Nagar, the railway terminus. It was early afternoon, and we were told that the next train for Pathankot would leave after two hours; and so we strolled once again through the now familiar bazaar street of the village.

A stall with huge cauldrons of hot milk -- assiduously stirred by a man with a long wooden ladle -- attracted my eyes and awakened my hunger; and so I said to my friend, 'Let's have a glass of milk and a bun; that will keep us until we reach Pathankot.' As we stopped before the stall, the owner was just holding out an earthenware bowl full of milk to a stray dog (a gesture of which I wholeheartedly approved); and when my friend told him in Punjabi what we wanted, he pointed, while rinsing the bowl, towards a shelf on the wall. 'What is he saying?' I asked my friend, and he answered, 'Well, he is a caste Hindu, and we are obviously non-Hindu, and therefore impure. He would not touch a vessel from which people like us would drink; and so he wants you to take down a glass from the shelf above, and he will fill it with water.'

Suddenly I saw red -- literally, a red fury boiling up in me and flimmering before my eyes. He had fed the dog with his own hand, and that was good -- but he refused to touch anything that might touch because I was impure! And to my shame I must confess that at that moment I lost all my composure and was filled with a fury such as I had never known before -- and, I hope, will never know in the future. 'Tell this bastard that I am a human being like him! Tell him to take down that glass and fill it with his own hands, or I will smash his stall to pieces and pour all his milk onto the street!' Seeing my furious face and learning from my embarrassed friend what I had said, the stall owner tremblingly took down the glass from the shelf. I tore it from his hand, and got hold of the ladle and filled the glass brimful with milk and let it overflow back into the cauldron, thus making all that milk 'impure'; and then I threw away the glass, and fished out a hundred rupee note from my pocket -- far more than the cauldron of milk had been worth -- and threw it at the shaking stall owner's face.

This was my first encounter with the Hindu concept of caste and purity and impurity . . . . [4]

Endnotes

1 *Dusserah* (Dassara, Dussehra) is the tenth and last day of Navaratri. According to Hindus on this day Ramchandra attacked Ravan; who will take bath in river Ganga on the occasion ten times of his sins will be forgiven. The Hindus celebrate it with much festivities. It combines many festivals in one.

cf. B. R. Gupta: *Hindu Holidays and Ceremonials.* Calcutta 1919.

2 Mahmud Ghaznawi (971-1039, r. 998-1030); son of Subuktagin; he frequently attacked India, including Somnath (1025).

cf. Muhammad Nazim: *The Life and Times of Sultan Mahmud of Ghazna.* Cambridge 1931 (reprinted: Lahore)

3 *Linga*, a word that means digging with a stick or primitive plough. Since both the plough and the phallus prepare the way for 'insemination' the term *linga* is also applied to the phallus, and to the regenerative religious symbol, particularly the phallic emblems of the god Shiva.

cf. Benjamin Walker: *Hindu World. An Encyclopedic Survey of Hinduism.* Vol.

I, London: 1968, pp. 594-597, also s.v. Sex Mysticism pp. 390-394; A. Miles: *Land of the Lingam*. London 1933.

4 From India, Asad despatched to the above-mentioned Swiss newspaper the following articles:

a) "Wer denkt an Kulu" (Who thinks about Kulu)
b) "Zu den Götter von Kulu" (The gods of Kulu)
c) "Die Götter tanzen" (Dance of gods)
d) "Tempel und Gottsucher im Himalaja" (Temple and god-seekers in Himalaya)
e) "Am Grat der Welt" (The Edge of the World)

Apart from some minor amendments and additions, Asad has reproduced all these articles in this chapter.

* * * * *

ISLAM AT THE CROSSROADS

by

MUHAMMAD ASAD

(LEOPOLD WEISS)

The author is an Austrian convert who embraced Islam several years ago. Lived in Medina -the Holy City- for nearly six years and carried out researches in Arabic Literature and Islamic History . . . .

The Cultural aspects of Islam and the Western Civilization and their reactions have been discussed in this book from a New and Original view-point . . . .

Neatly printed on thick Antique paper and bound in cloth Rs. 2-or 2*s*. 8*d*.—Postage extra

First edition of Muhammad Asad's book "Islam at the Crossroads" (Lahore 1934)

III
'ISLAM AT THE CROSSROADS' (1933-34)

I

During the year 1933, that is, during most of my stay in Lahore in the house opposite the Sheranwalah Gate, I had the opportunity of meeting many people of importance within the Muslim community, all of them curious to meet the European convert (a *rara avis* in those days) and one, too, who had lived for many years in Arabia and spoke Arabic better even than English, the *lingua franca* of India. And since, contrary to European custom, it is a time-honoured Muslim tradition to pay a visit to a new arrival rather than to expect a visit from him, most of those new acquaintances came spontaneously, without waiting for an invitation from my host; and since all of them were fluent in English, my days were filled with lively conversation and I became increasingly familiar with the social and political problems of that intriguing country.

In time, many of those new Muslim friends invited me into their homes, and I came to know their wives and their children, and to appreciate the easy familiarity with which I was invariably received, and to enjoy the delicious taste, or rather tastes, of *Moghulani'* food -- that cuisine introduced into India by a succession of Moghul rulers -- a combination of Turkish, Persian and Indian ways of cooking, very rich, very strong on spices, and probably the best fitted for India's climate. But most enjoyable of all was the genuine warmth with which I was received wherever I went, the unreserved acceptance of a newcomer as a Muslim among Muslims; and this made me gradually overcome my regret at having left Arabia. I began to realize that the change of my environment was but a change of form, with the substance remaining the same: I had been living among brothers and sisters there, and now I was among brothers and sisters here, once again at home, not a stranger among strangers . . . .

This feeling emboldened me to speak to my new-found Muslim friends with unhesitating freedom, to say 'Yes' to those facets of their social life of which I approved, and 'No' to those which, in my opinion, stood open to criticism. Although I did not know it at that time, this unexpected intellectual involvement of mine in the cultural problems of my community was destined to have far-reaching consequences for my own future inasmuch as it was to alter, by degree, the whole tenor and purpose of my life.

Ever since I could remember, I had been strongly influenced by the visual aspects of my surroundings, and this was reflected in my writings. Whenever I described a new phase of my wanderings -- whether it was the experience of an Arabian desert or of the bazaar in a Persian town or of the dramatic Muharram procession in Tehran -- the play of light and colours and movement and the constant changes of shapes gripped me so strongly that my experience flowed almost by itself into my descriptions and thus enabled me to convey it in full to my readers: and this explains perhaps my early reputation in the German press as a travel correspondent of special merit. And now, among my Muslim friends in Lahore, I was overcome by the same need to observe without cease the appearance of the people and things around me. I saw the beautiful high turbans on the heads of some of my Punjabi friends and noted how easily they gave up wearing them. I saw men dressed in elegant, form-fitting *achkans* and Jodhpore pyjamas, and a few days later I found that they had decided to exchange them for the formless garments of Europe. True, the women kept invariably to their becoming traditional garb -*shalwars* and tunics, or *saris* -- but they, too, together with their menfolk, frequently tried to conform to the ways and customs of the West in their furnishings, their daily life and, what was most disquieting to me, in their valuations of what was right and what was wrong in the social sense. In short, it soon became obvious to me that Muslim society was slowly being submerged in an imitation of an alien civilization not only in its appearances but also in its outlook and its aims; and I realized with the certainty of an instinctive knowledge that this trend was unavoidably leading to a step-by-step dissolution of all that was unique and precious in Muslim social and, in the last resort, spiritual life as well: and I was filled with a great desire, almost a passion, to fight against this deadening tendency towards an imitation of the West by the Muslims.

II

At about that time I was approached by one of the foremost Muslim foundations in the Punjab, the *Anjuman Himayat-e-Islam*[1] ('Association for the Protection of Islam') to deliver a public talk on how I had become a Muslim. I accepted the invitation as such, but only on the condition that I would be allowed to modify the theme as I saw fit; and the governing body of the *Anjuman* consented to my condition without any ado.

It was finally arranged that I would deliver not one lecture but two, on consecutive days.

In the first of these lectures, elaborated by me in writing (against my usual habit) and delivered before a congregation of several hundred people in the auditorium of the Muslim High School in Lahore, I outlined the essential characteristics of the two civilizations facing one another: the civilization of Islam, based on a definite ideology of its own, on the one hand, and, on the other, the pragmatic civilization of Europe, born out of the materialistic premises of Roman culture in conjunction with medieval Christianity and its dualistic antithesis of flesh and spirit symbolized by darkness and light. I endeavoured to show that the Unitarian concept of human life as revealed in the teachings of the Qur'an -- a concept bound up with God-consciousness -- could not possibly be reconciled with the man-centred, consumer-oriented outlook of Western civilization, which had long ago lost all contact with spiritual values and had no room for God in its considerations.

In the second lecture I stressed the fact that imitation *as such* is a deadly enemy of all creativeness, and that by imitating the aims or even the outward forms and aspects of another civilization the Muslims were, by implication, denying to Islam the role of a culture-producing power and, thus, the very right to existence. The world of Islam, I said, was now standing at a crossroads, with one road leading to cultural fulfilment and the other to dissolution and the Muslims still had the chance, though not for very long, to choose the road they were to take.

These two lectures created something of a stir among the Muslim community, first in Lahore and then, like ripples spreading on the surface of a lake, in other Muslim centres as well. People came to me in droves and requested me to address listeners in Delhi, in Bombay, in Madras . . . . could not possibly accept all of those invitations -- and so I decided upon another course: to elaborate the two lectures more fully and to publish the result as a book.

And so it came about that my first book on an Islamic subject --

Islam at the Crossroads[2] -- was born at the beginning of 1934.

III

It was a small book, for I had tried to condense within the compass of one hundred pages my perception of the essentials of Islam as a religion and a social programme. Apparently I had 'hit the nail on the head', as the saying goes, for the demand for it was so lively that it went through several reprints in the first year of its publication. After a year or so there was hardly any educated Muslim in India who had not read it or at least heard of it. To be sure, not all the reactions of my readers were positive. Many of the Western-educated Muslims were shocked by my condemnation of the tendency towards a 'Westernization' of Muslim society and regarded it as a reactionary attack on all that could be summed-up in the term 'progress'; and many of my conservative readers, on the other hand, especially among the self-styled 'guardians of the Faith' -- the *mullahs* -- vehemently criticized my rejection of all *taqlid* -- the blind acceptance and imitation of the thought-processes of the early generations of Islamic scholars -- and my insistence on the continuous necessity of independent thinking *(ijtihad)* by the Muslims of all times. And so a witty friend of mine once remarked, 'Muhammad Asad fights on two fronts at one and the same time -- both against the misters and the *mullahs.*'

This friend was Chaudhri Ilahi Bakhsh[3], an elderly retired Session Judge in whose house I was a frequent visitor. He was widowed; his children (I believe, two daughters) were now married and had families of their own, and so he lived alone in his comfortable bungalow on one of Lahore's beautiful tree-lined streets, looked after by a couple of competent servants, and ever-ready to receive his numerous friends at his table. One day he asked me to come to him in the evening, for, he said, 'Dr Muhammad Iqbal will be here, and I want you to meet him.'

Now the name of Muhammad Iqbal had a magical sound among the Muslims of India. He was a philosopher and a poet of great renown, and many of his verses were constantly quoted by high and low, men and women alike: for to them he was a seer who had grasped the innermost reality of Muslim life, of its virtues and its faults, of its errors and its great potentialities; and coming to know such a man was a prospect very much to my taste. I had, of course, heard of him long ago, in fact, ever since my arrival in India, but somehow I had never met him face to face. I knew that he had studied philosophy in Munich and had been called to the bar in London, but had given up his legal practice years ago and devoted himself nowadays only to poetry, meditation and to discoursing on Islam with his many friends and admirers.

My expectations were not disappointed. When I entered the living-room of Ilahi Bakhsh's house that evening, I found Iqbal sitting on the carpet, surrounded by about a dozen men of all ages who listened to his words in a hushed silence. My entrance broke up this concentration for a short while; but as soon as the introductions were over, Iqbal took up again the thread of his talk, and the others fell once more into silence. He spoke, I seem to remember, of some ancient phase of Muslim history, comparing that glorious period with the decadence of the present days -- like a lecturer addressing his students rather than conversing with his peers. He sat cross-legged, leaning in a relaxed manner against the wall-cushions, and spoke slowly, in a low voice, aware that he had the respectful attention of his listeners entirely at his command. Suddenly he interrupted himself and turned to me: 'I have read your 'Islam at the Crossroads' and I like what you have written. Only ... I disagree with your call for a new *ijtihad*. In itself, *ijtihad* is certainly salutary and necessary, but it is dangerous at a time of decadence -- a time like ours -- because it could lead to a chaotic divergence of views about Islam, and so to a still greater disruption of our social fabric . . . . '

I could not hold myself back and broke with some vehemence into his discourse: 'But, Dr. Iqbal, don't you agree that without a new, living *ijtihad* on the part of those Muslims who are able to think for themselves. Muslim society is bound to fall deeper and deeper into cultural sterility, without any hope of ever emerging from it? I am convinced that you are mistaken. I am convinced that it is precisely at a time of decadence like ours that we must find the courage to look at our ideology with new eyes, untrammelled by what the earlier generations of Muslims' thought about the problems of Islam! No, if we want to survive -- survive as a community and overcome our cultural decadence -- we must, whether our *mullahs* like it or not, try to exert our *ijtihad* even at the risk of committing errors! We must not be afraid of errors: we must be afraid of stagnation . . . .'

The circle of Iqbal's admirers sat as if thunderstruck, visibly shocked at the temerity of this young nobody who dared to contradict the great poet-philosopher so openly, so vehemently! One or another of them seemed about to protest; but Iqbal's voice silenced them once more. He sat there, softly smiling, obviously unruffled by my outburst, and finally said; 'We should talk about all this on another occasion, my young friend. Will you come to me at my house -- perhaps tomorrow?'

And thus began my friendship with this outstanding man – a friendship which lasted for the remaining four years of his life, until his death in 1938.

IV

The trait which distinguished Iqbal more than anything else was his inner quiet. Here was a man entirely at peace within himself and with God; a man who almost always spoke softly, often with a sweet, slow smile playing around his lips and lighting up his face. Indeed, he liked to smile on the least occasion, betraying a nature without guile and without rancour: and so one could easily understand why so many people regarded him not only with deep respect but also with love. Everyone with whom he conversed was made to feel as if he were the person most important to him in all the world: and that was the reason why he was listened to by all who knew him as no other man was listened to in his time.

One day we were sitting on the carpeted floor of his study, with Iqbal reclining as usual against the wall-cushions, the mouthpiece of his ever-present *hookah* between his lips, and I said: 'What the Muslims really need today is a prophet, for only a prophet could arouse them to new life and effort and bring them out of their stagnation ... But there cannot be and never will be another prophet after Muhammad -- and he is dead and lies in his grave in Medina, and we cannot hear his 'voice . . .'

Iqbal interrupted me and gripped me by arm: 'But we *can* hear his voice if we but listen! It is alive, for everyone to hear, even though he himself lies in his grave in Medina!'

I looked questioningly at Iqbal, and he said: 'The voice of the Prophet is alive in the *ahadith,* the Traditions of his sayings which have been transmitted to us, and which we can read in so many authentic compilations.'

I objected: 'But how many people read those Traditions? How many Muslims -- for instance, here in India -- know enough Arabic to be able to read and understand the Prophet's sayings? They are always obliged to turn to the *mullahs* who are reputed to know Arabic: but the *mullahs* offer only sermons to their followers and are unable really to teach and to guide them!'

Iqbal looked at me with a slow, sly smile: 'Why don't you, Asad, do something about it?'

I stared at him: 'I? What can I do?'

'You could,' replied Iqbal, 'translate some of the *ahadith* from Arabic into English. Take, for instance, the *Sahih* of Bukhari: it has never yet been translated into English; why don't *you* do it? Consider how many millions of Muslims in this country know English although they are ignorant of Arabic -- think of the many to whom you could make the Prophet's voice audible, if you but tried! Try it!'

And so it came about that I decided, there and then, to give up my journalistic work for good and to devote myself for years to come to translating, and commenting upon, the *Sahih al-Bukhari*.[4]

V

Very soon it became obvious to me that it would not be quite so easy to abandon journalism all at once. I had no means whatsoever apart from my revenues as a correspondent of the *Neue Zürcher Zeitung*. If I severed my connection with that newspaper I would have nothing with which to maintain my wife and child and myself;[5] and, on the other hand, I could not envisage living indefinitely as a guest under Maulana Abd Allah Kasuri's hospitable roof.

After much deliberation I arrived at what appeared to me the only possible solution of my dilemma; if, as Muhammad Iqbal had stressed, it was my moral duty to devote all my knowledge and all my literary experience to making the voice of the Prophet audible to my community, it was certainly the duty of the community to help me to achieve that end.

Almost all the friends with whom I discussed this problem agreed with me, and one of them suggested that the proper person to approach in this connection was the Nizam of Hyderabad, the richest and most influential among the Indian princes and widely known as the sponsor of many scholarly endeavours in the service of Islam. It would not be difficult, I was told, to get an introduction to that munificent ruler who was bound to realize the importance of my scheme and would surely support it.

This suggestion appealed to me in principle, but I was hesitant to approach the Nizam without being able to convince him *à priori* of my *ability* to do the work in question. In other words, I felt that I could not ask him to help me without showing to him at least a part of my translation and commentary in actual print. Thus, the initial problem consisted in producing the opening chapter or chapters of my work on the *Sahih al-Bukhari* well in advance of my approaching the Nizam. It may have been a quixotic idea, but on this point I was adamant.

My old friend Maulana Abd al-Qadir Kasuri (Abd Allah's elder brother) came to my rescue. He was not only prominent among the comparatively rare 'nationalist' Muslims but was, above all else, one of the most outstanding leaders of the *Ahl-e-Hadith*[6] movement, and therefore very much taken by the prospect of the *Sahih al-Bukhari* appearing for the first time in an English garb. 'The *Ahl-e-Hadith* community must help you,' he said, and forthwith approached the richest among them, the merchants living in the Phatak Habash Khan quarter of Delhi. Within a few days I received an invitation to visit them in Delhi.

The quarter -- or *muhallah* -- of Phatak Habash Khan[7] was one of the oldest I had ever seen. It consisted of quite a few extremely narrow streets -- so narrow that hardly more than two people could walk through them abreast -- with houses that showed to the street only blank walls but inside contained patios surrounded by luxuriously carpeted rooms, veritable warrens of rooms, each of them unmistakably displaying the owner's wealth: for, I was told, every one of these houses sheltered a millionaire or, rather, multi-millionaire. It was undoubtedly the richest and the most exclusive Muslim community in all of India.

I stayed as the guest of one of the most prominent among these new friends -- for, friends they clearly proved to be. Maulana Abd al-Qadir had already informed them of my ambition regarding the *Sahih al-Bukhari,* and I was able to explain my project to them in greater detail. My needs were threefold: firstly, means of livelihood during the initial stages of my work; secondly, a small library of Arabic books relating to the proposed undertaking; and, thirdly, the purchase of a set of Arabic and English type, seeing that no printing press in the Punjab or in Delhi offered the necessary facilities.

The response of the merchants of Phatak Habash Khan was prompt and exceeded all my expectations. Within half an hour they set up among themselves a fund which would secure my living expenses for the next six months. Another fund was established for the purchase of printing type (which I was to order from England). And as for the books, my host led me to a room filled with book-cases and said, 'Select for yourself whatever you need.' And indeed, my host's library provided all the books which I might need: they would be sent to me whenever and wherever I wanted them . . . .[8]

And so, since I suddenly saw myself freed of all my worries, I decided upon my next step: the choosing of a place where I could live at ease, within pleasant surroundings, during the coming months.

And I chose Kashmir -- a land which I had never yet seen, but which had always been a dream-land to me, and even more so since I had seen the Himalayas on my trip to Kulu.

VI

On one of the last days before my departure for Srinagar in search of a house to rent, I had lunch with Chaudhri Ilahi Bakhsh. As I was leaving his house he smiled and said, 'I have something funny to show you, Asad Sahib: have a look at this' -- and he handed me an open envelope. I removed its contents: a printed leaflet of four pages, displaying the word PAKISTAN in bold lettering and signed 'Rahmat Ali'.[9] I read it through quietly. It was no more and no less than a call for the separation of the Muslim-majority provinces of North-Western India from the rest of the country and the establishment of a sovereign Muslim state, to be called 'Pakistan' -- a name formed by the first letters of Punjab, Afghan Province (known as the North-West Frontier Province at the time of the British *raj*), Kashmir and Sind, as well as the last syllable of Baluchistan.

I felt as if my breath was about to stop, and I suddenly remembered a similar idea advanced many decades before by Jamal ad-Din al-Afghani:[10] a separation of Muslim and Hindu India along a straight line from Karachi to Delhi and eastwards to the Himalayas . . . .

I asked, 'Who is this Rahmat Ali?' And Ilahi Bakhsh answered, laughing: 'He is a student at Cambridge -- Chaudhri Rahmat Ali. Have you ever seen anything as ridiculous as this? To talk about a division of India! What a nonsense!'

I exclaimed: 'Oh no, Chaudhri Sahib! This is no nonsense: this is how the future *must* develop, as sure as you and I are now standing here!'

But my elderly friend only smiled: 'You are as yet new to this country, but in time you, too, will come to understand that what Rahmat Ali proposes is an impossibility, a pipe-dream . . . . '

A few days later I visited another acquaintance of mine, Sardar Sikander Hayat Khan.[11] After the Round Table conferences of the early Thirties the British had granted a limited form of autonomy to India's provinces, and Sikander Hayat was now the Chief Minister of the Punjab. I had come to know him well and met him often. And on that particular occasion I mentioned to him Chaudhri Rahmat Ali's leaflet which, of course, he had already seen. He listened patiently to my enthusiastic words, and then he pushed aside the pipe of his *hookah* and shook his head: 'You are a stranger in India, my friend. You do not --

you cannot -- understand the reality of India. If you did, you would realize at once that a division of this country is out of the question, utterly impossible. It will never come about, rest assured of that.' To which I replied, somewhat boldly: 'No, Sardar Sahib, it is not I who is mistaken. Pakistan *will* come into being, and you and I will witness it!'

But Sikander Hayat smiled, just as Chaudhri Ilahi Bakhsh had smiled. Neither he nor I could have imagined that a few years hence he would be one of the foremost leaders of the Pakistan movement . . . .

Endnotes

1 Anjuman-i Himayat-i Islam (Lahore) founded in 1884. Its main objectives are:
(i) to organize a mass movement in order to save the Muslims from the propaganda of the non-Muslims' missions,
(ii) to propagate the basic tenets of Islam,
(iii) to educate the Muslim children (male and female) according to the modern concepts of religious education and put them on the track of progress.

Anjuman has played a vital role in uplifting the Muslim conmmunity as a whole. Dr. Muhammad Iqbal was its member (April 1920-September 1924) and then the president (1934-1937) (see *Himayat-i Islām* (journal), 5 July, 1934).

(cf. *History of Anjuman-i Himayat-i Islam* (Urdu), no date (before 1947?), with an introduction by Sir Abdul Qadir).

A few months after Asad's arrival in the Subcontinent, he was invited to lecture on "Islam and Western Civilization" (January 1933). Organized by the Arabic Society of Islamia College, he delivered this lecture in the Habibiyah Hall of the College (5 February 1933), presided by Dr. Barkat Ali Quraishi, Principal of the College. (cf. *Inqilab* (daily newspaper, Lahore), 2 and 6 February 1933).

In the same month, he went to Delhi and Aligarh and lectured there. As reported by the Editor, Asad would give two lectures (on 22 and 23 February) after coming back from Delhi. (cf. *Inqilab*, 16 February 1933).

2 Asad's first book on Islam, published simultaneously from Lahore and Delhi (April and June 1934). In its 14th revised edition (Gibraltar, 1982), the author added nine footnotes;Urdu tr. by Mahbub Subhani, Lahore 2004; Arabic tr. by 'Umar Farrookh (1946).

According to Dr. Iqbal "This work is extremely interesting. I have no doubt that coming as it does from a highly cultured European convert to Islam it will prove an eye-opener to our younger generation."

See also Sayyid Sulaiman Nadvi's editorial note in: *Ma'ārif*, Oct. 1934, pp. 242-243.

3 No further information about the life of Chaudhry Ilahi Bakhsh, the host and close friend of both Iqbal and Asad, is extant. Even his name is not mentioned in the books which deal with Iqbal's contemporaries, friends and guests.

4 Before leaving Saudi Arabia, Asad intended to spend a few months in India and then proceed to various countries of Near East and South-East Asia, but after meeting Iqbal in Lahore, he changed his mind and decided to stay permanently in the Subcontinent. In the beginning of *The Road to Mecca*, he writes "...after leaving Arabia I went to India and there met the great Muslim poet-philosopher and spiritual father of the Pakistan idea, Muhammad Iqbal. It was he who persuaded me to give up my plans of traveling to Eastern Turkestan, China and Indonesia and to remain in India to help elucidate the intellectual premises of the future Islamic state which was then hardly more than a dream in Iqbal's visionary mind." (4th rev. ed., 1980, pp. 1-2)

For the relationship of Iqbal and Asad, see *Gift*, I: 225-230; Nazir Niazi (ed.): *Maktubat-i Iqbal*, Karachi 1957, pp. 161, 174-175, 178-179; ibid.: *Iqbal kay Huzur*, pp. 383-384.

It is entirely new information that Asad started a huge project of translating *Sahih Bukhari* into English on the suggestion of Iqbal.

In a letter (dated 17 June 1946, Dalhousie), Asad wrote to Malik Muhammad Ashraf (1915-1981):

"I cannot say anything about Iqbal as a poet. I know him well, but almost all our conversations were concerned with Islamic theology and jurisprudence."

Asad's two brief articles on Iqbal: "Sir Muhammad Iqbal is dead" (in: *Islamic Culture* (Hyderabad Deccan), xii/2 (1938), obituary notice; "Iqbal's Role in Muslim Thought" (in: *The Voice of Islam* (March 1957), pp. 633-634).

Iqbal as a President of Anjuman-i Himayat-i Islam tried to appoint Asad in the Department of Islamic Studies in Islamia College because he intended to make drastic changes in the prevalent curriculum of this department and considered this young converted European Muslim the most appropriate person who was fully conscious about the *Zeitgeist*. Unfortunately, Iqbal could not succeed in his efforts but his personal interest and incessant efforts explicitly show their relationship.

See Asad's letter to Iqbal (dated 12 July 1934, Delhi), reproduced in: M.A. Sherif: *Searching for Solace: A Biography of Abdullah Yusuf Ali*, Islamabad 1994, pp. 114-115, note 4.

5 As a correspondent of *Neue Zürcher Zeitung* (Swiss newspaper), Asad contributed to it for more than seven years. His first article "Arabische Reise" (Travel of Arabia) came out on 3 April 1927 and the last "Die indische Bitternis" (The Indian bitterness) on 22 December 1934.

6 *Ahl-e Hadith*, also called "Wahhabis" in Indian subcontinent who follow the teachings of Abdul Wahhab.

cf. Ibrahim Mir: *Tarikh-i Ahl-e- Hadith*, Lahore 1953 (reprinted Lahore)

7 Phatak Habash Khan (Delhi), built by Habash Khan (real name Sayyidi Miftah) during the reign of Shahjahan (1592-1666, r. 1628-1666). Very narrow and thickly populated area. Rich people of the Punjab lived here and they monopolized the import trade of the whole city.

(cf. Bashir ud-Din Ahmad: *Waqi'at-i Dar al-Hukumat-e Delhi*. Reprinted:

Vol. II, New Delhi 2001 (1919), pp. 255-256)

8 During Asad's internship, some leading Urdu newspapers appealed for the financial support of his family and for the continuation of his mammoth project of translating *Bukhari*. cf. *Sidq* (Lucknow, 2 August 1943)

On the suggestion of Iqbal, Asad started translating with explanatory notes *Sahih Bukhari* in English during his stay in Srinagar (August 1934-October 1936). He established his own printing press named Arafat Publications (cf. Asad's letter to Ch. Niaz Ali Khan, 22 November 1935, Srinagar). The first fascicule of this translation came out in December 1935. His financial resources were meager, so he first decided to dispose of this first part of translation. He offered special offers to different institutions and societies of the Muslims if they purchased in bulk, but he failed in his venture (cf. Asad's letter in: *Proceedings of the Anjuman-i Himayat-i Islam*, Lahore, 6 April 1935. In this letter, he informed that the complete translation would be in thirty fascicules). Only five fascicules were published (upto 1938), when he was arrested and imprisoned in a detention camp (1939-1945). After his disimprisonment, he could not continue this work. Afterwards, these five parts were reprinted in a book form (1981).

After Partition (1947), Asad saw the unpublished typed and hand-written scripts of this translation floating in a river Ravi. In a letter to Ghulam Rasul Mihr (28 September 1939), he expressed his bitterness in these words:

"Loss of freedom combined with a destruction of one's work is a bitter thing."

9 Chaudhry Rahmat Ali (1893-1951), who coined the name of 'Pakistan'. His oft-quoted pamphlet *Now or Never* was published in 1933, see his article "Contribution à l' étude problème hindou-musulman", in: *Revue des études islamiques*, 6 (1932), pp. 269-414)

See for detail. K. K. Aziz: *Rahmat Ali; A Biography*, Lahore 2008 (1987)

10 Jamal ud-Din Afghani (1838/39-1897), was one of the most outstanding figures of 19th century Islam; philosopher, writer, orator and journalist; his influence may be seen in these three factors: i) he refuted ideas that have become increasingly popular in the Muslim world since the late 19th century, including nationalism, Pan-Islamism, and the identification of many new ideas with Islam, ii) he was a charismatic speaker and teacher and iii) he travelled so widely in the Muslim world that he was able to have a direct impact in several countries.

cf. *EI*², vol. II, fasc. 29 (1962), pp. 416-419. *OEMIO*, vol. I, New York/Oxford 1995, pp. 23-27, art. Nikki. R. Keddie; M. Ikram Chaghatai: *Jamaluddin Afghani, a Promoter of Unity of Islamic Ummah* (Urdu), Lahore 2005; ibid.: *Writings of Jamaluddin Afghani* (Urdu), Lahore 2005; ibid.: *Jamal al-Din Afghani. An Apostle of Islamic Resurgence*, Lahore 2005.

11 Sir Sikander Hayat Khan (1892-1942); born in Attock; completed his education from Aligarh and England; prime minister of the State of Bahawalpur; an influential member of Unionist Party; appointed prime minister of Punjab (1937) afterwards joined the Muslim League.

IV
THE GOLDEN YEARS
(1934-37)

I

It was full summer when we shifted from Lahore to Kashmir. The heat lay heavy on the plains, and the journey by car to Rawalpindi seemed endless. But as soon as the car began to climb the steep mountain road to Murree with its countless hairpin curves, the cool air of the Himalayas enfolded us like a whiff from another world. The dusty plains were almost at once replaced by mountain slopes and sheer rocky walls, and after about an hour and a half we reached the hill station of Murree, seven thousand feet above sea-level: one single street shaded by innumerable trees and bordered on both sides by bungalows of all sizes and styles, as well as by shops that catered for the many visitors who were able to forget for a few months the smothering summer heat of the Punjab plain.

After a short stop-over at the *dak* bungalow we resumed our journey. A high pass was crossed, and almost immediately afterwards the valley of Kashmir lay open before us: a wide valley through which the Jhelum River flowed in majestic quiet, broadening into a succession of tree-and-flower-bordered lakes of such an unexpected beauty that I was reminded of an old Persian couplet which aptly summed up the poet's view -- and my first impression of -- Kashmir:

> *Agar firdaws bar rū-e zamin-ast –*
> *hamin-ast o-hamin-ast o-hamin-ast!*
> 'If paradise is to be found on the face of the earth –
> it is this, it is this, it is this!'

Never before had I seen and never afterwards was I to see another landscape of such perfection or experience a climate which could match that of Kashmir: it was truly a dream-land beyond compare.

Many house-boats were moored on the banks of the Jhelum and

of the chain of lakes into which it merged and from which it flowed out again as a river, lake and river glistening in the sun almost without a ripple. The lakes were dotted with movable, artificial islands: broad platforms made of rushes and covered with earth, out of which vegetables and flowers grew in abundance, tended by men and women to whom all those expanses of water seemed to be their natural element. Narrow *shikara* boats, each propelled by a long pole rhythmically wielded by a man, glided softly from island to shore, carrying vegetables and fruit and singing women; and that singing, as in time I came to know, was the most vivid, most entrancing sound that filled the summer days of Kashmir, as characteristic of it as the shimmering waters of lake and river or the immense snow-covered range of the Himalayas which enclosed the valley far to the north, a wall fifteen thousand feet high.

I hired a house-boat which was to be our abode until we found a house on rent ashore. It consisted of three rooms, simply but comfortably furnished, and a separate, smaller kitchen-boat, manned by the owner and his wife -- she to be our cook and he a man-of-all-work: and the rent of all that complex service amounted to less than the rent of one modest hotel room in the plains.

Our house-boat was tied up on the shore just below the town of Srinagar, only a walk of some ten minutes away; and so, early next morning I set out to explore it.

It proved to be a lovely town. The streets were narrow, the houses mostly old, built of brick and timber, with flat, only slightly-slanting roofs -- and most of the roofs were covered with a thick layer of earth, out of which flowers and wild grasses sprouted in colourful profusion: a unique, a lovely sight indeed.

II

I had a letter of introduction to the most important personage in the town -- the Mir Wa'iz,[1] or chief religious leader, of all Kashmir. He was a man of middle age, with a black-bearded, lively face, dressed in a turban and a voluminous Kashmiri cloak of the softest indigenous lamb's wool (known over all of Northern India as *pashmina*) and possessed of the most exquisite manners. He rose from the carpet on which he had been sitting and embraced me with the warmth of an old friend: and this warmth, I soon learned, was the most significant aspect of life among the Muslims of Kashmir.

We conversed in Persian, in which the Mir Wa'iz was fully fluent; and his first question after the usual inquiries about his guest's health was, 'Where are you staying?' And when I told him that I had rented a house-boat, he said reproachfully: 'You should have come straight to this house; it is wide enough, and always open to the friends of my friends . . . . 'After learning that I had come to Srinagar with wife and child, he made it clear that we must, at least, be his guests for the evening meal. I accepted his invitation, of course, and said that I would fetch my wife in the afternoon; but he rejected this suggestion and sent instead one of his sons to bring Munira and Talal to his house.

Very soon other people arrived, summoned by the Mir Wa'iz to meet his guest, and their women-folk went inside at once to join our host's family; and when my wife and child appeared, they, too, were whisked away to the women's quarters, from where the sounds of merriment soon became audible.

In the meantime tea was served. All the men were sitting on the carpet-covered floor, and I had my first taste of Kashmiri tea, which was prepared in front of us by one of the Mir Wa'iz's sons. It was quite unlike any tea I had ever drunk: a green, fairly broad-leafed tea, brewed with boiling water out of an immense brass samovar, very strong and diluted with hot, creamy milk. Instead of the conventional sugar, salt was added, and each guest's bowl was topped with a pat of butter! I tasted it, hesitantly at first, and then I emptied my bowl with great gusto: and ever since that day the salty, buttered Kashmiri tea has remained my favourite.

The evening meal, although prepared at such short notice, proved to be a veritable banquet. Large lamb ribs, delicately charcoal-grilled, appeared side by side with a sumptuous saffron-yellow *pilau* which could bear comparison with the best Irani *pilau,* studded with almonds and dried apricots, with highly-spiced meatballs and a fiery sauce on the side. And there were *kebabs* of various kinds, and apricot chutney, and thick, creamy yoghurt; and great, flat loaves of golden-brown bread such as I had not tasted since my days in Iran and Afghanistan; and robust, full-flavoured sweets of a kind never encountered in the rest of India . . . . It seemed to me that although I never wrote verses, I could easily have written a poem on a Kashmiri feast.

III

Within a few days a house was found for us by one of the Mir Wa'iz's men: a spacious bungalow just outside Srinagar, adequately furnished and surrounded by a small garden of lawn and flowering shrubs. Among the latter grew a good number of bushes known in that part of the world as *rat-ki-rani,* 'queen of the night', since its flowers open up at night and exude a sweet, entrancing scent.

And in that house I settled down to my work on the *Sahih al-Bukhari.* A carpenter came and built a row of shelves for the Arabic books which had been presented to me in Delhi: dictionaries (most prominent among them the twenty-volume *Lisan al-'Arab),*[2] commentaries on the Qur'an, various compendia of *ahadith,* and several volumes on the lives of the *rijal,* the accepted transmitters of Traditions. I was now fully equipped for the work which was to occupy me for a number of years; and I immersed myself in it almost to the exclusion of everything else. Almost, but not quite: for side by side with the daily routine of translation and commentary -- a routine made extremely enjoyable by my surroundings and the exhilarating climate of Kashmir -1 was on a permanent look-out for printing facilities.

What I had in mind was a printing press that could successfully produce the first part of the *Sahih* -- the part which I intended to present to the Nizam of Hyderabad both as a proof of my ability to accomplish the task that I had set myself and as a sample of how the work would look on completion. To this end I intended to print not only my translation and commentary but to reproduce the original Arabic text as well -- and to reproduce it in a form which had never been attempted before: namely, with a clear-cut visual separation of the substantive text of each Tradition, called *matn,* from its *isnad,* i.e., the line of the authorities responsible for its transmission from the time of the Prophet all the way down to Al-Bukhari. Seeing that in all the existing earlier editions of the *Sahih* (as well as of all the other compilations of *ahadith) isnad* and *matn* appear in one uninterrupted sequence, without interpunction or any other separation, and seeing, moreover, that Al-Bukhari's work abounds in frequent change-overs *(tahwil)* from one line of transmitters to another within the context of one and the same Tradition, it is obvious that a real understanding of the *Sahih* presupposes a certain scholarly acumen and experience. To facilitate such an understanding by my future readers, I decided -- for the first time in the history of *hadith*-literature -- not merely to produce a distinction between *isnad* and *matn* by means of different sizes of type, but also to introduce a definite system of interpunction -- another hitherto unheard-of innovation -- in the text of every *hadith* as such.

To produce a bilingual work to such specifications, I realized only too well, would not be an easy task for even a highly qualified printing press, and it was most doubtful whether such a press existed in Kashmir. My fears proved well-founded: several visits to the few printing establishments in Srinagar convinced me that the level of work which could be expected from them would be far below the standards visualized by me.

But I *had* to do my work in Kashmir simply because I was determined to live in this land as long as I could. And so I resolved to establish a press -- a small press -- of my own.

As already mentioned, some weeks earlier I had ordered -in anticipation of the difficulties which I was bound to encounter -- several sets of both Arabic and Roman type from abroad, and that type was due to arrive any day. What I still lacked by way of equipment was a small platen press -- but even the simplest kind was beyond the means then at my disposal. The thought of approaching my *Ahl-e-Hadith* friends in Delhi was repugnant to me – I remembered the old Arabian saying, 'A friend should be treated like honey: you may lick it from your fingers, but must never scoop it up in handfuls.'

Finally, after some inquiries, I found a solution: I could *hire* a platen press on a monthly basis from one of the friendly Srinagar printers -- a simple treadle machine operated by foot -- together with the services of one of his own workers, whose wages I was to pay as long as I employed him.

Within a few days the platen press was installed in one of the lower rooms of our bungalow, and the carpenter set to work on type-cases and composing-tables in accordance with a design supplied by me. After that I went on a short visit to Lahore to find a compositor able to do the work I envisaged and willing to live in Kashmir for an indefinite period.

In Lahore I had a friend who might help me in this task. His name was Muhammad Husain Babri[3] -- thus called after the first Moghul emperor of India, Babar[4], whose personal armourer was one of my friend's ancestors. Following this tradition, all his descendants had been and still were engaged in metal work of one kind or another. Muhammad Husain himself was an independent typewriter mechanic, and a very good one at that.

He was the best -- and certainly the most faithful -- of all the friends I have ever had: always ready to share one's worries and to help to overcome them in whatever way he could. We remained friends for well over fifty years, throughout the ups and downs of my life and all the changes of my habitat across three continents, until his death in 1985 at the age of well over eighty.

And so, to Muhammad Husain I turned in my search for a compositor. As it happened, he knew a man who might fulfil my requirements and who, moreover, had recently given up his job with a renowned printing press in Lahore and was still free. He was located and brought to me: a middle-aged, goatee-bearded man of small stature, Abd al-Haqq by name, and known to be fully experienced in composing in Arabic as well as in English. The prospect of spending some months in Kashmir -- always an allurement to people of the plains -appealed to him, and we quickly came to terms.

During my brief stay in Lahore I ordered a quantity of printing paper from one of the local wholesale dealers; it was forthwith packed and dispatched to Srinagar. When I returned there with my compositor in tow and installed him in a boarding house, I found that both the paper and the type had arrived; and after a few days the composing-tables and type-cases were ready and placed in my house next to 'my' platen press.

Thus -- since in the meantime a good deal of the manuscript of the first part of my work had been completed -- we started in all earnest on the first-ever publication of *Sahih al-Bukhari* in the English language.

IV

The whole of the summer and autumn of 1934 were spent in an unvarying routine. After an early breakfast I worked throughout the morning and afternoon on my translation and commentary, interrupting my labours by short visits to the press-room in order to supervise the work of Abd al-Haqq and to read the proofs produced in the course of the previous day. About the middle of the afternoon I went for a few hours' walk -- usually on the tow-paths along one of the many canals which criss-crossed the valley of Kashmir -- and came home only to eat my dinner, see some friends, and go to sleep. Only very occasionally did I allow myself an afternoon stroll through the lively bazaars of Srinagar, where by now I had many acquaintances. In particular, I liked to sit down for a while, cross-legged, in the shop of a carpet dealer who had become my friend: a small, black-bearded man with a partially paralyzed right hand and an inexhaustible store of information about people and happenings in Kashmir. We sipped green tea and -- since my Urdu had in the meantime become quite fluent -- we talked about everything under the sun until the time came for my return home and back to work.

Autumn passed, and winter came, and finally, as the first snows began to fall and one's footsteps went crackling over the crunchy layer of snow that covered the one-time greenness of the valley of Kashmir, and as flocks of ravens replaced the storks of summer and autumn -- at that time we printed the title page of the first part of my English version of *Sahih al-Bukhari* – containing the chapters on 'How the Revelation Began' and 'The Book of Faith' -- and set on the title page the imprint, 'Srinagar, Kashmir, 1935'.

On the evening of that memorable January day we had a small feast in my house. We sat down on the carpet around a white table-cloth -- the Mir Wa'iz, Muhammad Husain, Abd al-Haqq, my wife and I -- and offered a joint prayer of thanks to God, who had allowed me to convey the sayings of His Prophet to people who previously could not understand them . . . .

V

And here I must mention a discovery which seemed to me to be most significant, although it may not have been a really new discovery: but to me it was, and has ever since remained, most important.

From the very beginning of my immersion in the immortal *Sahih al-Bukhari* I had been struck by the inner difference between the language of *abadith,* on the one hand, and the language of the Qur'an, on the other. Whereas the former mirrors the purity and sharpness of the desert atmosphere within which the Prophet Muhammad and his Companions were born and grew up, the Arabic of the Qur'an is filled with a strange luminosity entirely its own above and beyond all influences of time and environment. The denseness of its phrasing covers and simultaneously reveals layers upon layers of meaning not to be reached by mere human diction and yet fully accessible to man's searching spirit: a quality not to be found in the day-to-day words of the Prophet and his Companions, although their speech, too, reflects the pristine Arabic as yet untouched by linguistic usages and thoughts derived from beyond the confines of their homeland. In short, the two modes of expression are so distinct from one another that no real scholar can ever confuse a saying of the Prophet, however lofty, with a passage from the Qur'an.

VI

My introduction to the Nizam of Hyderabad came about in an unexpected manner.

One day I was invited to lunch at the house of an exiled Afghan prince who was living permanently in Srinagar as a state guest of the Maharajah of Kashmir. His father, Ayyub Khan, had defeated the British Army in 1880 at the memorable Battle of Maiwand in an unsuccessful attempt to gain the throne of Afghanistan, and my host had now no chance of ever returning to his homeland. Nevertheless, he was deeply interested in everything that concerned Afghanistan, and so it was only natural that we talked about my travels and experiences in that country in 1925. In the course of our conversation we discovered that he had happened to have read one of my articles on Afghanistan which appeared in the 'Frankfurter Zeitung' in those far-off days -- an article entitled 'The State of the Wild Boys',[5] in which I had tried to elucidate the peculiar, unruly character of Afghan politics. He was full of praise for that piece of writing, and described it as 'the only correct appreciation of Afghanistan's socio-political life' that he had ever encountered in the European press (he was fully conversant not only with German but also with English and French). His flattering remarks led to a lively table-talk, in which one of the other guests, a grey-haired, elegant *nawab* from Hyderabad, fully participated. This latter person (whose name now escapes my memory) insisted that I must visit his country and meet the Nizam, who, he explained, was deeply interested in anything of importance that went on anywhere in the Muslim world.

'But this,' I said, 'is precisely what I intend to do: I very much want to visit Hyderabad and become acquainted with its ruler.'

'Nothing easier than that,' exclaimed the *nawab*. 'I will give you a letter to him and send an advance intimation to his secretariat, and you will be treated as an honoured guest . . . .'

And so it happened that one week later I found myself on a train steaming over days and nights towards the Deccan.

VII

Hyderabad was by far the largest and richest of all the princely states of India, and its capital of the same name fully justified its reputation. It was a widely laid-out white city free of any modern high-rises, but full of public and private buildings in the Moghul style, flowering gardens behind low, white walls, and tree-lined streets of a cleanliness not often encountered in India and -- what was even more remarkable -- free of the wandering, emaciated cows so characteristic of most Indian towns and cities.

At the railway station I was received by two white-turbaned men with red sashes -- employees of the state guest house that had already been alerted about my coming -- and was taken by car to my temporary destination.

I had hardly unpacked my suitcase and taken out the presentation copy of the completed first part of my *Sahih al-Bukhari*, bound in red Morocco leather and bearing a gold-stamped inscription 'To His Exalted Highness the Nizam of Hyderabad', when a young officer in a white uniform and a high turban appeared and informed me that the Nizam was expecting me for tea; a car was already waiting to take us to the palace.

Now 'palace' was not a proper designation for the Nizam's residence: what I saw before me on our arrival was a high white wall, and behind that wall, surrounded by a garden, an unadorned, three-storey building such as any well-to-do person in India might inhabit: and, indeed, that residence was never spoken of in Hyderabad as 'palace' but simply as *'kothi'* -- that is, dwelling -- or, to distinguish it from other dwellings, as *'King-kothi'*.

The salon in which the Nizam received me was large, with high ceilings and gilded scroll-work on the walls and velvet-upholstered Louis Quinze style chairs and sofas and low tea tables. The only really sumptuous things in the room were the exquisite Persian carpets which covered the floor from wall to wall.

The Nizam was alone, sitting on one of the sofas and toying with an amber rosary between his fingers. When I entered he rose and extended his hand in greeting and invited me to sit down on a chair opposite him, with a small glass-topped table between us: At that time he must have been about fifty years old, slight of stature and in no way physically imposing. He was one of the richest men in the world -- probably *the* richest – and yet he was dressed in a worn grey *achkan* with a frayed collar and a red Turkish *tarbush* slightly discoloured by sweat around the rim. I was not surprised, for I already knew that he was reputed to be a 'miser' in spite of his immense riches.

He was extremely polite and simple in his bearing, talking in English in a low voice and rarely smiling, even when he inquired -- as any Muslim host would do -- after my health and expressed the hope that my journey had not been too tiring. On the table before me teacups and saucers were already laid out, and almost immediately a turbaned servant appeared with a large teapot and poured out the tea -- first for the Nizam, as it should be, and then for me. Another bearer offered me a platter of small cakes and biscuits; I took one, and as the Nizam refused with a slight gesture of his hand, the servant withdrew behind my chair, ready to proffer the platter again as soon as I finished my little cake. I declined another, and the servant stood once again behind me. The Nizam glanced at him once, and then again, frowning, and when the cake-bearer did not take the hint, his master looked at him with visible annoyance and said sharply in Urdu: 'He has already told you he doesn't want more!' -whereupon the servant glided silently away. Was the Nizam afraid that I might change my mind and gobble a second cake?[6]

VIII

With all this he proved, as I was soon to learn, most munificent: indeed, without his generous help I could not have dreamt of proceeding with my work. The Nizam of Hyderabad was *not* a miser; he was a true eccentric -- and he loved Islam.

On the day following my first audience with the Nizam I paid my respects to Sir Akbar Hydari,[7] the Chief Minister and most influential person in Hyderabad. He was in his sixties, a stocky man with a small, pointed white beard and white hair and lively black eyes. When I entered his drawing room I found him surrounded by several men and women. There was his wife, Lady Hydari,[8] famed for her pioneer work in the cause of women's emancipation (she had been one of the first Indian Muslim women of the upper class to throw away her *burqah* and to induce other women to follow her example); and the two Turkish princesses, Durre Shahwar[9] and Nilofar[10]—both of them nieces of the last Osmanli Caliph, Abd al-Majid[11] -- who were married to the Nizam's two eldest sons. The elder of the princesses, Durre Shahwar -- wife of the Crown Prince -was one of the most beautiful women I had ever seen: tall and graceful in movement, with an almost Grecian face of utmost perfection (obviously inherited from a line of Circassian ancestresses); and the younger one, Nilofar, was almost equally good-looking.[12] Among the men present was Prince Akram Khan, grandson of the late Sultan Abd al-Hamid II and second in line of succession to the Osmanli throne, if that throne was ever to be restored. He was a tall, handsome man of about forty, elegant and -- as I learned years later -- very intelligent and world-wise.

After the introductions and the first cup of tea Sir Akbar Hydari shepherded me to his study for a private talk. There he told me that he had received a letter from Muhammad Iqbal, outlining to him my problem; 'and,' said he, 'it will most certainly be solved, God willing.'

And solved it was. A few days later Sir Akbar let me know that the Nizam had commanded him to place a very large sum of money at my disposal: so large, indeed, that it could cover the purchase of a complete small printing press.[13] 'You order whatever you need from abroad, and instruct the suppliers to send their bills to me.'

This was far more than I had expected; and yet it was not all. I was offered the post of editor of the quarterly 'Islamic Culture' in succession of its former editor, Marmaduke Pickthall,[14] who had just retired in order to devote himself to the translation of the Qur'an into English. The post carried with it a handsome salary and, since it was a quarterly, was not likely to consume too much of my time. I accepted, of course, but only on the condition that I would be allowed to do my editorial work from Lahore; and as I intended to establish my new press there as well, I suggested that I should be entrusted with the printing of the quarterly, too. Both these proposals were agreed to by Sir Akbar without any hesitation.[15]

IX

On my return to Srinagar I took stock of my new situation. Not only would I have a printing press of my own, but I was also assured of an income which would make me really independent of my earlier journalistic work, of which I was getting tired.

As I have already mentioned, I had decided against the setting up of the new printing press in Srinagar. The reason for this decision was partly technical and partly financial. It was impossible to find in Kashmir the many materials essential for a successful functioning of a press -- printing inks, paper and the hundred and one items necessary for the day-to-day work; everything would have to be imported, and for everything the Kashmiri excise duty would have to be paid. In addition, a printing establishment often demanded the services of a specialized mechanic -- not to speak of a permanent staff of workers -- and all these people would have to be brought from the plains and lodged and catered for in Srinagar at a great running expense. And so, whether I liked it or not, it had to be Lahore.

Very soon we found -- Muhammad Husain and I -- suitable premises for the new press: they consisted of two large, well-lighted rooms in a quiet side street, easily accessible and not very expensive. A signboard was placed over the entrance with the words 'Arafat Press' painted prominently in black and yellow. I had chosen this name because even then I was hoping one day to start my own monthly review, to be called 'Arafat' in commemoration of the plain of that name on which the annual pilgrimage to Mecca culminates: a symbol of the unity of the Islamic *ummah* and of every Muslim's individual responsibility for that unity. I did not know in those days that it would take well over ten years for this hope to be fulfilled and for my 'Arafat' to see the light of day . . . . Many years later there was to be a spate of journals calling themselves 'Arafat'; I like to think that it was I who pointed the way . . . .,[16]

In the meantime, the 'Arafat Press' came step by step into being. A lovely, fully automatic platen press arrived and was installed. The composing-tables came down from Srinagar, and the type-cases were filled with new Roman and Arabic type. A competent printer was engaged, as well as an additional compositor to assist Abd al-Haqq. I found, too, a young Anglo-Indian student who would read and correct the English proofs (the Arabic ones I reserved for myself). And to crown it all, I reached an agreement with a well-known Lahore publisher and bookseller who would take charge of the distribution of the many instalments in which my rendering of *Sahih al-Bukhari* was to appear over the coming years.[17]

X

For about two months I commuted weekly between Srinagar and Lahore. It was a very tiring period, for each two-way journey consumed three full days, and so the working time on my manuscript was halved. I began to realize that this could not go on much longer. Added to this was the nuisance of being shadowed by a policeman on every one of these trips to and from Lahore . . . .

As long as I had been living quietly in Srinagar I had been spared this unpleasant experience: the authorities apparently assumed that in Kashmir I was more or less innocuous, a sort of holiday-maker among so many others. But my frequent journeys to and from Lahore revived their suspicions, and once again, as had been the case during my stay in Maulana Abd Allah Kasuri's house, I had only to turn my head, whenever I walked in the street, to discover one of my 'secret' followers at some short distance.[18]

On one occasion I had to travel to Madras, where I had been invited to deliver a lecture: and, of course, one of my shadows went with me (they were always changing, for the C.I.D. apparently hoped that in this way I would not recognize them). I intended to stop in Delhi on my return journey and spend a few days with friends. However, during the three-day journey it occurred to me that I was losing too much time and

I decided to drop the stop-over in Delhi and to travel straight on to Lahore instead. To this end I had to change trains at Delhi and -- since my ticket was valid only that far -buy a ticket for Lahore. But I was told by the ticket collector that I would have only ten minutes between the arrival of our train and the departure of the one for Lahore.

And so, as the train steamed into Delhi railway station, I anxiously scanned the platform in the hope of finding some assistance. And there it was: as soon as the train stopped, I saw a man running from the third-class carriages towards mine -- and I recognized him at once, thanks to my previous experience, as my 'shadow'. I hailed him and he stopped, startled.

'Are you from the C.I.D.?' I asked him. 'Are you following me?'

He stammered in embarrassment: 'Do forgive me, *sahib,* I am only doing my duty...' I waved away his apology and told him rapidly: 'I have to change to the Lahore train and buy a ticket. The time is extremely short. Would you take care of my luggage and transfer it to the train for Lahore, second class?' -- 'Yes, *sahib,* I will!'

I ran down the platform and out to the ticket counter, bought my ticket and reached, breathless, the Lahore train just in time. My C.I.D. constable was awaiting me before an empty second-class compartment, and we both jumped in as the train began to move. My suitcase was already on the rack, and my bed-roll neatly spread out, ready to receive me. Nor was this all: my faithful follower held out to me a paper cup of hot tea which he had bought at the station a few minutes earlier. And so we went on, chatting about this and that, until the train stopped at the next station and my shadow left me to resume his seat in a third-class carriage.

However amusing that particular incident might have been, it was a nuisance always to be followed by a C.I.D. constable, and I wanted to end this rigmarole, if possible. To this end I secured an introduction from Sardar Sikander Hayat, the Chief Minister, to the Home Office in Delhi; and on my next visit there, about a fortnight later, I was sitting in the office of the Assistant Home Secretary, an Englishman, in charge of political security. To him I expounded my grievance, pointing out that -- apart from any other consideration -it was senseless to have me followed by 'secret' policemen whom I invariably recognized as such -- 'for,' I said, 'it is child's play to evade this supervision whenever I really want to. I could always enter a friend's house by the front door and leave by the back door, with my shadow waiting on the street till doomsday . . . .

Visibly annoyed, the Assistant Secretary answered with heavy sarcasm: 'Of course, you cannot compare our poorly paid constables with your subtle Gestapo agents . . . . ,

'But,' I rejoined, 'can't you see that a person of Jewish origin, like myself, would hardly be tempted to play the Nazi game? What, exactly, are you afraid of?' And so it went on, backwards and forwards, until my British *vis-à-vis* smiled and proposed that we make a 'gentleman's agreement': 'We shall withdraw this constant supervision if you promise to inform us, even by post-card, whenever you go on a trip outside Lahore . . . .' Naturally I agreed, and from that day on I was free of followers.

XI

Towards the end of 1936 it had become obvious that the Nazi regime was determined to get rid, in one way or another, of all the 'undesirable subjects' living in Germany. The first and main target was, of course, the Jews. I was greatly worried about the future of my father, sister, step-mother and her son who were still living in Vienna, for it seemed to be only a matter of time before Hitler extended his sway over Austria as well. Throughout the past years, ever since I had become a Muslim, my father had refused to answer my letters, but my sister -- who had in the meantime become a doctor of law and was assisting our father in his legal practice -- had always remained loyal to me; and so we maintained a steady correspondence. I did my best to persuade her -- and, through her, our father -- to leave Austria and to join me in India. At first my father was adamant; but gradually, when he came to understand that my conversion to Islam did not in the least interfere with my love for him, he relented and began to correspond with me. Still, he rejected the idea that Austria was in any danger from Nazism and was unwilling to contemplate giving up his home and his independence. And thus it went on and my worries increased rapidly.[19]

As for myself, I had already made up my mind that it was impossible to continue living in Srinagar, with the printing of my work -- as well as of 'Islamic Culture'[20] whose editor I now was -- going on in Lahore; and I was thus thinking of an alternative.

XII

About one year earlier, in 1935, I became acquainted with a man who was destined to remain one of my dearest friends until his death, many years later, at the age of ninety-four: Chaudhri Niaz Ali. He was an irrigation engineer by profession, and had served for a long time with the Government of the Punjab building canals and contributing quite a lot to the improvement of the province's irrigation system as a whole. When I met him for the first time he had just retired from government service in order to devote himself fully to the development of his large landed property in Jamalpur, near Pathankot. He was outstanding as a fruit grower. Not only were his plantations of citrus fruit among the best-managed in the whole of the Punjab, but he also introduced and successfully propagated new, exotic varieties of fruit trees from abroad -- like lichees, kiwis and persimmons -- and opened up new markets for his many imitators. But what he was most deeply concerned about was the propagation of Islamic thought and scholarship. To that end he established a foundation called Dar al-Islam and endowed it with some buildings on his estate, adjoining his own extensive, castle-like dwelling built of sun-baked brick around an enormous courtyard.

When we first met he was about fifty-five years old: a short, stubby man with a snow-white beard despite his relatively low age, full of verve and always in search of new activities. As soon as he learned that I intended to leave Srinagar and settle somewhere nearer Lahore, he urged me to make my home in Jamalpur, offering to build a house for me next to his own and to plant a fruit orchard around it.

This invitation and the warmth with which it was proffered appealed to me greatly, and I seriously considered accepting it, the more so as Jamalpur was not too far from Lahore. But there was a drawback to Chaudhri Niaz Ali's proposal: the climate of Jamalpur, which was only slightly milder than that of Lahore. I knew that I would not be able to work there during the hot season, that is, during two-thirds of the year; and since my work on *Sahih al-Bukhari* was bound to occupy me for years to come, I explained to Chaudhri Niaz Ali that I could not settle in Jamalpur, however much my heart drew me to it.[21]

After long cogitations I decided to transfer my residence from Srinagar to Abbottabad, a small town in the Hazara district of the North-West Frontier Province, situated in a valley about four thousand feet high and therefore enjoying a moderate climate. But what weighed most heavily in its favour was the comparatively short distance which separated it from the place where my 'Arafat Press' was established. Lahore could be reached by car from Abbottabad within five or six hours, and this would make my weekly commuting fairly easy.

In the end, Chaudhri Niaz Ali accepted my decision, albeit reluctantly, and I tore myself away from my beloved Kashmir and shifted with all our belongings to Abbottabad.

Our house there was small, very much smaller than the one in Srinagar, and there was no Mir Wa'iz to entertain us in his house and visit us in ours, and no Kashmiri shopkeeper with whom to drink green tea and talk about cabbages and kings. Abbottabad was only a small provincial town with hardly anybody to talk to -- unless it be with members of the caravans coming from the as-yet-uncharted Black Mountains in the north-east and carrying skins and felt carpets for the markets of Peshawar and Rawalpindi. And around the town there were only endless fields of maize, with jackals roaming through them and crying throughout the night . . . .

Still, because it was so devoid of all charm, Abbottabad was a good place to work. And work I did. The second instalment of *Sahih al-Bukhari* was printed, and I had completed the manuscripts of the third and fourth instalments and was labouring on the fifth.

Endnotes

1 Mir Wa'iz Yusuf Shah, a famous leader of Kashmir.

For the "suspicious" activities of Asad in Kashmir, see the report of the secret police, "Lieut-Col. L. E. Lang, President in Kashmir (Sialkot) to B. J. Glancy, Political Secretary Govt. of India, Foreign and Political Department (New Delhi), 31 January 1939." (in: British Library, India Office and Oriental (London), R/1/1/4670)

Around 1935, Asad came to Kashmir. He stayed there in a houseboat on the river Jhelum, near Lal Maundy. There, he met some Muslim scholars of Kashmir and the Mir Wa'iz (the hereditary office belonging to Jami'ah Mosque of Srinagar, of the Hanafi school) Mawlawi Muhammad Yusuf Shah (head of the Muslim community in Kashmir). He was introduced to Mir Wa'iz by Abdul Aziz.

According to Kalimullah Khan (author of the book *Islam: The Source of Universal Peace*, Delhi 2001) when Asad and Mir Wa'iz were talking to each other this man (Abdul Aziz) who was also present there, said: "Muhammad Asad talked to Mir Wa'iz Kashmiri in fluent Arabic. It was surprising to see this great man from Europe talking in fluent Arabic (according to Asad, in Persian) as Mir Wa'iz himself could not talk so fluently. So they had to take the assistance of an Arabic scholar, Husain Shah Wafayee, who acted as an interpreter between Asad and Muhammad Yusuf Shah."

During his stay in Kashmir, Asad delivered some lectures in the Islamia High School (Srinagar).

Just what Asad did in Kashmir is uncertain. But on learning of his presence, the Kashmir Government immediately wanted him "externed", although the police had no evidence to substantiate the intelligence report, and there appeared to be legal obstacles to "externing" a European national. The intelligence report had him spreading Bolshevik ideas.

(cf. Abroo Aman Andrabi: *Muhammad Asad. His contribution to Islamic Learning.* New Delhi 2007, pp. 27-28)

2 *Lisan al-'Arab*, by Ibn-i Manzur (1233-1312), an authentic voluminous Arabic dictionary, cf. Brockelmann 2:21, S 2:14.

3 Muhammad Husain Babri (1895-1980), a type-writer mechanic of Lahore but an intimate friend of Asad. He established Arafat Publications and published Asad's book *Islam at the Crossroads* (7th ed., Lahore 1955). Asad and his step-son, Ahmad Heinrich Schiemann frequently corresponded with him. See Muhammad Arshad: *The Reconstruction of Islamic State: A Critical Study of Muhammad Asad's Thoughts* (in Urdu); doctoral dissertation, Punjab University, Lahore, 2007. Asad and Pola frequently exchanged letters with Muhammad Husain Babri, mostly from Geneva and Tangier. After his death, this rare collection was safely preserved by his son, Maqbul Husain Babri (d. 2005) and now is in the possession of Muhammad Arshad.

4 Babur (1483-1530), first Mughal ruler in India; diarist and poet.

cf. *EI²*, ed., I (1960), pp. 847-850.

5 Art. "Der Staat der wilden Knaben", published in *Frankfurter Zeitung* (Frankfurt), 21 March 1926.

6 Nawwab Asif Jah (Mir 'Usman 'Ali Khan), 1886-1967, r. 1911-1948.

See V. K. Bawa: *The Last Nizam,* New Delhi 1992; Margrit Pernau: *The passing of Patrimonialism. Politics and Political Culture in Hyderabad, 1911-1948.* New Delhi 2000; Sidq Jaisi: *The Nocturnal Court. Darbaar-e-Dürbaar. The Life of a Prince of Hyderabad.* Trans. By Narendra Luther. New Delhi 2004; Omar Khalidi: *Muslims in the Deccan. A Historical Survey.* New Delhi 2006; Muhammad Saeedullah and Rasheed Shakayb (eds.): *Asif and the Mamlakat-i Hyderabad,* Karachi 1998; Anonymous (ed.): *The Last Emperor of Deccan* (in Urdu), Karachi 1991, pp. 33-48, art. by Nawwab Mushtaq Ahmad Khan.

7 Sir Akbar Hydari (1869-1942); served Hyderabad Deccan State in different capacities (1905-1941); appointed the Prime Minister of this state (1937).

"M. A. N. Hydari", in: *Eminent Mussulmans,* Madras 1926, pp. 491-507; T. V. Haranatha Baber: "Sir Akbar Hydari. The Forgotten Prime Minister of Hyderabad Deccan State", in: *Deccan Studies* (Hyderabad Deccan), January-June 2004, pp. 23-41.

8 For Lady Amina Hydari, Gail Minault: "Coming Out: Decisions to be Leave Purdah", in: *India International Center Quarterly,* 23, nos. 3-4 (Winter 1996).

9 'Abdul Majeed II, the last Ottoman ruler of Turkey, was dethroned (3 March 1924) and he permanently settled in France. Mir 'Uthman 'Ali Khan, Nizam of Deccan, financially supported the exiled Turkish ruler and the cordial relations between these two royal families ultimately resulted in the marriage of two Turkish princesses with the princes of Deccan (Maulana Shaukat Ali and Khwaja Hasan Nizami also contributed in this regard). One was Durr-i Shahwar (b. 1913 or 1914), a tall and beautiful woman who died at the age of

92. She rendered valuable services for the education and emancipation of women in the Deccan State.

10 The second Turkish princess was Nilofer (d. 1989). After her divorce (1952) she returned to Istanbul and married an American (1963).

For these two Turkish princesses, see Omar Khalidi: "Ottoman Royal Family in Hyderabad Deccan, India", in: *Journal of the Pakistan Historical Society* (Karachi), July 1998, pp. 89-97.

11 'Abdul Majeed II died in Paris (23 August, 1944).

12 The husband of Nilofer, Mu'azzam Jah, died in 1970; cf. *The Last Nizam*. By William Dalrymple. New Delhi: OUP.

13 *Inqilab* (Lahore), 3 Nov. 1941; in the beginning, Asad planned to publish the English translation (with copious notes) in 40 parts, but due to certain circumstances, particularly his internment (1939-1945), only five parts came out from Lahore and Srinagar (1935-1941).

14 Muhammad Marmaduke William Pickthall (7 April 1875–19 May 1936). English traveler, novelist, polemicist and educationist and British convert to Islam; founding editor of *Islamic Culture* (Hyderabad Deccan), January 1927.

See J. D. Pearson: "Bibliography of translations of the Qur'an into European languages", in: A. F. L. Beeston et al (ed.): *Cambridge history of Arabiac literature. Arabic literature to the end of the Umayyah period.* Cambridge 1983; Peter Clark: *Marmaduke Pickthall–A British Muslim.* London 1986; ibid.: "Pickthall's Busy years, 1931-32" (in: *Islamic Culture* (Hyderabad Deccan), October 1999); *EI*[2], Vol. VIII, Leiden 1995, pp. 305-306 (art. C.E. Bosworth); Muriel Pickthall: "A great English Muslim" (in: *Islamic Culture* xi/3 (1937), pp. 138-142; Zia ud-Din Barni: *'Azmat-i Raftah*, Karachi 2000, pp. 394-400; Sayyid Sulaiman Nadvi: *Yad-i Raftgan*, Karachi 1983, pp. 171-172; Iqtidar Husain Siddiqi: "Muhammad Marmaduke Pickthall and Islam" (in: *Tehqiqat-i Islami* (Aligarh) July-September 2000, pp. 97-110).

15 After Pickthall's death, Asad was appointed as the editor of *Islamic Culture.* Under his editorship of two years (1937-1938), eight issues were published from Lahore and he contributed two articles (cf. *Gift*, Vol. II)

16 In 1934, Asad established his own press in Delhi and planned to publish an English journal from here. (cf. *Ma'arif*, October 1935, p. 243)

17 Asad did not mention the name of the publisher. Perhaps, it would be Sh. Ashraf and Sons from where many editions of his book *Islam at the Crossroads* came out.

18 On the basis of the record of the Intelligence Department of the British Government, the following comprehensive report was proposed about Asad's activities in India: "History Sheet of Herr Leopold Weiss Alias Mohammad Asad Ullah Vyce. An Austrian Convert to Mohammadanism", prepared by the Intelligence Bureau of the Government of India, included in letter from E. J. D. Colvin, Political Secretary, His Highness Government Jammu and Kashmir (Jammu) to Lieut. Col. L. E. Lang, Resident in Kashmir (Sialkot), 30 January 1934."

(in: British Library, India Office and Oriental (London), R/1/1/4670)

19 Asad's father, Karl Weiss (alias Kiwa), (1872), died in concentration camp in 1942 (at the age of 70). His sister, Rachel Weiss (1906) and step-mother, Bertha Weiss (1885), breathed their last in a gas chamber (1944). Only his step-brother, Martin M. Goldenberg, fled from Austria and permanently settled in London.

20 "Islamic Culture", a quarterly English scholarly journal, appeared in 1927 under the patronage of the Nizam of Deccan (now Andhara Pradesh, India). Its first editor was Muhammad Marmaduke Pickthall, the famed English Muslim whose translation of the Qur'an would later become a classic in its own right. For more than eighty years this journal – an outstanding example of scholarly publication by Muslims, has remained without peer.

21 Chaudhary Niaz Ali Khan (1880-1976), with the constant consultation of Dr. Iqbal and Asad, laid the foundation of Dar al-Islam in Jamalpur, Pathankot, district Gurdaspur (now in India) for the propagation of Islam. On his invitation Mawlana Mawdudi (1903-1979), a reputed religious scholar, came from Hyderabad Deccan and took the charge of this newly-established institute. He was a close and sincere friend of Asad who acknowledged his excellent cooperation and help in order to facilitate his life and scholarly pursuits.

See *Gift*, I, pp. 330-337; As'ad Gilani: *Iqbal, Dar al-Islam and Mawdudi* (Urdu), Lahore 1978; Akhtar Hijazi (ed.): *Dar al-Islam*, Lahore 1995; Rihana Quraishi: *Dar al-Islam–a Research Study*, Lahore 2000; Safir Akhtar: *Ba yad-i Maududi*, pp. 4-26; Afzal Haq Qarshi (ed.): "Nadirat-i Iqbal", in: *Sahifa* (Lahore), Iqbal Nr. (Oct. 91973), pp. 229-230; *Wasa'ik-i Maududi*, Lahore 1984, pp. 84-85; Asad's letter to Ch. Niaz Ali Khan (22 Nov. 1935, Srinagar; 18 Nov. 1936, Model Town, Lahore); K. M. Azam (Ch. Niaz Ali's son): *Hayat-i Sadeed*. Lahore 2010.

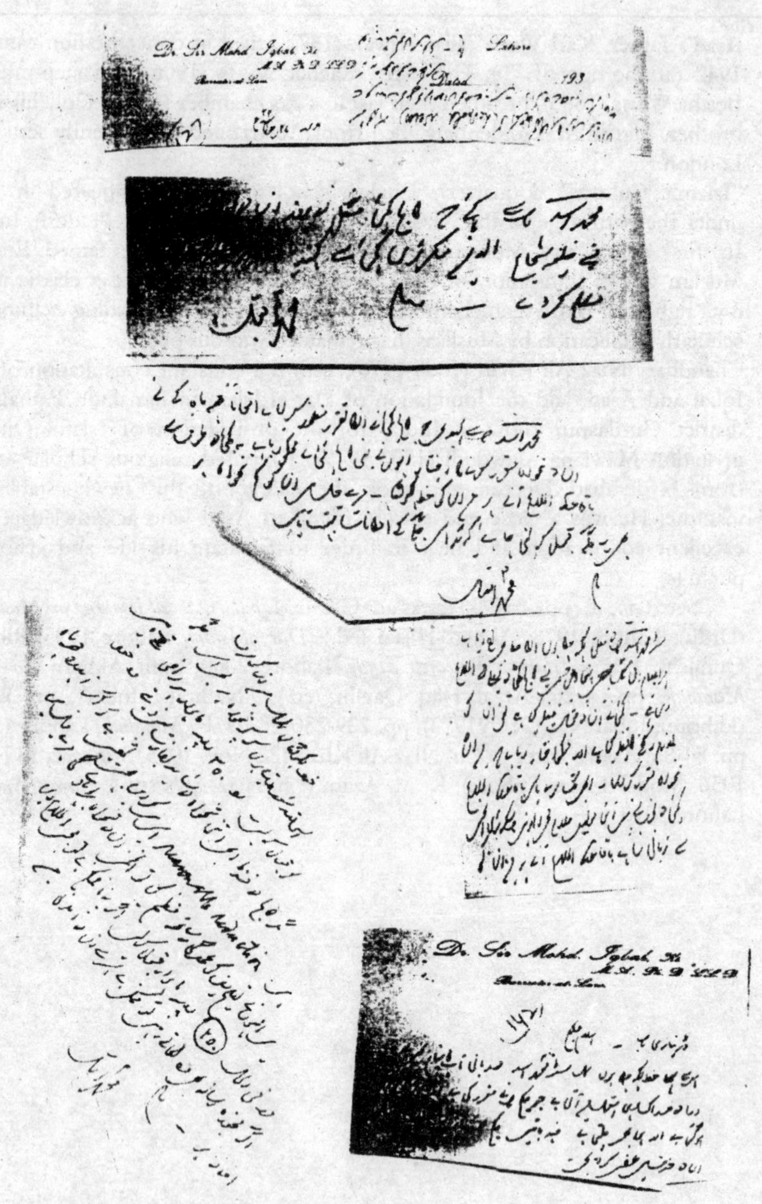

Dr. Sir Mohd. Iqbal Kt.
M.A. Ph.D. LL.D.
Barrister-at-Law

Lahore

Dated 193

Dr. Sir Mohd. Iqbal Kt.
M.A. Ph.D. LL.D.
Barrister-at-Law

Dr. Muhammad Iqbal's five letters (dated 27 June, 22 July, 28 July, 30 July and 18 August 1934) in which he wrote about M. Asad's appointment in the Islamia College (Lahore)

V
THE BLEAK YEARS (1938-45)

I

Whenever I came to Lahore I visited Muhammad Iqbal, and we spent many an hour talking about the prospect of Pakistan. Both of us were filled with enthusiasm about it and Iqbal had very definite ideas as to what consequences the establishment of the new state would entail. In his youth and his early academic years he had been an ardent Indian nationalist: in fact, his exuberant poem *Hindustan Hamara* ('Our India') had become -- and has remained to this day -- a sort of national anthem. But in the meantime Iqbal had shed his nationalist feelings and become fully imbued with the supra-national concept of the Islamic *ummah* and a burning passion for its realization in what was to become the state of Pakistan. Since this fully coincided with my own views and hopes, we would discuss for hours the forms in which that future state should be organized and the ways and means to persuade our political leaders to stand up boldly for our common ideal. Following Iqbal's advice, I wrote a series of articles about why Pakistan had to be established and had them published in various European newspapers and periodicals; some of those articles appeared also in an Urdu translation in a prominent Lahore newspaper.[1] In addition, I delivered some lectures on the same subject in Lahore and Delhi.

At about that time, in 1938, Iqbal's health began to fail; and one day, suddenly, a friend came running to me (I was sitting at my desk at my press, reading proofs) and told me, breathlessly, 'Iqbal is dead!'

I cannot describe my feelings at that shattering announcement; I only saw darkness.

Several of Iqbal's circle of friends were already in his house when I arrived there; none of us had expected him to die so soon. All of us stood wordless around his simple bed.

He lay there with lightly closed eyes and an expression of deep peace on his face, as if thinking a lovely thought. The merest hint of a smile played around his lips, and it seemed to me that at any moment he might open his eyes and say, 'I have fulfilled my task . . . .' It had been Iqbal who – perhaps inspired by a passing thought of that other great Muslim thinker, Jamal ad-Din al-Afghani -- was the first to formulate, in clear-cut political terms, the idea of an Islamic State in the north of India, and who thus gave it body and life. And it was he who, in turn, inspired -- directly or indirectly -- the young Cambridge student Rahmat Ali to put down the idea in print and to coin the name 'Pakistan' for the country-to-be. And thus it is understandable that throughout the Muslim world Iqbal is and always will be known as 'the Father of Pakistan'.

His funeral was the most impressive Lahore had ever seen. The bier was carried on immensely long poles by about forty men -- twenty on each side; and these bearers changed constantly, for every able-bodied man was anxious to be among those who carried Muhammad Iqbal on his journey to the grave. At least two hundred thousand men -- almost the whole adult male population of Lahore -- followed the bier, a mile-long cortège that wound its way slowly, for hours, through the narrow streets all the way to the Badshahi Mosque,[2] before which the funeral prayer was held. Thereupon Iqbal was laid to rest in the centre of the huge square between the Great Mosque and the Red Fort; and some months later a mausoleum was built over the grave.[3]

II

As the days and the months passed, an ominous rumble could be heard from Europe. Hitler occupied Austria, and one could almost physically feel the approach of a terrible catastrophe.

My desire to bring my father, sister and step-mother from Vienna to India became desperate; and even my father was now willing to leave his country. In view of the many thousands of refugees -- mostly Jews -- streaming out of Nazi Germany it had become extremely difficult for most of them to obtain visas for other countries; and India, with its highly labile political situation, was the most difficult of all.

As usual during my life, friends came to my rescue. One of them, Justice Din Muhammad[4] -- at that time Chief Justice of the Punjab High Court -- offered to give me a letter saying that he had engaged my sister as a 'governess' for his daughters; on the strength of this letter, stamped with the seal of the High Court, she was certain to obtain a visa from the British Consulate, in Vienna. I sent it to her forthwith. As for my father, no such fictitious 'engagement' was practicable; and so I importuned every person of high official standing known to me to help me in my endeavours. Sardar Sikander Hayat, Chief Minister of the Punjab, responded most generously. He personally intervened with the Home Secretary in New Delhi and prevailed upon him to issue, as a personal favour to himself, an immigration visa in my father's and his wife's names; and this exceptional grant was communicated telegraphically to the British Embassy in Vienna.

I wrote at once to my father and instructed him to present himself at the Embassy, have the visas entered on his and my step-mother's passports and leave Austria immediately. A few days later, to my horror, I received a letter from my sister informing me that she had somehow lost the Chief Justice's letter of engagement. It was almost like a death-wish!

On the same day I obtained a duplicate letter from my friend the Chief Justice and sent it express to Vienna. In a telegram I urged my father not to wait for this second 'engagement letter' to arrive, but to leave at once for Italy and await my sister there; she would follow as soon as she had secured her visa. Our father replied -- also by telegram -- that he would not leave Vienna without his daughter . . . .

This was in late August of 1939. A few days later the Second World War broke out, the British Embassy and Consulate were withdrawn from Vienna, and no visas could be obtained any longer; and I myself was arrested and -- because of my Austrian passport -- interned as an 'enemy alien'.

I was sitting in my study, immersed in my work, when a uniformed police inspector suddenly appeared and told me that a warrant had been issued for my arrest. I was thunder-struck, for, being conscious of my well-known anti-Nazi attitude, I had never expected such a thing to happen. But the inspector showed me a list -- a *printed* list, obviously prepared days or perhaps even weeks earlier -- with my name at its very top.

And so I went with the police inspector. As I was passing our front door, with my wife and our seven-year-old son Talal weeping and loudly protesting, our old maid-servant took hold of a copy of the Qur'an and held it over my head, thus invoking God that He protect my leaving and secure my return . . . . I had only time to tell Munira that she should immediately contact Chaudhri Niaz Ali and take shelter with him in Jamalpur, when the inspector politely but firmly urged me to go on.

III

A police car was waiting in front of our house, and we went to Rawalpindi. I was ushered into the police headquarters and found myself within a group of other internees-to-be, all of them refugees and holders of German or Austrian passports. I was told to stand in line with the others and await my turn for registration. When my turn came I was about to enter the room in which a police superintendent was filling in the registration papers, when one of my shoe-laces got loose. In order not to break the line I pushed the man behind me forward while I bent down and tied the shoe-lace. And so it happened that the registration number which had been meant for me -- 621 -- was assigned to my predecessor, whereas I was given the next number, 622. At that time I did not pay any attention to this detail; but months later, in the permanent internment camp at Ahmednagar, where I was the only Muslim among thousands of non-Muslims, a co-internee and friend of mine -- a Viennese painter by the name of Langhammer -- on hearing one day my number 622 at the daily roll-call -- suddenly exclaimed: 'Asad! Don't you know what this number signifies? It is the year of the *hijrah,* the year in which your prophet migrated from Mecca to Medina! How strange that it has been given to you, the only Muslim among us...'

And then I remembered that but for a loose shoe-lace my number would have been 621. Was it a sign from God that I had been awarded the most dramatic date in Islamic history as my internment number?

As it was, I badly needed such a sign, if indeed a sign it was: for, from the moment of my arrest in Abbottabad and the subsequent registration as an internee I felt enveloped by darkness; and it was only months after that day that I became reconciled to my destiny. I knew with absolute certainty that my internment would last for years. And I knew, too, that because of it -- because of my inability to pursue the exodus of my father, sister and step-mother from Austria into freedom – they were all doomed.

And doomed they were. As I learned years later through the Red Cross, my father died in 1941 or 1942, at the age of seventy, in the concentration camp of Theresienstadt, and my sister and step-mother perished at an unknown date in the gas chambers of Auschwitz. Only my step-brother, Martin, managed to evade arrest and, after escaping from Austria, joined the British Army, later settling down for good in England.

IV

A special train carried the internees -- several hundred men by now -- from the temporary, make-shift camp at Rawalpindi to a permanent one at Ahmednagar, near Bombay. Most of our group were Germans, with some refugees among them, and a sprinkling of Italians. We travelled for well over three days and two nights, tightly packed in locked third-class carriages, with a couple of armed guards in every carriage, as if we were criminals. The train stopped often, sometimes for hours, and at some stations, we were given food of a military kind -- mostly a thick vegetable soup ladled out of huge cauldrons, and bread. At every station groups of country people stared at us with curiosity, wondering what kind of dangerous criminals we were: for at each stop our police guards stood before the carriage door with their rifles at the ready. But there were no incidents, if for no other reason than that all of us were exhausted from sitting for days and nights on hard benches, with no room to lie down or to walk more than a couple of steps.

The Ahmednagar camp was installed in a one-time military complex. It was surrounded by two lines of high, tight barbed-wire fences with wooden watch-towers every fifty metres or so, guarded by Indian soldiers. Each barrack was filled with about sixty or seventy iron bedsteads with hard mattresses. An Indian cook with two helpers was to cater for each group of three barracks. We were assigned a money allowance sufficient for our day-to-day maintenance and the wages of the kitchen staff. Hence, we were free to decide what food we would like to have within the limits of our budget. To this end, the inmates of each barrack elected a committee of three or four men who were to manage our culinary affairs.

By that time the Ahmednagar camp contained about three thousand men, collected not only from all over India but also from Afghanistan and Indonesia. Most of them had been representatives of German and Italian multi-national firms like Siemens, Agfa, Bayer or Fiat, and almost all were Nazis or Fascists. Only about one hundred of us were confirmed anti-Nazis or anti-Fascists, and we naturally kept close together and aloof from the others. Most of our group were Jewish refugees from Germany and Austria; but there was also quite a number of non-Jewish socialists and liberals from Germany and Italy who had found it necessary, or at least advisable, to leave their countries of origin. We occupied two of the barracks at one end of the camp.

Immediately after our arrival we were informed of the daily routine which we were to observe. At six o'clock in the morning a trumpet-call awakened us. We were allowed fifteen minutes to wash and dress, and then we had to assemble for the daily roll call. Each man was called by his number, and each had to answer, 'Here!' The roll call was followed by a short physical fitness drill led by an army sergeant, and then we were free to do whatever we liked until nine o'clock in the evening, when another trumpet-call obliged us to return to the barracks. One hour later the Last Call was sounded, and the lights had to be extinguished.

And so it went on, day after day, week after week, month after month. I had no books with me with which to work on *Sahih al-Bukhari;* and in any case, work was unthinkable in a barrack filled with seventy men . . . .

Autumn passed into winter. In the outside world the 'phoney war' was going on, that early period of the Second World War when the two sides were only jockeying for position without any serious fighting. We were allowed some newspapers which went from hand to hand and offered ample material for discussion. Most of my co-internees were convinced that the war would end very soon and were making plans for the future. I was not so optimistic. I felt in my bones that I was destined to remain in internment for a long, long time, and this thought was the more bitter since all my sympathies lay on the side of the powers that had so senselessly locked me up. The Nazis, on the other hand, knew that they had been interned by their enemies; and this knowledge, combined with their certainty that the Axis powers would come out victorious, apparently made it easy for them to bear their internment with equanimity or even, it seemed to me, with a certain gusto. Added to this was the fact that most of them were swimming in money and spent a lot of it on drinks -and so they held 'open house' for the British officers entrusted with guarding the camp. Strangely enough, these officers, in their turn, did not mind being hosted by people whom they should have regarded as their country's enemies: on the contrary, they openly fraternized with the Nazi internees, and frequently dropped in for a glass or two of Scotch. No such facilities were available to them in the barracks inhabited by anti-Nazis or anti-Fascists who -- as already mentioned -- were mostly refugees without any financial means of their own; and, consequently, the officers of the guard visited them only rarely, and always cursorily.

When Christmas approached, the Nazi section of the camp resounded more and more with boisterous singing. To be sure, the religious aspect of this festival had long since, as in all Western societies, lost any meaning for them; but because the Germans are a sentimental people, Christmas and nationalist exuberance were, it seemed to me, inextricably mixed in their feelings. Songs like 'Silent Night, Holy Night' often flowed almost imperceptibly into the 'Horst Wessel' song or 'The Night of the Long Knives' and roused them to emotional tears, stimulated by alcohol and a hatred of all that stood in the way of the Nazi dream. More and more often they assembled in front of our barracks and hurled abuses and threats at the 'traitors to the Fatherland', promising us death by hanging at the moment of Nazi victory -- a victory which to them was a certainty.

On Christmas Eve their drunken exaltation reached its peak. Spurred on by the news of the Russo-German agreement which was meant to divide Europe into two separate but mutually friendly spheres of influence, and which led to the partition of Poland between the two powers and thus to the end of its existence as a sovereign state, the Nazi internees set about storming the barracks of the 'traitors' with the intention of 'making an end of them'. There were, as we knew and saw, about three thousand of them as against the one hundred or so of our anti-Nazi group; and the officers of the guard, probably immersed in their own celebrations, were nowhere to be seen. Faced by a growing threat -- a *real* threat -- we anti-Nazis readied ourselves for a desperate fight. We tore the iron legs off our army cots and hit right and left at the frenzied attackers. But even so we would have been overwhelmed by their vastly superior numbers had it not been for the fact that our adversaries were, to a man, entirely drunk -- so much so that hardly any one of them was steady on his feet. And thus it happened that in the ensuing melée several of the attackers were badly hurt -- as we later to came to know, one of them lost an eye and several suffered broken arms or legs -- whereas on our side not one man was seriously wounded, and only a few received minor scratches. It was almost a miracle.

Finally, a detachment of Indian soldiers, led by a British officer, marched in at a trot and separated the two factions; and a few days later a barbed-wire fence was erected between our barracks and theirs, and separate anti-Nazi and anti-Fascist enclosures came into being: an arrangement which henceforth lasted throughout the years of our internment.

V

And as the years dragged on and on, despondency grew among the anti-Nazis. The startling German victories of the spring and summer of 1940 -- their occupation of Norway and the fall of France and the open entry of Italy at the side of Nazi Germany, the aerial bombings of England in 1941 and the apparently successful invasion of Russia by the Nazis, the triumphant progress of their armies down to the Caucasus and the Black Sea -- all this convinced many among us that Germany was bound to win the war. To the Jewish refugees, in particular, this prospect meant the end. Several of them attempted suicide and were only at the last moment saved by the more balanced among our group.

As for myself, I somehow managed to keep my balance. I knew that a Nazi victory would put an end to all the efforts of the Muslim peoples to win their freedom from colonial rule: and this my mind could not accept. I felt with a certainty beyond certainty that a great future still lay ahead for the world of Islam, and that this future would never become a reality if the Nazi mentality prevailed -- and, therefore, it *could not possibly* prevail. It mattered little whether this conviction of mine had or had not a logical basis: it was firmly embedded in my mind and gave me the peace necessary for an emotional survival of my loss of liberty and the endless, grey years of internment as a solitary Muslim among so many non-Muslims.

What helped me greatly in that desolation was the attitude of the people charged with catering for our camp. As it happened, this task was entrusted to a Muslim business firm from Karachi. I slightly knew some members of the family concerned from the days before the war; but they knew everything about me, and they let me feel it almost from the very beginning of my internment. Whenever one of them entered the camp (they had free access to it in view of their duties), he brought me some titbits to relieve the monotony of our daily diet, and I shared them with a few special friends among my co-internees. Every year during the month of Ramadhan -- which I naturally observed by fasting from the first dawn until sunset -- a huge tray laden with the most delicious dishes was brought in for me at the time of breaking the fast; and always there was enough for five or six of my friends to share with me.

Another group of Muslims who did their best to alleviate the dreariness of my internment were the soldiers guarding the camp. Although we internees were strictly forbidden to approach the barbed-wire fence closely or to talk to the guards, this prohibition was overlooked by them and me, and we spent hours every day talking together in Urdu. They, together with their officers, belonged to a Punjabi regiment; and all of them felt closer to me, their fellow-Muslim, than to their overlords. On one occasion they even suggested that they might enable me to escape from internment and, one of them added, 'We will also give you a rifle to defend yourself, if need be . . . .'

However, I did not dream of escaping, for I did not want to give up my life in India and the prospect of working for the establishment of Pakistan, which by then was coming closer and closer to realization. And so I thanked my soldier-friends and assured them that one day I would meet them as a free man in a free country.

Such encounters and demonstrations of affection by my Muslim brethren contributed a lot to my peace of mind and to the hope with which I looked towards the future; they provided a counter-weight to the series of hostile 'interrogations' to which I began to be subjected during the third year of my internment.

VI

The purpose of these interrogations was to find out which of the internees could be considered harmless and might, therefore, be released without any risk to the established order, and which were potentially 'dangerous' to the war effort and hence should be kept locked up until the end of the war.

The first of these interrogators was a Czech refugee by the name of Wyscočil, who had been living for years in India; his nationality and perfect knowledge of German had made him most suitable for 'screening' the professed anti-Nazi internees, most of whom hailed from Germany and Austria.

When my turn came and I was led to a room in the Camp-Commandant's office, Mr Wyscočil answered my greeting with a sarcastic smile, and I felt at once that he was already primed and prejudiced against me. He appeared to be about forty years old, and was undoubtedly intelligent. After a brief pretence at reading and re-reading my 'dossier' he asked me -quite unnecessarily since he must have known it already -where I had been born. I told him, 'Lwów, or Lemberg as it was known in the days of the Austro-Hungarian monarchy; the capital of the Austrian province of Galicia.'

'Ah,' said Mr. Wyscočil with a smirk, 'by now Lwów has been incorporated into Russia; you must be happy about it, aren't you?' – thus clumsily insinuating that my sympathies were on the wide of Communism.

This silly remark angered me, and I retorted sharply, 'Just as happy as you must be at the German occupation of Prague, Mr. Wyscočil!' At that he nearly exploded, and I knew that I had made an enemy; but at that point I was beyond caring. After a few more desultory, mostly ironic questions and, from my side, bored answers the interview was over; and I knew that in Mr. Wyscočil's report I would figure as a 'dangerous' subject.

The reason of my indifference lay in my knowledge that some very influential Muslim personages were interceding at that time with the authorities in New Delhi and were pressing for my release. Foremost among them were the Chief Minister of the Punjab, Sardar Sikander Hayat, and the then Law Member of the Viceroy's cabinet, Sir Muhammad Zafrullah Khan (who later became the first Foreign Minister of Pakistan). The endeavours of these two men, I was convinced, were bound to bring about my speedy release. But as it soon transpired, I was quite mistaken. All those intercessions led to nothing, and I remained interned as before. Years later, when I was head of the Middle East Division in Pakistan's Foreign Ministry, Zafrullah Khan told me what had happened when he interceded in my behalf with the Home Secretary in New Delhi. The latter told him that the Government of India had nothing against me, and that the order for my internment had come from the Home Government in London. Since Zafrullah Khan was a fully trusted supporter of the British *raj* and held, moreover, a high position within the Indian Government, he was shown my file -- and there it was: I was supposed to have been instrumental in the Saudi Arabian grant of the concession for oil exploration throughout the Kingdom to an American group of companies and for the corresponding rejection of the British bid! This was, of course, utter nonsense. Although at the time I had vaguely known that negotiations about an American oil concession were going on, I played no role whatever in this matter and learned only much later, after ARAMCO had come into being, that the Americans had won the contest. Nevertheless, my file in the Home Office in New Delhi stated clearly that I had been responsible for the British débâcle and must, therefore, be considered an enemy of Britain. (Had this allegation been true, I would certainly have been a millionaire by then.)

And so, neither Zafrullah Khan nor Sikander Hayat succeeded in getting me out of internment. As soon as I learned of their failure in a round-about way, I decided to appeal myself to the Home Secretary; and the friendly British colonel commanding our camp promised to forward my letter to the addressee.

In that letter I asked the Home Secretary point-blank: 'Do you regard me as a Nazi or a Communist? The first is, you must admit, hardly plausible in the case of a man who was born a Jew and would always, even after his conversion to Islam, be regarded by the Nazis as a Jew. And do you, on the other hand, think that a conscious Muslim could ever sympathize with Communism, which is anti-religious by definition and, therefore, diametrically opposed to everything that Islam stands for? And if, as my friends have been told in your office, 'there can be no smoke without a fire', could you let me know what kind of smoke you have perceived in my case?'

My letter was, of course, not phrased in exactly these words, but that was its gist.

For long weeks I heard nothing -- until, finally, I was called to the Camp-Commandant's office and told that the Home Secretary had issued an order forbidding any letters from me to be forwarded to him in the future . . . .

VII

In 1942 our whole camp was transferred from Ahmednagar to Deolali, another town in the Bombay Province. We were not told why, but I think that it was done in the cause of the war effort: the Ahmednagar camp was fully fitted out for military purposes and was wasted as a mere internment camp.

The Deolali camp was quite different from Ahmednagar. There were no barracks there, only tents -- small tents with four iron bedsteads each and a large *shamiana* fitted with long tables and wooden chairs to house a communal dining hall. The smaller anti-Nazi and anti-Fascist wing was separated from the much larger Nazi wing by a high barbed-wire fence -adequate enough for preventing physical contact between the two wings, but not enough to protect us from the constant abuses and threats from the other side.

The same Karachi firm as in Ahmednagar was in charge of the catering for the new camp; and that was the one pleasant aspect of Deolali. For the rest, the change proved to be a miserable one. Instead of the solid barracks of Ahmednagar we were now housed in flimsy tents, and with the beginning of the monsoon season life became very difficult indeed. The heavy rains soaked through the fabric of the tents and dripped almost without cease onto the inmates. The bare earth under each tent became a quagmire, and at night one had to hang one's clothing and shoes on strings above our heads to prevent them from being soaked. Cases of colds, and sometimes even pneumonia, became the order of the day. Hardly anyone was free from muscular pains and aches, and coughing was the sound most frequently heard from all sides.

In time, however, this condition was to some extent improved. The camp authorities arranged for a second canvas cloth to be spread over every tent, and most of the dripping ceased or was at least greatly diminished. Gravel was spread over the earth surface within each tent to prevent it from being entirely water-logged. Still, living in the Deolali camp during the monsoon rains was just -- but only just -- supportable, and internment grew to be a nightmare.

By the middle of June, when the monsoon was at last ending, life gradually became easier- and for me a new ray of light came with the arrival at our camp of people with whom one could talk intelligently, without being exposed to the everlasting complaints and sentimental reminiscing of my refugee-companions, who could only talk about what they had lost in Europe and what they now missed so badly.

The new arrivals consisted of a group of ten or twelve German Jesuits who until recently had been allowed to continue their missionary work in the south of India and were only now, in view of the extremely difficult war situation both in Europe and on the Japanese front in Burmah, interned as possibly 'dangerous' subjects. All of them were educated people with intellectual interests, and it was a pleasure to talk with them, for a change, about things and problems far removed from the miseries of our own, personal existence. It was something that I had badly missed during the past two years of internment, and I readily availed myself of the new opportunity.

The unquestioned leader -- in every sense of the word -- of this Jesuit group was a Prince Löwenstein, descendant of one of the most illustrious families of Bavaria, probably as old as the royal house of Wittelsbach and certainly older than the Habsburgs. In addition, he was possessed of wide culture -- a culture far beyond the horizon of the average priest -- so that one could discuss with him many questions of religious philosophy and contemporary life. Thus, it was only natural that very soon something like friendship came into being between the two of us, facilitated by the fact that we were more or less of the same age and had both seen a lot of the world; and we would spend hours in animated talk, walking side by side along the circumference of the camp or sitting down in the *shamiana* for a cup of coffee.

Knowing that I was deeply interested in religious thought of every description, my Jesuit friend lent me a voluminous book on the history of the Catholic Church, and I went through its eight hundred pages within a couple of weeks. From that book I learned about a curious incident of history.

Shortly before the destruction of Jerusalem by Titus, the then bishop of that city had a dream which predicted the approaching catastrophe; and to save his people from that disaster, the bishop sent the whole small community, men and women and children, across the Jordan to the land east of it; and somehow they remained there, entirely cut off from the rest of the Christian world, for over two hundred years. Gradually times changed, Palestine became safe once again for Christians, and that particular community returned to the land of its origins. On their return, however, it was found that their beliefs greatly differed from those of the Christians who had remained in Palestine throughout the intervening two centuries: whereas the latter firmly believed in the Trinity and regarded Jesus as the Son of God and God Incarnate, the people who now returned from their voluntary exile saw in him a mortal human being -- a prophet who, like all the true prophets before him, had been elected by God to convey His message to the world and thus to lead mankind to a recognition of His oneness and uniqueness.

According to the history book which I was reading, this 'deviation' was a result of the group's isolation, over the centuries, from the main body of Christendom and, thus, of their loss of all contact with the central doctrine of the Christian Faith. To me, however, it became obvious on reading this book that what had really happened was the other way around: it was the Christians of Palestine who -- imbued with Pauline mysticism and probably also influenced by the then widespread Mithraistic beliefs -- had deviated from the original concept of God's oneness preached by Jesus and lost themselves in the dogma of the Trinity; whereas, on the other hand, the self-exiled small community who had lived for so long east of Jordan, totally isolated from all other currents of thought, had adhered to and brought back with them the untarnished, original doctrine of God's transcendental oneness: the same doctrine as was to be propounded a full century later by Arius, Bishop of Alexandria, and to be henceforth dubbed by Church historians as the 'Arian heresy'.

The reason of my conviction lay in the fact that history shows many instances of an inspired leader or hero growing in the minds of his later followers to the rank of divinity, but not a single instance of a personality once regarded as divine being 'degraded' to the status of a mortal man.

It was only natural that one day, while discussing with Prince

Löwenstein the book which he had lent me, I mentioned the history of that community which had returned from exile in Transjordan and gave him my interpretation of it -- an interpretation which he, of course, rejected out of hand as being fanciful. Nevertheless, since each of us had respect for the other's intellectual integrity, we continued our discussions on religious matters with, I hope, mutual enjoyment.

On one such occasion, my Jesuit friend suddenly remarked: 'You know, Asad, you were originally a Jew, unsatisfied with your religion: the right way for you would have been to become a Christian -- and instead you have chosen Islam!' To which I laughingly replied: 'Well, not all is yet lost. I am still prepared to embrace Christianity if you answer one question to my satisfaction. If you do, you may take me next Sunday to your chapel-tent and baptize me in public.' 'Well, what is that question?' asked Löwenstein eagerly. 'Would you,' I said, 'explain to me the meaning of the Trinity?'

My interlocutor thought for a long moment, and then said: 'Well, this is a mystery of the Faith, and cannot be explained in words; but it will become clear and understandable to your heart as soon as you attain to real faith.'

'This, then,' I rejoined, 'was the reason why I became a Muslim and not a Christian. Your religion tells me, 'Gain faith, and then you will understand' -- whereas Islam says, 'Use your reason, and it will *lead* you to faith.'

And that was that. Never again did my friend try to convert me; but we remained friends none the less.

VIII

As I could no longer address the Home Secretary directly, I did the next best: I wrote a long letter to the Camp-Commandant and handed it to him personally with the request that he convey its contents to the Home Secretary if he saw fit to do so: in that letter I sent out a definite proposal for the consideration of the 'higher authorities'.

The kernel of my proposal was an offer of my direct, active participation in the war effort in a special role. I explained in detail my association, over many years, with the late Grand Sanusi, Sayyid Ahmad ash-Sharif, and with the Sanusi movement in general; and I referred to my abortive mission, in 1931, to 'Umar al-Mukhtar in Cyrenaica.* My connection with the Sanusis had never been broken, and until my

* See the chapter on 'Jihad' in *The Road to Mecca,* pp. 312 ff.

internment at the outbreak of the war I had remained in contact, through letters, with the surviving leaders of the movement. Since the Sanusis had always been bitterly opposed to Italian rule over Libya, they were now opposed to the Germans as well in view of the Nazi-Fascist alliance, and they looked to the British in Egypt as potential liberators. In my letter I suggested that in view of my strong links with the Sanusis, my perfect knowledge of Arabic and my past experiences in Cyrenaica I was well fitted to organize an intensive guerilla activity behind the Italian lines, arousing the population to sporadic acts of resistance, destroying wells on the enemy's lines of communication, and so forth. Although I was well aware that this would involve risking my life a hundred times, I was prepared to do it not only to help the Sanusis but also to contribute something of value to the Allied struggle against Nazism and Fascism, and thus to avenge to some extent the murder of my family.[5]

This, in short, was the proposal which I asked our Camp-Commandant to place on my behalf before the Government of India or, if he so wished, before the War Office in London; and in time I learned that he indeed had done so: I learned it in the course of my next interrogation a few weeks later.

That interrogation was quite different from my sessions with Mr Wyscočil. Instead of one interrogator, there was now a group of six or seven men seated around a table in the Camp-Commandant's office. Some of them were -- as became obvious to me from their questions -- representatives of the Government of India; two of the others, I learned later, belonged to the Special Branch (the political section) of Scotland Yard; and the chairman, who seated himself on my right and was addressed by his colleagues as 'Colonel Hamilton', was almost certainly a member of the British Intelligence Service.

After a few desultory questions by one or another of my interrogators, Colonel Hamilton addressed me: *'Wy gavaritie pa rusku?'*

Because of my birth and upbringing in the Polish-speaking city of Lwów (in fact, my mother-tongue had been Polish)[6] I had some slight grasp of the closely-related Russian language, without being really able to speak of it. But I knew enough of it to understand Colonel Hamilton's surprising question, and so I turned to him slowly and answered in English, 'No, I don't speak Russian . . . .'

By now it had become quite clear to me that I was suspected of having Communist inclinations, and perhaps even of being a Communist agent. Mr. Wyscočil's insinuation of some weeks ago and now Colonel Hamilton's pointed question were obviously meant to bring home to me the nature of the authorities' suspicion and, thus, the real cause of my internment. This was to some extent astonishing in view of the fact that Soviet Russia was now an ally of Britain and America; but in time I came to know that, so far as the so-called 'upper classes' in Britain were concerned, their fear of Communism outweighed even their fear of Nazi Germany. Some of those 'upper class' British officers with whom I occasionally talked even made no secret of their pleasure on hearing that the Germans had occupied the whole of the Ukraine and had reached the Caucasus ; and one of them once said , 'We should be fighting on *their* side, and not against them . . . .'

IX

The bleak years of internment dragged on and on. After one year at Deolali our camp was again transferred -- this time to Dehra Doon in the province of the U.P. -- but the routine remained the same. Most of the anti-Nazi internees were gradually released, and only the most 'dangerous' among them -- myself included -- remained locked up. But even for us a change for the better came about towards the end of 1943 or the beginning of 1944, when a 'family camp' was established at Purandhar, in the hills near Poona, and those who had families were allowed to join them there. Until then, Munira and Talal had been living with Chaudhri Niaz Ali in Jamalpur; and now all three of us were brought together in the Purandhar camp.

It was a tremendous change from the three previous camps. Purandhar was a 'parole camp', that is to say, we were not subjected to any military routine, but had to undertake not to escape. There were no barbed-wire enclosures, no armed guards, and no barracks. Instead, we were lodged in bungalows (before the war Purandhar had been a summer resort), with each family enjoying its privacy and a monthly allowance of money. We were free to leave the camp on short excursions, and even -- with the Camp-Commandant's special permission -- occasionally to visit Poona; and since the Commandant was a humane, liberal Irishman, this permission was not difficult to obtain.

As for Talal, who was now twelve years old, he was sent by me as a boarder to the English school at Panjgani, a few hours away by car, and was able to spend every week-end with me and his mother.

But with all this, life in Purandhar was not a happy one. Whatever facilities there were at our disposal, liberty was far away. I was a prisoner, and had to obey the commands of others: and that was bitter to bear. In addition, during the years of internment Munira and I had become more and more estranged.

The year 1945 began, and April came, and Nazi Germany collapsed and surrendered, and D-day was celebrated throughout the Allied world: but I remained a prisoner, the very last in the parole camp of Purandhar. I now had books to read, but by far not enough to be able to continue my interrupted work on *Sahih al-Bukhari;* and so the useless, wasted days and months went by.[7]

Finally, on the fourteenth of December, 1945, I was called to the Commandant's office and informed that I was free. Two days later we left -- my wife and my son and I --, by train from Poona to Bombay and thence to the Punjab, straight to Chaudhri Niaz Ali's estate at Jamalpur. There I learned that immediately after my arrest at the outbreak of war that good old friends had shifted all the contents of my 'Arafat Press' as well as my library and my manuscripts for safe-keeping against my return. I was home once again . . . .

Endnotes

1 In those days, *Inqilab* and *Ihsan* were two widely-read newspapers of Lahore. Those translations would have published in any of these two.

2 Badshahi Mosque (Lahore), opposite to Lahore Fort:; built during Awrangzeb Alamgir's (d. 1707) period under the aegis of Koba Fidai Khan (1673); it is considered the biggest mosque in the world.

cf. M. Abdullah Chaghatai: *Badshahi Mosque*. Lahore: Kitab Khana-e Naurus.

3 In a register, still housed in the Iqbal Museum (Lahore), Asad's name is also included in the list of prominent personalities who attended the funeral procession of Dr. Iqbal (d. 1938). For Iqbal's mausoleum, see my book, *Iqbal, Afghan and Afghanistan*. Lahore 2006.

4 Justice Sh. Din Muhammad (1886-1965); born in Gujranwala, appointed as the Chief Justice of the State of Bahawalpur (1946); later on Governor of Sindh (1948-1952) and the minister of Kashmir affairs.

Cf. Ahmad Saeed. *Muslim India (1957-1947). A Biographical Dictionary.* Lahore 1994, p. 115.

5 During his stay in Saudi Arabia (1927-1932); founded by Muhammad ibn 'Ali al-Sanusi (1787-1859); the Sanusiyah is a Sufi brotherhood based in Libya and the Central Sahara. Asad tried to strengthen the Sanusi Movement. See *Gift*, (s.v. Index); *The Road to Mecca*; (s.v. Index).

'Umar al-Mukhtar (c. 1858-1931) belonged to a religious family connected to the Sanusiyah Sufi order in Cyrenaica (eastern Libya).

After the withdrawal of Turkey from Libya (1912), the Sanusi leader

Ahmad al-Sharif called for *jihad* and led a largely Bedouin force against the invaders (Italians). Later on al-Sharif was replaced by his cousin Muhammad Idris, and a settlement was made whereby the Sanusi retained large degree of autonomy. Soon, Italy came under the sway of fascism and the agreement broke down. At this stage, the struggle became a more purely Bedouin one led by 'Umar al-Mukhtar, a charismatic leader. His fighters became hunted groups, and on 11 September 1931, 'Umar himself was captured and hanged on 16 September.

cf. *OEMIW*. Ed. John L. Esposito, vol. 3, New York/Oxford 1995, pp. 473-474; *EI*[2], vol. IX, Leiden 1997, pp. 24-26, with bibliography; E.E. Evans-Pritchard: *The Sanusi of Cyrenaica* Oxford 1949; Mahmood Ahmad Ghazi: *The Sanusiyyah Movement of North Africa*. Islamabad 2001.

6 Cf. dr. Boguslaw Ryszard Zagorski: "The Relationship of Muhammad Asad and Poland," a paper read at the international symposium on "Muhammad Asad–A Life for Dialogue", organized by the Embassy of Austria (Riyadh, Saudi Arabia) in collaboration with King Faisal Center for Research and Islamic Studies (Riyadh), 11-12 April 2011.

7 As soon as Hitler captured Austria (March 1938), Asad hurriedly reached London so that he could help his close Jewish relatives. Unfortunately he failed in his efforts and came back to India (1939). Afterwards, he was arrested and spent about six years (1st September 1939-14August 1945) in the concentration camp.

cf. *Gift*, I: 339-342; Amir Ben David: "Leopold of Arabia" (*Ha'aretz*, 23 Nov. 2001), under the sub-heading "Behind the barbed wire fence"; Florence Haymann: *Un juif pour l'Islam*. Paris 2005, pp. 224-225; Asad's letter to Ghulam Rasul Mihr (22 Sept., 28 Sept. and 7 Nov. 1939, Ahmad Nagar, Bombay Presidency; *Inqilab*, (3 Nov. 1941).

* * * * *

VI
PARTITION
(1946-47)

I

The world to which I returned was quite different from the one which I had left on September 1,1939. The British *raj* was visibly coming to its end. India was nearing independence. Talks and negotiations were going on between New Delhi and London. Lord Mountbatten,[1] the last Viceroy, was ready to hand over his authority to a provisional Indian government composed of representatives of the National Congress in loose alliance with leaders of the Muslim League:[2] an uneasy alliance in view of the League's solemn adoption, in 1940, of the principle of Pakistan and of its separation from predominantly Hindu India.

The decision to establish Pakistan as a sovereign state had not come about all at once. For months and years the leader of the Muslim League, Muhammad Ali Jinnah,[3] had urged the Hindu leadership to accord to the Muslims the right to form autonomous units within the framework of an Indian Federation -- one in the north-west, comprising the Punjab, Sind, Baluchistan, the North-West Frontier Province and Kashmir, and the other in the north-east, consisting of Bengal and the Muslim-majority areas of Assam; and it was only after a categorical rejection of this proposal by the Indian National Congress, with Mahatma Gandhi's particular, unbending insistence on an undivided India, that the Muslim League voted unanimously in 1940 for a fully independent, sovereign Pakistan: a decision which was ultimately accepted, albeit reluctantly, by Lord Mountbatten and, on his advice, by the British Government as well -- in disregard of Gandhi's description of the Pakistan idea as 'a vivisection of Mother India'.

It was this reality which I encountered on my return after well over six years of internment.

The Muslim community was in a ferment, not only in the areas which were to become the State of Pakistan, but all over India. For the first time in many centuries they were faced with the prospect of an Islamic State -- a state based not on any national or racial affinities but solely on its people's voluntary adherence to a common religion and a common outlook on life. Their enthusiasm was so great that people who had been unknown to one another embraced in the streets; and although they did not know yet that such a need might arise, many of them were ready to lay down their lives in the pursuit of their common ideal.

And I, for my part, resolved to make a tangible contribution, in writing, towards a formulation of the ideological principles on which the future of Pakistan might be built.

And thus the monthly journal 'Arafat' -- the one-man journal of which I had been dreaming for years -- came into being.[4]

II

During those early months after my release from internment I lived, together with my family, with Chaudhri Niaz Ali at Jamalpur. His estate was so large and his house so roomy that none of us ever inconvenienced the others. But what was most important to me was the feeling of *belonging.* I was not considered by my friend nor did I consider myself a 'guest' in his house: I was truly at home. Free to stay, to come and to go as I liked, and to do what I liked.

At first I thought of resuming forthwith my work on *Sahih al-Bukhari.* All my books were already placed on shelves, all my manuscripts had been carefully preserved, the press furniture could be set up easily in one of the many outhouses on the estate, and the small staff which I needed could be easily arranged from Lahore.[5] Still, I hesitated. I was determined to start as soon as possible on the monthly journal which, I hoped, would help to clarify many of the ideological issues connected with the impending establishment of Pakistan. Could the two tasks be attended to simultaneously?

'Arafat' was not intended to be a periodical like so many others, with contributions by other writers, but rather something of a monologue, a vehicle for *my* ideas alone -ideas aiming at a fundamental reconstruction of our approach to the problem of the *shari'ah,* the Islamic Law as such. During the years of my internment, when I had nothing but my thoughts to comfort me, I had come to the conclusion that the true *shari'ah* had been so overlaid by the subjective speculations and deductions of generations and generations of scholars that its true purport had become almost entirely unrecognizable: and this, to my mind, was the main cause of Muslim decadence for so many centuries. To pare down that scholastic superstructure and reduce the concept of the *shari'ah* to its original conciseness and simplicity was, therefore, a condition *sine qua non* of Muslim re-revival. To draw the attention of our thinkers and scholars to this basic problem and to induce them to undertake an in-depth analysis of our past intellectual shortcomings -- in particular, the blind acceptance of all juristic conclusions of the early scholars (called *taqlid)* -- was the sole purpose of this journal-to-be,* and I was to realize this purpose single-handedly. Would I be able to do it side-by-side with working on *Sahih al-Bukhari*? Certainly not. Now which of the two objectives was the more urgent?

I decided that 'Arafat' must have precedence, and that the *Sahih* should be laid aside for a year or so. I did not intend to continue 'Arafat' indefinitely, it was to be only a clarion-call at the critical time of Pakistan's coming into being: and after I had sounded it, I would return to my lasting work.

III

It would have been senseless to open up my press and to engage staff for the printing of a monthly journal; consequently, this would be done at a reputable printing press in Lahore.

The first issue appeared in September of 1946, and hundreds of copies were sent out to select Muslim addresses all over India. The response was so good that 'Arafat' -- subtitled 'A Monthly Critique of Muslim Thought' -- became self-supporting by the end of that year.

The main theme of the September issue was the question 'Is Religion a Thing of the Past?' I answered it, of course, in the negative and showed that religion as such had always been one of the mightiest culture-producing forces throughout human history, and the only known source of ethics and morality. However, I argued, Islam had not merely the power to *produce* a culture but had always, because of its life-affirming world-view, acted as a steady, positive factor in the development of man's mind and knowledge, and had thus been able to shape and re-shape human society in accordance with the exigencies of time and circumstances: and in this respect Islam was unique among all the phenomena of religious faith and, *ipso facto*, timeless.

However, I argued, Islam could not maintain its legitimate role

---

* A more detailed discussion of the problems involved can be found in my book *This Law of Ours* published in 1987.

unless its spiritual constitution and its worldly 'program' could be fully visualized by its adherents: hence the necessity of making the *shari'ah*, the eternal Law of Islam, clearly understandable to every Muslim of average intelligence and maturity.

The next five issues of 'Arafat' were devoted exclusively to the one overriding problem: *how* to make the Law of Islam thus understandable to the community as a whole. The issue of May 1947 was entitled 'What Do We Mean by Pakistan?' In it I stressed the *real* purpose underlying the future establishment of Pakistan: that purpose did not consist in merely providing more economic opportunities or government posts to Muslims but, rather, in enabling them to live effectively as Muslims and to realize the spirit of Islam in their political forms, in their laws and social institutions -- in short, to bring into being the first truly *Islamic* state since more than a millennium.

In logical continuation of this line of thought, the July 1947 issue of 'Arafat' (published less than one month before Independence Day) consisted of a lengthy essay entitled 'Towards an Islamic Constitution'. It was, as far as I know, the first attempt ever made to outline the principles which must be incorporated in the constitution of any state that claims to be 'Islamic'; and, without my anticipating it at that time, this essay was destined to become the first -- however modest – step in the development of political thought as such in the modern world of Islam.

IV

To escape the summer heat, I rented a bungalow in Dalhousie,[6] a resort high in the hills of the Gurdaspur District, not far away from Chaudhri Niaz Ali's estate in Jamalpur; and there we transferred our temporary residence at the beginning of May 1947.

I did not know at that time -- none of us knew -- that when we shifted to Dalhousie we would be living on the very line which was to separate Pakistan from the rest of India.

Some months earlier, the British Government in conjunction with Lord Mountbatten had entrusted a well-known British barrister, Sir Cyril Radcliffe,[7] with the task of drawing that dividing-line in accordance with the country's communal configuration: that is to say, those districts of the Punjab in the west and Bengal in the east which were populated by Muslim majorities were to go to Pakistan, whereas the Hindu-majority areas would remain with India. In Bengal this division was relatively easy and did not cause any serious trouble; but as far as the

Punjab was concerned Sir Cyril Radcliffe allowed himself to draw, in one area, an arbitrary line in defiance of all communal realities. That area was the district of Gurdaspur, which was pre-dominantly Muslim in its population. However, if that district were to be awarded in its entirety to Pakistan, India would be left without any access to the State of Jammu and Kashmir, whose Hindu ruler, Maharajah Hari Singh,[8] had opted for accession to India despite the fact that the population of his country was overwhelmingly Muslim, with only sixteen per cent of Hindus in the Jammu Province and a bare seven per cent in Kashmir proper. This arbitrary 'accession' had been accepted by Lord Mountbatten, with tragic consequences; and it was widely rumoured that Radcliffe had been bribed by the Indian National Congress in unison with the Maharajah.

As I have said, all this was as yet unknown to us: all the Muslim residents in Dalhousie, together with its Muslim summer visitors, had taken for granted that the whole district of Gurdaspur (in which Dalhousie was situated) would go to Pakistan.

Hence, on the evening of August 14 -- a few hours before the Partition became a fact -- all of us were thunderstruck when we saw the flag of India being hoisted by the Hindu superintendent of police over the municipal building in Dalhousie. Still, many of us assumed that it must have been a mistake on the part of the superintendent, or, at the worst, an outcome of Hindu wishful thinking which was bound to be rectified as soon as Independence Day dawned. We did not know as yet that the great barrister Sir Cyril Radcliffe had committed a criminal blunder . . . .

V

On the same evening I went with Talal, who was now fifteen years old, on our usual walk over the mountain paths above Dalhousie. When we were returning long after darkness had fallen we suddenly heard the sound of a gunshot from the direction of the bazaar; and then another and yet another, in rapid succession. There could be no doubt about it: a riot was on.

No Muslim could have fired those shots because none of them had a gun at his disposal. A few days earlier all holders of gun permits had been ordered to bring their firearms to the police station for re-registration. It was only routine, they were told; their guns would be returned to them after a couple of days. But they were not returned -- at least not to the Muslims.

Talal and I were walking rapidly through the dark, empty streets of upper Dalhousie towards the safety of our bungalow when we beheld a man lying in a pool of blood in the middle of the pavement. We came closer, and at the same moment two other people appeared: I knew them -- they were Canadians, employed on some humanitarian work on behalf of an international agency. Together we bent over the man on the pavement. He had been literally hacked to pieces -- a bundle of flesh and bones and blood . . . . A last spasm passed over his body, and then he was dead. One of the Canadians shone his torch on the murdered man's face, and I recognized him: he was a Muslim, a cook in one of the summer visitors' houses, as inoffensive a man as ever could be. *Why* had he been killed?

We ran to our bungalow, where we found Talal's mother and our faithful Kashmiri man-servant huddled in the living-room. I bundled her off to our bedroom, and we three – Talal, the servant and myself -- decided to spend the night on guard in the living room. We had no arms except for an old cavalry sword which had been left behind in the house by some earlier occupant, and an axe normally used for cutting wood. But what was even worse than the lack of arms was the front wall of the room: it consisted almost entirely of glass -- large French windows opening onto the verandah, glass from top to bottom, meant to let in the sunlight, without any shutters.

Since anybody could see us from the outside, I turned off all the lights, and we sat down in the darkness, expecting an onslaught at any moment, for the sound of gunshots -- now accompanied by frenzied screaming -- came nearer and nearer.

However, nobody attacked us, and the screaming and shooting gradually died down.

The morning found all of us exhausted from lack of sleep and the long, tense night-watch. We could not even *think* of food. In mid-morning a man came running to our house -- a servant of one of my Muslim friends from Lahore who lived not far from us. He came with the urgent message to pack our belongings and shift to his master's house -- one of the largest in Dalhousie -- where already several other Muslim families had assembled for safety's sake.

And so we did. We packed our suitcases as fast as we could and carried them over the empty streets to our friend's house. It was filled to the brim by a crowd of men, women and children -- at least one hundred of them -- who had been sheltering there throughout the night. The women prepared a make-shift breakfast from what food stores were to be found in the house: they did not amount to much, considering the many hungry mouths that had to be fed.

Our host, a Mr Rahimullah, tried to phone the police station, but the line was dead: apparently the wires had been cut. Someone said, 'It is the Swayam Sewak Sangh[9] . . . .' We all knew what this meant: the most fanatical band of Hindu zealots, who had sworn to prevent the threatened 'vivisection' of Mother India at whatever cost.* Later we learned that even before the Partition became a fact that they had started killing Muslims in the villages around Amritsar and Lahore; and they were actively supported by the Sikhs who now put their *kirpans* to bloody use. The Muslims, of course, retaliated and began slaughtering Hindus and Sikhs wherever they could, and a cloud of death and destruction was spreading over the border-lands of West and East Punjab.

We refugees in the house of Mr. Rahimullah took stock of our arms. It was not a long stocktaking, for we had nothing beyond two pistols -- a small automatic and a 0.22 one-shot Flobert pistol -- plus an old elephant gun which had belonged to our host's grand-father and had somehow escaped the 're-registration': a good weapon originally, but now in a deplorable state, with a rusted cock-and-hammer and with the butt half broken off and tied with wire to the barrel. Only five or six cartridges had been left, and I was doubtful whether the ancient gun could still bear the shock of firing or would explode in one's face . . . . However, as the old proverb has it, 'beggars can't be choosers'; and so I took over the elephant gun and hoped for the best.

Nothing much happened during the day except for a few sporadic gunshots in the distance and occasional shouting from the bazaar in lower Dalhousie. But as soon as night fell we could see shadowy figures slinking through the bushes on the slope below the garden, and a muted call sounded off and on. There was no doubt that we were besieged, and so the three of us who had firearms stood or sat by the windows throughout most of the night, relieving one another from time to time.

It was an eerie night. We three crouched at the windows of the darkened room, straining our eyes in a constant effort to discern any sign of movement in the blackness. No sound came from outside, apart from the usual playing of monkeys on the tin roof of the house -- a scurrying to and fro of many tiny feet, and an occasional squeak: friendly

---

* It was one of the bitter ironies of history that it was this very group which, less than six months later, murdered Gandhi, the most determined opponent of partition.

little sounds, friendly little animals that wanted nothing more than their amusement and sometimes a bit of stolen food . . . . Never before had I been so taken with the monkeys' nightly dance on the roof.

At about three o'clock in the morning I heard an abrupt, subdued shout from the lower reaches of the garden, immediately answered by another shout from the hillside above the house; and at the same moment a few moving human shapes could be dimly discerned through the bushes: was an attack finally to start?

I felt that I would not take any further risks; I was the only one in our group accustomed to handling firearms. Hoping that my elephant gun would not explode, I took aim and fired. A crash like a cannon-shot boomed through the night and the recoil almost bowled me over. I heard a shout outside, and then there came an uncanny silence. Had I hit somebody, or missed? I never knew; but no further outside movement became visible or audible throughout the rest of the night. To make quite sure that the siege was over, I borrowed the automatic from my companion, covered my white shirt with a jacket and set out as noiselessly as possible on a tour around the compound. Nothing happened and no hostile figure appeared.

At sunrise we were hailed by a shout from below the garden -- and there stood a young British officer. He called out to us: 'Is everything all right?'

He was a subaltern in charge of a platoon of Gurkha soldiers who now became visible between the bushes. They had come to our relief. And from them we learned that during the night a score or more of Muslims had been slaughtered in lower Dalhousie . . .

VI

Eight or ten lorries were ready to transport us and all the other Muslims from Dalhousie to Lahore, with an escort of a Gurkha sergeant and a few of his men in two jeeps. All our moveable belongings were loaded onto open lorries and we huddled on top of them in tight groups -- women and children and men. And so the convoy -- preceded and followed by the two jeeps with Gurkhas -- started on its slow journey down the winding mountain road, with steep hills on one side and a precipitous chasm on the other.

The convoy stopped before every culvert and the Gurkha soldiers made a thorough search underneath for possible explosives -- for, as they told us, the Swayam Sewak Sangh men had publicly sworn not to let us pass alive. However, no explosives were found; instead, something potentially worse happened.

The first few lorries of our convoy were rounding a hairpin bend when suddenly a huge boulder came thundering down, and then another. Both missed us. It was an ambush. We could discern the faces of several men who were lying on top of the hill and were rolling more boulders towards its rim. Our Gurkhas fanned out and fired their rifles upwards in the direction of the attackers, while more and more boulders came rolling down: but, as if by a miracle, each one of them -perhaps badly aimed -- bounced off an outcrop of rock and went in a curve high above our lorries and down the chasm on our right; and suddenly, as it had begun, the shower of boulders ceased: the ambush had failed.

We reached the plains without further incident, and by afternoon we were in Lahore.

VII

Lahore was in complete chaos. Streams of Muslim refugees were daily, almost hourly, arriving from India, most of them entirely destitute and many suffering from illnesses as well as from wounds received during the communal riots which preceded this exodus. All available sanitary personnel, hospital nurses and doctors, as well as scores of voluntary workers exerted themselves day and night in taking care of the sick and trying to provide food and shelter for those who were able to move.

The new Government of West Ṗunjab was not yet functioning properly. There were not troops enough to man the new frontiers and to help the Punjab police and constabulary – themselves greatly reduced in number by the departure of Hindu and Sikh officers -- to maintain law and order: for, just before Partition, the then Prime Minister of the Provisional Government of India, Pundit Jawaharlal Nehru (who had also held the portfolio of Defence), had seen to it that most of the Muslim army units were transferred from what was to become Pakistan to the South-Indian province of Madras and the State of Travancore, so that now only about one thousand Muslim troops remained in Pakistan. Added to this was the extreme scarcity of road transport caused by the constant, two-way flow of refugees, so that the exhausted, ragged Muslims coming from India had to be marched on foot to temporary shelters scattered all over the city, whereas the sick and badly wounded had to be carried by volunteers to one or another of the improvised emergency hospitals.

It was in this utter confusion that I tried to find out what had happened to Chaudhri Niaz Ali and his large family, whom I had last seen at Jamalpur before leaving for Dalhousie. All my frantic inquiries led to nothing, and so I assumed that he was still stranded in Jamalpur, which was now part of East Punjab; and I knew, too, that he had a group of other Muslims living on his estate: Maulana Abu'l-Ala al-Mawdoodi,[10] a youngish scholar from Hyderabad, and the latter's followers who in time were to organize themselves into a revivalist movement called *Jam'at-e Islami,* 'the Islamic Association' or 'Community'. All these people would certainly perish unless they were brought to Pakistan.[11]

I turned to the man who had been placed in charge of Lahore's chaotic transport system: a good friend of mine who, like me, had been one of the intimate circle around Muhammad Iqbal. His name was Khwaja Abd ar-Rahim.[12]

I found him in a government office, surrounded by a crowd of excited people all desperately needing a car or a lorry or even an oxcart. Khwaja Abd ar-Rahim was obviously trying his best to satisfy all these demands, pleading, shouting, arguing to the left and right, and obviously not succeeding in bringing some sort of order into an utterly confused situation.

I pushed my way through the unruly throng and placed my problem before Abd ar-Rahim. Trying to outshout the others, I asked him to assign to me a few lorries and a military escort to save all those people bogged down in Jamalpur. Khwaja Abd ar-Rahim, who knew them almost as well as I did, shouted back in desperation: 'How can I give you transport if none is available? Don't you see that I am helpless?'

I insisted: 'I *must* have it! I won't leave until you give me what I need!'

And so it went on, backwards and forwards, both of us growing more excited, banging our fists on the table and almost -- but not quite – hurling abuses at each other. And suddenly, just before both of us exploded, Khwaja Abd ar-Rahim gave in. 'Wait! Perhaps I *can* do something . . . .'; and he grabbed the telephone and spoke to somebody at the other end of the line.

I had won. I got a written order for some municipal buses and was told that by afternoon a small escort would be assigned to me.

And so it happened that early next morning I set out for Jamalpur in a convoy of three empty buses, accompanied by four fully-armed Punjabi infantrymen, probably the best in the world. The salvage expedition was on.

VIII

Once again I was entering hostile territory. At the frontier post near Gurdaspur town we were let through without much difficulty: an arrangement had shortly before been concluded between the authorities of Pakistan and India, allowing for the free transit of refugees from one country to the other. Nevertheless, we were looked over suspiciously by the Indian frontier guards, who made sure that we were not carrying contraband arms apart from the legitimate equipment of our military escort.

When we arrived at Chaudhri Niaz Ali's estate in Jamalpur we found his fortress-like compound surrounded by a milling crowd of at least one thousand Muslim men, women and children who had abandoned the surrounding villages and were now desperately anxious to be brought -- or led -- to Pakistan. I was, of course, unable to accommodate all those multitudes in my three buses; but I promised their spokesman that on my return to Lahore I would make some arrangement for them as well. (In fact, most of them were later shepherded by a contingent of Pakistani soldiers to Lahore.)

To my immense relief I found that no serious ill had befallen Chaudhri Niaz Ali, his family or his guests, Abu'l-Ala al-Mawdoodi and his followers. My three buses were just enough to transport them provided that they did not take more with them than the barest necessities and that some of them would be prepared to travel on the roofs of the buses. And I warned them *explicitly* against taking any arms with them (Mawdoodi's people had brought a few rifles and shotguns to Jamalpur), since the Indian frontier guards were certain to insist on making a thorough search of the buses.

Late in the afternoon, after only a couple of hours or rest, we started on our return journey. All three buses were packed to the brim with people and luggage, and each of them carried at least a score of men on its roof. I myself sat next to the driver in the leading bus, and the soldiers of our escort squeezed themselves among the refugees.

Shortly before we crossed the frontier we were held up by a man who stood gesticulating in the middle of the road: an old, white-bearded Sikh with a sword in his hand and an arm raised high, imploring us in a loud voice to stop.

The driver beside me called out: 'No, we must not stop! It is an ambush!' But I somehow sensed that he was wrong, and that the old Sikh had no hostile intentions. And I was right.

As soon as the convoy came to a halt, the old Sikh approached us and cried, 'Listen, I have a Muslim family hiding in my place!' And then he told us that those Muslims belonged to his village and had taken refuge with him when the slaughter started on the day before Partition. 'For three days and nights I kept them in my house, and my four sons stood guard before the house with drawn swords. But then it became too dangerous for us to keep them, because other Sikhs in the village had become furious with us for protecting our enemies. And so I hid them in my sugar-cane fields. Take them with you; I cannot hide them any longer!'

The driver remonstrated with me: 'How *can* we take them! As it is, the buses are too full!'

But I overruled him and told the good old Sikh to bring his protégés to us. A few minutes later they appeared: three men and a woman carrying a child in her arms. They were so frightened that they could hardly speak. Somehow -- I don't know how -- places were found for them in our three buses. I blessed the old Sikh for the goodness of his heart, and on we went.

IX

On arriving at the Indian frontier post I had a shocking surprise. One of Maulana Mawdoodi's men confided to me that he and his friends had brought their rifles and shotguns with them despite my prohibition! These arms, I was told, had been packed in a carpet and were now at the bottom of all the luggage heaped up in one of our busses . . . .

I was struck dumb. If a search was made and the firearms were found, my whole expedition would be in vain, for the frontier guards would most certainly turn back our convoy and would not allow the refugees to cross over into Pakistan. And since we were already halted in front of the post, it was too late to jettison those guns.

I was almost in despair- but then, suddenly, an idea flashed through my mind.

I put my solar topee (sun helmet) firmly on my head and strode purposefully towards the table in front of the Indian post. My complexion and the colour of my hair and beard was right: nobody could doubt that I was a European.

I faced the Indian soldiers and engaged them in polite talk, pretending to be a Swiss representative of the Red Cross, and none of the Indians thought of asking me to show them my identification papers. I pronounced myself full of disgust at my humanitarian charge, and complained about the trouble which these blasted refugees were giving me with their undisciplined behaviour and their constant lamentations.

The Indian sergeant and his soldiers sympathized with me and invited me to have tea with them, and we chatted for a while about this and that, and I was full of pins and needles while I gulped down my hot tea and was offered a second, very welcome cup. No one thought of searching the buses, and after a while I was told that we could proceed. And so we did, and a few minutes later we crossed the frontier and India was behind us.

Thus ended another chapter of my life -- but not without a bitter postscript.

Some weeks later I learned that my library at Jamalpur had been looted and destroyed by marauding Sikhs. Together with the Arabic books (which had probably been regarded by the looters as 'unclean'), all my manuscripts on *Sahih al-Bukhari* -- nearly two-thirds of my entire work, as yet unprinted -- perished in that outburst of senseless fury: and so, the labour of years dissolved into nothingness.

A few days after my return to Lahore I happened to be walking on a tow-path along the River Ravi, which was still swollen from the monsoon rains. All manner of flotsam was sweeping along -- tree branches, broken pieces of wood, rags and papers -- and I thought that among all that floating rubbish I could discern some remnants of my manuscripts by their colour: for I had always been using paper of a light-blue tint; and now I saw scattered leaves of light-blue paper floating down the Ravi . . . .*

X

Lahore was more chaotic than ever. Together with the steady, distressing influx of refugees, alarming rumours floated through the city: rumours of an impending Indian invasion. In the direction of Amritsar the frontier was only about four miles distant, and it was said that the Indians were massing troops on the invisible line which divided the countries. Whereas some of our people were still jubilating, others were filled with a dread anxiety, for – as already mentioned – Pakistan had in those days no real army worth speaking of: all that we had at our disposal was one battalion of the Baluch Regiment and one company of

* Many years later a part of this work was published under the title of *'Sahih al-Bukhari: The Early Years of Islam'*.

the 8th Punjab Regiment; all the rest of the Muslim troops were still in South India.

In addition to the frightening rumours about India's hostile intentions, Lahore was swept by new waves of uncertainty and speculation. Many of its citizens seemed to regard the establishment of Pakistan as no more than a source of personal aggrandizement. People were jockeying for government posts and contracts, each of them eager to secure a promising niche for himself before the Government was fully organized and settled on its course. Meanness was in the air side by side with popular enthusiasm and readiness for self-sacrifice: jubilation, fear and greed were shockingly intermingled.

In view of this perplexing situation the new Chief Minister of West Punjab, the Nawab of Mamdot, turned to me -- who had a reputation for being vocal -- to do something to counteract the growing confusion: and so I embarked on a series of daily radio broadcasts under the heading 'Calling All Muslims'.

Every morning I sat down at my typewriter in one of the Government offices, hammered out the broadcast talk of the day in English and delivered it myself at noon; and each of these talks was immediately translated into Urdu and broadcast on the same evening.[13] I do not know what effect those talks had on civic morale, but some of my friends told me that many of our people had been encouraged and uplifted by them.*

Apart from this activity, I laboured every day, together with scores of other volunteers, on the reception of the unending stream of Muslim refugees from India. One day we received a telephone call from the station-master at Ferozepore in Indian-held East Punjab informing us that an unscheduled train of refugee women had just left and was due to reach the frontier at Kasur within a few hours. A group of volunteers, myself among them, set out immediately for Kasur in a hastily-assembled convoy of lorries.

At our destination we were met by my dear old friend, Maulana Abd al-Qadir Kasuri, and his son Mahmud Ali,[14] and together we drove to the railway station. One hour later the train arrived.

It was full of women of all ages -- at least two hundred of them – and to our horror we saw that all had been stripped naked . . . . They were Muslim women, most of them accustomed to veiling themselves in a *burqah* from head to foot, and all -- even those who had never worn a

* See 'This Law of Ours and Other Essays'.

burqah -- brought up to a high sense of woman's modesty and self-restraint: and now they tumbled out of the carriages as naked as they had been born, young and middle-aged women, and grandmothers, and barely adolescent girls . . . .

We had by far not enough blankets with us to cover them all, and so the volunteers took off their jackets and shirts and threw them over the sobbing, unhappy victims of Hindu and Sikh savagery. Still, there were not enough jackets and shirts to go around, and nothing could be done until we delivered the wretched women at hospitals and makeshift shelters in Lahore. It was one of the most harrowing experiences in all my life.

Endnotes

1 Lord Mountbatten (1900-1979); British naval and military leader; great-grandson of Queen Victoria; last viceroy of India (1947); governor-general of India (1947-48).

2 Muslim League is the successor in Pakistan of the All-India Muslim League (Dacca, 1906) which spearheaded the movement for the creation of Pakistan. The Muslim League ruled Pakistan intermittently from 1947 (when Pakistan became a reality) to 1958 and then again for short periods during the 1960s, 1980s and 1990s. It is still one among several political parties of the country, where it has continued to play a significant political rone.

cf. A.B. Rajput: *Muslim League. Yesterday and Today.* Lahore 1948.

3 Muhammad Ali Jinnah (1876-1948), founder and first governor-general of Pakistan, commonly called Quaid-i-Azam ("Great Leader").

cf. Stanley Wolpert: *Jinnah of Pakistan.* New York 1984.

4 Asad had a long practical experience of working as a correspondent to the leading newspapers of Germany, Netherland and Switzerland. When he came to India (1932), he soon decided to publish a journal of his own under the title "Arafat" but certain unfavourable circumstances hindered him from publishing it. Finally, after his release from the concentration camp (1945), he settled in Dalhousie (now in Himachal Pradesh, India) and from there the first issue of this monthly English journal "Arafat" came out (September 1946). In its introduction he describes the three reasons of naming this journal:

"It is on the plain of Arafat...that the yearly congregation of Muslims, clad in the all-levelling pilgrims' garb, became truly the symbol of an *ummah*, a community in which there are no differences of race, nation, social function; no difference of sect or "school of thought"; a community, in short, of Muslims without any qualifying adjective. Secondly, the pilgrims' meeting on the plain of Arafat has been likened by our Prophet (upon whom the blessing and peace) to that greater meeting on Resurrection Day when every soul will await the Judgment and in the meantime will try to render account to itself about its doings, in the world: and the Muslims of today need such a reminder more than anything else: because they need self-criticism more than anything else. And, thirdly, it was at Arafat, during the Prophet's Farewell Pilgrimage, that the words are revealed: "Today I have perfected for you your religion, and fulfilled My favour unto you, and willed that Islam should be your religion" (5: 3)–an eternal reminder to us that we need only the Qur'an and the Sunnah, and nothing else, to know what Islam is."

'Arafat' was a journalistic monologue, *e.g.* every issue (32 pages) consisted only of Asad's articles. Nine issues were published from Dalhousie (1946-47) and the next issue, under the same title, appeared (March 1948) when Asad was appointed as the Director of the Department of the Islamic Reconstruction (Lahore). All these Asad's articles in *'Arafat'* (all ten issues) have been reprinted in *Gift*, Vol. II.

In a letter to Malik Muhammad Ashraf (Gujrat, Pakistan), dated 24 Jan. 1946 (Lahore), Asad writes:

"There is so much to settle and to do after more than six years of absence that I could hardly call an hour of my own. At present I am at Lahore, trying to find a house, a terrible problem here. As soon as this is arranged, I hope to settle to work, both in connection with the Islamic Research Institute of which I am to be the Director, and with my translation of *Sahih al-Bukhari*. This later publication will have to wait for some time because of the paper shortage. But in the meantime I shall Insha a-Allah publish a book which I had been working for some time past and which will be completed within three months or so. Also a complete revised edition of *Islam at the Crossroads* is in preparation and will come out soon together with its Urdu translation."

See also Abdul Mājid Daryabadi's article "Future of a Scholar" (in Urdu) in: *Sidq* (Lucknow), 25 May 1946.

Asad explained the aims of publishing 'Arafat' in a letter to Muhammad Ali Jinnah (6 Sept. 1946, Dalhousie) and later's reply (letter dated 10 Sept. 1946, Delhi), see Khwaja Razi Haidar (tr.): *Quaid-i-Azam in the Light of Letters* (Urdu), Karachi 1985, pp. 432-433.

Dr. Zakir Husain (1897-1963), ex-President of India, wrote a letter to Asad (29 Sept. 1946, Delhi), in which he comments on the first issue of 'Arafat':

"I looked in 'Arafat' as soon as I got it, and – I could not put it aside before I had finished it. The very very first issue justifies the sub-title that you have given it. It is a real critique of Muslim thought. It is critical and constructive, it is thoughtful and thought-provoking. I shall look forward with the keenest interest to your presentation of the ethical, social and political realities of the *Shari'ah*. You have undertaken a service of fundamental import to the future of Islam as a culture-forming force of world-historic significance. Few are as qualified as you to undertake this essential service."

(in: *Arafat*, Nov. 1946)

5 Originally, Asad intended to complete this English translation (with commentary) of *Sahih Bukhari* in eight volumes (each comprising five parts) but he published only five parts (December 1935–May 1938, Srinagar and Lahore). He devoted ten years to this huge project and, according to him, the rest of three-fourth part of the work had been accomplished but the whole hand-written and typed material was lost during the Partition (1947). The printed five parts of this translation have been published together in one volume (Dar al-Gibraltar, 1981, with a new introduction by Asad).

6 Asad's letter to Malik Muhammad Ashraf (Gujrat, Pakistan), 24 Jan. and 17 June 1949, Lahore and Dalhousie.

7 For Radcliff's Award, see

"Radcliffe's Betrayal and Sikhs", in: *Quaid-i-Azam Jinnah. As I knew him.* By M.A.H. Ispahani. 3rd ed., 1976, pp. 240-251.

8 Maharajah Hari Singh Dogra (1895); son of Amar Singh, ascended the throne as the ruler of Jammu and Kashmir (1925); in 1947 he finalized an agreement with Indian government and his state became the part of India; settled in Bombay but died in Delhi.

9 Rashtriya Sewak Sang (RSS); an extremist political party of India.

10 Sayyid Abu al-A'la Mawdudi (1903-1976), Islamic ideologue and religio-political leader. He was one of the most influential and prolific writers of contemporary Muslim thinkers. His interpretive reading of Islam has contributed greatly to the articulation of Islamic revivalist thought and has influenced thinkers and activists of the whole Muslim world. He founded Jama'at-i Islami, an Islamic revivalist party in Pakistan, on 26 August 1941.

In 1938, Maulana Mawdudi came from Hyderabad Deccan to Jamalpur (now Himachal Pradesh, India) where he headed Darul-Islam, a religious educational project conceived by the poet-philosopher Iqbal but materialized by the combined efforts of Ch. Niaz Ali and Asad. At Darul-Islam Mawdudi devised a model Islamic community, which he hoped would spearhead the reform of Islam in India. Here Asad and Maulana Mawdudi spent a few years together.

cf. Sayyid As'ad Gilani: *Maududi: Thought and Movement.* Lahore 1984; Masudul Hasani: *Sayyid Abul A'ala Maududi and his Thought.* 2 vols., Lahore 1984; Charles J. Adams: "The Ideology of Mawlana Mawdudi" (in: *South Asian Politics and Religion*, ed. by D. E. Smith, Princeton 1966, pp. 371-397; ibid: "Mawdudi and the Islamic State", in: *Voices of Resurgent Islam.* Ed. by J. L. Esposito, New York 1983, pp. 99-133; Aziz Ahmad: "Mawdudi and orthodox Fundamentalism of Pakistan", in: *Middle East Journal*, Summer 1967, pp. 369-380; Seyyed Vali Reza Nasr's doctoral dissertation, published in 2 vols., under separate titles.

11 Asad put his life in danger and saved not only the life of his benefactor, Chaudhry Niaz Ali and his family members but also brought safely Maulana Mawdudi from Pathankot to Lahore. For the relationship of Asad and Maulana Mawdudi, see *Gift*, I: 330-337.

[12] Khwaja Abdur Rahim (1908-1974); a high-ranking civil officer and a lawyer.

[13] All these speeches were published in a pamphlet entitled, *Calling all Muslims*; seven broadcast talks delivered from Radio Pakistan in September 1947. Lahore: Department of Islamic Reconstruction, 1947 (pp. 30).

cf. Muhammad Asad: *Aims and Objectives of the Department of Islamic Reconstruction*, Lahore 1947, pp. 1-22; ibid.: "Memorandum; Enforcement of *Shari'ah* in Pakistan" (in: *Iqbal* (Lahore), July 1998).

Asad's colleagues and staff-members of this Department were:

Mawlana Muhammad Hanif Nadvi, Mawlana Ja'far Shah Phulwarwi, Sayyid Nazir Niazi, Dr. Husain al-Hamadani, Mawlana Abu Yahya Imam Nawshahrwi, Mazharuddin Siddiqi, Iftikhar Husain Chisthi and Muhammad Hasan (Stenographer).

[14] Mahmud Ali Qasuri (1910-1987); son of Abdul Qadir Qasuri and a reputed lawyer of Pakistan.

* * * * *

VII
ISLAMIC RECONSTRUCTION (1947-50)

I

One morning in October 1947 the Nawab of Mamdot[1] called me to his office. He was at that time in his middle forties, a tall, handsome man of a quiet disposition and a clear mind. Before Partition he had been the nominal ruler of a minor state -- in reality, only a *jagir,* a fiefdom bestowed on one of his ancestors by a seventeenth-century Moghul emperor -- and had for years been prominent in the Pakistan movement and had sacrificed almost all of his personal wealth in its cause. As the *jagir* was situated in East Punjab, Mamdot left it at the time of Partition and established himself in a modest villa in Lahore. Fully aware of his loyalty and incorruptibility, Muhammad Ali Jinnah appointed him as the first chief Minister of West Punjab on the very day of Pakistan's birth, and ever since then he was considered one of the Quaid-e-Azam's most trusted lieutenants.

As soon as I entered his office, Mamdot came to the point: 'It seems to me, Asad Sahib, that we must now do something tangible about the ideological problems about which you have been talking and writing so much. What do you suggest? Should we approach the Prime Minister?'

I had been expecting something like this for days and weeks, and so I had my answer ready:

'Since the Central Government has not tacked these problems so far, it is for you, Nawab Sahib, to take the first step. To my mind, it is *you* who ought to establish, here in the Punjab, a special department to work out the ideological premises on which Pakistan should rest -- and in time, God willing, the Government in Karachi might perhaps take over this task. At present, it seems, they are simply overwhelmed by problems of foreign policy and none of them -- neither the Prime

Minister nor even the Quaid-e-Azam himself -- is likely to think of anything else . . . .'

With his usual decisiveness, Mamdot expressed his agreement at once: 'All right, then. What should the department be named?'

'It should be called the "Department of Islamic Reconstruction" ', I answered, 'for this is exactly what we are aiming at: a reconstruction of our social life and thinking along genuinely Islamic lines.'

'Well,' said Mamdot, 'so it shall be. You may prepare a scheme for the organization of the Department and work out a provisional estimate of the budget required. You will be officially appointed as Director, with a salary -- let us say – equivalent to that of the Director of Information. Will that suit you?'

I had not expected such a quick decision; but that was the way of the Nawab of Mamdot . . . .

Within a few days the scheme was set forth in a formal Memorandum, the budget estimate discussed and approved in conjunction with the Head of the Finance Department, and an official notification issued. The Department of Islamic Reconstruction – the first and only in the entire Muslim world – came into being.

I asked some of the more prominent Muslim scholars of Lahore -- foremost among them Maulana Da'ud Ghaznawi,[2] leader of the *Ahl-e-Hadith* community -- to find for me two assistants, well-versed in Arabic, who could be of help in the time-consuming task of going through innumerable large tomes of *hadith* literature in the search for texts and quotations necessary for the formulating of my future proposals; and in due course two young, well-qualified men were found and engaged.[3] In addition, I secured the part-time services of an enthusiastic student from Punjab University.[4] As for the running of the office as such and for accounts work, I relied on – and obtained -- the whole-hearted support of a very good friend of mine, Mumtaz Hassan,[5] who held a high post in the West Punjab Finance Department and later became its head.

II

Being now a government servant, I was allotted a house, free of rent, in the beautiful tree-lined Chamba House Lane (thus called because the Maharajah of Chamba -- a Hindu state on the spurs of the Himalayas -- had his palace there before Partition). The house, surrounded by a small garden, had belonged to a Hindu businessman who had since emigrated to India and most probably had been allotted the abandoned dwelling of a Muslim who had come over to Pakistan.

Until then, ever since my release from internment, my son Talal had been living as a boarder in a Catholic school (the very best in Lahore) administered by Irish Dominicans; but since his mother and I were now established in Lahore, he henceforth lived at home and attended his school as a day-scholar; and this was a very satisfactory arrangement.

One morning -- it was January 30, 1948 -- as I was leaving my house to drive to the office (for I had been allotted an abandoned car as well), I met our neighbour and friend, Sardar Shaukat Hayat,[6] a nephew of Sir Sikander Hayat Khan. His face wore a deeply troubled expression and he exclaimed: 'I have just heard on the radio that Gandhi[7] has been shot dead! Please God, I only hope that the murderer was not a Muslim!'

I fully shared his worry. We both knew what would happen to the Muslims left behind in India if it indeed had been a Muslim. But a few hours later the All-India Radio made it clear that Gandhi had been killed by a member of the Rashtriya Swayam Sewak Sangh -- the same group of fanatics who had been murdering Muslims in Dalhousie . . . .

III

The work of the Department of Islamic Reconstruction was proceeding steadily.[8] We were immersed in the problem of *zakat* and *'ushr* -- the basis of all taxation in a state to be ruled by the *shari'ah* -- when Mamdot invited me again to his office. As soon as I entered, and without further preliminaries, he said: I have just read your essay 'Towards an Islamic Constitution'[9] in your 'Arafat'. Would you prepare a memorandum on those lines? Mind you, not a blueprint -- just an outline of basic principles. I intend to bring it out on behalf of the Government of West Punjab, and then, perhaps, the Central Government will be moved to do something about it . . . .'

And so my paper on 'Islamic Constitution-Making' was produced in 1948 and published in English and Urdu under the auspices of the West Punjab Government. Some weeks later the Prime Minister summoned me to Karachi.

It was, of course, not the first time that I had met Liaquat Ali Khan;[10] I had known him in the days before the birth of Pakistan, and had always found him to be open-minded and willing to listen attentively while smoking one cigarette after another (in fact, I have never seen him without a tin of fifty State Express cigarettes in his hand or on his desk). This time, too, I was not to be disappointed. He offered me a cigarette, called for coffee, and asked me to enlarge upon my ideas on the subject of an Islamic constitution. I was aware from our earlier meetings that he had been seriously thinking about this problem; 'but,' he added 'we cannot embark at this juncture upon the framing of a constitution. There is so much to be done just to keep our heads above water: there is the Indian occupation of Kashmir, and the attempt -- the abortive attempt -- by our Pathans to capture Srinagar. And there is the fact that India is militarily so much stronger than we are. And we have not yet been able fully to organize the government machinery. All this takes time and effort. We simply cannot allow ourselves to proceed all at once with so far-reaching a task as the drafting of a constitution . . . .'

I thought then -- and I think now -- that it was a really handsome gesture on the part of the Prime Minister to speak to me so frankly about the difficulties besetting his Government. I knew, too, that he was as keen as myself to see Pakistan evolve to a truly Islamic stature, but could not as yet see his way to working towards that end. And therefore I silently agreed with him when he concluded the interview with the words, 'For the time being, we must confine ourselves to theory alone . . . .'

During my subsequent talk with the then Secretary to the Cabinet, Chaudhri Muhammad Ali,[11] I learned that one of the gravest difficulties with which our Government was faced was the lack of financial stability. The Quaid-e-Azam, I was told, had requested the extremely rich Nizam of Hyderabad to lend to Pakistan some millions of pounds sterling in gold bullion, to be deposited -- in the Nizam's name – as a coverage for Pakistan's currency; but the Nizam, always intent on keeping his enormous riches in his own hands, refused point-blank; with the result that some months later, when Hyderabad State was incorporated into India and ceased to *be* a state, all of the Nizam's gold bullion was taken over by the Indian Government and thus lost to himself and his descendants – and to Pakistan -- forever.[12]

And as I was talking with Chaudhri Muhammad Ali I vividly recalled the Nizam's private treasury, part of which I had been shown by his Finance Minister during my second visit to Hyderabad, in 1939: rooms upon rooms with rows upon row of chests containing gold bars and precious stones, and metal trays full of pearls on the floor: an unbelievable, lifeless hoard attesting to one man's morbid, fantastic avarice . . . .

IV

The struggle for Kashmir, alluded to by Liaquat Ali Khan during our conversation, had always been uppermost in my and every other

Pakistani's mind. Because of its geographic, ethnic and communal configuration, that lovely land had appeared to us predestined to become part of Pakistan. Its population was overwhelmingly Muslim; and all its great rivers, the Indus, the Jhelum and the Ravi -- flowed into West Punjab, and all of its economy was closely connected with the latter. The Maharajah's accession to India, made possible by Radcliffe's fraudulent assignment to it of the Muslim-majority district of Gurdaspur, amounted to an outright denial of the principle underlying the Partition as such, and no Pakistani could willingly accept it. But since Pakistan, with its truncated army, could not risk at that point in time a war with India, the Quaid-e-Azam ruled out any military intervention. And thereupon a warlike segment of Pakistan's population – the Pathan tribes from the frontier areas and adjoining Afghanistan -- took the matter into their own hands and started out on the conquest of Kashmir in the name of Pakistan.

This tribal invasion took place as early as October 1947. Large contingents of Mahsuds, Waziris and Afridis swept across the border into Kashmir and occupied the towns of Baramula and Muzaffarabad almost without a fight. The Maharajah's army around Srinagar, composed mostly of Muslims, mutinied and prepared to join their Pathan brothers who now saw the way to Srinagar open before them. But then something calamitous occurred: instead of marching straight on to Srinagar, the Pathans surrendered to their age-old instinct for plunder and began to loot the town of Muzaffarabad. Two full days were lost, and those two crucial days allowed Mountbatten and Nehru to organize a counterattack. In conjunction with the British army command in New Delhi, a hastily-arranged airlift of Hindu and Sikh army units and weapons -- including some light artillery -- enabled the Indians to occupy and fortify the airfield of Srinagar. A steady flow of air transport, utilizing all available military and civil aircraft, rapidly carried a large number of Indian troops to Srinagar, from where they subsequently fanned out to other points of the Maharajah's realm. The Pathans were gradually routed and their *jihad,* so enthusiastically undertaken, was hopeless frustrated.

None the less, the fight for Kashmir did not cease. New tribal forces came in and unavoidably, little by little, units of the Pakistan Army were drawn into the fray. However, the Valley of Kashmir proper remained in the possession of India, and the dividing-line, with its dugouts and trenches on both sides, now stretched -- and has remained thus stretched to this day -- from the Pakistani area of Gilgit towards the icy highlands of Ladakh and Kargil.

Finally, the conflict over Kashmir was brought by Pakistan to the United Nations, and the latter resolved upon a plebiscite which would determine the fate of the region. Reluctantly, the Government of India agreed to such a plebiscite; but knowing full well that the people's verdict would result in Pakistan's victory, the Indians postponed it again and again, until the scheme became a dead letter- a lasting, unsurmountable obstacle to normal relations between Pakistan and India. And the soldiers of both countries still face one another in their hostile trenches . . . .

In September of 1948, after the monsoon rains had stopped, I decided to visit the Kashmir front.

V

A jeep provided by the army command in West Punjab carried me and my escort of two soldiers into the spurs of the Himalayas. Beyond Murree the road became more and more narrow and precipitous, with only a few widenings at rare intervals so as to enable two vehicles coming from opposite directions to by-pass one another.

In order to avoid being machine-gunned by India aircraft which were flying frequent sorties over that road, we had to travel by night and without lights; thus, our progress was very slow, a mere crawling between mountain-wall and precipice, allowing ourselves only very occasionally, and for a few seconds, to switch on our headlights.

We circumvented Muzaffarabad and climbed higher and higher into the cold mountains and reached the first army outpost just before dawn. From there we proceeded for an hour or so on foot, guided by an infantryman, up a steep path to a one-time goatherd's hut which now served as a relay for ammunition supplies and troop relief as well as a first-aid station for the wounded brought in from the trenches.

Roughly built of stone and roofed with slates and tree branches and half-hidden in a cleft between two vertical walls of rock, the hut was full of soldiers when we entered; some of them had just come down from the trenches and others were preparing to go up. A single paraffin lamp hung down from the low ceiling and shed its light upon several *charpais* -- the usual Pakistani bedsteads made of wood and bast-ropes -- on which some wounded men were lying. They had been provisionally attended to by their company medic and were now awaiting transport to the field hospital lower down in the valley. Two men, in particular, attracted my attention. They were lying on their *charpais* next to one another, both of them, I was told, badly wounded and not likely to survive; and yet they were cheerful and -- heart-breaking to an onlooker like myself -- they teased one another. One of them said, 'well, soon I will meet you in hell' -- but the other answered, 'No, we won't go to hell, because if we die, we die as martyrs, for we were fighting in God's cause . . . .'

At that moment a young subaltern officer appeared, sent by the sector-commander to lead us to the trenches.

How they had been dug with mere hand-shovels out of the hard-frozen ground was a mystery to me; but for the most part they were deep enough to walk through them provided one kept one's head and shoulders very low. I saw several machine-gun nests with their barrels in an almost vertical position -- obviously meant to protect the trenches from attacks by low-flying enemy aircraft -- and their crews at the ready although for the moment all was quiet. Most of the soldiers were sitting or lying about in more or less relaxed postures, chatting or smoking, while others busied themselves with cleaning their rifles or repairing their cartridge belts. In this particular sector all of the troops were Punjabis from around Jhelum and Rawalpindi -- splendid types of men, mostly tall and spare, with some of their profiles pure Greek in cut, reminding one of the fact that the armies of Alexander the Great and his successors had remained for generations in that part of the Punjab and must have sired a lot of offspring there . . . .

I stayed for about an hour with the sector-commander, a youngish major, and had tea with him. He and his troops were visibly pleased at receiving a visitor who so clearly admired their morale and shared their enthusiasm for the cause which they were defending. I conveyed to them the personal greetings of the Chief Minister of West Punjab and, through him, of the leadership of all Pakistan. I knew – and made no secret of my knowing it -- that there are no better soldiers in all the world than Punjabi soldiers; and they, on their part, responded with frank enjoyment, without any self-consciousness, to this appreciation of their military virtues.

This first visit of mine to the front-lines made me eager to see more of the kind, and I promised myself that it would not be my last one.

VI

A new opportunity offered itself, unexpectedly, late in December 1948 or at the beginning of 1949 – I am not sure about the exact date.

One day I was browsing among some newly-arrived books in Lahore's largest book-shop when I perceived Major-General Hamid[13] engaged in a similar task at the back of the store. I knew him well -- as I knew most of the prominent people in Lahore -- and so, being aware that in spite of his comparative youth (he was in his early forties) he held an important command on the Kashmir front, I asked him what he was doing in Lahore. He told me that he had availed himself of a temporary lull in the fighting to have a couple of days of rest; he intended to return to the front the next morning. 'And,' he added, 'why don't you accompany me?'

The invitation was very tempting, but I could not drop my work in the Department of Islamic Reconstruction at so short a notice; 'However,' I answered, 'I might be ready to go within a week or so.'

'Well, then,' said General Hamid, 'next week it shall be. Before I leave I will provide for your transport and escort from Jhelum to the front. I don't know exactly where I will be at that time, so I shall give you a letter to one of our sector-commanders, and he will take charge of you. I am sure that you will like him.'

VII

A week later I was travelling in a jeep from the town of Jhelum towards the east. The driver, by whose side I sat, was a corporal from the 8th Punjab Regiment; a second soldier sat in the back behind a machine-gun anchored to the jeep's floorboards.

This time we were not going into the mountains. Our road led through a softly rolling landscape in the direction of the Kashmiri province of Poonch, which was said to be held by considerable numbers of Indian troops -- according to our reports, about one hundred thousand men.

As soon as we had crossed the nominal frontier between the Punjab and Kashmir we arrived at a large encampment of the Pakistan Army -- hundreds of tents and a large contingent of infantry, established well within the Poonch province and protected at regular intervals by heavy machine-guns and mortars. Apparently the Indians were not yet ready to attack us, for the atmosphere within the encampment seemed to be relaxed in spite of the discipline which was evident in every movement of men and weapons throughout the camp. I also saw small groups of Pathan scouts in their picturesque, individually-varied accoutrement -- baggy *shalwars* and *kurtas* and turbans, with bandoliers full of cartridges across the chest, rifles slung over the shoulders and daggers at their belts: hard fighters all, now gradually getting accustomed to real army discipline. (As a matter of fact, most of Pakistan's frontier guards consisted at that time of Pathan tribesmen who proved very effective during those first few years of our existence as a state.)

I was led straight-away to the tent of the sector-commander, Lieutenant-Colonel Yaqub Khan.[14] He was younger than myself -- perhaps thirty-five years old -- and he received me with open arms: 'You will stay in my tent, of course, and I hope that you will enjoy your visit!'

A son of the one-time hereditary Prime Minister of Rampur state, the wealthiest and most important Muslim principality in North-India (which, of course, by then had been integrated into India), my host proved to be highly cultured and of an extremely pleasant, open disposition, so that we readily 'clicked'; and I may mention here that we have remained friends, even at a great distance, to this day. Many years later, after having attained to the rank of general, he was sent out as Pakistan's Ambassador to Washington and subsequently appointed by President Zia ul-Haq as his Foreign Minister.

'General Hamid wants to see you as soon as possible,' said Colonel Yaqub Khan, 'so, if you don't mind, I will send you over to his headquarters early tomorrow morning.'

This suited me well, for I was keen to see as much of the front as possible.

After a simple but tasty and substantial dinner, and after many cigarettes and several cups of tea, we went to bed in the tent.

I was ready well before dawn, and after we had finished our *fajr* prayers in a congregation of several hundred of Yaqub Khan's men and had eaten our breakfast of bread, salted cheese and tea, I took temporary leave of my host and set out in my jeep, with the same two-man escort as before, on my drive to headquarters.

We arrived there about an hour later and found Major-General Hamid in conference with his staff officers, studying a large-scale map of the Poonch province. I wanted to withdraw, but General Hamid held me back: 'No, don't go away! We have no secrets from you- in fact, I am going to show you some more secrets today . . . .'

And then we started, this time in the General's jeep, on the road leading towards the town of Poonch and the Indian lines.

VIII

For a while we drove northwards. After a few miles we turned off towards the west and then continued in a wide semi-circle over side-roads back to the main road, leaving the town of Poonch -- invisible to us -- somewhere in the centre of the semi-circle.

There was not much movement on the road. Here and there small groups of soldiers were lounging on the roadside, and once an army lorry passed us by in the opposite direction. Far away on the right I saw a dense woodland, invitingly shady, but there, too, nothing seemed to move. After we had passed it the General turned to me and asked, 'Did you see anything interesting in that wood?' I answered, 'Why, nothing in particular, only trees . . . .'

General Hamid smiled. 'You may as well know it. In that small wood there is camouflaged more than half of Pakistan's entire artillery. The road to Poonch, and beyond Poonch, is now fully covered, and when we start our offensive tomorrow the Indians in Poonch will find themselves entirely cut off from both directions. Since our artillery strength is at the moment far greater than theirs, they will be unable to break through -- and since it will be too late for them to bring in reinforcements from India, they will have either to surrender or be annihilated, for we now have a whole army corps massed in this sector. And then, insha-Allah, we will push on towards Srinagar. For us it is now or never!'

However, General Hamid's confident anticipation was to prove unfounded. As soon as we returned to headquarters he received a severe shock. On the same evening a coded signal had come through by field telegraph from the Commander-in-Chief of Pakistan's armed forces: on specific orders from the Prime Minister, Liaquat Ali Khan, the offensive planned for the next day was to be cancelled . . . .

It was weeks later that we learned what had happened.

At the moment when the Indian Army command got wind of what was planned on our side -- which, of course, was unavoidable sooner or later -- Pundit Nehru[15] contacted the British Prime Minister, Clement Attlee,[16] by telephone and told him that the Pakistani offensive must be stopped at all costs because India was unable to reinforce the troops around Poonch in time, even by air-lift. If those troops were to be overcome -- as they must be -- by Pakistani forces, India would immediately withdraw from the Commonwealth and turn elsewhere for political support (and by 'elsewhere' clearly Soviet Russia was meant). On the other hand, if Pakistan could be persuaded to call off its offensive and leave the Poonch district in India hands, Pundit Nehru would agree to a plebiscite on Kashmir to be held in the very near future.

The telephone lines between New Delhi and London were humming through the whole of that night. Prime Minister Attlee, faced by the prospect of losing India, immediately consulted with Lord Mountbatten (who had relinquished the Governor-Generalship of India by the end of 1948 and was now resting on his laurels in England) and asked him, as the man most experienced in the affairs of the India sub-continent, to use all his influence with Pakistan in the sense suggested by Nehru. Within a couple of hours Mountbatten contacted by telephone Pakistan's Foreign Minister, Sir Muhammad Zafrullah Khan,[17] and conveyed to him Nehru's offer of a plebiscite together with Attlee's urgent personal request to cancel the offensive; whereupon Zafrullah roused Liaquat Ali from his sleep and did his best to persuade him to pay heed to Attlee's entreaties.

In order to appreciate fully the role played by Zafrullah Khan in this tangle of influences, one must recall his antecedents and peculiar loyalties. He was a fervent follower of the Ahmadiyya sect, regarded as heretical by all other Muslims. The originator of that sect had been one Mirza Ghulam Ahmad of Qadian,[18] who had once enjoyed some reputation as an Islamic scholar. Fairly late in his life he became convinced that he was a prophet chosen by God to 'complete' the – according to him as yet uncompleted -- mission of the Prophet Muhammad: a claim that was categorically rejected by the bulk of the Indian Muslim community, *sunnis* and *shi'ahs* alike, for the simple reason that the Prophet Muhammad is described in the Qur'an as the Last Prophet, with none to come after him: and since Mirza Ghulam Ahmad's claim offended against this basic tenet of Islam, he and his followers have hence forth been regarded as being 'beyond the pale'. The British rulers of India, on the other hand, were highly pleased with the Ahmadiyya movement because Mirza Ghulam Ahmad made it ***obligatory*** on his followers to be always loyal to the established government, irrespective of whether it was Muslim or non-Muslim. Hence, the members of the Ahmadiyya sect were invariably favoured by the British-Indian authorities and placed in highly influential government posts; and Sir Muhammad Zafrullah Khan was certainly the most influential, as well as devout, of them all -- in fact, throughout his entire life he was more pro-British than the British themselves.*

None the less, since Zafrullah Khan was an extremely able Foreign Minister, Liaquat Ali Khan lent ear to him. In addition, he was swayed by Nehru's promise of a plebiscite on Kashmir, hoping that the conflict which had for so long been consuming so much of Pakistan's energies would at last be laid to rest: and so he gave the order to cancel the Poonch offensive. But as soon as he had done it and the Pakistani forces were withdrawn from Poonch to the 'international' frontier, Nehru reneged on his promise of an immediate plebiscite and once again postponed it to an indefinite, never-never future.

By then the damage had been done and could not be rectified. The Indian forces in the Poonch area were greatly strengthened and Pakistan, deprived of the element of surprise, could not regain its one-time advantage.

The Prime Minister's order struck the Pakistani troops around Poonch like a bomb-shell. When it became known that the offensive had been called off, many officers and men wept unashamedly; their hopes of freeing Kashmir from Hindu domination and making it part of Pakistan had been shattered, for nobody seriously believed that the promised plebiscite would take place now or in the foreseeable future.

General Hamid shut himself up in his quarters and I did not see him again until months later, after he had resigned from the army . . . .

As I had just written the above lines (on August 17, 1988) in a mountain village in the south of Spain, I received a telephone call informing me that the President of Pakistan, General Zia ul-Haq,[19] had been killed in an airplane crash over Pakistan.

This news shocked me to the core, because I had loved him not only as a personal friend but also, and more than anything, because he was the best that Pakistan had brought forth for many years. Honest and strong and yet without a trace of arrogance in his make-up, imbued with a great love of his country and, above all, of the Faith for the sake of which that country had been created, Zia ul-Haq had already proved himself the most outstanding leader of Pakistan since the death of Muhammad Ali Jinnah. And now he had been assassinated -- for from the moment I heard this news I was convinced that his death was not due to an 'accident' at all, but was the result of careful planning by

---

* As a curious illustration of this fact I may mention here that on the death of King George VI Zafrullah ordered the entire Pakistani delegation to the United Nations -- myself among them -- to wear black ties for a whole month as a sign of mourning. I have never worn that tie since . . . .

people who hated his assistance to the Afghan *mujahidin,* as well as his efforts in the cause of bringing Pakistan closer to a truly Islamic way of life.

Endnotes

1 Iftikhar Husain Mamdot (1906-1969), son of Shahnawaz Khan Mamdot (1883-1942); the first Chief Minister of Panjab after Partition (15 August 1947–25 January 1949). See Humayun Adib: *Pakistan Movement, Punjab and Mamdot,* Lahore 1987.

2 Maulana Da'ud Ghaznawi (1895-1963); a prominent religious scholar of *Ahl-i Hadith* and an active member of the Khilafat Movement.

See *Hazrat Maulana Da'ud Ghaznawi.* Edited by Sayyid Abu Bakr Ghaznawi, Lahore 1974; *Nuqush-i 'Azmat-i Rafta.* By Muhammad Ishaq Bhatti, Lahore 1999, pp. 11-122; *Ghaznawi Khandaan.* By Abdur Rashid 'Iraqi. Karachi 2004; *Gift,* I: 319-322.

3 Among these "young and competent religious scholars", Maulana Muhammad Hanif Nadwi (1908-1987), Maulana Muhammad Ja'far Shah Phulwarwi (1907-1982, see *Bazm-i Arjmandan.* By Muhammad Ishaq Bhatti. Lahore 1999, pp. 351-399), Sayyid Nazir Niazi (1907-1981) and Abu Yahya Imam Khan Naushahrawi (d. 1996) were assisting Asad to achieve the prescribed aims and objectives of the Department of Islamic Reconstruction.

4 Perhaps, this energetic young man was Iftikhar Ahmad Chishti who afterwards was employed in the Government College (Faisalabad) in the department of Islamic Studies.

The title of Asad's interview was:

"Building up an ideological community. Aims of Islamic Reconstruction Department."

(in: *The Pakistan Times* (Lahore), 19 October 1947).

5 Mumtaz Hasan (1907-1974); an Iqbalist, renowned littérateur and an expert economist.

6 Sardar Shaukat Hayat (1913-1998), son of Sikandar Hayat, the first Chief Minister of Punjab. His autobiography was *Gumgashta Qaum* was published from Lahore (1995). Also available in English: *The Nation that has lost its soul.*

7 Mahatama Karam Chand Gandhi (1869-1948) a great political leader of Hindus.

8 Immediately after Partition (1947), the West Panjab Government decided to establish Department of Islamic Reconstruction under the directorship of Muhammad Asad. In an interview (in: *The Pakistan Times* (Lahore), 19 October 1947), Asad explained the basic aims and objectives of this institution in these words:

> "All that we are expected to do–all that we can legitimately do–is to help the community to co-ordinate its spiritual and intellectual resources, and to revive the moral strength of which the *Millat* must be capable of virtue

of its being the *Millat* of Islam: in other words, to help the *Millat* to re-create the Islamic atmosphere so necessary for a revival of Islamic Life in its practical aspects."

9 The title of his article is "Towards an Islamic Constitution", published in *'Arafat* (Dalhousie, No. 9, July 1947; reproduced in: *Gift*, II: 933-949.

10 Liaquat Ali Khan (1896-1951); first Prime Minister of Pakistan who was assassinated.

Ziauddin Ahmad: *Liaquat Ali Khan, Leader and Statesman*. Karachi 1970.

11 Chaudhry Muhammad Ali (1905-1980); Prime Minister of Pakistan (1955-1956) and the author of *Emergence of Pakistan* (New York, 1967)

12 The thriftiness of Mir 'Usman 'Ali Khan, Nizam of Hyderabad Deccan, is a known fact; see Mir La'iq Ali's book *The Great Tragedy*.

13 Major-General Hameed; during Yahya Khan's (d. 1980) period (1969-71), Lieut.-General was the Chief of Staff of the Pakistan Army.

14 Sahibzada Ya'qub 'Ali Khan (1920-); see his book: *The Story of Soldiering and Politics in India and Pakistan*, Lahore 1978 ("I join the Pakistan Army", pp. 113-164)

15 Jawaharlal Nehru (1889-1964), the first Prime Minister of India.

16 Clement Attlee (1883-1967), British Prime Minister.

17 Sir Zafrullah Khan (1893-1985); see his autobiography under the title *Tahdees-i Ni'mat* (Lahore 1971, repr. 1994); see also K. K. Aziz: *Remembering some Great Men*. Lahore 2002, pp. 76-84.

18 Mirza Ghulam Ahmad, the founder of Ahmadiyah, a messianic movement in modern Islam. He was born in the late 1830s in Qadian, a village in the Indian Panjab. He died on 26 May 1908.

See Muhammad Zafrullah Khan: *Ahmadiyyat: The Renaissance of Islam*. London 1978; Y. Friedmann: *Prophecy Continuous: Aspects of Ahmadi Religious Thought and Its Medieval Background*. Berkeley, 1989; *EI²*, Vol. II (Leiden), pp. 301-303 (art. W. C. Smith).

19 Muhammad Ziaul Haq (1924-1988), ex-President of Pakistan (1977-1988).

* * * * *

VIII
FOREIGN SERVICE: MIDDLE EAST DIVISION (1949-51)

I

In January of 1948 Liaquat Ali Khan called me again to Karachi -- this time not to remonstrate with me about my proposals but to place before me a proposal of his own. 'You are one of the few people in Pakistan with an intimate, first-hand knowledge of the Middle East; and you have, I am aware, full command of Arabic and Persian. We *need* a man like you in the Foreign Service. I would strongly suggest that you join it and, for the time being, put aside your work on Islamic Reconstruction. Would you consider this suggestion?'

Coming as it did from the Prime Minister of Pakistan, this request could not easily be rejected. However deeply my emotions were bound up with the Department of Islamic Reconstruction, I realized that Liaquat Ali Khan had made a strong point. Pakistan's Middle East policies were, as yet, erratic. No clear-cut aim was discernible in them. We were, of course, committed to supporting the independence movement within the Muslim countries that were as yet subjected to foreign rule; but beyond that we seemed to be floundering without any definite direction. The prospect of being able to contribute something tangible to a formulation of Pakistan's foreign policy in the Middle East was extremely appealing, the more so as the past years of my life had given me an intimate -- and perhaps unique -- insight into what was going on in that part of the world and what its peoples felt and wanted. And there was an additional temptation at the thought of coming once again face to face with a world so much wider than the one in which I had been immersed for so many years, perhaps for too many years. I loved my work in the Department of Islamic Reconstruction, it was my 'baby', so to speak, but by now it was well launched on its way, and surely other people could be found to pursue the task which I had so clearly outlined . . . .?

II

And thus I accepted Liaquat Ali Khan's request and agreed to enter the Foreign Service, which was then being organized. The man who was in charge of organizing it was an Irishman, Sir Terence Craigh-Coen,[1] who had been a highly-placed member of the Indian Civil Service and at the time of Partition had opted for Pakistan. I had some preliminary talks with him, and he informed me that under the existing rules I would have to pass -- purely as a formality -- an examination by the Civil Service Commission.

On the day appointed for the examination I presented myself before the Commission. Its chairman was Hassan Suhrawardy, a brother of the then Chief Minister of East Pakistan. He was a professor of history at one of Pakistan's universities -- not merely learned in the academic sense but possessed of a deep culture and a wide range of intellectual interests.

About eight or ten other candidates for the Foreign Service were already in the room when I entered, all of them very young men. Hassan Suhrawardy[2] took them one by one in the order in which they had presented themselves and put to them questions relating to geography and modern history. I had to laugh when he asked one of them, 'What is the name of the capital of Ethiopia?' -- and was answered by the candidate's perplexed silence. Suhrawardy glanced at me briefly and proceeded with the next candidate: 'Can you tell me the name of the last Emperor of France?' Again silence. And so it went on and on, with the young men answering the simple questions correctly or incorrectly or not at all; and every time Suhrawardy noted his marks against the candidate's name.

Finally my turn came. Professor Suhrawardy smiled and said, 'I know you by reputation, Asad Sahib, and so I will not bother you with school-book questions. However, since I have to examine you for form's sake, could you tell me something about European politics, say, between the end of the Seven-Years' War and the post-Napoleonic period?'

I happened to have been familiar with the subject ever since my school days, and so I started with an exposition which after a few minutes developed into a kind of lecture. I had not come to the end of it when Suhrawardy interrupted me: 'That will do. You have passed the examination.' And after the session ended, he took me aside and said, 'I am placing you as Number One of this year's successful Civil Service candidates.'

A few days later I met Craigh-Coen in one of the corridors of the Foreign Ministry, and he let me know that he had assigned me the position of Number Three on the list of Foreign Service officers, immediately after the Permanent Secretary and the Joint Secretary, both of them, of course, ex-members of the Indian Civil Service. 'But,' he added, 'I am not sure that my suggestion will be accepted by the higher-ups: I am afraid that the colour of your skin will be a disadvantage to you . . . .'

And so it happened. Several more Civil Service men -- all of them with somewhat darker complexions than mine and with proper antecedents in the Indian Civil Service -- were placed ahead of me.

III

On my joining the Foreign Service shortly afterwards, I was told by the Permanent Secretary -- an amiable, easy-going man of approximately my own age named Ikramullah[3] -- that the Prime Minister had ordered my appointment a Deputy Secretary in charge of the Middle East Division. I was assigned a large, cheerful office in the Foreign Ministry (then situated in the Clifton suburb of Karachi), together with the services of a young, competent Personal Assistant, who was located in a small room adjoining mine.

My Division was to comprise the whole Arab world, including North Africa, as well as Iran. I had very definite ideas as to the policies which, in my opinion, Pakistan ought to pursue in that part of the world.

Immediately upon assuming office I ordered a large-scale map of the Persian Gulf and had it placed on one of the walls of my office; it was so high that it covered most of that wall.

Simultaneously, I sat down to prepare a long, explicit memorandum for the Foreign Minister, Sir Zafrullah Khan, outlining my policy proposals in some detail. On completion, this memorandum contained some outspoken criticism of the policies until then pursued by the Government and had, therefore, to remain confidential, I typed the whole of it myself with my two-finger stroke.

The gist of my proposals was this:

Since Pakistan had been established on a purely ideological basis -- a non-nationalist, non-racial groupment of peoples bound together solely by their adherence to a common religious and cultural ideal -- it had to pursue a dynamic policy with a view to the Muslim world as a whole. If it did not conform to this essential demand arising from its very nature, Pakistan was *bound* to lose its ideological coherence and thus, in time, its *raison d'être:* and it was, I pointed out, precisely our total failure in this respect that had placed us at so great a disadvantage *vis-à-vis* our main adversary, India, and had brought about, among other things, the loss of Kashmir. In order to counteract that failure Pakistan must embark on a two-pronged foreign policy: on the one hand, we should immediately set about to work, in cooperation with the Arab states, for the creation of something like a League of Muslim Nations; and, on the other hand, we should aim with all our strength at expanding our influence over all of the Persian Gulf, which was politically as well as economically our predestined life-line. In view of the fact that the British had withdrawn from the Gulf at the end of the Second World War, we should *supplant* them there instead of allowing ourselves, as we had hitherto been doing, to be overawed by the British shadow in that area. After all, I pointed out, Great Britain was now so exhausted that it could act only in submission to the power of the United States -- and why could *we* not turn directly to the latter? The United States could not well aim at a Persian Gulf policy of its own without overstretching its political and military lines of communication, and so Washington would certainly approve of our endeavours in the interests of the 'Free World'. In short, we should cease to be the slaves of slaves, and should go straight to the source of power.

I marked my memorandum 'for the attention of the Foreign Minister' and sent it on as 'top secret' through the official channels, that is, via the Permanent Secretary.

The next morning Ikramullah asked me to see him in his office. As soon as I was seated opposite his desk, he exclaimed, 'I have read your memorandum, and I am shocked! Asad, you simply *cannot* criticize the Foreign Minister and, yes, the Prime Minister in this way!'

To which I replied, 'Well, I am doing it. At the most I shall be placed against the wall and shot for my impertinence -- or, rather, what you Civil Service people regard as impertinence. Do, please, send it on to the Foreign Minister.'

Ikramullah signed, 'On your head be it, then . . . .'

As it happened -- and as I came to know after a couple of days -- Zafrullah Khan was not in the least offended by my criticism. On the contrary -- as he himself told me later -- he endorsed it and sent it on to the Prime Minister. Afterwards he had several copies made for 'obligatory reading' by the heads of divisions in the Foreign Ministry.

IV

Finally, Liaquat Ali Khan sent for me to discuss my policy proposals with him.

He opened the interview with a faint smile: 'You have been harsh on us, Asad . . . .' and pointed at my memorandum, which lay on his desk. As I remained silent, he continued: 'You know, of course, that we are nowadays negotiating a broad alliance in our part of the world; is that not activity enough for you?'

He was obviously referring to the talks that were going on at that time between ourselves and the United States, Britain, Turkey, Iraq and Iran, aiming at the establishment of some sort of *cordon sanitaire* around the south-western flank of Soviet Russia. I had always felt that this plan -- known among the participants as 'the Baghdad Pact'[4] -- was not only useless but also highly dangerous for Pakistan because it was bound to force Soviet Russia into open hostility towards us and, consequently, into an ever tighter, more active alliance with our main enemy, India. Until that morning I had not regarded myself as placed high enough to object openly to a plan of such magnitude, and so I had remained silent. Now, however, since the Prime Minister himself had broached the subject, I felt free to enlarge upon it; and I did so with all the insistence at my disposal. (In any case, that famous 'pact' proved to be stillborn and fizzled out shortly afterwards.)

Liaquat Ali Khan listened to me patiently, as was his custom, and let me ramble on. When I had finished he said neither 'Yes' nor 'No', but turned straight-away to the proposals set out in my memorandum:

'You suggest that we should engage ourselves actively in the affairs of the Persian Gulf and should make our influence felt there both politically and economically. But don't you realize how difficult our economic situation is at present? We are only *beginning* to be productive industrially. Our monetary situation is most precarious, as you know; our currency is fluttering up and down for lack of substantial coverage. We cannot compete with the Indian rupee, and so the Indians are gaining daily more and more ground in the Gulf, not only economically but also politically. How can we think of an extension of our political influence without the backing of a strong currency?'

'Sir,' I answered, 'I am convinced that in this respect we could -- and should -- turn to the United States for economic assistance. If we place the prospect of Pakistan's gaining *real* influence in the Persian Gulf before the Americans, and if we persuade them that such an expansion of our political influence is the only realistic alternative to the chimera of a 'Baghdad Pact' -- don't you think, sir, that they would be bound to assist us in our endeavours? After all, they are as deeply concerned as we are about preventing a Russian breakthrough to the warm waters of the Gulf -- and if this can be achieved by political instead of military means, the better for the United States and for Pakistan.'

The Prime Minister remained silent for a while; in the end he said: 'You have a point there. We shall think about it. And now to your second proposal -- a League of Muslim Nations. Can you tell me something more about that?'

As this had always been a pet subject of mine, I had no difficulty in expounding on it in detail. I referred to the weakness of the disjointed states of the Middle East and to Pakistan's great prestige in that area. After all, we were the largest Muslim state in the world, and so it was for us to take the lead in a movement which might result in a re-birth of the strength of Islām after so many centuries of political decadence.

'At the same time, however,' I concluded, 'we must make it clear to the Arabs -- and, in particular, to the Egyptians -- that we do not aim at leadership of the Arab world: that role must be reserved to Egypt in view of the fact that it is the largest and most highly developed Arab country. As it is, the Egyptians are extremely jealous of their position and would certainly refuse to cooperate on any scheme which might jeopardize it. Hence, our first step must be to convince them that in our view, too, it is they who must remain the leaders of the Arab world and that, moreover, Pakistan has no desire for 'leadership' as such, but aims at no more than a unification of Muslim political endeavours.'

V

A few days later the Prime Minister suggested that I should go as soon as possible on an official tour of the Middle East and sound out the reactions of the individual governments to the idea of a League of Muslim Nations. I could not remember when I had been as happy as I was now.

The first thing I did was to summon our Passport Officer and instruct him to issue a passport to me. He asked, 'What shall I enter as your nationality?'

I was astonished: 'Pakistani, naturally.'

'But, sir, as yet there *is* no such thing as a Pakistani nationality. A citizenship bill is now pending before the National Assembly, but it will take some months before it is passed. In the meantime we have an informal agreement with Britain which authorizes us to mark every new passport as 'British subject'.'

'Nonsense,' I rejoined. 'I have never been a British subject and do not intend to become one now. Write 'citizen of Pakistan'.'

'I can't do that -- it would be illegal. Shall I mark your passport as 'Austrian citizen'?'

'Worse and worse', I replied. 'Do you seriously suggest that I should go on an official tour, as a representative of the Government of Pakistan, with a passport saying that I am the citizen of a foreign country?'

And so it went on, backwards and forwards, until I got tired of it. Finally I rang up the Personal Assistant of the Prime Minister: 'Please arrange for me an interview with the P.M. It is urgent!'

Within a short time I entered Liaquat Ali Khan's office and informed him of my difficulty. He immediately told his secretary to call the Passport Office, and as soon as the latter appeared the Prime Minister told him to make out a passport for me as 'citizen of Pakistan' . . . .

And so I obtained the very first passport marked 'citizen of Pakistan'.[5]

VI

Before starting on my exploratory journey I discussed it with the diplomatic representatives in Pakistan of three Arab countries: the Ambassadors of Egypt and Saudi Arabia and the minister plenipotentiary of Syria. All three had been close friends of mine since I had entered the Foreign Service.

Foremost among them was Abd al-Wahhab Azzam,[6] the Egyptian Ambassador. A scholar of considerable attainments (he had been a professor of the Persian language and literature at the University of Cairo), he was endowed with great sensitivity and a penetrating intellect, and could converse freely in several languages. His particular admiration was reserved for Muhammad Iqbal, a good deal of whose poetry Dr Abd al-Wahhab had translated into Arabic. We soon established a personal relationship which went far beyond the usual diplomatic contacts between the representatives of two friendly countries. We met almost daily at each other's home and talked about everything that occupied our thoughts, and most often about what was happening or probably would happen in the world of Islam. Our minds seemed to function on one and the same wave-length, and we remained close to one another until his death, as Rector of the Saudi University in Riyadh, some years later.*

Next to my deep affection for Abd al-Wahhab came my friendship with the Syrian Minister Plenipotentiary to Pakistan, Umar Baha al-Amiri. He descended from an ancient, aristocratic family of Aleppo and was a poet of distinction. Since he was half-Turkish from his mother's side, he was almost predestined to be of a pan-Islamic bent of mind; in fact, he regarded himself as a follower of Hassan al-Banna,[7] the inspired founder of the Muslim Brotherhood[8] in Egypt, and was connected with the Syrian branch of that organization. Being of a very lively and humorous disposition, he was a pleasant companion to spend one's time with; and this was facilitated by the fact that his Legation was situated very near to the house in Clifton which had been allotted to me by the Government. He, too, had a great liking for Abd al-Wahhab Azzam, and so we often found ourselves together in our free hours.

The third person to be mentioned in this connection was Shaikh Abd al-Hamid al-Khatib, Ambassador of Saudi Arabia. He was a Meccan, and thus he represented for me an unforgettable segment of my past. Although, having been born and bred in the Hijaz -- with a good deal of Indonesian blood in his veins -- he could fully appreciate the truly *Arabian* quality of Najdi life, so dear to me from my past experiences, his literary education and, in particular, his love for ancient Arabian poetry enabled him to understand completely *my* feelings about Central Arabia and its people: and so we, too, had a lot of common ground between us.

These were the three persons (apart, of course, from my colleagues and superiors in the Government of Pakistan) with whom I discussed every possible aspect of my forthcoming journey to the Middle East, and from whom I received personal letters of introduction to various people in their respective countries, in addition to the official messages from my Prime Minister and my Foreign Minister.

---

* As it happened, Abd al-Wahhab's younger brother, Salem Azzam (now Secretary-General of the Islamic Council in London, which he himself founded) became later on -- and has remained to this day -- as intimate a friend of mine as Abd al Wahhab had been.

Endnotes

1 Sir Terence Bernhard Creagh-Coin. Born in 1903, joined Indian Civil Service (1927); Deputy High Commissioner, Dera Ghazi Khan (1931-1932); Registrar Lahore High Court (1933-1935); Joint Secretary, Foreign Office (1947-1950).

2 Hassan Shaheed Suhrawardy (1891-1964); elder brother of Husain Shaheed Suhrawardy, the Prime Minister of Pakistan; Ambassador of Pakistan in Spain; Chairman of the Federal Public Service Commission.

cf. Afzal Iqbal: *Diary of a Diplomat.* Karachi 1986.

3 Muhammad Ikramullah (1903-1963), first Foreign Secretary of Pakistan; Ambassador in Canada (1952), France (1953), Portugal and Great Britain (1955); husband of Shaista Ikramullah (1915-2000) and father of Nuzhat who is the wife of Prince Hassan (Jordan).

4 Baghdad Pact, a defence agreement against Russia. Pakistan was its member. (3 Nov. 1955) but resigned in 1972. In 1979, this Pact was permanently ended.

5 Asad was a citizen of Pakistan. After Partition (1947), he surrendered his original Austrian passport. He was the first Pakistani citizen who got the passport of the new country (Asad's letter, 6 August 1982, in: *Nawa-i-Waqt* (Lahore), 10 September, 1982).

6 Abdul Wahhab 'Azzam (d. 1959), Egyptian Ambassador in Pakistan (1952-1954); translated Iqbal's Persian books (*Payam-i Mashriq* and *Asrar-o-Rumuz*) in Arabic (Lahore 1978, 1981); see *The Pakistan Times* (Lahore), 24 January 1959; *Mah-i Nau* (Lahore, Urdu journal), April 1959, pp. 11-14, art. by Ziaul Hasan Musawi.

Abdul Wahhab 'Azzam wrote an introduction to the Arabic translation of Asad's *Road to Mecca*, by 'Afif al-Ba'albaki, Beirut 1956 (new ed., Riyadh, 1997).

7 Hasan al-Banna' (1906-1949), founder of Muslim Brotherhood of Egyptian religio-political party; cf. Rif'at al-Sa'id: *Hasan al-Banna'*, Cairo 1977. *OEMIW*, vol. I (New York/Oxford), 1995, pp. 195-199 (art. Olivier Carré).

8 Muslim Brotherhood (al Ikhwan al-Muslimun), founded in Ismailiyah (Egypt) by Hasan al-Banna', is the parent body and the main source for inspiration for many Islamist organizations in Egypt and several other Arab countries, including Syria, Sudan, Jordan, Kuwait and some North African states. The movement was initially announced as a purely religious and philanthropic society that aimed to spread Islamic morals and good works.

cf. *OEMIW*, ed. John L. Esposito, vol. 3, New York/Oxford 1995, pp. 183-201.

● ● ● ● ●

SAHÎH AL-BUKHÂRÎ

TRANSLATED FROM THE ARABIC

WITH EXPLANATORY NOTES AND INDEX

BY

MUHAMMAD ASAD-WEISS

IN 40 PARTS

WITH ARABIC TEXT

For particulars apply to:

ARAFAT PUBLICATIONS

MODEL TOWN · LAHORE

Title page of a part of Ṣaḥiḥ al-Bukhāri (first edition)

IX
IN SEARCH OF UNITY
(1951)

I

The season of the *hajj,* the annual pilgrimage to Mecca, was close at hand as I was setting out on my Middle Eastern tour; hence, I chose Saudi Arabia as its first stage and changed at Karachi, before boarding the airplane, into the traditional pilgrim's garb, the *ihram,* which I would wear during the coming weeks: two white sheets, one of them tied at the waist and covering the lower part of the body, and the other slung loosely over one shoulder, leaving one arm bare; and a pair of sandals on my bare feet. It was to be my seventh *hajj.*

The plane was full of Pakistani pilgrims, most of the men already attired in their *ihrams,* like myself, and all the women in long dresses and with their faces uncovered, in accordance with the *shar'i* rules prescribed for this occasion. A happy excitement vibrated through the cabin in expectation of the great event, which to most of them would be the only one throughout their entire lives.

The huge airport of Jidda was filled with scores of aircraft that had come from all parts of the Muslim world, and the chaos produced by the thousands of newly-arrived pilgrims could only with difficulty be controlled by the overworked Saudi pilgrim guards. But despite all the milling and jostling and shouting there hung an air of happiness over all those crowds, and one felt that this was really a gathering of brothers and sisters of one single, huge family, now assembling for a purpose common to them all. As for myself, it was a return to one of the happiest periods of my life -- a backward flow of years that had passed but would never cease to be . . . .

I was received at the airport by several old friends, among them Shaikh Muhammad Sarur as-Sabban,[1] who in my Arabian days had been an official of the finance department and was now Minister of Finance.

We embraced, and I kissed his dear, black face and he kissed mine, and it was as if we had parted but yesterday: all the warmth of Arabia lay in that embrace.

Sarur took hold of my luggage ticket and instructed one of his men to collect my suitcase from customs; and while we waited for it we talked of the old times. After half an hour the man returned and informed us that the suitcase could not be found; it had not been on the plane. (Afterwards we learned that in the pre-pilgrimage chaos at Karachi airport it had been loaded by mistake onto a plane leaving for Bangkok; it was delivered to me in Jidda about a week later.)

So there I was in my *ihram,* without a single stitch of clothing at my disposal . . . . 'But,' said Shaikh Sarur, 'don't worry. Tomorrow we will proceed to Arafat, and the *hajj* will be over, and then I will fit you out: we are more or less of the same height.'

I slept that night in Sarur's house, and early next morning we left by car for Arafat.

By car . . . what a change it was from my early years in Arabia...

When I had last performed the pilgrimage over eighteen years earlier, I had ridden on a dromedary in the midst of thousands and thousands of white-garbed Najdi beduins, and we swept across the plain of Arafat in a thundering gallop: and now the same plain was filled from horizon to horizon with thousands of cars and lorries crawling in twenty or more lines towards the Jabal al-Rahmah, the 'Hill of Mercy', in the centre of the great plain . . . .

Between the lines of that endless procession of mechanical transport stood men of the King's bodyguard -- hundreds of them -- trying to control the chaos and to make the progress as orderly as possible: a most difficult task. And suddenly, among those men, I saw Amir Faisal,[2] the King's second son and Viceroy, taking part in that logistic effort: he stood there, armed with a thin bamboo stick -- the same kind of stick that a dromedary rider would use to guide his mount -- and tried, as any ordinary traffic policeman would do, to keep the flow of cars and lorries in some sort of order. But then, since it was connected with the *hajj,* it was a religious duty to him, just as was the sweeping and washing of the floor of the Ka'bah in Mecca which the King himself undertook every year . . . .

I did not wish to bother either the King or Amir Faisal until after our return to Jidda. And there I was informed that King Abd al-Aziz[3] expected me at a banquet to be held in Mecca on the conclusion of the pilgrimage.

In another book, 'The Road to Mecca', I have described how I met Amir Faisal again after an interval of eighteen years and how I addressed him with the words, 'Thou wilt have forgotten me, O Long-of-Age!' -- whereupon he answered with a loving smile: 'How could I have forgotten thee!'

And it was the same Faisal with whom I had spent so many of my Arabian years -- eighteen years older, more self-possessed than ever, but unchanged in his demeanour and filled with an inner quiet which illumined his whole being.

II

Next morning I paid an official visit to the King (he had not been well the night before, and so Amir Faisal had acted as host at the *hajj* banquet).

The King was sitting slumped in a broad easy-chair, visibly ill and too weak to rise to his guest, as had been his custom in earlier times. He had aged beyond words during the eighteen years of my absence from Saudi Arabia. My heart contracted on seeing his tired face and the effort behind his faint attempt at smiling. His eyes lit up for a moment when his trusted adviser, Shaikh Yusuf Yasin,[4] who was standing beside his chair, bent down to him and said, 'Muhammad Asad has come to pay his respects to thee, O Long-of-Age.' Thereupon the King raised his head a fraction; for a second the old eagle's look passed over his face, and he whispered, '*Ahlan wa-sahlan,* O my son . . . .'

I was deeply moved, but I did not want to tire him yet more, and so I withdrew. That was the last time that I was to gaze on the very dear, beloved face of Abd al-Aziz ibn Saud . . . .

On the other hand, I saw a great deal of Amir Faisal in the days of my stay in Mecca. He was Foreign Minister of Saudi Arabia in addition to being Viceroy of the Hijaz, and so it was to him that I explained the purport of my visit. He welcomed my idea of a League of Muslim Nations without the least reservation; in fact, he told me, he himself had already started on the first step towards that great goal -- a unification of the Arab states as the core of that league-to-be.

As we sat in his simple office at the Foreign Ministry and talked about the dream common to us both, neither of us knew, of course, that twenty-four years later, when he had almost succeeded in bringing the Arabs together to form one single, unified force, an assassin's bullet would put a full stop to his efforts and shatter his dream.

But I was still destined to meet him many more times in many other places before that terrible tragedy . . . .

III

I could not leave Saudi Arabia without seeing Medina once again. So many years had passed since I had lived there, but to me it had never ceased to be the dearest city in the world.

I booked a seat on the regular flight from Jidda: Medina now had an airport and could be reached by airplane from many parts of the world. Times had certainly changed . . . .

But they had not yet quite changed Medina itself – that was to come later. Of course, there were now cars in the streets, and some multi-storied modern buildings raised their ugly heads, arrogantly, above their ancient, stone-built neighbours, which were still dreaming with their windowless walls in narrow, winding lanes. But there was still the same air of peace as in the old days, and one had the feeling of being welcomed.

The Prophet Muhammad, I thought, must have had the same feeling when he set out from Mecca, pursued by the hatred of his pagan compatriots, and rode towards the distant town, then called Yathrib, which was destined to become known as *Madinat an-Nabi,* 'The City' par excellence. And I recalled his prayer: 'O God, Thou has willed me to leave the place of my birth, the place that I have loved best: guide me, then, O my Sustainer, to the place which *Thou* lovest best!' And since God answered His Prophet's prayer by bringing him to Medina, some of the great Islamic thinkers of the past attributed to it an even greater sanctity than that of Mecca: -- for it was Medina which God Himself must have loved best . . . .

I visited those of my friends who were still alive: there were not many of them left. Among the latter was Ibn Ibrahim, the old Amir of Medina, white-bearded now but as sharp of eye and as straight of body as ever. And again, *'Ahlan wa-sahlan'*, and the round of tiny cups and the talk about what had happened to each of us since the old days, the beautiful days . . . . .

I had a last look at the huge *Al-Manaqah* square, where the caravans used to alight in times past: but now the resting-place of the hundreds of camels of former days was occupied by scores of cars and lorries, and there were no beduins around any more selling clarified butter in goat-skin bags . . . .

IV

The next stage of my journey was Egypt.

At the airport of Cairo I was received by the Pakistani Chargé d'Affaires, and we drove straight to the old Shepherd's Hotel, which had always been my favourite. I did not know then that I would be one of the last patrons of that lovely, old-fashioned hostelry with its velvet hangings in every room and silent-footed bearers in turbans gliding back and forth across the marble floors and sumptuous carpets; I did not know then that shortly after I left Cairo the historic hostelry would be sacked and destroyed by rioting mobs.

I had known Cairo since the very first time that I set foot on a continent outside of Europe, in the autumn of 1922, and I had visited it many times since then: and every time it had been an unforgettable experience. There is a strange magic about this city on the Nile and in the soft, hardly-perceptible breeze that causes the fronds of the many palms on the river-bank to sway and whisper old tales into one's ears. I felt young once again and full of happy memories and of hopes.[5]

The city was as full of noise and bustle as ever, even more crowded but -- so it seemed to me -- poorer than before: many of its sidewalks were beds of misery, with homeless people and derelicts lying about on straw mats or rags or on the bare stones, and one had to tread gingerly so as not to step on a sleeping body. The magic of the Nile and of the palms on its banks did not reach this far . . . .

V

On the first morning after my arrival I paid a call on the Foreign Minister, Salahuddin Bey. He had been advised of my coming by Abd al-Wahhab Azzam and received me in a friendly, if somewhat reserved, manner. Very soon I understood *why* he was so distant. Hardly had I begun to explain the purpose of my visit when I saw his features visibly stiffen; and then he said with a half-smile, 'In *our* country we are not in favour of mixing religion with politics . . . .'

At that moment I was vividly reminded of my encounter in 1926 with Zaghlul Pasha,[6] the father of Egyptian independence, and of his reaction to my youthful enthusiasm about the role of Islam in man's social and political life. He had turned his pale face towards me and said pontifically, 'The time of religion has passed, my young friend. Our time is a time of nationalism.'

I seemed to hear an echo of Zaghlul's remark in the words which Salahuddin had just uttered, and I realized that it would be useless to talk any longer to him about a League of Muslim Nations.[7] None the less, I had to do my duty, and so I continued for a while, stressing our conviction that the leadership of the Arab world was the birthright of Egypt and that Pakistan, moreover, had no ambition to 'lead' other Muslim countries -- and so forth and so on until we had drunk our obligatory cup of thick, sweet Turkish coffee and it was time to leave.

On the evening of the same day I met Abd ar-Rahman Azzam Pasha,[8] the founder of the Arab League and the uncle of my good friend Dr Abd al-Wahhab. Himself an ardent believer in the necessity of Muslim unity, he agreed with me that it was a hopeless task to attempt a conversion of the Egyptian government to our ideas. 'Later, perhaps,' he said, 'but certainly not in the near future. Our politicians have still a lot to learn: they should learn from their own people's feelings . . . .' *

I stayed on in Cairo only two days and then left for Damascus.

VI

I had not seen Damascus since 1923 when, after a long, long march on foot across the mountains from Palestine, I had smuggled myself into Syria without a passport or visa because the French authorities -- apparently still lost in a perverse remembrance of the Great War -- had refused to grant me a visa on my Austrian passport.[9]

The contrast between those far-off days and the present went very deep. Syria was now free and independent, but the scars of the past were still painfully evident. In 1925 the entire centre of Damascus had been destroyed by French artillery in the course of the last -- and successful -- Syrian uprising against the 'Mandatory Power'. Innumerable old buildings, indeed whole streets, were still heaps of rubble, left possibly in that state as a reminder of foreign occupation or, more probably, because of a lack of funds on the part of the Syrian Government. Damascus had been deprived of its ancient glamour; a large segment of its history had been wiped out.

None the less, there was no trace of despondency about Damascus. Its people went about with their habitual resilience and optimism, the shops were filled with goods, and everyone seemed to be

---

* Years later, in the early Sixties, while I was residing near Geneva, we met again, several times. With regard to my forthcoming translation of and commentary on the Qur'an, he remarked: 'With this work, too, you are a hundred years before the times'; but he still encouraged me to complete it, which I did in 1979, in Tangier. Abd ar-Rahman was not only a great statesman, but he was also a very good and perceptive man.

confident of a better future. The sea of gardens and orchards that surrounded the ancient city were still unchanged, and the autumnal breeze which wafted a scent of roses and jasmine and orange blossoms over the ugly rubble in the streets was like a heavenly promise.

The political atmosphere, too, was free of resentments and hidden jealousies; a pleasant openness manifested itself in the behaviour of high and low within the Syrian Government. The Prime Minister, Shukri Quwwatli, received me in his office like an old friend -- as, indeed, he was. In 1929, when Shukri was living as a political exile in Saudi Arabia, we had spent many pleasant, animated days in my house in the mountain town of Taif, and neither of us had forgotten them.[10]

He was neither frightened nor surprised by the idea of a League of Muslim Nations. 'Indeed,' he said, 'we have been expecting something like this to come from Pakistan ever since you became a state. After all, this is what you have been created for.'

We discussed the scheme in all its aspects, and Shukri Quwwatli promised to have a memorandum of his own ready for me to place before my Government on my return to Karachi. He suggested, too, that I should see Faris al-Khouri, the Grand Old Man of Syria.

VII

The description 'Grand Old Man' fitted Faris al-Khouri extremely well. When I visited him the next day in his lovely house on the slopes of the Muhajirin Hill outside Damascus, I found a man of about eighty years, white of hair but full of mental vigour and wisdom. He was -- nominally, at least -- a Christian, but the prospect of a League of Muslim Nations filled him with something approaching enthusiasm. In his younger years he had been an ardent Arab nationalist, foremost in the ranks of the Syrians who, at the time of the World War of 1914-18, had allied themselves with Great Britain and France in a revolt against the Ottoman Empire, of which Syria was in those days a part.

'That was our great mistake,' said Faris al-Khouri. 'We did not realize at that time, although we should have, that the Ottoman Empire was the *only* power that could guarantee our independence. Indeed, if the Turks had not been defeated, Enver Pasha would have succeeded in his great plan to reform the Empire as a dual monarchy with Istanbul as the capital of the Turkish part and Aleppo as the capital of the Arab dominion, both of them internally independent and yet united, with the Sultan residing half a year in each city. But the Ottoman Empire broke down -- to a large extent to our, the Arabs, political imbecility and misguided nationalism – and Enver Pasha's dream went up in smoke.'

I marvelled at the Christian Faris al-Khouri's views about the Islam-inspired, stillborn project of Enver Pasha and even more about his unreserved approval of the present idea of a League of Muslim Nations. 'How come,' said I, 'that you, a Christian, welcome our proposal? Do not misunderstand me, Sayyid Faris, I am most happy to learn that you agree with us; but I must confess that I am somewhat surprised -- pleasantly surprised -- by your readiness to visualize the Arab world within an Islamic political configuration . . . .'

Faris al-Khouri leaned forward and gripped my arm: 'Yes, I call myself a Christian, but this is only an empty word. Christianity is now a dead formula, a memory. The only *real* force that is still alive in the Arab world is Islam, and let there be no doubt about it! Without Islam, the Arabs are bound to remain a plaything of the Western world: and do you wonder that I, an Arab patriot, am not willing to contemplate such an eventuality?'

I understood now what Shukri Quwwatli had in mind when he insisted on my meeting Faris al-Khouri . . . .

And so, my mission to Damascus fully accomplished, I continued on my journey -- this time to Baghdad.

VIII

Whenever I visited Baghdad (and this had happened several times in the course of my wandering life) I was invariably struck by that city's tawdriness and utter lack of character. No trace remains of its one-time legendary splendour: the Mongols who invaded Iraq in the thirteenth century had been too thorough for that. Although the conqueror, Hulaku Khan,[11] afterwards regretted the senseless destruction of that unique city and had some of the gutted buildings restored, Baghdad was never able to regain its former appearance or its importance. It is a *has-been* of a city, without any beauty of its own apart form the majestic flow of the River Tigris on whose banks it is situated. No edifice of any architectural merit relieves the visual monotony of its crowded, noisy streets, and there is nothing to remind one even distantly of the irrevocable past; the Mongol holocaust was too complete and the city never recovered its body or its soul . . . .

As soon as I felt rested from my two-days' journey by car from Damascus across the immense, flat Hammada Desert (I preferred to go overland rather than to fly), I paid my respects to the Prince Regent, Abd al-elah, who was ruling over Iraq on behalf of his nephew, the late

King Faisal's son, at that time a boy of fourteen or fifteen years and also named Faisal. Abd al-elah received me in the red-brick royal palace which -not surprisingly -- was as devoid of character as the rest of the city; but his friendliness outweighed by far the insignificance of our physical surroundings. He was about thirty years old and of a pleasant, outwardly open countenance; how he *really* was I had, of course, no means of guessing -- either then or even a couple of years later, when we met again in New York -- for, as I was aware from my earlier experiences, it is never easy to know what is going on in the mind of an Iraqi. In contrast to the Arabs of the Najd and even of the Hijaz, who are invariably direct and humanly comprehensible, the people of Iraq are, as a rule, somewhat opaque and difficult to read . . . .

Nevertheless, as I have mentioned, our interview was pleasant and friendly, although Prince Abd al-elah made no secret of his disappointment at Pakistan's rather hesitant attitude -- largely due to my influence -- towards the 'Baghdad Pact'. Still, he seemed to be genuinely interested in the idea of a League of Muslim Nations, and this was in tune with the Iraqi tradition going back to the time of the First World War, when Iraq -- alone amongst all Arab countries -- wholeheartedly supported the Ottoman Empire as a symbol of Muslim unity.

In the course of our conversation, Abd al-elah told me that the Prime Minister, Nuri Said,[12] was ill and would not be able to see me, 'But,' he said, 'you will find our Foreign Minister very receptive to your Government's proposals.'

And he was. The Foreign Minister, Fadhil al-Jamali, proved to be more than just 'receptive' to the purpose of my mission: he openly stated that he had not come across a more important project throughout the whole of his official career. We discussed it from all possible angles, and at the end of our conversation Fadhil al-Jamali assured me that Iraq would wholeheartedly support our endeavours. However, he, too, like Abd ar-Rahman Azzam, was deeply pessimistic about the attitude of Egypt -- 'and without Egypt,' he added, 'it will be very difficult to bring the Arab world together into a common front. Still, we must try, and try at one -- for if we lose our momentum and allow the project to cool down, it is bound to fizzle out . . . .'

I left Fadhil al-Jamali with the feeling that I had gained a real friend, whatever the future might bring. And I was not to be disappointed. Whenever we met in later years -- and we were destined to meet often -1 found Fadhil al-Jamali to be closer to my way of thinking, to my hopes and my ideas than almost any other statesman in the

Muslim world.

IX

And so on to Turkey. I flew to Istanbul and had once again, after so many years, my fill of the beauty and stately splendour of the one-time Imperial City: its mosques, symphonies of stone and tile and gleaming domes and heaven-pointed minarets; and the Golden Horn with its ships and boats of all sizes and flags; and the many-faceted bazaars full of colours and scents and living sounds: two whole days filled with ever-new enchantment. And then, with something like regret in my heart, on to barren Ankara and the prospect of not very hopeful discussions.

I knew that it would not be easy to persuade the Turkish Government even to *consider* my proposals with an open mind. Although Kemal Atatürk[13] had been dead for more than fifteen years, his shadow still lay heavily over Turkey . . . .

How heavily became vividly, almost tangibly, obvious to me on the very first day of my stay in Ankara. True, there was now a civilian government in office, but all *real* power still remained in the hands of the generals, who regarded themselves as the only true heirs to Atatürk's 'reforms'. Their aversion to anything that smacked of Turkey's Islamic past manifested itself in the day-to-day life of Ankara, in the drabness of its people's appearance. The men were still forbidden to wear the fez or the high fur *kalpak* on their heads, and the women were obliged, whether they liked it or not, whether young or old, to dress in what was considered, 'civilized' apparel: with the result that both, men and women alike, now resembled nothing so much as out-of-work crowds in a proletarian suburb of any Western European city. One felt strongly that this mode of dress had been forced on them, and it *had* been forced, for no other reason than to divorce them from all visible associations with their past and to convert them into 'Europeans' by governmental *fiat:* a pitiful undertaking, as destructive in its effects as was the banishment of the Arabic script from all schools and public institutions and its replacement by the Roman alphabet – destructive, because with one stroke of the pen it cut the Turks off from all their past literature and, thus, from their cultural roots. Whether he intended it or not, Atatürk -- the 'Father of the Turks' -- had transformed the Turks, his own people, into a race of cultural half-castes, neither entirely Western nor fully Eastern ... a race of cultural bastards . . . .

However, on the day after my arrival in Ankara, I realized that

Kemal Atatürk's imitative endeavours had not entirely succeeded, and that in their innermost being the Turkish people had not ceased to be what they had always been -strong Muslims. This realization dawned upon me when the Pakistan Ambassador, Bashir Ahmad, reminded me that it was Friday and took me with him for the noon prayers at the main mosque of Ankara.

That unpretentious but very large mosque was so full of worshippers that we could find no place either in its interior nor even in its enormous courtyard; and so we had to spread our prayer mats in the street together with thousands upon thousands of other people, men *and* women, who had not forgotten -- and indeed, could never forget -- that they were Muslims. And then and there it became clear to me that no Atatürk, no general who sat on top of Turkey by the sheer force of the arms at his disposal, could ever really cut off this nation from its consciousness of being followers of Islam . . .

On our return from Friday prayers I had a touching experience of the brotherhood of Muslims. Somehow, in the throngs that milled around the mosque after the end of the prayers I had lost my fur cap, and as it was the only one I had with me on my travels, I asked one of the Embassy secretaries to guide me to a place where I could buy a new one. He brought me to a furrier's shop owned by an old man and his son and told them in Turkish (with which I was not acquainted) that I wanted to purchase a *kalpak*. They had none in stock because that kind of headgear was strictly 'out of bounds' in Turkey; but they promised to make one for me within a few hours. When I returned to the shop later in the afternoon a beautiful *kalpak* of grey Astrakhan was awaiting me. As I took out my wallet to pay for it, the father and son refused to accept money from me, 'because,' the old man said, 'we could not take money from a brother, and our brother you are . . . .'

X

It was with this unexpected feeling of encouragement -- first engendered by the sight of the many thousands of worshippers at the mosque, and then by my experience at the furrier's -- that I had my first conversation with the Prime Minister of Turkey, Celal Bayar,[14] and the Chairman of the Legislative Assembly, Adnan Menderes.[15] While we sipped our coffee I explained to them my plan to bring about a League of Muslim Nations in which, of course, Turkey was bound to play a prominent part in view of its large population, its military strength and -- most of all -- of the centuries of their history as 'the lions of Islam'.

Both Bayar and Menderes approved of Pakistan's endeavour, and Adnan Menderes added: 'We have indeed placed our hopes on Pakistan. May God allow your country to become the forerunner of Muslim revival all over the world . . . .' At the same time they made it quite clear that they themselves would have to proceed very slowly and cautiously because the destructive heritage of Kemal Atatürk was still very powerful in the land, and especially in the cities, and that *too* strong an accent on Islam might provoke a violent reaction on the part of the powers-that-were.

Neither of those great Turkish leaders had on that day any inkling of *how* violent that reaction would be, and that both of them would soon end as martyrs on the gallows . . . .

XI

That same evening I received a terrible blow: news came to the Embassy by telephone that Liaquat Ali Khan had been assassinated.

He had been shot dead while addressing a huge public meeting in [Rawalpindi] by a man whom nobody knew and nobody would ever know: for, one second after he had fired his deadly shot, the assassin himself was shot dead by the police inspector in charge of the Prime Minister's security . . . .

And so, with the unknown murderer's death, the 'why' of his deed remained -- and remains to this day -- completely obscure.

As for myself, I saw immediately that this was the end of my Middle East tour and a full stop to our plans for a League of Muslim Nations. I immediately packed my bags and took the first plane back to Karachi.

On my return I learned that before he had set out on his tragic last journey to [Rawalpindi], Liaquat had made some notes for a public speech which he intended to deliver on the following morning. Those notes were found on his desk. They consisted of only a few words, all of them heavily underlined in red: 'League of Muslim Nations' and 'Constitution' -- apparently relating to the speech that was never to be delivered . . . .

Since then I have often asked myself: Was there a connection between Liaquat Ali's death and the purport of those notes? Was I, thus, indirectly responsible for his death? I do not know . . . .

XII

I reached Karachi too late to attend the Prime Minister's funeral, but not too late to witness the people's shock and sorrow. The question 'why' lay on everyone's lips, and there was no clear answer. Various conjectures were put forward, fantastic rumours floated about -- but in the end all speculation amounted to nothing in the face of the unknowable identity of the assassin. One thing was certain: there was no trace of any previous relationship between him and his victim, and so all *personal* motivation had to be ruled out. It must have been a politically-motivated murder, with its perpetrator no more than an instrument set up by somebody who remained in the background and could not be seriously guessed at . . . .

After a few days a new Prime Minister -- a nobody -- was chosen by the National Assembly from among the leaders of the dominant party, the Muslim League. He was a politician from East Pakistan by name of Muhammad Ali[16] (not to be confused with the Secretary-General to the Cabinet of that same name who later, too, became Prime Minister).

And so life went on. I submitted a full report on my Middle East tour to Zafrullah Khan, the Foreign Minister, who read it through carefully and then put it aside. My search after Muslim unity became a file in the archives of the Foreign Ministry.

XIII

During my visit to Damascus the Syrian Prime Minister, Shukri Quwwatli, had expressed his desire to see a treaty of friendship concluded between his country and mine; and now the Syrian Minister Plenipotentiary, my old friend Baha ad-Din al-Amiri, placed the project formally before his Government. As the head of the Middle East Division I was entrusted with the task of negotiating that treaty with the Syrian envoy.

From the very outset I suggested that we should entitle our draft as a 'Treaty of Friendship and *Brotherhood*', and not just a 'Treaty of Friendship' as was customary; and Baha ad-Din agreed with me wholeheartedly. We did our best to bring out the special character which ought to govern the relationship between two nations belonging to the community, the *ummah,* of Islam; and I believe that we succeeded in our common effort.

As soon as the draft was ready, I submitted my copy to Ikramullah, our Secretary-General, who exclaimed at once: 'But, Asad, the term 'brotherhood' does not *exist* in the language of diplomacy!' -- to which I replied, 'Well, in that case we are innovators. Why should we fight shy of introducing a *new* concept into diplomatic terminology?'

We wrangled for a while and finally agreed to leave the decision to the Foreign Minister who, after some consideration, gave the go-ahead to my suggestion. And so, for the first time in modern diplomatic usage, the term 'brotherhood' appeared in the treaty which was formally concluded and signed by both parties. It was a small step in my quest for Muslim unity.

XIV

One day a most welcome visitor appeared in my office: Habib Bourguiba,[17] the exiled leader of the Tunisian struggle for independence.

He was a man of approximately my own age or perhaps slightly, older, visibly tired from his long peregrinations in Europe and various Arab countries and had, finally, after many disappointments, come to Pakistan in search of moral and material support for his movement; and here he was not to be disappointed. One of our Foreign Minister's greatest virtues was his feeling of solidarity with the Muslim peoples who were struggling against colonial domination -- and this attitude of his was genuine -- a solidarity which was not affected by Zafrullah's personal, deep-seated involvement with the Ahmadiyya sect or his emotional 'loyalty' to Great Britain. Before sending Bourguiba to me, he had discussed with him all the problems confronting Tunisia's independence movement, and we three then continued those discussions in several sessions. The result was a solid undertaking on the part of the Government of Pakistan to aid Bourguiba -- and through him, his movement -- not only morally and financially but in other ways as well: and we saw to it that this undertaking was fulfilled in spite of the obvious risks which it involved for Pakistan on the international scene.

Bourguiba never forgot my modest role in those discussions and subsequent developments; and many years later, when I had retired from the Foreign Service and he was President of Tunisia, he let me feel this in unmistakable terms.

XV

My work at the Middle East Division was coming to an end. One day Ikramullah informed me that the Foreign Minister had decided to send me abroad -- perhaps to get me out of the way? 'Where to?' I asked. 'As Chargé d'Affaires in Buenos Aires, to establish our new embassy there,' was his answer.

'But, Ikramullah Sahib, I am a *Middle-East* man -- my field is the

Arab world, or at least the *Muslim* world! What have I to do with South America?'

'Well,' rejoined Ikramullah, 'you will have to talk it out with Zafrullah. It is *his* decision, not mine.'

And to Zafrullah Khan I went and protested against my proposed posting to Argentina on the same grounds as I had advanced to the Secretary-General; but Zafrullah insisted on my going to Buenos Aires.

'In that case, sir, I am now going straight back to my office to write out my resignation from the Foreign Service!'

As I turned to the door the Foreign Minister called me back: 'Don't be too hasty, Asad. I will think it over . . . .'

He apparently did think about it, because the next day my posting to Buenos Aires was rescinded and for the time being I was to stay on at my old job.

Endnotes

1 Muhammad Surur al-Sabban (1898/99-1972), a Meccan merchant and the first secretary-general of the Muslim World League (Rabita Alam-i Islami), Mecca, (1962-1972); minister of Finance and National Economy; ex-Director of Pilgrimage.

(cf. Reinhardt Schulze: *Geschichte der Islamischen Welt im 20. Jahrhunderts.* München 2002, s.v. Index).

2 Faisal ibn 'Abdul 'Aziz al-Sa'ud (1906-1975) Foreign Minister (1930) and then king of Saudi Arabia, who was assassinated by a nephew on 25 March 1975. Cf. Willard A. Beling (ed.): *King Faisal and the Modernisation of Saudi Arabia*, Boulder 1980.

3 'Abdul 'Aziz ibn al-Sa'ud, the founder of Saudi Arabia (d. 9 November 1953, at the age of 73); see also above 1.

4 Shaikh Yusuf Yasin (1900- ?); Private Secretary to H.M. the ex-King Ibn Saud; Councellor, Deputy Minister for Foreign Affairs; Head of the Political Department in the Royal Court; Delegate to the League of the Arab States.

cf. *Schulze*, p. 164.

5 Asad's first visit of Cairo, see *The Unromantic Orient.* Tr. by Elma Ruth Harder. Lahore 2005, pp. 1-20.

6 Sa'd b. Ibrahim Zaghlul (1860-1927). Eyptian jurist and politican, president of the Egyptian Wafd party (1918-1927) and in 1924 Prime Minister. Cf. *EI*², vol. VIII (Leiden, 1995), pp. 698-701 (art. R. Schulze). For Asad's meeting with him, see *The Unromantic Orient*, op. cit., pp. 114-121.

7 Arab League; primarily Egypt proposed for the establishment of an Arab League. Representatives of the Arab states met in September 1944 in

Alexandria (Egypt) and eventually agreed on a structure in which member states would retain their sovereignty and resolutions would be binding on all member states only when voting was unanimous. Arab representatives met in Cairo and signed the Pact of the League of Arab States on 22 March 1945.

The Arab League comprises six major bodies and their goals have been extensive, including encouraging close cooperation of the member states in political, security, economic, communications, cultural, social and financial matters.

It is often said that the Arab League is a mirror of Arab politics.

cf. Ahmed M. Gomaa: *The Foundation of the League of Arab States.* London/New York, 1977.

8 Abd ar-Rahman 'Azzām (1893) a pro-Ottoman Egyptian nationalist; Ottoman officer in Cyrenaica (1916) and for a short time was advisor to Tripoli Republic General-Secretary of Arab League (1945-1952); his book (in Arabic 1946) has been translated by Caesar E. Farah and published under the title *The Eternal Message of Muhammad* (Mentor Book, 1964).

cf. *Schulze*, pp. 161, 164, 173.

9 Asad described his experiences and observations during his stay in Damascus, see *The Unromantic Orient*, op. cit., pp. 96-110.

10 On the special instructions of the first Prime Minister of Pakistan, Liaquat Ali Khan, the first official delegation of Pakistan was sent to Saudi Arabia (1951) under the headship of Mawlawi Tamizuddin Khan (1889-1963), speaker of Constituent Assembly. Asad accompanied this delegation as its secretary. He used his personal contacts with the rulers of Saudi Arabia and laid the strong foundation of mutual friendship between the two countries.

cf. *Nawa-i Waqt* (Lahore), 27 August and 28 October 1982)

Immediately after Partition (1947), India tried to have diplomatic relations with Saudi Arabia on firm footing. Pandit Jawaharlal Nehru, the first Indian Prime Minister, officially toured Saudi Arabia and established the first Indian Embassy in Jiddah. At that time, Pakistani Embassy was not existed there and the Ambassador of Embassy of Pakistan in Cairo, Hajī Abdus Sattar Ishaq Seth (1896-1988), was looking after the diplomatic affairs.

In 1951, an official delegation was sent to Saudi Arabia and Muhammad Asad was its secretary and interpreter. After many years, he met Abdul Aziz Ibn Saud and King Faisal (Foreign Minister) and according to Muhammad Yaqub Hashmi (ex-Secretary Education and Information, Government of Azad Kashmir and one of the members of the delegation) the cordial relations of Asad with these most influential members of ruling family played a vital role in achieving the many diplomatic goals, including the opening of Embassy in Saudi Arabia (see his letters to Sadiq Quraishi, 1st August 1982, Muzaffarabad and 20 Feb. 1983, Rawalpindi). In a letter to Muhammad Sadiq Quraishi (23 Dec. 1982, Tangier), Asad writes:

"With reference to my discussions with the Government of K.S.A. in 1951, I can only say that the then Foreign Minister and Crown Prince (later king) Faysal who was an old and beloved friend already at that time and remained so until his tragic death, had a great love for Pakistan. It was not difficult, therefore, to remove whatever misunderstanding may have existed."

He also toured different countries of Middle East like Syria, Lebanon, Egypt, Iraq and Turkey with Ch. Zafrullah Khan, Pakistan's Foreign Minister, and submitted several memorandums to the concerned authorities, based on his personal experiences and observations. In a letter to Altaf Husain, Editor of *Dawn*, (16 June 1953, New York), he writes:

"...the many memoranda which I wrote on major problems of Pakistan's foreign policy in the Middle East, the reports of my official tour in 1952 (undertaken in the company of Pakistan's Foreign Minister) as well as the recommendations I submitted in the context of these tours to our Government would bear out my contention that whatever influence I may have possessed was always directed at the strengthening of the bonds of unity between the various components of the Muslim world and at the combating of all trends that might be inimical to the interests of the Muslim world and especially of the Muslim Middle East."

11 Hulaku Khan (d. 1264, r. 1251-1264), grandson of Chingiz Khan and founder of Ilkhanid Dynasty in Iran.

12 Nuri al-Sa'id (1888-1958), commander-in-chief, Minister of Defence and then prime minister of Iraq (1921-1958). In a military coup he was killed with Faisal II. *EI*[2], VIII (1995), pp. 140-143, art. P. Sluglett.

13 Mustafa Kemal Atatürk (1881-1938); founding father of the Turkish Republic; his ultimate objective was the achievement of a genuine and modern nationhood, responsible for and answerable to its citizens individually and collectively.

cf. Uluğ Iğdemir et al: *Atatürk Biography* (1963). Translated by the Turkish National Commission for UNESCO; complete translation of the entry "Atatürk, Gazi Mustafa Kemal" in *Islâm Ansiklopedisi*, vol. I, fasc. 10, pp. 719-807 (Istanbul 1949).

14 Jalal Bayar (1883- ?), a famous politician of Turkey; Prime Minister (1937) and then President of the country (1950); arrested (1960) and sentenced to death which was changed by life imprisonment.

15 Adnan Menderes (1899-1961), Prime Minister of Turkey (1950); dethroned and sentenced to death.

16 Muhammad Ali Bogra (1909-1963). Prime Minister of Pakistan (April 1952-August1955).

17 Habib Bourguiba (1903-1996). President of Tunisia; see Asad's letter to Muhammad Husain Babri (14 August 1970, Tangier).

* * * * *

ISLAMIC CULTURE

The Hyderabad Quarterly Review

EDITOR'S OFFICE:
MODEL TOWN
(LAHORE, INDIA)

18th November, 1936.

Ref

Muhammad Asad's office in Lahore, as editor of "Islamic Culture"

ادارۂ دار الاسلام

DAR-UL-ISLAM INSTITUTE

AN ISLAMIC CULTURAL CENTRE

Dar-ul-Islam (Pathankot, Panjab)
India

Rly. Station Sarna

دار الاسلام (پٹھان کوٹ۔ پنجاب)

ریلوے سٹیشن سرنا

Dar u-Islam Institute where Muhammad Asad worked
With Ch. Niaz 'Ali and Mawlana Mawdudi

X
AT THE UNITED NATIONS
(1951-52)

I

Early in December 1951 Zafrullah Khan asked me whether I would not like to go to the United Nations. He advanced this suggestion in a very tentative manner because he knew from his previous experience that I held definite views about what could or could *not* be my field of activity. He was a very subtle man. He pointed out that during its coming session the United Nations would be largely concerned with the status of Europe's North African colonies and 'protectorates' and their quest for independence and, 'Since all of them are Arab countries, it would be most useful for us to have as one of our representatives a man who is fully conversant with their problems and speaks their language. What about it, Asad?'

I did appreciate the Foreign Minister's cautious approach to the question of my posting, and I agreed with him at once that North Africa was well within my range of interests and my competence. At the same time, however, I did not fail to notice that he referred to my future position as '*one* of our representatives' -- which obviously implied that I would not be given the charge of our mission. Once again it seemed, the light colour of my skin had stood in my way, as Terence Craigh-Coen had so clearly predicted on my joining the Service. But I did not mind too much: I was looking forward to defending the rights of Muslim North Africa, and I knew that I could do it far more effectively than any titular head of our mission, whoever he might be.

Very soon I learned who it was to be. The Prime Minister's and Foreign Minister's choice fell upon one Ahmad Shah Bokhari,[1] a former professor of English literature at one of Lahore's colleges. He was appointed Pakistan's Ambassador to the United Nations, and I was to be his second-in-command with the rank of Minister Plenipotentiary.

We did not know one another personally, and neither of us had as yet any inkling of how badly matched we would prove to be . . . .

II

It took me a couple of weeks to wind up my work at the Middle East Division and to hand over its charge to my successor, who was -- of course -- a former member of the Indian Civil Service without any previous acquaintance with the problems, let alone the languages, of the Middle East. But I was by now used to these sudden shifts after several years of Government Service and at that point I no longer cared about what might happen to the Middle East Division. I had already felt in my bones that after the death of Liaquat Ali Khan my days in the Foreign Service were numbered. None the less, I looked forward with some expectation to the coming months at the United Nations and to the chance of furthering personally North Africa's march towards independence.

During the winter of 1951-52 the United Nations was holding a special session in Paris, and so to Paris I went. I landed at Orly airport close to midnight on December 31, 1951, and thus found myself once again in Europe after an absence of exactly twenty-five years -- to the day -- that is, for the first time since January 1, 1927, when I left Berlin for Egypt . . . .

Several members of our delegation were already in Paris, but not Ahmad Shah Bokhari: he had remained in New York to prepare the newly-acquired Pakistan House as the permanent headquarters of our mission. The Paris session was to be attended by Zafrullah Khan, who on this occasion intended to lead the Pakistan delegation in person. In his absence I took charge of it as the senior most officer present.

Our Ambassador in Paris -- probably anxious to dispel the impression that Pakistan was a poor country -- as it was -- had provided us with very sumptuous living quarters: all of us were lodged at the Plaza Athenée, then the most luxurious hotel in Paris. The suite which was assigned to me as the temporary head of mission consisted of a bedroom and a huge salon furnished with genuinely antique pieces and exquisite carpets: a truly extravagant show in view of Pakistan's economic condition. But since the choice had not been mine, I moved in without demur, and then I and my staff settled down to work in our makeshift office (also in the Plaza Athenée) as well as in the General Assembly, whose routine was new to all of us.

There was not much for us to do in the General Assembly

except to listen to the more or less permanent slanging-match between the representative of the United States, Mr Gross, and the Soviet delegate, whose name I have forgotten. At the beginning this display was amusing to witness, but in time it became monotonous and -- what was more significant – entirely fruitless: so much so that as soon as either of them rose to address the Assembly, one was invariably tempted to leave the hall temporarily, get acquainted in the corridors with members of other delegations and spend half an hour or so in animated talk with people who knew the world and could converse with one another without bitterness or rancour.

During the hours when the General Assembly was not in session, either in daytime or in the evenings, I wandered through the streets of Paris -- sometimes accompanied by one or another of the mission staff, but mostly alone -- occasionally having a wonderful soupe à l'oignon before dawn at Les Halles in the midst of workers and lorry drivers who were bringing all manner of foodstuffs to the city markets. I came to like the working class of Paris far better than the brusque and often rude 'better class' people, and so I usually omitted my breakfast at the Plaza Athenée and had my coffee and croissant in one or another bistrot instead, chatting with this man or that, and always wondering how they could start on their heavy day's work fortified with a solid glass of aquavit . . . .

After a fortnight Zafrullah Khan arrived and began to 'organize' our mission, attributing to its work far more weight than our role within the General Assembly warranted. There was no question at that time of North African or Middle Eastern problems coming to the fore, and our conflict with India over Kashmir was certainly *not* on the agenda. In fact, no matter of any real importance was, for the moment at least, before the Assembly, and even the perennial verbal duals between the United States and Soviet Russia were predictable in their utter futility.

None the less, we *had* to be 'organized': and to this end Zafrullah instituted a daily conference, at nine o'clock in the morning, which had to be attended by all officers of the mission, with a view to laying down Pakistan's attitude on this or that irrelevant point of the day's schedule. I suspected that he wanted to impress us with his supposed earnestness *vis-à-vis* the Assembly's deliberations and so to justify our living it up at the Plaza Athenée . . . . Anyhow, all of the four or five mission members were expected to be present at every morning's conference, and that was that.

It was only much later, in New York, that Pakistan began to play a really essential role at the United Nations, and I was to be its instrument.

III

As the Paris session was to be only temporary, my wife had remained for the time being in Karachi -- and, for that matter, what would life in Paris have meant to an Indianized Najdi woman? My son Talal was now studying architecture in London: and so I decided that it would be best for all concerned if his mother would live with him until the end of his studies. Consequently, I took a short leave of absence and flew to Karachi to wind up our household there and to bring Talal's mother to London. Since the Paris session was approaching its end I did not propose to return to Paris but to proceed from London straight to New York.

In London Munira and I were received by a secretary from the Pakistan High Commissioner's office and lodged, of all places, at the Dorchester, again an extravagance which seemed to have been dictated by an exaggerated notion of 'prestige' on the part of Pakistan's diplomatic representatives.

But comfortable it was, and in sharp contrast with London's over-all drabness at that time. The destruction caused by the bombings during the war was still everywhere in evidence. Whole blocks within the City were but heaps of bricks, twisted iron girders and rubble, surrounded by wooden hoardings and waiting for a regeneration. Nothing could have been more depressing than the face of London in that first decade after the war.

Very soon I found a suitable furnished flat and installed Talal and his mother there. After that I flew to New York – a long, tedious flight in a propeller plane, with a short stop at Shannon Airport and then, because of the weather conditions, on a circuitous route towards the north and a lengthy stop in icy Newfoundland. Finally, after a flight of some nineteen hours, I reached New York's international airport, where a car and a third secretary from the Pakistan Mission awaited me. During the whole flight, first from Karachi to London, and then from London to New York, I had been attached by handcuff to a suitcase carrying our new code, with the result that two cracked ribs suffered during a fall in a garage in Karachi the day before my departure -- and, of course, ignored -- broke through and probably became the cause, several years later, of a serious bout of pleurisy. So much for Foreign Service . . . .

During our drive from the airport to the city I was told that originally, in view of my rank, a room had been booked for me at the Hotel Pierre; but this had been vetoed by my boss- to-be as being 'too expensive'. Thus, I was to stay at a second-class hotel: this was the first hint of my future relations with Ahmad Shah Bokhari.

The next day I found him ensconced in a very luxurious suite of rooms in one of the most exclusive hotels in New York's East Side. It was the first time we met, but I knew at once that we would never be friends. No doubt, he was extremely intelligent and well read and, at least outwardly, well-bred, but at the same time he was very vain and 'full of himself', and it soon became obvious that he could not tolerate any opinion, on any subject, that conflicted with his own. But what was even worse was his inner urge to dominate anyone whom he regarded as subject to his 'authority' -- and that, to be sure, did not go down well with me at all. Despite my current involvement in government service I had always remained independent in my views; and whereas this, precisely, may have attracted Liaquat Ali Khan to me -- he was never a petty man -- it proved to be a serious stumbling block in my relations with Ahmad Shah Bokhari. Possibly he suspected, quite wrongly, that I aimed at undermining his position and taking away something of this 'prestige' as the sole moving force with the Pakistani delegation, and so he never missed an opportunity to 'put me in my place' whenever I voiced an opinion different from his to any political problem under discussion, be it in private or in front of other people. In consequence, our mutual relations were always strained, and I never had the feeling that we were members of one and the same 'team', working towards common ends.

IV

Contrary to the dullness of the Paris session, the scene in New York was, to me at least, animated and full of interest. From the very first days I had plenty of occasion to meet and make friends with various representatives of Arab countries who attended the sessions of the United Nations either as representatives of their respective governments or -- as was the case of politicians from North Africa -- as observers. Outstanding among the latter was Allal al-Fassi,[2] the leader of Morocco's Istiqlal Party. An Islamic scholar of great standing and, what was even more important, an original, bold thinker, this man soon became a close friend. He realized at once that the freedom of his country was as much a concern of mine as his own, and that I identified myself with the interests of North Africa to no lesser extent than with the interests of Pakistan; there *could* be no conflict. In fact, to me, as a Muslim, both were not merely parallel but *identical* inasmuch as the achievement of independence of one Muslim country strengthened the position of all others. There was, to my mind, nothing 'unpatriotic' or 'disloyal' in this attitude, but later I was often to be accused in Pakistan of being 'too pro-Arab' . . . .

We spent many hours together planning the tactics to be adopted at the United Nations and acquainting one another with our past experiences. Allal al-Fassi described to me the nine years of his exile in Gabon, the tropical West African colony to which he had been deported by the French, and I narrated to him the story of my conversion to Islam more than twenty-five years earlier, of the happy years I had spent in Arabia, and of my work and my ambitions for Pakistan. Our views about the problems facing Islam as such coincided in most points, and both of us looked forward to a fruitful collaboration in the cause of Morocco and North Africa as a whole. The friendship which began at this time lasted for many, many years, in fact until his death, when I was already residing in Morocco.

I also came to know intimately the representatives of Tunisia's Destour Party -- the party led by my absent friend Habib Bourguiba -- and, in particular, Bahi Ladgham, who later became the first Prime Minister of an independent Tunisia, as well as his colleague and partner, Salah ben Yusuf, who later became the victim of political assassination. At that time neither of them could do more than work in the corridors of the Assembly and try to gain as much support as possible from among the accredited members of other delegations, both Muslim and non-Muslim; and in that sense we -- the Tunisians and I -- worked hand in hand.

And there I met again my old friend Faris al-Khouri, who attended the session as representative of Syria and who, because of his bad eyesight, could take cat-naps behind his dark glasses during the more boring exchanges, which was often. I found him as firm as ever in his conviction that Islam was the *only* force that could safeguard the independence of Middle Eastern countries and bring freedom to North Africa as well.

And there was Iraq's Foreign Minister, Fadhil al-Jamali, and there were observers from Algeria and Libya, and several other personalities whom I had met during my recent wanderings in the Middle East. In short, my days and evenings were full of friendship and with planning a common course of political action.

V

In the meantime I was able to arrange my personal life on a more permanent basis. I did not like to stay indefinitely in a hotel room, and so I found for myself an independent flat on the top floor of a residential hotel on the West Side of New York -- four well-furnished rooms and a large roof terrace -and settled in together with my trusted Pakistani servant, Ashraf. He was an ex-soldier and an experienced driver, and I had been thinking of employing him in that capacity. Unfortunately, however, because of his inability to read and write in English he could not obtain a New York driving licence. And so I kept him on as my personal servant and cook -- and in the latter capacity he proved to be very satisfactory. He could cook quite well, Pakistani style, and this suited my taste. Moreover, he was so good at it that I could invite friends to my flat and regale them with quite a selection of spicy dishes.

And it was at this time that I met the woman who was destined to become my life companion.

It happened at a reception given by our press attaché. In the throng of guests who crowded the large salon of Pakistan House I suddenly saw a young and beautiful woman whose appearance caused my heart to contract in a strange way: not just because she was beautiful but because she stood out among those people as a being remote from their world, lost in an inner silence which seemed to envelop her like a transparent veil -- something difficult to grasp and still more difficult to describe. I asked our host, the press attaché, who she was; and he told me that she was an American of Polish origin who worked for the Voice of America, that she was apparently unhappily married and, so my friend thought, on the brink of divorce. 'Do you want me to introduce you to her?' he asked. 'No, thank you', I replied, 'I will introduce myself.'

I still recollected the remnants of my mother-tongue, and so I went up to her and addressed her in Polish. Startled, she turned round to me and replied, in English. 'I do not know much Polish . . . .' Whereupon I introduced myself formally and we began to talk. She was very reserved, almost shy, but gradually she relaxed somewhat and told me that when she had seen me first she had thought that I was an Arab, and since she knew several of the Arabs attending the U.N. session she had been interested in making my acquaintance. This, then, was mutual. We talked for a while about her family background and I learned that her mother had been born at a place in eastern Poland about two hours distance from where I had been born, and this provided an unexpected connection between us. We talked and talked, and I found that she had a lively, perceptive mind, and I knew that I had fallen in love with her . . . .

I asked her to have dinner with me, and she agreed. We dined at a Turkish-Armenian restaurant on the East Side called 'The Golden Horn' and to my regret she told me that she was due to go away next morning to visit with some friends on Long Island and would not be back before five days or so. However, I obtained from her the telephone number of her friends and said that I would call her.

After our dinner I accompanied her to her apartment on the East Side and we took leave of one another. It was May 7, 1952.

VI

Five days later Pola[3] returned to New York and from then on we met daily, usually for lunch. She was working at the Voice of America as editorial assistant to a well-known radio commentator, Raymond Gram Swing, and since this gave her great insight into the contemporary political scene, we had a lot to talk about. Before her present job she had been employed at the State Department in Washington as secretary to the head of the European desk, and was for some time in charge of the secretarial pool at the U.S. Delegation to the United Nations, and it was in that capacity that she had become acquainted with some Middle Eastern and Pakistani representatives since she was responsible for introducing American VIPs who visited sessions at Lake Success to the heads and members of the various delegations.

And to my surprise -- a very pleasant surprise indeed -- I learned that Pola had embraced Islam a few months earlier; and this was a further bond between us -- almost like predestination.

By and by I came to know how that had happened. There was not much of a religious atmosphere in Pola's family. Her father, who had recently died, had been a second-generation American of Polish descent and more or less a free-thinker; her mother was only conventionally Catholic, not much given to religious observances, while her two older sisters did not care even to set foot in a church. In contrast to them, Pola had felt from early childhood a religious urge -- so much so that even at the age of five or six she would go alone to the neighbourhood church to attend Sunday mass. However, after growing up, having been taught the catechism and received 'confirmation' at the age of thirteen, she began to be dissatisfied with what her priest was teaching her. And since her longing after spiritual truth had remained undiminished, she began to read book after book about other religions.

Hinduism did not move her. The teachings of the Buddha attracted her in some measure, but its negativism, instinctively perceived by her young mind, left her unsatisfied. Finally, as a last resort, she began to read about Islam -- and almost immediately she felt that this was what she had been groping for. The more she read about the fundamental teachings of the Prophet Muhammad, the more she realized that the Islamic postulate of an approach to faith through reason was closest to what she sought.

As I have said, almost from the beginning of our acquaintance I saw to it that Pola and I met every day, usually during the lunch interval which I, for my part, tried to extend as long as possible. We would stroll for hours along the paths of Central Park, whose leafy splendour was beginning to unfold into the abundance of early summer. Grey, bushy-tailed squirrels were scurrying from tree to tree, wild pigeons were flying overhead or alighting at our offerings of breadcrumbs or biscuits -- a steady accompaniment to the happiness which I felt and which, I hoped, Pola was beginning to share with me. We would have lunch at a small, unpretentious place called 'The Russian Tea Room' on South Central Park -- a one-room establishment with a few tables for two, each one bearing a huge bowl of lilac blossoms in the centre. After a light meal and another stroll through the park we separated, each of us going back to our work and arranging to meet again for dinner.

VII

In the meantime, Ahmad Shah Bokhari tried to make me 'innocuous' to his own position by shunting me off to an activity which, he obviously thought, would keep me fully occupied and at the same time free him of my presence at the sessions of the General Assembly. And so he hit upon the idea of assigning me to the Commission on Non-Self-Governing Territories, which he regarded as a side-issue of little importance.

That Commission was composed of about ten or twelve representatives of member states of the United Nations, each state to be given a seat and a voice in it by rotation. In 1952 it was Pakistan's turn to be represented. The agenda of the Commission's forthcoming session, comprising the problems of the French protectorates in North Africa, was very much to my taste.

I told Ahmad Shah Bokhari that I would need a special secretary to work with me throughout the session, and he agreed readily enough, happy to have me off his neck. I declined the offer of a secretary from within the staff already employed at Pakistan House, who were chosen mostly for their appearance, and stipulated that I would engage one myself; and to this, too, he agreed without demur. I placed an advertisement in a couple of daily newspapers, and within a few days I had several applicants. Finally I chose the one with the best references: a girl of about twenty, small and dumpy and not at all pretty, but with intelligent eyes and a ready smile; her name was Rosie. I warned her that her task would not be an easy one and that there would be no limitation on our working hours. She was not frightened, and the next few weeks showed that I had made an excellent choice: never before had I had a secretary of a similar willingness and aptitude.

So as not to be disturbed, I decided to work in my apartment instead of my office room in Pakistan House. To begin with, I ordered copies of all the French documents and statistics relating to Morocco and Tunisia, especially the latter, which was first on the agenda. Most of these documents were obtained from the U.N. Secretariat, and the rest were secured for me through them from French sources. The result was a stack of cyclostyled papers nearly one metre high, and I set about with Rosie to go through each of them carefully. We read and re-read every scrap of those papers and made copious notes, until both of us were fully conversant with every item of importance. Rosie proved to be an admirable assistant, far better than an ordinary secretary would have been. Her memory was so keen that later on, during the sessions of the Commission, she always had the relevant document at hand, ready to be placed before me whenever I addressed a meeting.

We worked for nearly three weeks, every day from morning till lunch time, and then through the whole afternoon until late into the evening -- in the last days before the start of the session, until two or three o'clock in the morning. And then we were fully prepared.

VIII

The commission on Non-Self-Governing Territories met in one of the largest of the U.N. committee rooms. There was not only enough space for the official representatives and their staffs -- about twenty-five persons in all -- but a special gallery was provided for observers from countries not represented in the Commission as well as from such as were not U.N. members at all. Among the latter, naturally, the North

African observers predominated.

At the opening session it was proposed to elect the representative of Pakistan as chairman, and this proposal was accepted by a large majority. Before assuming my charge I took aside the representative of Great Britain (he was a First Secretary in the U.K. delegation and well-known to me) and placed before him the suggestion of a 'gentlemen's agreement': 'I shall refrain from attacking Britain or any British colonial administration on the condition that *you* do not interfere in any way with my tackling France. What about it?'

My British counterpart agreed without further ado, and I took my place as Chairman of the Commission. (From then on,whenever I addressed the meeting I stated at the outset whether I would speak in my capacity of Chairman of the Commission or simply as the representative of Pakistan.) After a few procedural questions and answers the meeting began in earnest.

In the midst of an expectant hush I declared that we would take up the internal conditions in Tunisia as the first point of discussion -- and I could see the French representative looking up at me with some apprehension. 'Unfortunately,' I went on, 'we have not been adequately supplied with documentation by the representatives of the Tunisian people as such, and therefore we are obliged to proceed exclusively on the basis of documents prepared by the Protective Power, that is, by the French administration of Tunisia . . . .'

At that, the French representative visibly relaxed while, on the other hand, the Tunisian observers -- in particular, Bahi Ladgham -- looked at me with some perturbation.

I continued: 'For a start, let us consider the arrangements made by the Protective Power in the matter of popular education'. . . . and Rosie, who was sitting behind me, immediately handed to me the relevant documents. 'Let us see,' I said. 'We have here the official statistics showing the allocation of places in elementary schools. From these statistics it appears that, for instance, in the city of Tunis about three hundred places have been allotted to native-born Tunisians, whereas a little over two *thousand* places have been reserved for pupils of European, that is; French descent . . . .'

(I must state at this point that the figures given by me here -as well as in the subsequent recital of the deliberations of the Commission -- are purely illustrative: they are based on memory alone, without any notes at my disposal at this time. Consequently, they must not be regarded as more than a remembered impression of a glaring discrepancy -- evident in the real figures appearing in the official documents -- between the treatment accorded by the French authorities to the 'natives' on the one side, and the Europeans on the other. The same applies to the figures given later on in this narrative with regard to hospital facilities, etc.).

The face of the French representative clearly registered his unease on listening to my recitation of the official statistics and their evidence of a brazen discrimination between the relatively small numbers of French residents and the masses of the indigenous population of Tunisia; and at the same time I could see that the Tunisians in the observers' gallery could hardly refrain from applauding my matter-of-fact enumeration of figures.

Next I brought up the question of hospital facilities (with Rosie placing unerringly the proper documents before me): 'We have here, as the official French statistics show, two hundred-odd hospital beds reserved all over the country for native-born Tunisians as against fifteen hundred beds reserved for Europeans . . . .'

And so it went on and on, from hospital beds to trade schools, from trade schools to clerical employment, and so forth and so on, always the same endless picture of discrimination and injustice.

After about half an hour's recital from the French statistics I declared: 'And now, gentlemen, I shall speak as the representative of Pakistan.'

Thus temporarily freed from the onus of partiality as Chairman of the Commission, I launched upon a clear-cut denunciation of French colonial policies, stressing the fact that the so-called 'protectorate' had reduced the powers of the Bey of Tunis to the point of total impotence and that, therefore, what we saw in that country was nothing but old-fashioned colonialism without any of the redeeming features which had been evident, for instance, in most of the British colonies: an impartial judicial system, a civil service with full native talent, and so forth. I concluded my speech with an appeal to the United Nations, of which Pakistan was a member, to speed up the process of a decolonization of Tunisia and North Africa as a whole.

The face of the French representative had by now assumed a greenish colour, and his angry reply was listened to without any evident support from most of the other Commission members, apart from the occasional fervent, 'Hear, hear!' by the Governor-General of the Belgian Congo, who was in person representing that colony at the Commission.

At the end of the meeting the observers from North Africa

crowded around me with happy faces and one after another of them embraced me.

IX

The sessions of the Commission for Non-Self-Governing Territories developed into a resounding triumph for me personally, and I presume that Ahmad Shah Bokhari regretted that he had shunted me off in this way: he simply could not digest the fact that this time it was I, and not he, who stood in the 'limelight'.

I must confess that I did not care much about his feelings, the more so as my private life was in those days extremely satisfying. I was deeply in love, and even during the weeks of absorption in the Commission work I found time to spend most of my evenings with Pola.

In those entrancing days of May and early June we discovered that despite the great difference in our ages and temperaments -- Pola was gay by nature, loved to laugh and to talk whenever she found herself in congenial company, whereas I was more self-sufficient and could remain silent for many hours -- we had many tastes in common. Like myself, she had discovered Lao-tse[4] at an early age and was fascinated by ancient Chinese landscape painting. Both of us loved oriental pottery and Persian carpets; both of us preferred the open country with its fields and forests to living in the midst of city blocks; to both of us dogs and horses and animals in general were far more attractive than cars and airplanes; and a painting by Rembrandt[5] or the sight of a medieval cathedral gave us both more pleasure than any of the 'wonders' of modern technology. In short, the better we came to know one another the more we became convinced that we shared common values and a common outlook on life and that, therefore, our living together would bring us happiness.

And having discovered all this, I asked her to marry me.

She was perplexed rather than surprised, and she turned slowly towards me and said, 'But, darling, you are already married -- and so am I.'

'Yes,' I replied, 'I am married, but I am no longer living with my wife and have no intention of living with her in the future. We have become estranged from one another, and there is nothing in common between us except our son. Moreover, I am a Muslim and my religion allows me to have more than one wife. Although I would not like to divorce her -because of our son -- we are already separated to all intents and purposes, and if you agree to marry me, her remaining outwardly my wife would not really play any role in your and my life. I would take care of her financially, and she could go on living with Talal, or alone, or with Chaudhri Niaz Ali and his family in Pakistan -- as she may prefer. As for Talal, you are so close to each other in age that you could become like brother and sister' (this was, of course, naive of me, but I really believed it at the time).

Naturally I realized that for a woman born and bred within Western society the idea of being a 'second wife' must be extremely difficult to absorb. But I knew, too, that Pola and I were already bound together and that to neither of us a life without the other was conceivable. She remained lost in thought for some time, and in the end she looked into my eyes and said slowly, 'Yes, I agree to be your second wife, although it will not be easy . . . .'

Thereupon I wrote to Munira in London and laid the situation before her. I assured her that even though we would not live together, she would still be formally my wife and that I would remain responsible for her maintenance on the same level as she had been accustomed to. I also appealed to Talal to try to help his mother to accept this solution; he had already had an intimation from me in Paris that I was seriously considering marrying another wife, and this many months before I had even *met* Pola.

In the expectation of Munira's answer and of further developments, Pola's and my life went on as before. We made plans for her flying to Mexico to obtain a quick divorce. We were meeting daily and discussing our future. And both of us were happy . . . .

Munira's reaction was swift and violent. She not only refused point-blank to accept my proposal, but she went straight to the Pakistan High Commissioner in London and told him that I intended to *abandon* her. She raised such a scandal that the High Commissioner not only saw fit to address to me a highly offensive letter of 'admonition', but also - quite unwarrantably -- wrote to the Governor-General of Pakistan, Khwaja Nazimuddin,[6] asking him to intervene directly in the matter. It goes without saying that all this proved highly damaging to my position in the Foreign Service, to the delight not only of Ahmad Shah Bokhari but many other envious or ambitious people. And then there appeared the 'fine Italian hand' of Zafrullah Khan, who had his own particular interests in mind.

Under the existing rules, if a Foreign Service officer wanted to marry a non-Pakistani national he was required to apply for special permission from the Governor-General. The application had to be accompanied by a formal letter of resignation from the service: if the permission was granted, the letter of resignation would be returned to the applicant; if not, the resignation would be regarded as final. I had no doubt about the outcome: I proposed to marry an American -- that is, the national of a country with which Pakistan had most friendly relations -- and a convert to Islam as well. And since recently a very junior member of our Foreign Service had been granted permission to marry a German girl, I was sure that I would be accorded the same treatment. To make doubly sure, I requested Zafrullah Khan -- who had known Pola for well over a year before I made my appearance on the scene and had often lunched with her during his many visits to New York -- to put in a word with the Governor-General, which he promised to do. And so I sent in my application.

About a fortnight later I received a staggering answer; my application had been rejected and my resignation accepted. Munira's intervention with the High Commission in London had born bitter fruit . . . . I had no alternative but to divorce Munira because after the scandal which she had caused there could no longer be any *possibility* of remaining man and wife, even in the most formal sense of the word.

It was about this time that I received a brief letter from my son Talal declaring, 'My father is dead.' Although I realized that this was an emotional response, it did, of course, hurt me very deeply. A few weeks later he turned up, unannounced, in New York, having borrowed the airplane fare from my step-brother Martin[7] in London. His purpose: to persuade me not to marry Pola. Both Pola and I tried, of course, to make Talal understand that this was not, nor ever could be, a break with him nor the end of the world, but he returned to London almost immediately, obviously unconvinced.

And life somehow went on, for all of us.

Endnotes

1 Patras Bukhari (1898-1958). Principal of the Government College, Lahore (1947-1950) and a famous satirist of Urdu literature.

cf. *On this Earth Together. Ahmad S. Bukhari at UN, 1950-1958.* Compiled and edited by Anwar Dil. Islamabad etc., 1994; Col. Ghulam Sarwar: *Patras–A Study* (in Urdu), Rawalpindi 1985; Dr.Daud Rahbar: *Tasleemat*, Lahore 2004, pp. 104-118.

2 Muhammad 'Allal al-Fāsi (1906-1973); statesman, politician and educationist; forced to leave Morocco (for the nationalist activities), 1932, returned (1934); imprisoned (1935-1936); leader Hizb al-Istiqlal since 1956; Minister for Muslim Affairs (1981); authored *The Independence Movement in Arab North Africa* (1954); a member of Muslim World League (Mecca) and was among the partisans of the divergent currents of the neo-Salafiyah.

Al-Fasi was an intellectual, historian, legal scholar, teacher, poet, political leader and founder of the Istiqlal Party.

He was an Islạmic modernist and reformer, advocating Islamic renewal, a return to original sources, Arabic language reform and avoidance of imitating the West. He was an early critic of the protectorate and an advocate of Moroccan independence.

cf. *Schulze*, pp. 126, 156, 203, 219; Annon Cohen: "Allal al-Fasi, his Ideas and his Contributions towards Morocco's Independence" (in: *Asian and African Studies* 3 (1967), pp. 121-164); Attilio Gaudio: *Allal El Fasi, ou, l'histoire de l'Istiqlal.* Paris 1972; see the English translation of his book by Hazim Zaki Nasiba: *Independence Movement of Arab North Africa.* Washington D.C. 1954.

3 Pola Hamida Kazimirska (1926-2006), Asad's last wife who was also a converted Muslim. He married her on 1st November 1952 and dedicated his *The Road to Mecca* to her. She was twenty-six years younger than Asad. His first German wife, Elsa, was twenty-two years older than her husband.

cf. Asad's letters to Altaf Husain (Editor of *Dawn*), 16 June 1953, New York and to Zahid Husain (ex-Governor, State Bank of Pakistan), 8 July 1953, New York.

4 Chinese religion of the sixth century B.C.

Wing-tsit Chan: *The Way of Lao Tzu.* New York, 1963.

5 Rembrandt (1606-1669), Dutch painter and etcher; leading representative of the Dutçh School of painting and master of light and shadow.

6 Khwaja Nāzimuddin (1894-1964), Prime Minister of Pakistan (1951-1953).

7 Martin Manfred Goldenberg (1916-), step-brother of Asad. He wrote an article on Asad's death (1992):

"From Galicia to Granada", in: *Association of Jewish Refugees from Germany in Great Britain. Information*, June 1992, p. 7.

* * * * *

PART TWO

(Pola Hamida Asad)

ملو جمال پور۔ ضلع پٹھانکوٹ (پنجاب)

3 اکتوبر

مخدومی - السلام علیکم و رحمۃ اللہ۔ نوازش نامہ ملا۔ [illegible]

[illegible]

والسلام۔

خیر اندیش

نیاز علی خاں

Ch. Niaz 'Ali's letter (3 Oct. 1937) to Mawlana Mawdudi. The names of Iqbal and Asad are also mentioned.

XI
'THE ROAD TO MECCA' (1952-54)

At this point in time -- 1952 -- the manuscript of Muhammad Asad's memoirs comes to an end. It has been difficult for me, his wife, to persuade him to undertake it at all; for years I have been pressing him to do so, and many of his friends supported me. He insisted, 'There cannot be a second 'Road to Mecca', and I agreed with him. But what I wanted him to do was to set down for the record, so to speak, some of his experiences, some of his accomplishments over the rest of his life -- a large part of his life -- after leaving Arabia in 1932. 'The Road to Mecca' was, of course, a *spiritual* autobiography, not only about his inner self but about Islam and his beloved Arabia, the land that gave birth to Islam, and about the royal House of Ibn Saud, with which he was destined to remain so closely and indissolubly linked until his death.

From now onwards, from the year 1952 to 1992, the story of my husband's life can only be related by simple narrative, and only by me. Although I shared the last forty years of that fantastic life, I am not a writer and can only present, so to speak, the bare bones of that life. Any lapse of memory or error in dates and circumstances -- and I am convinced that there will not be many — will be mine alone. But our long life together began exactly at the point at which he laid down his pen: with 'The Road to Mecca' -- the first book ever to have been dedicated to me. . . .

I

Some time during the late summer of 1952, during which the personal and governmental decision about my husband's future in the Foreign Service were being discussed, he came together with an old friend, or rather writing acquaintance, from the Twenties: Quincey Howe, the editor of a well-known American journal that had translated and published a number of his articles about Middle East which had been written originally for the 'Frankfurter Zeitung'.[1] He, in turn, introduced Asad to Joseph Barnes, then literary director of the famous publishing house of Simon and Schuster.

In the foreword to 'The Road to Mecca' entitled 'The Story of a Story' my husband described this first meeting with Joe Barnes, and how insistent the latter had been that the story of his conversion to Islam and his subsequent life in Arabia *must* be shared with the reading public. Actually, the idea had been brewing in my husband's head for a long time but he never had the necessary stimulus, or opportunity, to do anything about it. And now it occurred to him: When I leave the Foreign Service I shall sit down and write the story of my early life and all that drove me towards the most important decision of my life: that of embracing Islam.

And so, when his resignation was accepted and he was once again the free man that he had always been up to the time of his government service, Muhammad Asad returned to his writing career, the only one that had really been his own and the only one that truly satisfied him.

We were married on the first of November at a civil ceremony in a small town in upstate New York, with the obligatory two witnesses; thus it was in that sense fully in keeping with the concept of an Islamic marriage -- that is, proclaiming our union before two witnesses and the world at large.

Shortly before, Asad had found for us a small but elegant apartment on one floor of a three-storey town-house on Manhattan's East Side. The location, 3 East 80th Street, was excellent because it was just off Central Park and within walking distance of the Metropolitan Museum of Art, bus-stops, etc.. While I was at my office during the daytime he would prowl the second-hand shops on Second Avenue where he found excellent pieces of used furniture, some of them antiques, at very modest prices, which was all we could afford with my modest pay and his equally modest advance for his prospective book, not a line of which had yet been written.

The day on which we were married was what they called in America an 'Indian summer day', a false and short-lasting warmth preceded and followed by real October chill and November frost. We had a small party in the evening for a few friends at, I remember, a restaurant called 'The Polonaise'.

And that's how our new life started. During the daytime he sat down to writing, while I was at my office, and in the evening, having cooked a light meal together -- usually Pakistani food -- we often took a walk along Madison Avenue, looking into the shop windows along the way at the displays of carpets and antiques.

As mentioned earlier, we shared a taste for Chinese landscape painting, Middle Eastern pottery and Persian carpets. There was no question of buying these things in antique shops, but we began to frequent the pre-viewing of auction houses such as Parke-Bernet and other lesser known places -and in the course of the next few years picked up, literally 'for a song', several beautiful examples of all these things. There were not many collectors of this kind of art in New York of those days; our only competition was the knowledgeable Armenian dealers, but for the most part we concentrated on smaller auctions where those experts were less liable to turn up. I can still remember the oriental expertise of my husband in keeping his *sang froid* at auctions, something which I was entirely unable to do, as I was unable to bargain in our later years in the Middle East and Pakistan. With all his Western upbringing, Asad was entirely an 'oriental' in such matters and he always remained a harmonious combination of what was best in the West and the East without the least contradiction. In much later years I was to meet another man who contained within himself that ability to 'fit' into the Western world without losing or sacrificing anything of his Eastern self. He became our closest friend: his name was Shaikh Ahmad Zaki Yamani -- but I am years ahead of myself.

Speaking of friends, we had a small number of them during our two years in New York. There was Joe Barnes, who aside from his professional relationship with my husband, became a friend as well. There were Asad's two cousins who, after leaving Austria just in time before Anschluss, had eventually settled in New York -- the one, Fred Taubes,[2] having become a well-known and successful painter and the other, John Taeni,[3] a Wall Street broker, equally successful. Other friends were Rudolph and Marysia Rathaus, prominent Polish emigrés and old friends of my first husband's and more recently of myself and Asad. And there were occasional pleasant encounters with Dorothy Thompson and her husband Max Kopf; she was at that time very much involved with The American Friends of the Middle East, an early, fairly useless attempt to set the record straight about the Arab-Israeli conflict. Of our Pakistani friends at the Mission, only Akbar Tyabji and his wife Sorayya, a beautiful and intelligent Indian princess, remained loyal. Akbar was then either first or second secretary at the Mission; he later went on to become Pakistan's Ambassador in Morocco and afterwards in Indonesia.

Years later, Akbar told us about a conversation that took place in his presence at that time between Amir Faysal, who had come on a visit to the United Nations, and Zafrullah Khan, the Foreign Minister who manoeuvered Asad's exit from the Foreign Service. Amir Faysal, who had observed that my husband was no longer present in the Pakistani delegation, inquired about what he was doing, where he was, etc.; Zafrullah's only answer was, 'He is no longer *with* us', which carried -- as it was intended to carry -- a hint of disloyalty.

In fact, false and misleading rumours about the *reason* for my husband's leaving the service started to come in from all sides. There was always the hint of disloyalty, or worse. Reports that Asad had 'abandoned Islam' and 'reverted to Judaism' were circulated; also that he had married a Polish-American Jewess (I had been a Catholic up to the time of my acceptance of Islam). All these and many other rumours had one thing in common: they originated either in Pakistan House in New York or in the Foreign Ministry itself. Finally, my husband wrote to Zafrullah Khan and requested him to put the record straight by making a statement of the true facts; his reply: 'I cannot run around chasing rumours . . . .'[4]

Fortunately, we had some very loyal friends in Pakistan itself who did not for a moment swallow such tales. Chaudhri Niaz Ali, Chaudhri Nazir Ahmad[5] (former Attorney-General of Pakistan), Mumtaz Hassan (Finance Minister), the Egyptian Ambassador in Pakistan, Dr. Abd al-Wahhab Azzam, the Syrian Minister Umar Baha al-Amiri, the Saudi Arabian Ambassador, Abd al-Hamid al-Khatib, and many, many others. And, of course, Asad's beloved friend, Muhammad Hussain Babri, the typewriter mechanic from Lahore, possibly the most loyal friend a man, or woman, ever had. A few years later, all these friends of Asad's came to know me and became *my* friends as well. Our friendships were always shared.

Only about a month after our marriage, with the first chapters of 'The Road to Mecca'[6] well under way, we received a visit from two Arab friends who were visiting New York: Shaikh Mustafa al-Zarqa, a well-known Islamic scholar and dignitary from Damascus, and Said Ramadhan, at that time still the most active member of the Muslim Brotherhood of Egypt. His wife, Wafa, whom we met a few years later, was the daughter of the founder of the Brotherhood, Shaikh Hassan al-Banna: with her gentle simplicity and loyal support for her husband in good times and bad, she was and is a worthy daughter of that great and often misrepresented Muslim leader.

These friendships lasted throughout our lives and the friends from those early days who are still alive have tried to support me in my days of sorrow.

II

of course, shortly after our marriage on the first of November Asad and I went up to visit my family in Boston, to acquaint them with my new husband. My father had already died before we had met and my mother was now living with one of my sisters, Wanda, and her husband. My other sister, Regina, lived nearby; shé was married to a gigantic American of Scots-English provenance, David Sherwood. He eventually became President to Prudential Assurance of America, a short time after my sister's early death at the beginning of 1965.

The danger in writing about shared life is that, without realizing or intending it, one writes too much about one's *own* life, and mine is really unimportant to anyone but myself. I shall try to avoid this and touch upon persons and events that primarily concerned my husband.

Towards the end of 1954, except for the final chapter, 'The Road to Mecca' was practically finished. Simon and Schuster were eminently satisfied with the result of the last nine months' work and there were no suggestions about re-writing or making any changes. Publication was planned for the spring. Then, as often happened with Asad, with just the final pages to be completed, he caught the flu. The result was that the publication date had to be put off until autumn and that it was highly unlikely that we would be able to be present at the time of publication and launching: a very important time for the author of any new book.

The reason was financial. With the completion of the work, we could hardly expect any more advances before the publication itself. I still had my job, but that was not enough. We were still sending remittances to Talal and his mother in England, but how long could this continue? Also, Talal had dropped out -- from lack of real interest, he later admitted -from his studies at the Royal Institute of Architecture to which Asad had with such difficulty got him to be admitted. Now he had taken a job to help financially and was still groping his way to his future career as an academic. He eventually became a most successful, perhaps brilliant professor of social anthropology, for many years in England at the University of Hull, and, at the time of this writing, in

New York City at the New School for Social Research. But I am supposed to be writing of *our* years in New York from 1952 to 1954 . . . .

While we were in a quandary about our immediate future, Asad was introduced to the owners of Germany's most important publishing house, S. Fischer Verlag. Before the Hitler period it had been the biggest publisher with the advent of the Nazis they had moved to Sweden, where Mr Bermann, the husband of the Fischer heiress, continued the business. After the war they had re-started in Germany, and both Mr. and Mrs. Bermann-Fischer were very much impressed by 'The Road to Mecca', which they had read in manuscript. Although they were Jews by religion and German by culture, they were also very liberal and deeply-cultured *Europeans*, and it was obvious that Asad's having been born to a Jewish family as well as his openly-stated anti-Zionism did not trouble them at all. They wanted to publish a German translation of 'The Road to Mecca',[7] but only on the condition that it would be Muhammad Asad that would translate it -- in short, re-write it -- in German. He agreed to this, but insisted that it was impossible for him to write in German after so many years of writing exclusively in English without spending a period of time in Germany itself, where he would once again speak German, think in German and, consequently, *write* in German. And so we decided to go to Germany. We literally had to 'borrow' from my mother the fare for the Norwegian freighter which was to take us from Brooklyn Harbour to Antwerp.

A few weeks later we took fond leave of my family in Boston and friends in New York, several of whom we were never to meet again . . . .

III

It was very pleasant on the Norwegian freighter, where we had a small stateroom with bath. There were several cultured people on board, one of whom was a German photographer who had published a number of art books on Tuscany and other places. The company, thus, was excellent, the food execrable; but that didn't matter. We were very happy and it actually was like a honeymoon trip because in New York we had neither the time nor the money for such a luxury. This was my first ocean voyage, and Asad's first trans-Atlantic one, but neither of us felt the least hint of sea-sickness. It was a beautiful week or so -1 can't exactly recall how long it took the small ship to cross the rough Atlantic. Then, one late afternoon, before sunset, we arrived at Flushing, just outside Antwerp. The flat light-blue waters reflected a thin coat of gold from the sun, wavering and shimmering like satin; I don't remember ever having seen anything quite so beautiful, and the memory of it remains to this day, nearly forty years later.

Our author-photographer friend from the ship was planning to go on to Bruges, but our straitened finances could not bear even this small side-trip, and so we went on alone to Brussels, where we found a cheap but comfortable hotel. This, remember, was my first experience of Europe, and even Asad had never been to Belgium.

We spent several days taking in the 'sights' of Brussels -- it was very charming then -- and enjoying the exquisite Belgian cuisine in quite inexpensive restaurants. Never since then have I had such lovely omelettes and green salads, or so it seems to me now. One day we were sitting in the Grande Place, the physical and architectural heart of Brussels, where they were retouching with fresh gilt the wrought iron splendour adorning the beautiful buildings and arcades. Suddenly, a couple of youngish men -- prosperous Americans by their dress -- sat down at the table next to us; one of them turned to his companion and asked, 'What is this old junk?', contemplating the world-famous square. This was my first experience of an American stereotype, a hold-over from America's more naive days which you rarely come across today – or so I hope . . . .

We soon had to leave Brussels, with much regret, for we were expected in Frankfurt, where the German publishing house was located. There, after some preliminaries, we came to the decision to go on to Hamburg, where Asad intended to begin working as soon as possible.

Was it in Frankfurt or in Hamburg -- or in Hannover -- that we met Asad's stepson Ahmad Schiemann,[8] and his wife Ruth? Asad had been reunited with Ahmad, or Heinrich as he was called in Germany, in Pakistan after the war where Ahmad, now adult and married and an engineer who had worked on space research, I believe at Peenemunde, spent a year or more on some project in Karachi and stayed with Asad and his family there. He was still in Karachi at the time of Asad's leaving the Foreign Service, but reacted in a just manner, in spite of some affection for Talal and Munira, and remained very close to Asad -- and thus to me -- until the present day.

I think the reason we went to Hamburg was that an old friend of Asad's, a publisher named Claasen -- since dead -lived there. He lived in a beautiful bourgeois town-house on the Alster, but he himself was anything but bourgeois. We took a small apartment in a private house and began to work in earnest. Hamburg was fun for both of us, and for me an eye-opener in many ways, but what we really needed was a small house in the country in order to be able to concentrate. So, after giving a series of talks on German Radio, which were later to be collected and published in book-form,[9] we left for the Black Forest, where we had arranged to rent what proved to be a fairy-tale cottage in a beautiful little resort town called Badenweiler. The owner was a well-known German lady-writer of earlier times, Annette Kolb. She was ancient by now and we never did get to meet her because she resided elsewhere. She was reputed to be an illegitimate daughter of the mad Ludwig of Bavaria -- or was it granddaughter?

We had some pleasant neighbours in Badenweiler -- a Mrs Schickele, widow of another well-known German writer, and Mrs Wally Ruge, the widow of a prominent doctor from East Germany, Dresden I believe, who had fled to the West. All of us were living in adjoining cottages outside of the little, elegant spa-town, and we spent many happy hours together. This was just the atmosphere that Asad needed for his entirely free re-writing of 'The Road to Mecca' into German, and he was very successful.

During the winter in the Black Forest we went to Bonn, at the invitation of the West German Government, and stayed later with Asad's old friend, the Pakistani Ambassador to West Germany, an aristocratic bachelor who put his whole luxurious house at our disposal. He gave several amusing dinner parties, among whose guests were highly-placed politicians and industrialists with somewhat questionable past credentials, but they were all civilized and charming and one didn't ask questions of people who were so friendly. The Ambassador's residence in Königswinter had once been the home of the Nazi Minister, Robert Ley. It was there that I had my first, and only, experience of a bathroom -- our bathroom -covered with Persian rugs. As for the rest of the house, it was also literally smothered in carpets of the finest kind; the Ambassador was a great collector, and these were his private property. It is a pity that I can't recall his name now; my husband would have. Every day his lunch consisted of two *meringues Chantilly* delivered to his home by the best of the many local patisseries . . . .

Our life in Badenweiler that winter and spring had a kind of enchantment never experienced by me before or after, except perhaps in Switzerland many years later. The winter was a harsh one, but we had German tile-stoves in all the rooms and even a young fraulein (actually a refugee from the east) to help us stoke and clean them and to look after the little, lightly-furnished cottage.

Apart from the main occupation of Asad's writing and my transcribing it into German -- a language which I neither knew nor liked – on a borrowed typewriter, we indulged during those months in long walks through the forest (after all, we *were* in the Black Forest) amidst snow-covered firs and tinkling icicles blowing in the lightest breeze. Asad invested in the first of his many walking sticks, and one for me as well, and we tramped along the logging paths and through the deserted forests of Germany, a delight not to be described in words. One day we set out early and entered the forest. The path, and then the logging road which we eventually stumbled onto, went on and on until suddenly we realized that it would not be possible to return the same way back to Badenweiler in the dark. But I was young and Asad only fifty-five years old, and he had always been a great walker. So we continued, tired but not exhausted, until we reached what was obviously a main road, and almost exactly opposite there appeared an old inn with smoke rising from its chimney. It was like a dream. I can never forget the smell that assailed us as we entered the door: of wood-smoke, beer, good cooking, human warmth . . . .

After inquiring and learning that in a few hours a bus would pass by which would take us back to Badenweiler -- not so far away as the crow flies but a great distance on foot through the forest as we had come -- we sat down to an inexpensive but glorious meal of *pfankuchen* -- thin German pancakes -- accompanied by *feldsalad* -- a wild green salad, small-leafed, which grew on the hillsides. Years later I was to encounter this salad again in Switzerland, where it was called 'rampon' and in Morocco, where it had been introduced by the French under the name 'doucette' -- but it never had the same taste as that first-ever *feldsalad* -- nor did any of the many happy ones in the future ever have the nostalgic quality that did that particular day when we hiked to Amsteg. Neither of us ever forgot it. Years later, when we went back on a visit, it was not the same. Nothing ever is . . . .

IV

But soon it was time to leave our temporary paradise. We went to Frankfurt again, where Asad had a stiff battle with the Jewish literary director of Fischer Verlag, who had obviously taken an immediate dislike to both the author and the book. But Asad remained firm in his conviction that it was a very *good* German book that he had produced, and the future reviews proved him to be right. He had, after all, for many years before the Nazi period, been famous for the quality of his language while writing for 'The Frankfurter Zeitung'; and his German was not tainted by the Nazi period, when so many German writers came to accept and use a somewhat debased language. Till this day, I am told, the German language has never really recovered from this unfortunate experience.

As usual, when the book was ready for printing and publishing, we were unable to stay on and enjoy the fruits of our labours. Again the problem was mainly financial. One day, still in Badenweiler, I came across two separate letters with the same return address in Pakistan lying unopened on Asad's work-table. This was an old habit of his -- a very bad one -which I had already discovered in New York: when I married him I found a whole drawer full of unopened, and thus unanswered, letters. This time, however, I put my foot down and insisted on his opening them. They contained an offer by an Islamic foundation in Pakistan to finance the writing of a book on the political principles of Islam and to have it published by the University of California Press in Berkeley, California. Of course this work was right down Asad's alley, so to speak, and he immediately answered and accepted.

Meanwhile, Asad had been longing for the Arab world, with all its human and climatic warmth, and he decided, almost overnight, that we would go to Genoa by train and find a ship to take us across the Mediterranean to Beirut. From thence we would go to Damascus, a city which he loved very much from his time there in the early Twenties.

So we took leave of our various friends in Germany – Germany had been kind to us and was nice in those days when people were still poor, a bit apologetic and very pleasant. We went by train by night across the high, mysterious Alps, gleaming in the moonlight; of course we didn't sleep. Very early in the morning we arrived in Genoa and looked for and found an inexpensive *pension*. Asad had been to Italy before, and had lived in the north, near Lake Como, for some time with his first wife Elsa, and had been very, very poor and happy. We were still poor and happy and he did not yet know Genoa and so we 'discovered' it together and have always loved it since. It is a genuine and very unpretentious city, proud, not living from tourists. We arranged there for a cabin on a boat which would be leaving shortly for Beirut; on returning to our *pension* we found that our whole room -- a very large one -- smelled of the huge single peach which we had bought earlier and left there for a few hours. There was never before such a sweet-scented peach; never again the taste of such a peach, although I was to eat them in many other lands. Like my husband's much earlier experiences of a watermelon eaten in Seistan in distant Iran, or the green-and-red apples of the Kulu Valley in the north of India -- these experiences are not exaggerated by the memory -- they really *were,* and they are not repeatable . . . .

V

Genoa provided the first taste of the East for me. The early renaissance churches and palaces with their black-and-white striped marble arches were to be repeated in the mosques in Syria, whence the style probably originated. But most of the palaces, subsequently turned into business offices and elegant banks, were purely Italian. It was, and is, a lovely, unsung city.

The boat which we took – I think it was a regular Egyptian line -- stopped at Naples, where we spent half a day exploring it, in the company of a young Syrian sister and brother on their way back from studies in Europe. Lovely Naples, with its strong Spanish undertones which I came to recognize only years later, in Spain itself. The dirt and the poverty were there, of course, but overshadowed by the charm of its sinuous, almost oriental, passageways and the liveliness of its people.

When we took ship again that evening I had had my first real inkling of the Mediterranean world -- a highly-civilized world, unique. When we landed -- several days? a week? -- later on the other side of the Mediterranean, I began to realize how very *real* were my husband's descriptions and appreciations of this peculiar Mediterranean world, especially its eastern side, in 'The Road to Mecca' I had so much to learn from him, and from life itself . . . .

I have often recalled since how, just after our marriage, I had said to my husband: '*You* have seen so much of the world; I will never be able to catch up with you.' And he replied, 'You just wait,' And he was right; although I never did 'catch up with him', in his matchless company I visited many countries and continents that I had never dreamed would come within my ken. And in the company of *such* a guide; he knew so much about so many peoples and places and events -- so much about *everything.* I never came to fully understand how so much knowledge had been acquired by him, and his memory for dates and places was prodigious -- although he often forget a *face* which should have been remembered, a strange lapse indeed and not quite comprehensible . . . .

And then, one morning, we sighted the shores of Lebanon in the hazy distance, and then the bustling port of Beirut, with the high bluish mountains in the background: *my* first sight of the East, albeit a familiar one to Asad since his first visit in 1922 . . . .

Endnotes

1 The present name of this newspaper is *Frankfurter Allgemeine Zeitung*.

2 Franziska Taubes.

3 Heinrich Feigenbaum *alias* Heinrich Taeni.

4 Asad strongly refuted the rumour that he gave up Islam, and again accepted Judaism. See for this controversy *Nawa-i Waqt* (Lahore), 28 October 1982, *Sidq-i Jadeed* (Lucknow), 15 January 1954.

According to Asad, the man behind this obnoxious campaign was Patras Bukhari (see his letter to Mumtaz Hasan, 17 June 1953, New York), supported by Zafrullah Khan, the Foreign Minister. *The Star* (English weekly) spearheaded this offensive against Asad (esp. 4 April 1954). On the contrary, Asad wrote many letters to his friends and press notes to various Arabic, English and Urdu newspapers and refuted this baseless propaganda.

See his letters written to Mumtaz Hasan, Zahid Husain, Ch. Nazir Ahmad Khan, Dr. Abdul Wahhab 'Azzam and Muhammad Husain Babri, Hameed Nizami, etc.; classifying statements sent to newspapers *Dawn, Nawa-i Waqt* (22 Dec. 1953), *Ihsan* and religious journals like *The Voice of Islam* (Karachi), Jan. 1954, *Sidq-i Jadeed* (Lucknow), 19 Feb. 1954, *The Islamic Literature* (Lahore), Feb. 1954.

A concerned passage of Asad's letter to Zafrullah Khan (6 July 1953, New York) is as under:

"I have no doubt that the ease with which the Government of Pakistan dropped me from service, in spite of the fact that a more generous interpretation of the existing regulations was possible, has greatly contributed to the impression that I was in some way a *persona non grata* with my own Government (Perhaps I am, but, if so, I should like to know why?)"

5 Chaudhry Nazir Ahmad Khan (1898-1980). Attorney-General of Pakistan (1959-1961) and the editor of a journal *al-Ahibba* (Lahore); see his autobiography *Dastan-i Hayat*, Lahore 1975.

6 *The Road to Mecca* (1st ed., New York/London: Simon and Schuster, 1954) or the spiritual journey of the author, is still a most popular book. Several editions and the translations in many languages, including Arabic and Urdu, have been published.

cf. Asad's letter to Altaf Husain (Editor, *Dawn*) 16 June 1953 New York: Muhammad Hūsain Babri (22 Feb. 1953, New York) and 15 Sept. 1954, Hamburg; Mumtaz Hasan (17 June 1953, New York).

According to Martin Kramer, "*The Road to Mecca* cannot be read as a document on historical truth about Arabia, Ibn Saud, or even the author's life. It is an impressionistic self-portrait that suggests more than itself. The face of its subject is in half-shadow." (*Gift*, I)

7 German edition of *The Road to Mecca* was published under the title *Der Weg nach Mekka* (Berlin–Frankfurt a.M.: S. Fischer, 1955). Soon it became very rare and now one can hardly find it, even in the big libraries. For its review, see *Der Spiegel* (1956).

8 Heinrich (Ahmad) Schiemann (1916-2002), the step-son of Asad's first German wife, Elsa (Islamic name 'Aziza Muhammad'). He spent some years in Pakistan as an employee of a company. For his article "Verwandschaft und Familie", see H. Becker et al (eds.): *Erziehung und Politik. Minua Specht zu ihrem 80. Geburtstag.* Frankfurt a.M. 1960, pp. 356-366.

9 For the list of Asad's German articles, see

Günther Windhager: *Leopold Weiss alias Muhammad Asad. Von Galizien nach Arabien, 1900-1927*: Vienna 2002, pp. 206-208; ibid.: *Muhammad Asad–Leopold Weiss (Travels in Saudi Arabia).* Arabic tr., Riyadh 2011, pp. 80-83.

Asad's first German book *Unromantisches Morgenland. Aus dem Tagebuch einer Reise* (Frankfurt a.M., 1924; now available in English tr. *The Unromantic Orient*, op. cit.) is primarily based on these articles.

* * * * *

Vol. XII N

ISLAMIC CULTURE

The Hyderabad Quarterly Review

April, 1938

EDITED BY MUHAMMAD ASAD-WEISS

"Islamic Culture" (Hyderabad Deccan, April 1938), edited by Muhammad Asad

XII
THE FERTILE CRESCENT
(1955-57)

I

I seem to recall that we were met at the dock in Beirut by our old friend Said Ramadhan[1] -- my 'twin', because he and I were born on the same day, month and year. Later I came to learn that we had many qualities -- and faults as well -- of temperament in common, both of us being very thin-skinned and nervous, but also impulsive and quixotic. We were to go on immediately to Damascus, where Said's wife, Wafa, and the children were living; I believe that she already had one or two of her children by then.

We went by car through the rolling, already slightly desert landscape of the road from Beirut to Damascus -- which I was later to know so well -- stopping over in Chtoura in the Bekaa for a lunch of Lebanese dishes, until that time unknown to me but much loved by my husband -- especially *tahina, humus* and the salad dishes so beloved by those inhabiting the Fertile Crescent, as well as those abroad, non-Arabs as well. I never did come to appreciate them, but later the sweets of Damascus -- the best in all the Arab and Muslim countries and perhaps in all the world -- and the wonderful slightly chewy ice-creams and sorbets, caught and held my taste-buds for life.

And then we reached the Lebanese-Syrian border, to be told: 'You are not allowed to enter Syria; you are on the blacklist!' My husband was astonished. Both the President, Shukri Quwwatli, and Faris al-Khouri were old and dear friends of his. Then, after much conversation and some insults, Asad and Said were told the reason: the false rumours that had been spread about Asad's leaving the Pakistan Foreign Service and becoming a 'Jew' had reached the Ministry of the Interior and had apparently been accepted at face value!

There was nothing that we could do but return to Beirut, where apparently no such rumours had been spread, or at least been accepted. We spent a few hectic days there, where Asad insisted upon exposing me to instant dysentery on the theory that Americans had to build up resistance by eating *everything,* including salads and unpeeled fruit. Since *he* had never experienced a similar misery, it simply did not occur to him that on practically the very first day of my stay in Lebanon and Syria, I would come down with an infirmity that I would not get over for several years -- that is, until we reached Pakistan, where the hot spices apparently had a medicinal effect. And it never happened again.

After a few telephone calls to Damascus the 'misunderstanding' was cleared up and when we arrived there a few days later we were met by many old friends. Asad was received at his office by Shukri Quwwatli with great warmth, and we both called on Faris al-Khouri, by now a fast friend to *both* of us, in his lovely traditional house in the hills above Damascus. How many more times were we to meet that sweet little man; the last time in Geneva, when we resided there some years later. And he never changed, just becoming a little bit more bowed, until finally he faded away. Our last meeting in Geneva I remember well: he was quite ill and almost blind already, and in the course of our always lively conversation he remarked: 'I wish I could die with the faith of old women . . . .' I understand now what he meant; it is a very *special* kind of faith -- no questions asked, no questions needed . . . .

II

Asad knew Damascus extremely well. He loved it particularly and he often described it to me. It was *really* an oriental city that time, in spite of so much of it having been permanently destroyed by French shelling. But the *souks,* even the partially restored Hamidiyya bazaar, were full of oriental goods, together with those of Western provenance, and most of the women were covered in long black outer garments, although not all were veiled. It was in the street of the Hamidyya bazaar that I was pinched on the bottom for the first, and I hope the last, time – hardly a place where one would have expected such a thing to occur. I remember that I did not tell Asad what had happened until long after the event; I think that he would have reacted violently, although he was never a violent man.

In Damascus we called on Shaikh Abd al-Aziz bin Zayd, the Saudi Arabian Ambassador. He had been a great friend of my husband's in Arabia, and he treated Asad's young and very inexperienced and entirely unveiled wife with grave courtesy -- that peculiarly *Arabian* courtesy which I was to experience over and over in later years, up to the present day. By this time I had come to understand *why* my husband had literally fallen in love with the Arabs so many years ago. The true Arab gentleman – and lady, for that matter -- has often been described, but no words can really do justice to what this noble race is *really* like . . .

Outside of Damascus we visited the romantic house which Asad's friend, Shaikh Abd al-Hamid al-Khatib, had built for his new Syrian wife. He had been Saudi Arabian Ambassador to Pakistan in Asad's Karachi days, but had retired in Damascus, where he had recently married. The house was in the open countryside on a huge property planted with every kind of tree, flowering and fruit. Through the middle of his large, marble-floored and, of course, oriental-carpeted drawing room a stream had been led through, with a fountain in the centre interrupting the flowing water and continued on into the garden. It was a revelation of Arab taste, culture and comfort, and somehow it did not even overwhelm one because it was so lovely. A pale reflection it was of the promise of Paradise in the Qur'an -- it really *had* a Qur'anic flavour because in a strange way it was also modest.

In Damascus friends -- Faris al-Khouri among them – suggested that we should spend summer in a rented house in one of the cooler resorts, either Bloudan or Zebadani. We made the mistake of choosing the latter, because it was cheaper, and came to regret it: nay, we practically *fled* from it . . . .

III

At that time, early 1955, very few tourists came to Syria; it was also a time of political agitation both in Syria and in Egypt. Gamal Abd al-Nasser[2] was then at the peak of his popularity. When one spoke English in taxis, the drivers and other passengers looked askance. I remember Asad putting one such driver in his place by telling him, 'This is *our* country, as well.' The driver became furious, thinking that we were European 'colonialists' -- until Asad explained that we both were Muslims and on *his* side, as against the British and French. He immediately changed his tune and became, indeed, very, very friendly. After a short time I came to understand why the Arabs then carried such a 'chip on the shoulder'; they had been so much misunderstood and misused by most of the Western powers . . . .

But Zebadani was different; it simply wasn't used to foreigners *as such,* and plainly didn't welcome them -- us. Innocent little children were encouraged to throw stones at us in the street, there was hostility everywhere except from the local government administrator (mayor?), a handsome young Syrian nationalist, a member of the Ba'ath Party, but not hostile to the foreigner; he behaved like what he was -- a Syrian gentleman.

During these few months in hostile Zebadani we often called on Faris al-Khouri, who always summered in the neighbouring, more sophisticated mountain town of Bloudan. Since summer was almost over, there was no point in our shifting there, but with its gardens full of enormous, heavily-scented, dark red damask roses and its best hotel serving a magnificent international fare, it was pleasant to visit and somehow reassuring.

IV

Now we decided that with the agitation going on in Damascus because of the Suez Canal crisis, and the onset of winter, which can be very hard in badly-heated Damascus, to return to Beirut and sit down to write. After all, Asad was *supposed* to be producing a book!

We took an apartment in central Beirut, but neither of us had anticipated how incredibly noisy it would be. We furnished it very sparsely, waiting for our household goods to arrive from New York, where they had been in storage for several years. But the noise was overwhelming and I, in particular, had and have no immunity to noise. There was the noise of the street traffic, the noise of the church-bells, the noise of the loudspeakers on the mosques, the noise of the people in the flat above pounding in a mortar for hours on end – usually at the break of dawn – the cracked wheat to be used for their favourite dish, *kibba*, which I in any case heartily detested. None of this was conducive to turning out a book, and a very serious one at that. And so we decided, on the good advice of our dear friend Dr. Mustafa Khalidy, to take up quarters on one whole floor of his palatial summer house in the mountains of Aley; he even provided the servants who lived there throughout the year. The idea was an excellent one but, unfortunately, when we returned from our investigation of the possibility of living alone, cut off from most of our friends, in the hills (cold in winter), Asad began to feel ill. That evening we had a rendezvous with, of all people, Zafrullah Khan, who was passing through Beirut and had somehow learned of our presence there. We met for dinner -four of us, for Zafrullah was accompanied by a handsome young Syrian who, it turned out, was the brother of Zafrullah's 'intended'; the marriage was to take place shortly in Damascus and Bushra, that was her name, was a member of the Ahmadiyya sect, so all should have gone swimmingly. (As a matter of fact, it didn't; not long after their marriage they were divorced and Zafrullah never married again. He was already well into his seventies at that time.)

During dinner, which was somewhat strained, what with all that had passed with regard to Asad's 'forced' resignation -never even referred to again by any of us -- Asad started to have violent abdominal pains and we had to break up earlier than expected. After a bad night Dr Khalidy insisted that he go to hospital – a Catholic hospital with an excellent reputation. There, upon examination it was pronounced that he had gall-bladder trouble and would have to be operated at once. I had the sense to protest, and the decision was postponed. He was recovering with treatment and rest and diet when he began to suffer from the cold in the unheated room; although it was December and there was central heating, it was never turned on. The result was that he came down in hospital with pleurisy! His suffering was enormous. Even when we were finally allowed to leave to go up to the 'summer house' in Aley, he was still suffering, although I recall that we had some kind of heating, at least in the bedroom. A kind friend obtained from his doctor a vial of morphine to be taken only in case of unbearable pain. I sat through long nights with him when he was hitting his head against the wall in pain, but when he was finally cured of his pleurisy -- or, rather, by miracle survived it -- I found the unused vial of morphine untouched and we got rid of it. Later we were told by old Shaikh Abd al-Aziz bin Zayd that, had he known of it, he would have sent us an experienced beduin who would have 'burned' it; and it is really true: drastic and 'primitive' as it may seem, it would have cured him quickly and avoided much long-drawn-out and totally unnecessary suffering . . . .

V

This was in some ways a 'nightmare period' for both of us. But we were fortunate in having several very good friends and that made all the difference. Foremost among these was Philippe Khoury -- or Khwaja Philippe as he was called by the local Druze peasants. Philippe was a Greek Orthodox Christian, not particularly religious, but traditionally so, and extremely open-minded to people of other faiths, including members of the so-called 'fanatical' Muslim Brothers. He came from a wealthy family from an area in northern Syria which had been annexed by Turkey, and had lived for many years in Cairo, dealing in the cotton exchange. He was a wonderful friend and, since he lived not far from our 'summer home' all the year round -- he enjoyed hunting for hares and pheasants in winter -- we had his excellent company on bitter winter evenings as well. He managed a hotel called 'The Green House' in the mountain resort of Bhamdoun. This hotel was owned by the Greek Orthodox Church, but in summer the clients were both Muslim and Christian. It was a moderately-priced 'family hotel' and beautifully lorded over by Philippe, who was urbane and kind and as great a gentleman as we would ever meet. He also owned a large paint shop in Beirut -- he was agent for ICI there. He often shopped for us when he went down to Beirut -- he always used a driver -and helped us in innumerable ways during Asad's long illness. After we left Lebanon we maintained close contact with him by letter throughout the years in Pakistan and Switzerland and finally Morocco. He already had cancer of the stomach when he visited us in Tangier in the middle of the Sixties, and he died shortly afterwards in Beirut, always remembering us to mutual friends -- and he sent us a last brief letter announcing his impending, inevitable death. He was a very brave man and a complete gentleman . . . .

Another frequent visitor to us in the hills was Abd al-Hakim Abdin, one of the leaders of Egypt's Muslim Brotherhood, in exile after Nasser's take-over in Egypt (the brave but foolish ones met with prison and torture and often death -- and they met it bravely). Abd al-Hakim was married to a sister of Hassan al Banna, as against Said Ramadhan's being married to his favourite daughter. At that time Said was the most active and vocal leader of this group in exile, but Abd al-Hakim attempted to displace him and there was little love lost between the two. And, then, Abd al-Hakim was always on the lookout for a second -- or third? – wife . . . .

Still, with all his obvious defects, Abd al Hakim was very kind and extremely helpful to us in his peculiar way and he visited us often. One day Asad mentioned how fond he was of *fool mudammass,* an Egyptian dish of cooked dried favas and lentils, eaten with olive oil and lemon and pepper over it. This is the classical breakfast dish -- a very substantial one -- of Egyptians, whether rich or poor. It is a wonderful dish. Abd al-Hakim, on hearing of our fondness for it, arrived the next day with all the necessary ingredients, including the necessary pot, prepared it and stressed that it had to be cooked over a minimal fire, preferably charcoal, all night long. The next morning we were awakened, early, by the smell of burning – no *fool* for us but many good intentions.

As the pleurisy improved slowly it became obvious that Asad

was still not really well, and one of our doctor friends -and we had many, and they invariably refused payment, being Muslims -- strongly suggested that we take an X-ray of Asad's lungs. In it appeared a shadow the size of a walnut and the alarmed technician insisted that Asad and I should go to the excellent government sanitorium for lung diseases high in the mountains above Beirut. There he was treated, for what specifically I do not know, but there was a dark hint of lung cancer which I kept to myself and never conveyed to my husband. Later, after he was well, it turned out that he had an old embedded amoeba which had probably caused all the trouble in the first instance. He never had a 'gall bladder attack' again in his life, although if he had had an operation, as originally suggested, he would certainly have had future trouble. But for the rest of his life, because of the pleurisy contracted in a first-class hospital, he always suffered from air currents, possibly a souvenir of these adventures in the Lebanon. Later, medical care in Beirut improved enormously and the hospital of the American University, in particular, was excellent. But I, for my part, never had confidence in a Levantine doctor again -- I put my confidence in Pakistani ones, who are among the best in the world.

Somehow or other, during all these ups and downs, the book suggested and subsidized by the foundation in Karachi was completed. It was translated into Urdu and later Arabic as well and published in the original English by the University of California Press in the U.S.A. under the title 'The Principles of State and Government in Islam';[3] it was a very important book, although written in such trying circumstances. The translator into Arabic -- Mahmoud Sharif -- later edited an important newspaper in Amman and is currently Minister of Information in Jordan. His brother, Kamil Sharif, a very dear friend for many years and also prominent member of the Muslim Brotherhood in those early times, eventually became ambassador of Jordan in many countries and later Minister for Religious Affairs.

'The Principles of State and Government in Islam' -- a very short and concise book -- was highly regarded, and still is, throughout the Muslim world and two of the best rulers of Pakistan, Ayyub Khan and Zia ul-Haqq, appreciated it so much that they utilized at least some of the ideas which it set forth. It is another of Asad's books that are 'before their time', if it ever comes . . . .

VI

In the meantime, while we were still in Germany, 'The Road to

Mecca' had come out in America, and was a great literary success. The prestigious 'Saturday Review of Literature' had a picture of Asad in his Arab dress on its cover and a glowing review of the book inside. We also learned that the Book of the Month Club had seriously considered it for their choice but that finally, because the five judges had to be unanimous in every choice, it was vetoed by one member, Clifton Fadiman, who happened to be a Zionist: financially it did not come to much.

Also, it was published shortly afterwards in Great Britain by Max Reinhardt and received excellent reviews, although for obvious reasons, not so warmly as it was in America; after all, Britain still had colonies and the bleary, somewhat tarnished memory of 'Lawrence of Arabia'. Later, the German edition received the same enthusiastic reception by the reviewers but did not, somehow, reach the general reading public. Years later we were to learn in Switzerland that almost the whole German edition had been bought up and taken off the market by some mysterious Jewish group or organization; we never bothered to try to track it down.

When we had first arrived in Beirut we had learned, by pure chance, that a Lebanese publisher had, without permission, translated 'The Road to Mecca' into Arabic and that it was in the press. This was found to be sadly true to the traditions in the Muslim world, but we stopped it in time to repair a *little* of the damage caused by a very bad translation. It never was good, but at least it was correct. Most of the famous lyrical passages describing the Arabian desert had been dropped because, according to the Lebanese translator, 'all Arabs know what the desert is like.' When Asad asked how this was so, he replied 'We have been across it by bus many times.' There was little that could be done with such a mentality, but in spite of the very mediocre translation the book became quite famous in the Arab world. And the publisher of the book and his charming, and innocent of these dealings, Palestinian wife became close friends of ours. My husband could never 'harbour a grudge' -- and neither could I.[4]

Over the years there have been more than a dozen authorized and possibly even more unauthorized translations and publications of this extraordinary book (as well as many of his others). Early in the Fifties there were Dutch and Swedish translations and subsequently French and Japanese and Serbo-Croat and many, many others. In our library downstairs there is a shelf covered with these many translations. But the thrill of that first publication shared by us, and dedicated to me in the first instance, has never worn off. The book has since become a classic, especially in the context of the old, pure Saudi Arabia of the time of the great Abd al-Aziz ibn Saud, upon the foundations of which the modern Saudi Arabia still stands. May it stand still solidly forever . . . .

VII

Beirut in the second half of the Fifties was the motor of the Arab world. Arabs from every country -- and especially Saudi Arabia and the Gulf -- flocked there in summer, building or renting houses in the mountains above the city. And so we were permanently meeting many old and new friends. One day there was a knock on the door of our modest rented house in Bhamdoun, and in came Dr. Zakir Hussain,[5] the first Muslim President of India. He had been a famous intellectual and educator in pre-Partition India and one of Asad's closest friends in the sub-continent. It was he who said to my husband, in the days before Partition: 'Asad, if I *really* believed that Pakistan would develop on the Islamic lines which *you* are propounding, I would join it. But you will see that it will be run only, or primarily, in the economic interests of a very small group of people . . . .' During this brief and completely unexpected visit, he and my husband spent several hours talking mostly about the past times in India; they never met again.

Another *new* acquaintance, later friend, was the Saudi Arabian Director of Information, Shaikh Abdallah Balkhair, whom we first met through our mutual friend Said Ramadhan. Shaikh Abdallah was visiting Beirut in the company of his bride, Aida, the beautiful young daughter of a prominent Jordanian family. Their happiness was almost palpable, and we understood it well, having ourselves been married for only four years.

Shaikh Abdallah was one of the first Saudis to have been sent abroad for education in the time of the great King Abd al-Aziz; I believe that he attended the University of Beirut. In any event, he was a middle-size, handsome, urbane man with a large stock of stories about the period almost immediately following Asad's departure from the Arabian scene -- the early oil period. He had been present at the famous conference between Ibn Saud and President Roosevelt[6] on the former's yacht off Casablanca; it was the first and last such meeting off the soil of Arabia of the great King, and it was a very successful one. At the time when we met Shaikh Abdallah in Beirut, King Saud was still in power; when he was finally removed in the ensuing conflict with Amir Faysal, it was only natural that Shaikh Abdallah left with him, but it was a pity because the services of such an able man should never be dispensed with, and he was still relatively young and very active. But usually new rulers, even in non-monarchic systems, prefer to have their 'own' men around them; and this is perfectly natural. But Shaikh Abdallah remained a prominent figure in Saudi Arabia and his articles in various newspapers and journals, reminiscing about the 'good old days', are said to be both very accurate and most entertaining. To this day one is always hoping for a book of his memoirs to be published, but perhaps because he was so close to events he prefers to keep silent on many subjects about which he is uniquely well-informed. As for his relations with Asad, they remained close and cordial to the very end, and when he visited us in our home in Tangier many years later, with his still lovely wife, we enjoyed ourselves immensely.

VIII

Although we lived in Beirut, we visited Syria often and I got to know Damascus very well. Apart from the usual sights – the *souks,* the lovely ancient mosques, the narrow, winding streets through which only humans and donkeys could pass -Asad took me to visit the grave of one of the greatest Muslim scholars of all times -- Ibn Taymiyya[7] -- which was situated in the grounds of Damascus University, surrounded by a simple wrought-iron fence. But I was horrified to find the enclosure filled with old tin cans and bottles: in short, it had become a kind of rubbish dump! We received a similar impression when we visited the tomb of one of Islam's greatest heroes and rulers, Salahuddin al-Ayyubi,[8] the famous 'Saladin' of Crusader fame. The largish enclosure was full of ladders, cackling chickens and the like, and we were both deeply shocked. And there were on the dangling, naked light bulbs which palely – and uglily -- illuminated the interiors of some of Damascus's finest mosques. All this distressed us so much that, upon my insistence, Asad took the matter up with some of his friends and it was finally openly discussed in the Syrian Parliament -- and, I believe, the situation was eventually rectified.

That was the period in which Asad made his only unsuccessful speech -- and before the same Syrian Parliament, at that. It was in commemoration of the great spiritual founder of Pakistan, Muhammad Iqbal, and the Pakistan Embassy approached my husband not only because he had been a close collaborator of Iqbal, but also because none of the Embassy staff had a sufficient knowledge of Arabic to be able to present such a speech. Now Asad had always been able to express himself in fluent, 'classical' Arabic. But the custom in the parliament and universitites of the Arab world, at all such public representations, was to speak in a particular, rather stilted and artificial way which my husband had never liked or bothered to master. Still, he had to do it and the speech was written out in that particular manner and so could not be spontaneous, as was his way of speaking in all languages. In addition, the lighting at the lectern was dim and Asad was long-sighted. The result was that he somehow got through the speech, but there was rustling and occasional rude snickering in the audience, and afterwards Asad said that he would never again address an Arab audience in that way. And he never did. But he always had a very thick skin and never took such incidents to heart. It was I who suffered on these very rare occasions . . .

We had been living almost three years in Syria and Lebanon when my husband received an invitation from the University of Lahore in Pakistan to organize an International Islamic Colloquium there. As we had for some time been considering returning to Pakistan, he decided to accept the invitation. Our farewells to our innumerable friends were not dramatic because we felt that they were not final, and most of them were not. Still, when we boarded the plane at Beirut I wondered if I would ever see that lively city again -- and I never did, except for a brief stopover of one day on our way to *hajj* in 1966, a little over ten years after our departure for Pakistan.[9]

Endnotes

1 Sa'id Ramadhan (d. 1995); staunch follower-founder of an Islamic movement in Egypt and Syria named Ikhwan al-Muslimun (The Muslim Brethren); son-in-law of Hassan al-Banna' (1906-1949); editor of "Al-Muslimun" (Cairo); obtained doctorate from Berlin; Egyptian nationalist President Jamal Abdul Nasir (r. 1951-1970) declared his party illegal and severe measures were adopted to crush this movement. Sa'id Ramadhan migrated from Egypt and spent some time in Pakistan. Later on, he laid the foundation of an Islamic Centre in Geneva which was linked with World Islamic League (Mecca).

cf. *EI*[2], (Leiden), vol. III, 1970, pp. 1068-107, with bibliography (art. G. Delanoue).

2 Jamal Abdul Nāsir (1918-1970), Egyptian soldier statesman and proponent of Arab nationalism; leader of the group of Free Officers which overthrew King Faruq in 1952, Col. Nasir became Chairman of the Revolutionary Command Council in 1954 and was elected president of the Egyptian Republic in 1956, a post which he held until his death.

cf. Robert Stephens: *Nasser, a Political Biography*. London 1971.

3 *The Principles of State and Government in Islam*, Berkeley 1961 (translated in Urdu by Ghulam Rasul Mihr, Lahore 1963) and Muhammad Arif Gill (Lahore 2000).

4 Arabic translation by 'Afif al-Ba'albaki, 2nd ed., Beirut 1964, introduction by 'Abdul Wahhab 'Azzam (1956); see Letter of Pola Hamida to Muhammad Husain Babri (13 April 1956, Beirut).

5 Roosevelt (1882-1945), thirty second president of the United States of America (1933-1945).

6 Dr. Zakir Husain (1897-1969). President of India. Cf. *Puraney Chiragh* (in Urdu), by Syed Abul Hasan Ali Nadvi, pt. II, Karachi 1981, pp. 62-86.
Islamic Culture (Hyderabad Deccan), April 1969.

7 Ibn Taymiyya (1263-1328), Hanbali theologian and jurisconsult; a prominent, influential and sometimes controversial thinker and political figure.
cf. *EI*², III (1971), pp. 951-955.

8 Salahuddin al-Ayyubi (Saladin), 1138-1193; the founder of he dynasty of Ayyubids and the Champion of the *Jihad* against the Crusades.
cf. M.C. Lyons and D.E.P. Jackson: *The Politics of Holy War*, Cambridge 1982; Hannes Möhring: *Saladin, the Sultan and his times, 1138-93*, tr. by David S. Bachrach. Baltimore, MD, John Hopkins Univ. Press, 2008.

9 For Asad's writings and speeches during the extensive travelling of Germany and the Middle East, see his letters to Muhammad Husain Babri (15 September 1954, Hamburg; 15 December 1954, Badenweiler; 17 February 1955, Badenweiler; 8 June 1955, Zebdani, Syria; 28 August 1955, Bhamdoon; 13 April 1956, Beirut; 26 December 1956); and to Mumtaz Hassan, 17 June 1953, New York.

* * * * *

XIII
PAKISTAN INTERLUDE
(1958-59)

I

At Karachi airport we were met, for a change, by old friends of *mine,* M. J. As'ad and his wife Farrukh. I had known As'ad in my pre-marriage days at the United Nations in 1950, and after his return to Pakistan in 1951 -- when he married Farrukh -- we had remained in close touch. They both were members of the Ahmadiyya community, and he had been the constant companion of Zafrullah Khan at the United Nations in New York. But these religious differences did not affect in the least the close friendship we always felt, nor As'ad's great admiration for the personality and work of my husband. As'ad lost his wife at far too young an age in 1988, and I my husband in February 1992; the friendship remains.

After a few days in Karachi -- a rather nondescript but not unpleasant port city -- and meeting other old friends of my husband, we proceeded to Lahore, where we found our beloved Muhammad Hussain Babri, the typewriter repairman, anxiously awaiting us. I well remember our stay at Faletti's, an old colonial landmark of Lahore, at that time the best hotel in town. It was singularly old-fashioned in its comforts as well, but we loved it. It was located in the heart of the 'new' city and from its windows you could gaze down upon the colourful population of Lahore at their labours, and smell the burning pats of cow-dung used to fuel the fires for their outdoor cooking; it rose in grey spirals to join the dusty air. It was an indescribable smell, somewhat acrid but surprisingly pleasant and somewhat evocative. I, for one, was enchanted by the colourful scene around me. And the food in the hotel itself was excellent, genuinely Pakistani and not toned down for tourists, of which at that time there were very few indeed.

Papaya for breakfast, rich *pilaus* and *achars* (pickled fruits and vegetables) for lunch and dinner and occasionally *nan,* the delicious bread of the Northwest Frontier Province, and of Afghanistan and Iran as well: thin, but soft inside, and crisp on the outside -- one of the best breads in the world and the only really good one in Pakistan or India.

At the university we called on the Vice-Chancellor, who was cold but polite. I immediately had the impression that he didn't like Asad and was perhaps unhappy at his choice as organizer of the forthcoming Colloquium because he, in the first instance, was the official host. But Asad, with his deep knowledge of Islam, his complete command of the Arabic language and his acquaintance with many of the personalities who were to participate in the conference, was the logical choice for organizing it and he had not the slightest intention of usurping the Vice-Chancellor's prerogatives. And, moreover, he had never solicited the post. Still, at the beginning, it seemed to promise well. A small office was assigned to him at the University, a male Pakistani secretary, not very bright, put at his disposal, and it was decided that I would assist in a purely honorary way, that is to say, without any 'position' and, of course, without salary. From the very outset I put my heart into it and we two devoted ourselves to this work with great enthusiasm, arriving by horse-drawn *tonga* for work and returning in the late afternoon to our rented house.

At first we rented a house in the same tree-shaded Chamba House Lane where Asad had been assigned a similar, neighbouring house in the time of his service for the West Punjab Government as Director of Islamic Reconstruction. It was a beautiful area, with old colonial-style houses having ample gardens redolent of *rat-ki-rani* ('queen of the night') -- called so because it gave off its heavy, almost overpowering scent only after dark. But when the monsoon rains began, we learned that the vaulted brick ceilings were not sound and awakened after the first rainfall to water almost pouring over our beds, so we had to find a new place. The new house which we rented at a very moderate rate from an old friend of Asad's, Sardar Shaukat Hayat Khan, was in the Model Town district, outside of Lahore, where most of the big new villas were located. It had been built by his brother-in-law, but before occupying it he had died and his widow was not yet certain whether and when she would take up residence in it. It had a very large garden and adjoined the property of Shaukat Hayat, so we were very fortunate in our neighbours, who showed us great friendship while respecting our privacy. Also, our furniture had arrived from Beirut just before we moved in, and so we were able to furnish the house in a style which it deserved. The car that we had purchased in Beirut just before leaving also arrived, and we no longer had to depend for transportation on the picturesque but not very comfortable *tongas,* which was a great relief because the treatment of the poor horses caused me great distress and often provoked me into protesting to the *tongawala,* who could not understand what could be the matter.

As for Asad's old friends and hence to some extent his former wife's as well, except for a few, who were quite nasty, the majority of them took me to their hearts -- especially Muhammad Hussain Babri, and later Chaudhri Niaz Ali Khan when we visited him and his large family on his vast lands in the country,[1] and Chaudhri Nazir Ahmad Khan, the former Attorney General of Pakistan, and his wife Hamida, who bore the same Muslim name that I had adopted. He was tall, extremely handsome and aristocratic in his bearings; she was tiny, not very pretty and most intelligent; they loved each other in a way which one rarely encounters in the East or in the West.

We often met Mumtaz Hassan, the Finance Minister, both in Karachi and in Lahore. He himself was from Lahore and he had several brothers, all prominent in one way or another; the one I remember best was Nasim Hassan,[2] a well-known barrister who lived and practised in Lahore. And there was A. D. Azhar[3] -- who practised yoga even to the end of his not very long life, when he shouldn't have. And there were so many others whose names I have since forgotten, but whose kindness to me -- a shy stranger with a 'cross to bear' in the intrusive 'presence' of a former wife -- can never be forgotten. All these people, who contributed so much to Pakistan's early political and cultural life, were gradually shunted from the regions of power, to the permanent loss of Pakistan itself . . . .

During a break in our work at the University, Asad took advantage of the opportunity to show me something of the vast country. We had been invited by General Bakhtiar,[4] the military commander of the Northwest Frontier region and a good friend of Field Marshal Ayyub, who later became President of Pakistan, to stay with him in his headquarters in Peshawar, and he arranged for us to visit the fascinating region, where we were cordially received by the local Pathan chieftains and regaled with delicious open-air meals of *kebabs* and other delights in various places all the way up to Landi-Kotal.

On the return journey we visited a number of Buddhist ruins, half-fallen *stupas* in an abandoned countryside. Pakistan is a land of many contrasts with its Attok forts and its jewelbox mausoleums for dead princesses, and some of the most beautiful mosques in the world, most particularly my favourite, the Badshahi Mosque in Lahore, to my mind the most beautiful mosque in the world, with the possible exception of that in Cordoba.

II

Our only problem, and our immediate reason for having come to Pakistan in the first instance, was the Colloquium, or rather the Vice-Chancellor of the University. Although Asad was supposed to have a free hand in the choice of the scholars and Islamic-oriented personalities to be invited to the Colloquium, he kept interfering and questioning the right of this or that person to be invited, and suggesting some definitely inappropriate ones. It had been decided from the outset that there would have to be more or less 'official' delegations from all the Muslim countries, which was somewhat delicate because of the obtrusive presence of Nasser in and outside of Egypt, but my husband believed that it would be possible to accommodate both pro-Nasser and anti-Nasser elements since this was presumably to be a *scholarly* conference. However, the petty-minded Vice-Chancellor chose to make an issue of it and brought his influence to bear on several 'big guns' on the committee, particularly Maulana Mawdoodi, who by this time had achieved a considerable following among certain factions in Pakistan.[5] Although he had defended Asad's reputation when he left the Foreign Service, they had never been particularly close, and never friends; he found my husband's ideas about Islam too liberal and although my husband had a certain respect for him as a scholar, their political and social ideas -- both based on their own concepts of Islam -- were poles apart.

I myself had met Maulana Mawdoodi only once -- and it was quite enough: a chance meeting at Lahore airport, where my husband introduced me to him. Of course I knew better by then than to give him my hand, after certain embarrassing experiences in Damascus, but I was really shocked when he did not answer my greeting of *as-salamu alaykum* – the traditional Muslim greeting -- probably because he did not approve of my European dress, although it was extremely modest, or the fact that I didn't cover my face and head, let alone my *hands*. This lack of response to the greeting of 'Peace be upon you' had never happened to me before, even with the most conservative of Muslim scholars in Syria, and it never happened to me again. It was like a pointed insult -- as it was probably meant to be.

Anyhow, the upshot of all these intrigues and shadow-plays -- unfortunately very Pakistani in nature -- was that my husband decided to hand over the work to the Vice-Chancellor himself and to step aside. Everything had already been accomplished. I believe that even the air tickets had been issued, and it did not much matter to Asad that he would not even be a *participant* in the Colloquium, although in view of his standing as a scholar both in Pakistan and in the entire Muslim world it appeared, to the other participants, very peculiar.

And so we were experiencing a repetition of what had happened to us in New York.[6]

Many of the Colloquium guests made it a point to contact my husband, and we were made particularly happy by the presence of Dr Abd al-Wahhab Azzam, the former Egyptian Ambassador to Pakistan. Now I finally met this tall, elegant gentleman-scholar, one of the last to carry proudly on his head a tall Turkish-style *tarbush* which was the headgear of all the upper classes of Egypt in earlier times. His personal warmth and the fascination of his broad and lively mind captivated me, as it had earlier captivated Asad, and when we learned several years later of his death in Saudi Arabia, we were deeply grieved. After Nasser's conquest of political power in Egypt, such moderate Islamic elements as the Azzam family, the natural leaders of Egypt, were no longer welcome, and Abd al-Wahhab went to Saudi Arabia, where he was appointed the first Rector of King Abd al-Aziz University, a fitting choice. His daughter was married to one of King Faysal's outstanding sons, Muhammad, who was later to found a series of Muslim -- Islamic -- banks not based on the payment of interest. It was a bold and not completely successful attempt, in view of the complicated ways of banks in the Western world which completely dominate all others -- but it was a bold step in the right direction. We came to know Prince Muhammad and his immediate family many years later, in and outside of Arabia.

III

Apart from our personal disappointment, life in Pakistan was not its best in this period, although I felt completely 'at home' there. The central Government's popularity had never been so low; it was neither Islamic nor even efficient. Corruption was rife, the people were understandably dissatisfied, and it was time for a change. But at that point no one really expected that it would come from the best and most disciplined element in the country -- the Army.

And so Asad, always ready and able to make a change, decided that Pakistan was not for us and, after many discussions about life in Europe with various friends, we decided that to go to Switzerland and start to write again would be a wise choice. I had already suggested to Asad that he should undertake a translation of and commentary on the Qur'an: for years he had received innumerable inquiries to recommend an English-language translation of the Holy Book, which he could not do in good faith. Muhammad Ali's translation and brief commentary was very respectable and probably the best, but not quite adequate; Arberry's language was excellent, except for a few lapses, but it was viewed from non-Muslim eyes; Yusuf Ali's English was too flowery and his footnotes not always to the point; and so on and on. In short, none was even nearly satisfactory and really it is not an easy task because -- as Muslims always rightly insist -- the Qur'an, 'the *Arabic* Qur'an' is not really translatable. However, after his many years in Arabia among the beduin, whose Arabic was still at that time the closest to that of the Qur'an, and with his years spent in translating and commenting on the Traditions of the Prophet, the *Sahih al-Bukhari,* Muhammad Asad was indeed uniquely equipped to undertake this difficult task, and I shared his enthusiasm at this prospect. And so we decided to go to Switzerland and to work there in peace.

Before leaving the area, we decided that it would be a pity to depart without my having seen something of neighbouring India. There was great tension between the two countries at that time, and we were not even allowed to take out money. However, as we were to be the guests in New Delhi of the Saudi Arabian Ambassador to India, Shaikh Yusuf al-Fawzan, -- an old friend of Asad's and related, in addition, by marriage to our dear friends the Shaya family -- money would not be too great a problem. And so we arrived in New Delhi and were put up at an excellent hotel and I proceeded to have elegant *sari* blouses made for the many *saris* I had already acquired and to which I was already long accustomed from my New York days. After provincial Lahore, New Delhi was like Paris to us and in addition the Ambassador invited us often and there were a number of receptions at the Embassy. There we met for the first time the Saudi Minister of Commerce Muhammad Ali Reza, a member of one of the Saudi Arabia's foremost old merchant families; I believe they originated in the south of Iran, as the name would indicate, but had been Saudi Arabians not only in name but in all other customs and matters for a long time. Many of the old merchant families hailed from outside: for example, the Qusaibi family had their roots in Bahrain.

Shaikh Yusuf had a special place in the Saudi royal family's heart. I believe that it was his father, a prominent Arab merchant in India, who had lent money in time of great need to Abd al-Aziz ibn Saud; the royal family never forgot their 'debt' and Shaikh Yusuf was the more or less permanent Saudi Ambassador to India and represented them well. His wife was from Basra, and although they never had children and had wanted them, it never occurred to Shaikh Yusuf to take a second wife. They, like ourselves in later times, kept dogs -- golden retrievers . . . .

Staying in New Delhi, we made a side trip to Agra and to the Taj Mahal, which my husband had never even once visited in spite of his many years in pre-Partition India. He had never been a 'sightseer' and it was only at my strong insistence that we went to see it at all. He did not regret it and we were fortunate to have it entirely to ourselves, as rare an occurrence in India as it is, nowadays, in the Alhambra of Granada, which we also had the good fortune to have entirely to ourselves -- and our two salukis, Arabian gazelle-hounds -in October 1964. Today this would be unthinkable.

After this very pleasant interlude, we returned to Karachi to take our farewells. At the last minute -- only a few days before our departure -- Asad's old friend, comrade and admirer, Mumtaz Hassan, the Finance Minister, came up with a last-minute proposal which, he hoped, would change our minds. Asad was offered the co-directorship of a soon to be established Institute -- or Academy? -- of Islamic Studies.[7] But it was too late, and in any case my husband was rightly tired of resigning from -- or being pushed out of -- government posts -and he realized all too well that a co-directorship could never work, even with the best of will on both sides. At that time an editorial appeared in 'Dawn', the principal daily newspaper, to the effect that 'Muhammad Asad had not done badly by Pakistan' . . . . What an effrontery!

IV

And so, with something like relief in our hearts, we boarded the ship at Karachi which was to take us to the Persian Gulf as a stopover on our way to distant, and still unknown to us, Switzerland.

After several days' ploughing uneventfully through the calm sea, we arrived at Muscat, to which we had been invited by one of the diplomatic representatives at the British Embassy in Karachi. Thus we were the guests of the British Resident there, who very kindly showed us the 'sights' of that colourful place -- then so very much 'off the beaten track'; in fact, I believe, it was not easy to get permission to visit Muscat at that time. This was not my first contact with real Arabian life because in Syria we had visited beduin encampments and been their guests at feasts and admired their falcons -- but the forbidding aspect of Muscat was most interesting. The then-ruler of the country, still under British protection, was a harsh man, not loved by his people as his son was later to be. I will never forget the scent of the bees-waxed furniture in the Residence -- one of the nicest smells of British colonialism.

From there we went on, again by ship, to the *real* Persian Gulf, staying in Kuwait, Bahrain, Sharjah and Qatar, always the guests of either the local ruler or of prominent business people. We were very much impressed by Amir Salman, the ruler of Bahrain because he was a man of great distinction, culture, with a love of Arab tradition, of salukis and highbred horses. His son 'Isa inherited this tradition and is now the ruler of liberal Bahrain.

In Kuwait we stayed with the Al-Shaya family, an old merchant clan from pre-petrol days. They were very kind to us -- we had first met them in the mountains of Lebanon, where they had a summer home near us -- and it was thanks to them that my husband was free to concentrate on his work in Switzerland without pressing financial problems, because they offered on this occasion to supplement the small pension which my husband had been receiving from Saudi Arabia ever since his illness in the Lebanon. This Saudi pension was, of course, at the instance of Shaikh Abdallah Balkhair and, we learned much later, came from the private purse of Shaikh Muhammad Sarur as-Sabban, the then Saudi Arabian Financial Minister. Later it was to be regularized, in the time of King Faysal, into a government pension which has continued even after my husband's death. Years later, as life became more and more expensive, it was upgraded at the instance of his Majesty King Fahd, always a generous man. Although the Shaya family always remained anonymous about their earlier help to Asad for his work on the Qur'an, we remained deeply grateful and conscious of the fact that, without them, perhaps the work would never have come to fruition.

In the emirate of Sharjah we were the guests of Shaikh Saqr bin Sultan al-Qasimi, another friend from the years in Syria and Lebanon. He was a fairly good poet but unfortunately not a good politician. He sided too openly with Gamal Abd al-Nasser and was eventually deposed by the British, who were still ruling in the Gulf. He later tried to regain his lost power, such as it was, by force and unfortunately killed the new ruler, his cousin, in the attempt. For years afterwards he was kept in humane imprisonment -- but still imprisonment -- in the United Arab Republic. His virtues and faults were both excessive, but we always remembered him with great affection. We met him again in Switzerland and, for the last time, in Tangier -- after he had finally been allowed his freedom. Shaikh Saqr, too, remained reasonably faithful to the beduin tradition of keeping salukis and pure-bred Arabian horses, but I am convinced that his more and more frequent visits to Europe in the Sixties and Seventies had a negative effect on him -- a great pity.

Next we visited Qatar, where the old Shaikh still ruled the roost and the Darwish family ran it. Although we both were received by the Shaikh and his family at the palace, we were the guests of the Darwishes there. The eldest brother, Abdullah, the founder of the family fortunes, was usually in Saudi Arabia, and was at that time still a powerful financial figure. The next brother, Jasim, took little part in business affairs and was interested more in religion -- a basic sort of religion. Abd ar-Rahman, the youngest brother, was a handsome, personable man in his middle thirties who often visited Europe and enjoyed the 'good life'. We were to know him better in Geneva, which was a second home to him. And I also got to know the various, in some ways very impressive, Darwish women.

All of these friends and acquaintances, each in their different ways, were very kind to us, and thus our memories of the Gulf were pleasant ones.

V

And then we flew to Baghdad, where we were again the guests of private persons, a solid middle-class Iraqi family whom we had known in the Lebanon. Baghdad was still entirely undistinguished, even shabby, without even one distinctive building -- with the exception of the Qazimayn Mosque, a *shi'a* shrine which I visited wearing a black *abaya* but with my face uncovered. Here for the first time I witnessed women weeping and touching the grille around some saint's grave, and I came fully to understand why such practices are prohibited in the Prophet's Mosque in Medina. As for the uncovered faces of most Iraqi women, I was told by our hosts that usually the fully-veiled ones were taken for prostitutes, which they often were, the veil being ideal for anonymity. Anyway, that is what I was told.

Our Iraqi hosts had a summer house in Samarra, and they took us there. It was on the edge of a reservoir which had recently been constructed, and you could still see the fronds of tall palm trees marooned above the water. And there was a salmon-run where we watched hundreds upon hundreds of salmon leaping up an artificial waterfall -- quite astonishing in the midst of what had shortly before been desert. Not far away was the ziggurat-like -- or perhaps it *was* a ziggurat – building which had been used by astronomers in Samarra in very ancient times. And ruins everywhere of other, pre-Islamic civilizations.

I remember that I inquired from one of our friends if they had any remnants of ancient pottery (I had been presented with a lovely little Graeco-Buddhist stone head in northern Pakistan), and the next day they came to me proudly bearing an ancient pottery pitcher, intact, but they had scraped away all the turquoise glaze from it, thinking that they were improving things; I wanted to cry at the sight, but controlled myself. Since those times the Arabs have become far more sophisticated and knowledgable about their own and other peoples' antiques, but at that time there was very little interest in these wonderful things. In Syria, I had found earlier, they had been almost stripped of many art objects and artefacts by the French occupants, who knew what they were about. But all is fair in love and war -- and many of these precious objects have been preserved from destruction in this way.

Our stay was drawing to a close. The shoes which Asad had given for repair were not yet ready, and so we left with one less pair of shoes. We never went back to collect them. Three weeks later the revolution broke out and toppled the monarchy, followed by a series, as unending series, of successful and unsuccessful *coups d'état,* and we just never went back. Iraq had never been a favourite of my husband's, even in the early Twenties when he had travelled there and had deeply sympathized with the people's desire for independence from British rule. But there is a strong undercurrent of violence in that strange land, perhaps a heritage of the pre-Islamic past – of Sumeria, of Assyria, of Babylonia and all that passed away before them . . . .

Endnotes

1 After Partition (1947), Chaudhry Niaz Ali permanently settled in Jauharabad and there he also established Dar al-Islam.

cf. *Sidq-e Jadid* (Lucknow), 29 July 1960 and 9 April 1965.

Once Asad and Pola went to Jauharabad to meet him (1957). For the photograph of their meeting, see *Gift*, vol. II.

2 Nasim Hassan, a younger brother of Mumtaz Hasan and a leading lawyer of Lahore.

Muhammad Aslam: *Wafyat-i Mashahir-i Pakistan*, Islamabad 1990.

3 Ahmad Din Azhar (1900-1974), was born in Sialkot; joined Indian Civil Service; also served as Finance Secretary, Punjab Government.

Cf. Muhammad Aslam: *Khiftgan-i Karachi*. Lahore, 1991.

4 Liet.-General Bakhtiar Rana (1908-1998).

5 Despite certain religious and ideological differences, the mutual respect and friendly relationship between Asad and Maulana Mawdudi continued.

See *Gift*, I; *Correspondence between Mawlana Maudoodi and Maryam Jameelah*. Delhi 1969, p. 15 (Maudoodi's letter, 25.2.1961)

6 In September 1953, an international Islamic Conference was held in Princeton University of America on the subject "Colloquium on Islamic Culture: in its Relation to the Contemporary World" in which many orientalists, reputed scholars and widely known Islamicists participated. For the abstracts of their scholarly-papers on different topics on Islamic history and culture, see *Colloquium on Islamic Studies,* Princeton University, 1953. Sayyid Amjad Ali, Ambassador of Pakistan in America, attended a few sessions of this Colloquium and was highly impressed. Afterwards, when he was appointed the Finance Minister of Pakistan, he decided to hold such Conference in the country and contacted the Vice-Chancellor of the Punjab University for making proper arrangements for this international assemblage. As proposed by Allama Alauddin Sidduqi (Head of the Department of Islamic Studies, Punjab University, 1950-1969) with the consultation of eminent religious scholars (like Ahmad Ali Lahori) Asad was invited to come and make arrangements for the Colloquium.

International Islamic Colloquium (29 December 1957–8 January 1958 was held in the Punjab University, Lahore in which all distinguished scholars and experts of Islamic studies of the Middle East, India, Europe and America participated. For the summaries of their scholarly contributions, see *International Islamic Colloquium*. Papers. Lahore: Punjab University Press, 1960.

In early 1957, Asad was officially invited by the Vice Chancellor of the Punjab University, Mian Afzal Husain (1869-1970), to come and make the proper arrangements for this Conference (cf. Asad's letters to Muhammad Husain Babri (26 Nov. 1956, 28 Dec. 1956, Bhamdoun and Sayyid Abul Hasan Nadvi (12 Feb. 1957, Beirut). He accepted the invitation and came to Lahore with his wife, Pola (8 March, 1957), who assisted her husband as the secretary without any salary or other official benefits (cf. *Proceedings of the Chancellor's Committee*, 30 April 1957). As Director, Asad completed his assignment with great fervour and enthusiasm but a few weeks before this Conference's opening ceremony, he had to submit the resignation through his wife.

In a report, the following three differences of opinion between Asad and the Vice Chancellor have been given:

(a) "...provision of adequate staff for the Director's office,

(b) appropriate and timely arrangements for the translation into Arabic of

English papers to be read at the Colloquium and vice versa, as well as for trained interpreters required the Colloquium and

(c) unnecessary delays in the various administrative and organizational matters."

After reading this report, Asad differed on certain points and clarified his position in these words:

"In the issues of your newspaper of Monday, Dec. 2, there appeared report about my resignation from the directorship of the International Islamic Colloquium. This report contained several inaccuracies which I would request you to correct.

(i) I was not engaged by the Pakistan Government but by the University of the Punjab.

(ii) My engagement was not for a "term of two years" or for any specified period. My task was to organize the Colloquium and, presumably, also to edit the final report on its proceedings; but this last point was mentioned in the exchange of letters on the basis of which I assumed my task.

(iii) I have never submitted any "budget" to the Colloquium Committee. The responsibility for the budget has never been entrusted to me, and all financial dispositions relating to the Colloquium have been and are being made by the Vice-Chancellor, University of the Punjab. What I did do, at the request of the Vice-Chancellor towards the end of October, was to prepare and submit an estimate of expenditure. Reference to the memorandum in which that estimate was included was made in the Progress Report which I submitted to the Colloquium on Nov. 30.

(iv) During the period in which my wife was assisting me as Colloquium Secretary in an honorary capacity (that is, from the time of my assumption of the directorship in March last until her resignation on Oct. 23), my office staff consisted of a stenographer and one peon. The assistant mentioned in your report joined my staff only after my wife's resignation.

(v) The Vice-Chancellor has never refused to accept my proposals regarding accommodation arrangements for the participants.

The main point at issue between the Vice-Chancellor and myself was the question of making suitable arrangements for a good translation into Arabic and English of the papers to be read by the participants (and to be printed for distribution during the Colloquium sessions) – a point I consider to be of utmost importance to the success of the Colloquium. The arrangements which the Vice-Chancellor has seen fit to make are, in my opinion, both belated and inadequate.

Another important point of disagreement was my insistence on an early finalization of the programme of the Colloquium."

(*The Pakistan Times*, Dec. 4, 1957).

See for detail:

Bayard Dodge: "The Islamic Colloquium, Lahore" (*Muslim World*, April 1958, pp. 170-173; July 1958, pp. 192-204); University of the Punjab, *Proceedings of the Chancellor's Committee*, 30 March 1957, 25 Jan. 1958; Asad's letter to Vice-

Chancellor (30 Nov. 1957, 4 Dec. 1957); Muhammad Aslam Khan's letter to Muhammad Sadiq Quraishi (6 Dec. 1992, Jauharabad); Abdul Mājid Daryabadi *Siyahat-i Majidi* (in Urdu), Lahore 1988, pp. 291-299; *Hundred Years of Punjab University: History.* By Dr. Ghulam Husain Zulfiqar, Lahore 1982.

7 In a letter to Muhammad Husain Babri (20 April 1959, Geneva) Asad writes:

"As regards your suggestion that should take charge of the Institute of Islamic Culture at Lahore [founded in 1950], this will unfortunately not be possible. I think I wrote to you in one of my earlier letters that I had been offered as even more important job by the Government of Pakistan – namely the Directorship of the Islamic Research Institute in Karachi [now shifted to Islamabad] with the rank and salary of a Vice-Chancellor. But circumstances did not allow me to accept that office, and similarly it will not now be possible for me to contemplate the Lahore post mentioned to you."

* * * * *

ARAFAT

Quarterly Journal of

Islamic Reconstruction

Edited by

MUHAMMAD ASAD

Rates of Subscription:

Pakistan and other Rupee-Countries	**Rs. 7/8 p.a.**
All other Countries	**Sh. 12/6 p.a.**

Published by the

DEPARTMENT OF ISLAMIC RECONSTRUCTION

Government of West Punjab

LAHORE

'Arafat (Lahore), cf. Pakitan Times (30 March 1948)

XIV
SWITZERLAND
(1959-64)

I

As the plane dropped low over the smiling Lake of Geneva, surrounded by its tidy green patches of fields, we both realized that this well-ordered land would be the ideal place for Asad to settle down and begin work on his Qur'an translation -- and so it proved to be.

We took rooms in a small *pension* in the Old City of Geneva, and decided to search for a house to rent in the vicinity. About a week after our arrival, while crossing the long bridge across the swift-flowing Rhône -- the Pont de Mont Blanc -- we came face to face with Asad's son Talal and his mother. I realized later that it couldn't have been fortuitous. Talal had somehow learned of our presence in Geneva and had come to ask his father to take back his mother! They had been having serious financial difficulties in London and at his subsequent meeting with his son Asad suggested that his mother return to Pakistan to live with Chaudhri Niaz Ali and his family on his country estate. After all, they had been a *real* family to both of them for many years and it had been with Chaudhri Niaz Ali that Munira had lived during the six long years of Asad's internment during the war. This would also make it easier for Talal to pursue his studies in social anthropology which he had finally elected. Munira eventually did go back to Pakistan but she was never really satisfied with country life, even in such comfort and among such intimate friends; she later chose to live with Talal for some time in the Sudan, where he was preparing his thesis for his PH.D. Still later she went to live with her family, which had since become very wealthy, in Saudi Arabia, eventually to die there in the presence of her son.

In Geneva we found our old and loyal friend, Said Ramadhan, and his family. He had gone there to found an Islamic Centre -- a project which my husband had proposed and drawn up some time earlier. But since Said had already put this project into effect, there was no longer any question of my husband's participation in it, although Said, of course would have welcomed it. And in any case we had already decided that he was to devote his entire energies to the translations of the Qur'an.

One day we visited the head office of Rolex watches in connection with some adjustments to the beautiful watch that had been presented to me by the Darwish family while we were staying in Qatar. And in this way we met Mr Edi Peter, who was then Rolex representative for the Middle East and Africa. He was an enthusiastic admirer of the Arabs and we immediately 'clicked'. He had already read 'The Road to Mecca' and so the name of Muhammad Asad was known to him. Then and there Edi insisted that we come home to his apartment for lunch and there we met his petite, vivacious wife Friedl. This was the beginning of a deep friendship which was to last long after we left Switzerland.

From Geneva we began to explore the little towns in the neighbouring Canton of Vaud. One day we visited Coppet, thirteen kilometres outside of the city, and with the help of a friendly grocer were put in touch with a 'notaire' who found for us a house for rent in Commugny, only a few kilometres above the lake. This little village house, a converted wine press, was ideal for us. It was situated in a cobblestoned courtyard adjoining the main house, a large late seventeenth century farmhouse belonging to an elderly Swiss lady of Huguenot descent and her middle-aged, unmarried daughter, Gigitte, who bred chickens for local consumption, their large lands having been sold off because it was impossible for two elderly ladies to continue the agricultural pursuits of former days. And so we had a constant supply of fresh eggs when we settled down in the village. It was a charming place – genuinely Swiss -- for at that time there was not a single other foreigner residing there; at present the foreign population, mostly prosperous business people with interests in Geneva, by far outnumbers the indigenous population, and the charm is gone.

There was a tiny grocery shop in the village, an *auberge* and a cooperative *laiterie,* where we were supplied with fresh milk, butter and ice-cream. In the mornings we were delivered *ballons* (crisp white rolls) and *baguettes* from the neighbouring village-baker in Mies, and our daily necessities, fresh fruit and vegetables were delivered by our grocer friend Coppet; even medicines were delivered to the house from the pharmacy in Coppet. This was the warm friendliness and efficient service we experienced from what had often been described as the 'cold and impersonal' people of Switzerland. When we finally left Switzerland six years later, the younger of our two landladies predicted, 'Vous regretterez La Suisse' -- 'You will regret leaving Switzerland' -- and in many ways she was right.

II

In Commugny we settled down to work in real earnest, with occasional visits to Geneva, where we came to have many friends. It was then that Asad suggested that we acquire a dog -- the first of many to come -- not only for company but also as a reason for taking real exercise in the neighbouring countryside. Since his time in Arabia Asad had always wanted to have a *saluki* -- an Arabian gazelle-hound -- and so we contacted various breeders in England and found the right one. Her name was Azdar; she was golden in colour, with dark, almond-shaped eyes. And with her we used to tramp around the countryside, giving her freedom to run in the fields and in the nearby private wood. While she was racing about we would wander through the wood, often coming upon lilies of the valley and wild strawberries in hidden places. Once Azdar disappeared for hours; we had almost given up hope of her return when she showed up, panting with exhaustion, having abandoned her hopeless, and dangerous, pursuit of a wild boar which had somehow taken up residence in the wood . . . . And once, while walking between the tall, golden wheat-fields, she suddenly jumped high into the air and brought down a partridge and laid it at our feet. Since we would have been taken for poachers had we been seen, Asad wrapped the poor dead bird in his handkerchief for the return to our house, where we cooked it and offered it to Azdar. She refused to touch it.

And so our life took on a definite rhythm -- long hours of work at the translation, always followed by a walk, or run, with Azdar, and once-a-weekly visits to Geneva for shopping and meeting with friends. And the work began to take shape; and we were idyllically happy.

During this cloudless period, we received one day a telephone call from a complete stranger -- although not really a stranger because he was one of the sons of the late King Ibn Saud, and no member of that illustrious family could ever have been a 'stranger' to Muhammad Asad. Thus began a long friendship with Amir Nawwaf bin Abd al-Aziz al-Saud.[1] He was then perhaps in his early thirties at the most -- tall and courteous and extremely handsome, with the bearing of a true Saudi prince, grave and dignified. At that time there was a crisis in the royal family, and he decided to back the cause of Faysal, as my husband had advised him to do. He later became a counsellor to Faysal when he took over the rule of the Kingdom, and he, like most of the Faysal's other half-brothers, remained loyal to that great monarch.

Amir Nawwaf visited Geneva twice a year at least, and often we dined at one or another of Geneva's excellent restaurants: he was a *connoisseur* of good food and together we ate our first frog's legs -- at least his and mine.

And in the village we made several new friends. First, at a chance meeting in the tiny post office, we met David Walters, an Englishman, who shortly afterwards moved into the annex of an ancient house across the road from us. David was a man of many accomplishments. He was a free-lance professional translator, his principal foreign language being Russian, and he made several trips to then Communist Russia and had many interesting tales to relate of his adventures there. He was an all-round intellectual and so was his German-Swiss wife Marthe, a gifted pianist and harpsichordist who always refused to perform at public concerts. We were among the very few friends who were privileged to hear her play in their cosy little sitting-room. Their eventual 'landlords', Mr. and Mrs. -- or, rather, Monsieur et Madame -- Charles-Antoine Vodoz, also became fast friends of ours. They had purchased the main house, an ancient farmhouse, and 'done it up' in exquisite taste -- and so we now had *two* sets of friends across the way.

Almost every Sunday afternoon we had visitors to tea and scones: Muhammad Akram, the grandson of Sultan Abd al-Hamid of Turkey, and his beautiful French wife, Rolande, a former fashion model, and their son Ali. As mentioned earlier, Asad had met Prince Akram in pre-Partition days in Hyderabad. He was a man of the world but with a definite serious cast of mind, very proud of his Turkish-Muslim heritage but never arrogant. While we were still in Switzerland his wife was to die, far too young, in tragic circumstances. I do not recall the year in which Asad was invited to visit Saudi Arabia by Shaikh Abdallah Balkhair, who was then living mostly in Dammam. I, too, had been invited but it was quite impossible for me to leave Azdar either in a kennel or with friends. She was too close to us and would have suffered deeply. Asad stayed with Skaikh Abdallah and his wife for several weeks in Saudi Arabia; it was again a 'home-coming of the heart' for him, as was every one of his visits to Saudi Arabia in later years.

One day we called on Amir Faysal during one of his frequent

trips to Switzerland, having received a telephone call from our friend Fakhri Shaikh al-Ardh, who was currently Saudi Arabian Ambassador in Berne. He informed us that Amir Faysal was in Lausanne and invited us to visit him there. I was extremely eager to meet the man about whom my husband had spoken so often and with so much love. When we arrived at the Beau Rivage there was a small group of Arab personalities who had come to meet Amir Faysal, and I found that I was the only woman present, but I had been invited . . . .

After a brief wait there appeared suddenly the tall, gaunt figure of Amir Faysal, wearing elegant European dress. He had been ill and the tiredness which showed on his face brought actual tears to my eyes, that and the emotion which I felt on finally meeting this very great man. He and Asad embraced warmly and after I was introduced he led us to a divan in the salon surrounded by several chairs. I was astonished when he placed me at his right hand, and, when the waiter arrived bearing a coffee tray, he took the silver pot from the waiter's hands and poured the first cup for me, allowing the others to be served afterward. This was my first-hand experience of the courtesy of a great Arab king. He was really born to be a king, as one realized the moment one set eyes upon him. I was to meet him again when he really became King of Saudi Arabia, and to weep, together with my husband, when we learned of his tragic death . . . .

Asad's son, Talal, came once to visit us in our house in Commugny. I think that he came primarily to tell his father of his impending marriage to Tanya, a good-looking English social anthropologist whom he had met during his studies at Edinburgh University. We both hoped that this would be the beginning of a new phase in the relationship between father and son, for they loved each other very much; but this was not to be. It broke down one day with a clash between Talal and myself -- there was always a strain between us -- about something entirely unimportant. We were both very sad when Talal left, because we had really been hoping . . . . When we eventually met Tanya, after she had become Talal's wife, we found her to be very intelligent, reserved and possessed of a peculiarly English kind of beauty; she turned out to be the perfect companion for Talal.

III

And so the years went by, six short and very happy years. Asad had already completed, and published, the first third of his Qur'an translation.

One day he received -- out of the blue -- a letter from the then President of Pakistan, Field Marshall Ayyub Khan,[2] whom he had never met. The President had read "The Principles of State and Government in Islam" and was highly enthusiastic. In a subsequent exchange of letters he proposed to Asad that he return to Pakistan to become a member of a seven-man group of Muslim scholars -- people who both supposedly knew the world and were experts on Islam -- to advise him with regard to everyday matters as well as the drawing-up of a new, Islamic constitution for the country. But it was too late because it was now unthinkable for Asad to put aside his cherished work on the Qur'an, and so he regretfully declined.

IV

With the completion and publication of a part of his work, Asad began to become restless and to long for the warmth of Muslim countries -- as well as to have a home of his own. He began to think of moving on, in spite of our happiness and modest comfort in Switzerland.

In the meantime we had found a male companion for Azdar -- another saluki from the same lady-breeders in Oxford. We named him Afreet and he soon became an integral part of our lives. He worshipped his female companion, never to become his 'wife', and was gently dominated by her. And we, in turn, were dominated by our love for both of them and wanted to give them, as well as ourselves, a little more 'lebensraum'.

It was then that Asad hit upon the idea of settling in Cyprus, near but not quite *of* the Middle East. With several letters of introduction he paid a visit to Cyprus and actually *did* find an appropriate house for sale in the hills just above Kyrenia. It had belonged to the Spinney family, who owned an enormous food emporium in Beirut and probably other principal cities in the Middle East as well. After the guerilla war against British rule they had moved out of Cyprus, leaving behind their large house and enormous garden. Asad was enchanted with it and began to discuss its purchase. The high court judge to whom our friend Edi Peter had introduced Asad was extremely helpful, as were all the other Greek Cypriots whom Asad had the opportunity to meet. They were not anti-*Muslim* as such, but anti-Turk, and so they encouraged him to settle there and did everything in their power to assist him to this end. But at the last minute it occurred to Asad to contact the chief government veterinary in Nicosia with regard to the regulations or formalities to be followed in order to bring our two salukis to Cyprus. And there the trouble started. Before leaving for Cyprus Asad had written to the Cyprus High Commision in London and had been informed that in view of the fact that both hounds had been born in England and had from the beginning of their lives been inoculated against rabies, there would be no problem. But the official veterinary, a dour Turk, put his foot down and declared, 'When I took over from the British, Cyprus was *clean*, and it will remain so', and he refused permission, insisting that the dogs would have to be put in quarantine for six months. Upon this my husband requested to see the kennels and he immediately realized that it would be quite impossible and very cruel to subject any dog -- let alone two big coursing hounds that required large running space -- to such a fate, even for six months -- a long time in the life of a dog. He counter-suggested that we would surround the property with a high fence and a double set of gates and that the authorities could have a key and free access to the ground, to ascertain that the dogs never left the place. But the unfriendly Turk refused to budge, even when high-placed Greek Cypriot officials tried to intervene on our behalf, or probably *because* of it. In short, our moving to Cyprus was out of the question and Asad had regretfully to drop the project. It turned out to be a favour on the part of the nasty Turkish veterinary: three weeks later fighting broke out in the Kyrenia region between the Greek and Turkish Cypriots, and our prospective house was right in the middle of the fighting and later became part of the Turkish-occupied area in Cyprus. We would, had we settled there, have become refugees, with two large dogs, in the Lebanon, where the civil war was soon to break out. And so we were 'saved' by our dogs . . . .

After his return from Cyprus, deeply disappointed, Asad began to think of other alternatives, and one day, quite by chance, he picked up an English journal which carried an article about Tangier. In describing its lively international character, it mentioned that in the phone-book there were foreign names 'from A to Z'. It mentioned specifically the name of Craigh-Coen, the Sir Terence Craigh-Coen of Asad's Foreign Service days. This seemed to be almost like an augury. So Asad decided to visit Tangier, to investigate the possibility of having a home of his own there and, what was even more promising, the prospect of living once again in a Muslim country.

He was immediately enthusiastic. Terence Craigh-Coen introduced him to his many British friends and, more important, suggested several housing agents who might be helpful. And indeed they were. They finally found a lovely property on the hill above Tangier, and it was very inexpensive. It was a large, abandoned garden of seven thousand square metres with a prospect of palm and fruit trees and terraced with dry-stone walls and overlooking Tangier and the sea. The house was tiny and in bad repair but the possibilities were enormous. I remember the rough sketch that Asad sent me of the projected changes to the house; and when it was finally built, the result was astonishingly like the sketch which he had made in such a hurry. And it was to become our home -- the only *real* home we were ever to have – for nineteen long-short years . . . .

V

And so, with a few misgivings, we decided to leave 'La Belle Suisse', for better or worse. The misgivings were mostly mine because I didn't like the thought of Asad's interrupting his work on the Qur'an, which had been so successfully set in motion in Switzerland.

We left in October of 1964; our farewells were not sad because we had no intention of forgetting our friends of the past six years. We loaded our two faithful hounds into the station-wagon which we had recently purchased and started on our long drive to the 'promised land'. Down we drove through the Haute Savoie, the Côte d'Azur and across to Pau in the Gascoigne. Pau was empty in October, and it had an abandoned air, as indeed it was because it had long since ceased to be one of the resorts so loved and patronized by the British upper classes. But the food was still probably the best in all France. We, accompanied by Azdar and Afreet, sat down in one of the best of its many restaurants and waded through a many-course meal, probably the finest either of us had ever eaten -- and years later we could not recall *what* we had eaten, only that it had been so good.

From Pau we went down to Irun and crossed the Bidassoa into Spain. We spent the first night in a roadside hotel-restaurant outside of a small Basque town and there we had the best meal we were ever to eat in Spain. Basque cooking on both sides of the frontier was, and still is, exceptional. As so often in Spain, the electricity broke down and we spent the evening in candlelight.

Then we continued down to Burgos, a beautiful cathedral city in Castile; neither of us spoke any Spanish as yet. And finally we reached Granada, which was like home territory.

Granada is a very Spanish city -- but Moorish Spanish. From the very first moment we felt ourselves in a somehow familiar atmosphere.

When we visited the Alhambra (I remember it was on the day that Khrushchev[3] fell from power in Russia), we found it absolutely empty. We wandered without guide, or the need of a guide, through the vast, rambling buildings and grounds, always accompanied by our Arabian gazelle-hounds -- our precious salukis -- and it occurred to me that these were probably the first salukis to wander through the Alhambra and Generalife since the fall of Granada almost five hundred years before. The only person whom we encountered on the premises was Antonio Molina, who was in charge of restauration of the exquisite gypsum decorations covering the walls of the Alhambra. He descended from a long line of specialists who had for perhaps a century kept these delicate decorations from crumbling into dust.

We were later to visit this beautiful Spanish Muslim city many times, once for a period of two months searching for, without finding, a house there. How could it have occurred to either of us then that one day Muhammad Asad would be buried in the tiny Muslim graveyard in Granada... ?

And then down through the mountains to Málaga and the sea. At Algeciras we boarded the ferry for Tangier, which was almost within sight. When it actually did come into sight we gazed at the city lying beside the water with the small hill above -- 'the mountain' -- where we were to spend the next nineteen years of our lives and where Asad was eventually to complete his historic translation of and commentary on the Holy Qur'an.[4]

Endnotes

1 Amir Nawwaf bin Abd al-Aziz al-Saud.
cf. *Schulze*, p. 217.

2 Field Marshal Muhammad Ayub Khan (1907-1974), Commander-in-chief of the Pakistani Army and President of Pakistan who imposed first Martial Law in the country; authored *Friends not Masters*, his political autobiography. (Oxford: OUP, 1967).

3 Khrushev (1894-1971), Russian political leader, first secretary of Communist Party (1953-1964); premier of Soviet Union (1958-1964).

4 The translation of the first nine surahs (*Fatiha* to *Tauba*) with explanatory notes, published from Mecca (Muslim World League, 1964). It was banned by the World Islamic League (Rabita 'Alam-i Islami) but Asad continued his work and within a few years completed the translation of the whole Qur'an with explanatory notes.

* * * * *

درسِ قرآن کے سلسلہ میں آپ نے جو مشورہ دیا ہے میں خود بھی اسکی کمی اسلیم
میں محسوس کر رہا ہوں۔ مگر اب تک میں نے اس کی جرأت اسلیے نہیں کی ہے کہ مجھ پر کام کا
بار بہت زیادہ ہے اور تحقیق و مطالعہ اور غور و خوض کا وقت کم ملتا ہے۔ ذرا اس بار میں
کچھ کمی ہو جائے اور مجھے فرصت کے لمحات میسر ہوں تو ان شاء اللہ تفسیری مضامین کا ایک
سلسلہ شروع کروں گا۔ سرسری طور پر قرآن کی تفسیر لکھتے ہوئے خوف معلوم ہوتا ہے۔
مطالعۂ قرآن کے لیے جن امور کی ضرورت ہے ان کو ایک مضمون میں جمع کرنا
تو مشکل ہے۔ البتہ ایک ایک چیز پر ایک ایک مضمون لکھا جا سکتا ہے۔ بعد میں ان
مضامین کو جمع کر کے ایک کتاب کی صورت میں شائع کیا جائے تو قرآن فہمی کے لیے ایک
مفید مقدمہ ہو جائے گا۔ میں ایک عرصہ سے ارادہ رکھتا تھا کہ اس قسم کی ایک مستقل
کتاب لکھوں۔ مگر اب کتاب کی تصنیف تو مشکل نظر آتی ہے۔ زیادہ بہتر یہی
ہے کہ الگ الگ مضامین لکھنے شروع کر دیے جائیں۔ ان شاء اللہ عنقریب یہ سلسلہ
شروع ہوگا۔

محمد اسد صاحب سے حیدرآباد میں ایک مرتبہ مل چکا ہوں۔ ان کی کتاب
Islam on the Crossroads اور ترجمہ صحیح بخاری دونوں میری نظر سے گذری ہیں۔ میرا خیال یہ ہے
کہ دورِ جدید میں اسلام کو جتنے عالم یورپ سے ملے ہیں ان میں یہ سب سے زیادہ
قیمتی ہیرا ہے۔ اسلام کی اسپرٹ اس میں پوری طرح حلول کر گئی ہے اور
اسلام کو اس نے ان علماء سے زیادہ اچھی طرح سمجھا ہے جو پچاس پچاس برس سے
درس و تدریس میں مشغول ہیں۔ اگر یہ شخص آپ کے ادارہ کے لیے مل جائے تو
میں آپ کو مبارکباد دیتا ہوں اور نہایت خوش قسمت سمجھتا ہوں۔

Mawlana Mawdudi's letter to Ch. Niaz Ali (1955) in which he has referred Muhammad Asad

XV
TANGIER
(1964-83)

I

How can one condense into a few pages nineteen years of a shared life? It is literally impossible. But they were happy years, and fruitful years, and probably the best in our lives in many respects. With the help of friends we soon rented a temporary house as a base from which to build our permanent -- or so we then thought -- home. But then, what is permanent . . . ? We were advised by Moroccan friends not to entrust our work to an architect or a contractor, but rather to plan and oversee it ourselves, employing a Moroccan master-mason and local workers. We had practically to demolish the existing house; we tore down everything except the inner staircase and the garage, which we turned into a large kitchen. For calculating the foundations and supervising the building work, we employed the services of a Swiss-Italian engineer; but after some months he suddenly took off for the Belgian Congo (from which he had to flee with only the clothes on his back because of the outbreak of the bloody civil war -- God certainly works in mysterious ways), leaving us completely in the lurch, and pocketing some of our money into the bargain. And so it was we who had to control the work, and the workers; I remember how Asad climbed one day to the top of the roof (the house had two stories) to demonstrate how the tiles had to be joined at the corners. He had never seen such a thing before, but with his lively intelligence had worked it out and passed along his new-found knowledge to the Moroccan workers, who caught on very quickly.

They were nice people, those Moroccan workers. All of them were poor, some practically in rags, but I was impressed by the fact that every day they brought with them a cooked meal which they re-heated over open fires in the garden. This was Morocco, where people ate well, even if they were poor.

The *souks* in which they bought their food were filled with every kind of fresh vegetable, salads and fruit, fish and fowl – and everyone could afford it. Never before or after, even in the prosperous countries of Western Europe, did I see -- and eat -- such wonderful foodstuffs. Surely this is the basis of 'the good life' . . . . ?

And they were cheerful, those Moroccan workers, and easygoing and tolerant. This tolerance was the keynote of Moroccan life. Although as good Muslims as anywhere in the world, they were always tolerant of other peoples' customs. Probably this is why so many Europeans flocked to the country, and especially to Tangier and Marrakech, and always bitterly regretted it after having gone away.

Tangier was then even more colourful than it is now. Moroccan life was far more oriental in spirit than any of the Muslim countries west of Pakistan. As in Pakistan, the overwhelming majority of the people kept to their traditional dress, even many of the men, who are usually the first to don Western garb -- with the strange exception of Saudi Arabia, where it was the women who were the first to break radically with their native dress, which is really quite beautiful and in keeping with the climate. Almost all of the Moroccan women wore *kaftans* or *diffins* under their *jellabas* and veils; the peasant women from the countryside wore a picturesque red and white candy-striped shawl wrapped around their waists, reaching to the ankle, and an enormous straw sombrero on their heads. (And this, by the way, is the origin of the Mexican sombrero, which originated in the Yemen, was brought to Spain by Yemeni troops during the first invasions, and later travelled to Mexico by way of the Spanish invaders and introduced to the Indians there -- quite a long odyssey for a simple straw hat!)

They were very self-confident, townswomen and peasants alike, and would often jostle you while passing in the streets or *souks,* and it was the women, often heavily veiled, who were the most aggressive in this respect. And although they were often divorced by their husbands and left with small children, they thought nothing of re-marrying and trying again. Divorce was common in Morocco, especially among the 'lower classes', but so was re-marriage, and there was no stigma attached to a divorced woman, as was the case in Pakistan. All in all, the Moroccans enjoyed a very great measure of social and religious freedom and most of them were content with their lot. And they were blessed by having a ruler, King Hassan, who understood his people's mentality through and through -- and was thus able to govern a race that was basically unruly, as the French and the Spanish had learned to their cost.

It did not take long to realize that the Moroccans are not Arabs, as is commonly believed: they are essentially Berber in their descent and in their culture, especially in the mountains and countryside. Although their official language is Arabic, the majority of their uneducated population speak *darija,* an Arabic dialect strongly laced with Berber and many foreign words as well -- it is almost a separate language. Of course in school they learn classical Arabic -- it is, after all, the language of the Qur'an -- but even then it is spoken with a strong Moroccan intonation. And in the south and among the people of the northern Rif, they speak their own, Berber language.

In temperament, too, they are not Arabs. Although friendly by nature, there is always a slight suspicion of the foreigner. Of course, that is partly because they suffered until recently under a harsh foreign rule. But, even so, they are not really 'open' as are the true Arabs, and the Egyptians as well. And thus, although it was very pleasant to live among them -they left you alone, so to speak -- one didn't make as many friends as one did among the Arabs of the East. And although they are extremely hospitable by Western standards, they are much less so than the real Arabs and much more formal in their entertaining. Even in a prince's or a millionaire's home in Saudi Arabia, there is very little formality connected with the process of eating and entertaining. That is where the much-vaunted hospitality of the Arabs is really to be found. But 'East is East and West is West' -- and the meaning of *maghreb* is West . . . .

The Moroccan cuisine is magnificent and again entirely different from that of the Arab East, much better in my opinion and more refined. But as with many people with sophisticated cuisines, their desserts are mediocre, to my taste -- nothing like the sweets of Damascus. Their bread -- or, rather, breads, for there are many kinds -- is usually prepared at home and sent to be baked in the small 'professional' ovens which exist in every neighbourhood, patronized by rich and poor. And such breads, so many *kinds of* bread! Raised white bread, raised brown bread, raised wholemeal bread, flat breads, every kind of bread imaginable. No wonder that the French were so happy in Morocco with such an excellent cuisine at their disposal . . . .

II

After nine months our house was finished. The bees-waxed mahogany beams had been posed on the ceilings of the long sitting room and drawing room; the *fer forgé* grilles placed on the windows, the heavy, panelled mahogany Spanish-style door was mounted with the bronze door handle and hinges which we had bought in Madrid -- we had made a special trip in order to acquire these beautiful things. And we moved with our furniture and carpets and household goods of every kind into the 'Villa Asadiyya', the 'Villa of the Lioness', which Asad named after me . . . .

But almost before we had settled down Asad was invited again to Saudi Arabia, and off he went again. He could never resist the siren song of Arabia . . . .

This time it was an Islamic conference of some sort, remarkable only for one event: there Asad met for the first time the already well-known Minister of Petroleum Affairs, Shaikh Ahmad Zaki Yamani.[1] Asad had been sitting, quite alone, at one of the small tables laid out for the lunch break when a handsome, middle-sized man with soft, sweet but penetrating eyes approached him and said, 'May I join you? I am Zaki Yamani . . . .' That was all that Asad recalled on returning from this particular conference. Who could ever forget his first meeting with Shaikh Zaki Yamani?

The house was built, our journeys for the time being over, and it was high time to resume work, which we did with a will. Asad would sit down to work after a good breakfast, not stopping for four or five hours at a stretch before laying down his pen. Then he would join me and the dogs in our vast, slightly overgrown garden -- that was my 'baby' -- or we would drive to one of the long, often deserted beaches on the Atlantic or, when the sea was rough, to one of the intimate little coves on the Mediterranean side of the Straits. Later, when we came home, we would cook our dinner together, we always preferred our *own* kind of food -- fluffy cheese souflées and salad, or Pakistani fare, of which we both were masters. And I learned to produce a wonderful French *soupe à l'oignon.* If we had the time and energy, we would set ourselves to producing a wonderful fish soup -- a combination of a French *bouillabaisse* and a Spanish *zarzuela de pescado* -- because in the two principal fish markets of Tangier one could find every kind of fish imaginable, and very cheap in those early days.

We also had a full-time gardener. But, especially in the earlier years, I myself would spend most of the day planning and working in our beautiful, exuberant garden. We had more palm trees and pear and apricot trees than we could use, and I added rows of needle cypresses and innumerable flowering bushes, and I never became tired of embellishing my first *real* garden. And on one of the many terraces we had an enormous umbrella pine -- often called stone pine, the tree *par excellence* of the Mediterranean, and thus had at our disposal pine-nuts for some of our exotic Italian dishes. And there were innumerable lemon and orange trees, and even one that produced the famous Seville orange for the home-made marmalade that I myself produced.

The long garden walks were all paved with 'crazy stones', with grass and small flowers growing between them and there were almost countless terraces going up and down, all made of cut stone. Near the front of the house there was an enormous bougainvillaea -- it must have been well over a hundred years old; it was already a tree which spread its purple branches all over the walls. And, of course, there was jasmine -- jasmine which really *smelled* -- and *misk al-layl* which we both remembered so well from Pakistan, where it is called *rat-ki-rani*. I loved that garden -- *my* garden -- with a real passion. It was a romantic garden, an enchanting garden, and I learned to become a gardener in that garden. But although Asad appreciated my enthusiastic efforts -- and their results -he never really shared my passion for gardening, or even gardens, as such. In this he was a true Semite: he liked to look at or stroll in a garden, but not to *work* in one -- and that is where the passion lies. This was the only interest -- passion – which we never were able to share completely, so that in time I was to lose a lot of my early enthusiasm and, with it, very much indeed that was really necessary for my nature . . . .

Meanwhile his work went on steadily until it reached the point at which I could *really* take part. As I transcribed his crabbed but very legible handwriting into my typewriter, many times over, we would read the work through, discussing it, polishing its language like ivory, until we both were satisfied.

And it *was* satisfying labour. There were days when Asad worked for hours on end without finding exactly the right word in English -- or even whole phrases -- which would bring out the full meaning of this or that passage of the Qur'an. And then I would tell him: 'Leave it until tomorrow and sleep on it; it will come to you by morning' -- and it always did. How fortunate we were able to do the work which we both loved and to live in such beautiful surroundings! God was very good to us.

The result of this work is there for all to see. The process by which it was accomplished was only witnessed by me. Never have I experienced such complete self-surrender, such honesty, such integrity and such humility as I witnessed during the long years which Muhammad Asad devoted to this, his greatest work . . . .

III

In spite of this almost total concentration on his work, Asad and I enjoyed a lively social life in Tangier, especially in the first ten years -- the best- that we spent in Morocco. We had in our immediate vicinity on 'the Mountain' many foreign neighbours -- we ourselves were foreigners in Morocco -- British, French, Belgian -- many of them holding distinguished titles, and some of them became real friends. There were so many that it was impossible to enumerate them, and it would be unfair to mention one without another. Apart from neighbourly visits, 'dropping in', there was a constant round of parties and it was impossible to attend all of them. In turn, we invited our friends to dinner and buffet parties -- for we always reserved the daytime for our work -- and we regaled them with our own particular kind of food -- mostly Pakistani *moghulani* dishes and often Iranian ones, for we both loved the exquisite food of Iran; in fact, I had, and have, cookbooks of both the northern and southern cuisines of Iran, a cuisine so refined and so unknown to Westerners and despised by the few Arabs who have been exposed to them.

There were many foreign consulates at that time in Tangier, and so we had the opportunity of meeting and discussing foreign politics -- always one of my passions -- with highly-educated people and, of course, there were many retired diplomats residing there. It was a very full life indeed.

And from time to time we had visitors from the East, old and new friends. We deepened our relationship with Shaikh Salem Balamash, a Saudi Arabian businessman of Hadhramauti origin, one of the most deeply religious Muslims I have ever met, and one of the most tolerant. He was almost always accompanied by Abu Bakr Bakhashab, the only son of his partner, Bakhashab Pasha, a very rich businessman who had, among other things, a fleet of ships and dealt mostly with Italy, for they, too, were of Hadhramauti origin and had close contacts with Abyssinia, and therefore with Italy as well. The Pasha's son, Abu Bakr, became a very close friend, as did his second wife Khadija, a woman of great fascination and herself a brilliant businesswoman. Abu Bakr's children by his first marriage were sent to the American School in Tangier after their mother's death, and we loved to visit them at school and felt almost as if we had a family of young children ourselves. Later Abu Bakr built a house very close to our own on 'the Mountain' and we used to spend long summer days in his palatial Moroccan-style house with its vast lawns and gardens. Even his servants were our friends -- we knew them from older times -- and we used to drop in and have a coffee in his absence in the winter months -- his 'home' was in Jidda. It was dear -- now sadly dead -- Abu Bakr who saw to it that Asad's unmatchable Qur'an translation finally saw the light and helped us to publish it.

IV

During this long, rich period of our life in Morocco, we were able to travel abroad together, thanks to the presence of servants, who lived in a small, separate house on the property. We were thus assured that Azdar and Afreet were properly looked after, no matter how much they missed us. The Moroccans, unlike most other Muslims, are generally very good to animals and they harbour no unfounded prejudice against dogs. When we did go away, however, it was never for more than two or three weeks at a time , and we were always happy to return home -- for it *was* a home to us . . . .

Early in 1966 Asad was invited to Saudi Arabia by Shaikh Muhammad Sarur as-Sabban, no longer Finance Minister but now the Secretary-General of the Muslim World League -- the *Rabitah al-Alam Islami* -- an organization based in Mecca composed of scholars and Islamic personalities from all over the Muslim world. The *Rabitah* had originally been prepared to sponsor the publication -- not the work, which was done independently by Asad and with precious little money at his disposal throughout all the long years which he spent on it. But differences had arisen among some of its scholars -- some of whom were not of the first rank -- about this or that of his interpretations. The principal movers in these objections -almost never the same -- were Pakistanis -- in short, the followers of Maulana Mawdoodi of our Pakistan days. Since these people were the only ones really conversant with English, however bad, they presented their various objections to the Arab scholars from their own particular point or points of view, often quite incorrectly. But the damage was done and the *Rabitah* decided not to publish the work unless my husband agreed to their arbitrary censorship, that is, to change a handful of his honestly-arrived-at conclusions into line with their own. This was, of course, impossible for any really honest man to do -- and Muhammad Asad was a completely honest man. He had worked with full integrity and consciousness of his duty to God over many, many years, always conscious that he was an ordinary human being -- and thus fallible -- but not prepared to be dishonest with his own *self* and, in the final resort, with God. The financial gain would have been tremendous had he been prepared to compromise with his conscience, but it would have been fatal to his integrity; he would never again been able to have lived with himself. I, of course, entirely agreed with him.

On his return from a kind of inquisition in Mecca, Asad informed me that Shaikh Sarur -- who remained his friend throughout but who, not being a scholar in any sense of the word, was helpless to intervene in the organization which he himself had founded -- Shaikh Sarur had invited me to Mecca for the forthcoming *hajj:* I had to be prepared to leave in about a week's time! We quickly had some *jellabas* made up for me as my pilgrim's garb and Asad unearthed his Arab dress which had lain unused since many years.

And so we arrived in Jidda in the rush of the pilgrim season. Some of Sarur's staff came to meet us at the airport and whisked us off to Mecca. Asad had made eight pilgrimages during his years in Saudi Arabia and Pakistan, but this was *my* first experience of the *hajj,* as well as my first experience of Saudi Arabia itself. Again we met Said Ramadhan and his wife and spent most of the time together in Mecca, Arafat and Medina. This was Asad's first visit to Medina after many years, and I remember how saddened he was to find the beautiful City of the Prophet so changed. Many of the dignified old stone houses and indeed even the old city walls had been demolished to make way for 'American style' buildings of the worst possible taste. And, of course, most of the luxuriant date orchards surrounding the city had been laid waste. Medina had once been Asad's favourite Arabian city, and his son Talal had been born during his sojourn there. Only the Prophet's Mosque had not been spoilt; on the contrary, they had already begun to enlarge and enrich that sacred spot, and it was very beautiful.

Indeed, it was in the Prophet's Mosque that we had an unusual experience. Since the time of Ibn Saud's rule pilgrims had been discouraged and even forbidden to approach the bronze grille that surrounds the Prophet Muhammad's grave because the ruling Najdis were strongly against what seemed to them often fetishistic worship of saints' graves -- and even of that of the Prophet of Islam. Recalling my earlier experience in a mosque in Baghdad, I could easily understand their reasons, and sympathized with them, as did my husband. To prevent this behaviour on the part of well-intentioned but ignorant visitors, there were posted Najdi 'guardians' with sticks in their hands to prevent such misguided people -usually hysterical women -- from coming too close to the Prophet's grave. So, after saying our prayers, Asad and I stood at a distance while he explained to me the position of the Prophet's body within the enclosure. Suddenly, one of the 'guardians' approached us and asked us if we didn't wish to come closer to the grave and proceeded to lead us right up to the grille. I never really understood this entirely unsolicited behaviour of this simple, and certainly fanatical man, but I was deeply touched by it. This was one of a series of similar exceptional situations which I have encountered while visiting mosques -- one in Ronda in Spain, the other in Fez in Morocco.

Once, during one of our many visits to Ronda, the last important Arab town in Andalusia to fall to the Christians, I decided to visit a small church which, it seemed to me, had the 'feel' of an old mosque. This actually proved to be a fact, for the prayer niche had been uncovered some time earlier. On leaving this church-mosque, descending the steep stairs to our car where Asad and the salukis waited, I was suddenly accosted by two little Spanish urchins who first asked me, 'Mora?' (Moor, meaning Muslim woman) and when I shook my head negatively: 'India?' (Indian). Since I was clad in a skirt and blouse and my hair and skin were fair, it seemed to me a strange cognition of being on the part of two little, uneducated Christian boys . . . .

Another moving experience occurred when Asad and I visited Fez, in Morocco, and went first to the famous Qayrawaine Mosque. For some unknown reason, women are almost never allowed to visit mosques in Morocco, apart from the prayer times, where they are allotted a specific place, separated from the men. And foreigners in general are discouraged from visiting mosques there -- quite in contrast to all other Muslim countries, with the possible exception of neighbouring Algeria. Since I had not thought to put on oriental attire, I was hesitant to enter the outer courtyard of the mosque, let alone the interior -- and when I reluctantly did so, out came the doorkeeper shouting that 'foreigners are not allowed into the mosque'. By that time a large group of curious onlookers had gathered outside, many of them Moroccan women who themselves were not allowed entry, and we were becoming more and more embarrassed. With his usual patience, Asad quietly explained to the doorkeeper that we were indeed Muslims, but he remained sceptical. At that, I suddenly turned to him and said in my very broken Moroccan kitchen *darija:* 'I have been in the *haram* in Mecca and visited the Prophet's grave in Medina and that is enough for me!' -- upon which the previously hostile doorkeeper, as usual a very simple man, entirely changed his attitude and practically *dragged* me into the mosque, where my husband and I were allowed to pray and gaze upon the beautiful interior.

From there we proceeded down the winding allies to the Moulay Idris Mosque, and again we were met -- but this time by a group of religious dignitaries who insisted upon our entering and pointed out to us the grave of the great man and suggested that we might pray before it. This, of course, was against our own principles, and we politely but firmly desisted. When Asad asked them how they had known that we were both Muslims, one of them gravely replied, pointing to his heart, 'We know it here.' And, believe it or not, they had *not* been advised of our coming to the mosque by the door-keeper at the Qayrawaine . . . .

Such unexpected and inexplicable experiences are beautiful to remember; and they reflect the faith of the majority of Muslims all over the world.

V

As I have said earlier, the year of this, my first, *hajj* and of Asad's eighth was 1966. I had wanted very much to visit Jerusalem on the return journey, but we were terribly short of money at the time and, being guests, we did not like to impose such a request on our host, although he would certainly have granted it and could easily afford it. We were later to regret this unnecessary modesty -- typical of both of us I am proud to say -- because a year afterwards another Arab-Israeli conflict broke out and Jerusalem was taken from Jordanian rule and shamelessly occupied by the Israelis. And so I never did visit Jerusalem, *al-Quds,* 'the Holy' . . . . This leaves me something to look forward to: visiting a freed, unoccupied Jerusalem, but with whom . . . ?

The following year, in the early autumn of 1967, Asad and I were officially invited to visit Tunisia. The invitation came about after a chance meeting with several government personalities at the house of Si Abdullah Gannoun,[2] the foremost Islamic scholar of Morocco and the only one to be dispensed with the kissing of the King's hand. Asad had been invited to dine with Si Abdullah at his small town palace in the *casbah* of Tangier. After a pleasant time reminiscing about the old days of Tunisia's struggle for independence during which Asad himself had played so active a role at the Foreign Ministry in Karachi and later in the United Nations, the Tunisian guests, on taking leave, accepted Asad's verbal message to the Prime Minister, the Bahi Ladgham of former days at the U.N., conveying his warmest regards.

A week later we received a telephone call from the Tunisian Ambassador in Rabat, Habib Chatti,[3] inviting us both to visit Tunisia at whatever time suited us.

And so, one lovely autumn day we arrived in Tunis, to be state guests of the Tunisian Government for the following month. There we met Bahi Ladgham again, who protested that we had chosen to make our home in Morocco instead of 'our own country' -- and the following day we were received by President Habib Bourguiba and his wife in the beautiful official residence at Carthage. Bourguiba had not changed much from the days when Asad first knew him as a more or less penniless political refugee in Pakistan. He was still very outspoken, almost to a fault, and direct -- and he made us both feel very much at home. I was instantly taken by the directness of this famous man and by his supreme self-confidence as a statesman -- for a statesman he was. Although he had been savagely mauled by most of the Arab press when he had recommended acceptance of a partition plan for Palestine, in later years the Palestinians themselves were to turn to this solution and to adopt it as their own; by that time they had suffered and, consequently, matured. He was a true statesman, as I have said, but his scope was sadly limited by the size of his country. It was then that I told him: 'You and Nasser should exchange countries because Egypt would give you a larger scope . . . .' He laughed loudly and later, when I was out of hearing, in the company of the President's wife and her daughter, Asad was to listen to an almost scabrous description by Bourguiba of Gamal Abd al-Nasser, whom he, of course, heartily detested, as did every other moderate Arab leader.

Of all our experiences as guests of Tunisia, there is one I particularly remember. It was on the occasion of the national holiday and we were to go to Bizerta, where we were to witness a military parade and take part in the reception. We left Tunis by car very early in the morning, for all the male guests were to receive the President when he arrived there by helicopter. I was accompanied by a young lady from the foreign office, as on many other occasions, and on our arrival Asad was immediately taken aside and told that he would be greeting President Bourguiba, together with all the diplomatic representatives of all foreign countries. When he joined them he was astonished to be informed that he would be the first in the receiving line. Asad demurred, saying that he had no diplomatic status, but whoever was in charge of protocol insisted: 'But you are our guest . . . .'

Later, reviewing the parade, the President placed my husband at his right, while I sat opposite on a balcony with the First Lady and other prominent Tunisian women.

This was Bourguiba's -- and thus Tunisia's -- way of showing to Asad how much they still appreciated his great assistance in the days before they achieved independence. We both were deeply touched by this consideration and gratitude and long memory.

During the month that we spent in Tunisia, travelling all over the country, we met Habib Bourguiba and Bahi Ladgham on many occasions. All the countries of the Maghreb are lovely, but in Tunisia one had the feeling of being surrounded by history, which we were -- Carthaginian, Roman, Berber, Arab and Turkish -- and the cultural level was very high.

VI

And thus the years in Tangier -- with occasional trips abroad -- passed almost unnoticed while we were engaged on Asad's work on the Qur'an . . . . 'row upon row of happy years'.

At the beginning of 1972 our beloved saluki bitch Azdar died of leukaemia after many months of our suffering and hers. At the end we had to have her 'put down', as it is euphemistically expressed, in order to avoid more suffering. And this was the beginning of a period of wandering in Spain twice a year or so -- always accompanied by Afreet, and later by Farouk as well, another male saluki whom we brought later from England as a companion for Afreet -- nothing could replace Azdar. We used to cross by ferry to Algeciras and to cut across the Costa del Sol, which we never had liked, directly into the 'real' Spain. Using secondary roads whenever possible, over the next few years we really explored the country in depth, visiting all parts except, unfortunately, Cataluria and Asturias. And I 'fell in love' with Spain somewhat in the manner that Asad had so long ago fallen in love with the Arabs -- but there lay the difference: I fell in love with the landscapes and towns of Spain, whereas Asad had fallen in love with the *people* of Arabia . . . .

It was on one of our last journeys through Spain -- in 1976 -that we lost our very beloved Afreet, the early companion of our equally beloved Azdar, who had died five years earlier. Afreet had been operated in Tangier for a large growth but seemed to have recovered, and the veterinary thought it would be all right for him to travel -- which had always been his favourite amusement; he actually *liked* to travel in

Spain, where everybody admired him and asked, 'How much is he worth . . . ?'

On this fatal trip -- it was towards the end of May -- the weather suddenly turned unseasonably hot and when we arrived in Madrid, after spending two nights on the road, he suddenly more or less collapsed. He was unable to urinate; obviously it was a breakdown of the kidneys. We were staying in a hotel on the top floor and the room was torrid. As we were wondering where to turn for help, I recalled that a Spanish veterinary surgeon whom we had known in Tangier and who had become a friend in the process of looking after our hounds was now living in Madrid. And we found him in the telephone book -- Dr Antonio Molina-Larré -- and he came to the hotel immediately. He tried to do what he could for Afreet, and together Asad and he took him to a hospital to be X-rayed. It appeared to the X-ray specialist -- he was a professor- that Afreet had been *kicked* in the kidneys. And it immediately occurred to us that shortly before he collapsed we had been invited to lunch at the apartment of some Spanish friends and that afterwards Asad and I had gone out with his wife -- I went reluctantly and only at their insistence -leaving Afreet and Farouk in our 'friend's' apartment, something which I was loath to do and had never done before. On our return -1 had been anxious throughout our shopping excursion and insisted on going back -- we were met at the door by a furious host. Apparently Afreet had suddenly needed to go out for a call of nature and had 'made a mess' just in front of the closed door to the balcony. Obviously our very unobservant host had not responded -- and Afreet was an extremely clean and well-trained dog, but he had had a sudden attack of diarrhea. It even happens to humans . . . .

Although our gracious host had a maid -- a Moroccan maid -- in his apartment, he had left the 'mess' uncleaned, obviously in order to demonstrate the 'wickedness' of our poor Afreet. I immediately apologized on his behalf -- how can a dog apologize? -- asked for a bucket of water and some rags and, going down on my hands and knees, cleaned it up myself, leaving his precious little carpet spotless. During the process, my husband, our hosts and the Moroccan maid looked on silently. In the meantime, Asad observed that the two hounds were extremely uneasy in the presence of our host, and Farouk actually growled at him, a most unusual occurrence.

We left as soon as we could politely do so, and on the short walk back to our hotel I observed that Afreet could no longer walk properly and we just managed to get him back.

In spite of all his efforts, our veterinary friend was unable to save Afreet and after three days of frantic effort and little or no hope, he died. I asked Dr. Molina how we could bury him, and he replied sadly that in 'normal' circumstances one could dig a hole somewhere in the country, but he was so *big* . . . . It is worthy of note that in all of Madrid there was no place for domestic animals to be buried and the only alternative was the rubbish dump . . . .

And suddenly I remembered that the son of a Catalan lady-friend in Tangier was living in Madrid. We also knew that he, like his wonderful mother, loved dogs and that he looked after many abandoned ones in a small country place that he had outside of Madrid. He immediately responded to our call and said that we could bury Afreet on his property; but then he discovered that there was nobody there who could dig the grave, and he himself was partially crippled. And so he turned to his own friends -- the Casados -- who had a house and large garden in Alcala de Henares, and requested that Afreet be buried in their garden, where several of their own dogs had their graves. There *are* people in Spain who love and respect animals . . . .

And so we took Afreet to Alcala de Henares and buried him there. As I have said before, he had always intensely enjoyed travelling and it was on a travel that he was to die. Although he was a few days short of fourteen and very old, it was a terrible blow to both of us. We returned home to Tangier via Portugal with only Farouk, who did not enjoy travel, to accompany us . . . .

VII

During the first half of the Seventies, Asad had again met his old friend, King Faysal, on two occasions. We had visited him in Geneva, where he received us very cordially in his suite at the Hotel Intercontinental. This time he was in Arab dress and surrounded by many courtiers, most of whom were known to Asad from earlier times. Asad and he discussed many subjects, the principal one being the perennial, apparently unsolvable conflict in Palestine, about which all three of us felt very strongly and were in complete agreement. Shortly before asking permission to leave -- for an Arab king never 'dismisses' a guest -- Asad asked the King if he could help him to untie his knotted relations with the *Rabitah* in Mecca, and the King diplomatically replied that he should visit Mecca again, turning to me: 'With my sister Hamida', and work out the problem directly with his antagonists -- and they *were* antagonists. Of course the King was right in not intervening in this matter, but naturally we were disappointed. But, to my knowledge, the wise King Faysal never made a move or decision when it was not indicated . . . .

The second meeting was in Rabat, where the King was paying an official visit. Asad had been invited by our old friend Fakhri Shaikh al-Ardh, who by then was Saudi Arabian Ambassador in Rabat. Like my husband, Fakhri and his entire family -- aristocratic Damascenes by origin -- had had a long and close association with the Saudi royal family from the days of the great Abd al-Aziz. His elder brother, Medhat, had been personal physician as well as adviser to three kings. So it naturally occurred to Fakhri to invite Muhammad Asad to visit the King in Rabat. (Although I accompanied him, these formal occasions were strictly for men, and so I remained in the hotel). During the first reception held by the Saudi Arabian Ambassador, Asad mingled with the other guests, many of them friends, and then it was announced that 'official' visitors were invited into an inner salon to meet the King -- *both* kings, because King Hassan would also be present. Asad moved on with the others into the adjoining salon, to be confronted by a Moroccan security man demanding to see his 'credentials' -- this could never happen in Saudi Arabia -- and when informed that he had none, tried to prevent Asad from entering the room. But Asad ignored him. He was standing quietly to one side of the salon when Faysal entered, glanced swiftly around the room and his gaze alighted on my husband. With one graceful gesture the King went directly to Asad and embraced him warmly, Asad kissing him on the forehead and nose-tip in the old Najdi manner (he never kissed the hand of any king, even the great Abd al-Aziz; it was not expected of him or anyone else in Arabia, an essentially very democratic country). This warm greeting was a spontaneous gesture from a man, a powerful monarch, who was rarely given to spontaneous gestures. And it was the last time that Asad was to gaze on that familiar, beloved face . . . .

At noon on the twenty-fifth of March, 1975, we turned on the news broadcast of the BBC, as was our wont, and were shocked to learn of the assassination of that great man just a few minutes earlier. It was the first and last time that I ever saw Muhammad Asad cry. He went straight to the telephone and called Fakhri Shaikh al-Ardh in Rabat. Fakhri had not yet heard the terrible news and I feel certain that he, also, cried.

VIII

During the second half of the Seventies, Asad was invited a number of times to various conferences in London, many of them sponsored by the Islamic Council, of which our good friend Salem Azzam was Secretary-General. Salem, a younger brother of Asad's great friend Dr Abd al-Wahhab Azzam, was now an Islamic personality in his own right. When the Azzam family joined their destinies with that of Saudi Arabia, Salem had entered the Saudi diplomatic service and had become an Ambassador-at-Large, with headquarters in London. Later he was to leave the diplomatic service, but the Islamic Council, his own brain-child, remains and is very active to this day.

During one of these many visits to London -- this time accompanied by me -- Asad met for the second time, and I for the first, the Saudi Minister of Petroleum Affairs, Shaikh Ahmad Zaki Yamani. He was accompanied by his lovely young wife Tammam and his two equally lovely daughters from his first marriage. The occasion was the opening of a new publication called '*Arabia*'[4] which was to devote many of its pages to the works of Muhammad Asad and to champion his translation of the Holy Qur'an.[5] At the same meeting we met King Faysal's son, Prince Muhammad, whom we already knew and whom we were later to meet many times. And there we met Said Ramadhan and other old friends, as well as several of the Al-Wazir brothers from the Yemen, whose father had been an outstanding patriot and had been beheaded by the father of Imam Badr; all of this family were of great stature and fervent Muslims, and one of them, Ibrahim, was an outstanding and liberal Islamic scholar.

These last years of the Seventies were extremely eventful, and the events were mostly happy ones.

With his Qur'an translation and long commentary completed, Asad was invited to visit the large, active Muslim community in South Africa, who were almost all of Indian descent and therefore English-speaking. There he undertook a series of informal lectures, which he always preferred to making speeches. The talks were mainly about the Qur'an itself, and he was received with great comprehension and warm hospitality by this tight, religious community. On arriving in London on his return journey, extremely exhausted by the long flight -- not first-class -- he went to a hotel where, on entering, he tripped over a shallow marble stair, difficult to discern against the marble of the floor itself. He fell, recovered himself and thought nothing more of it, but on meeting him at the airport in Tangier the next day I found him looking unusually tired.

About a month later we had a visit from Talal. His mother had died shortly before in Riyadh, and he had taken temporary leave from his teaching post at the University of Hull to spend the last months of his mother's life with her. On his return to England I wrote to him myself and told him how sad we both were to learn of Munira's death from cancer and how glad we were that he had been with her. I reminded him that he still had a father who loved him very much, and asked him to come out to visit us. He and his wife Tanya had visited us in Tangier only once or twice during our many years in Morocco and I very much wanted him to maintain, and if possible deepen, his relations with his father.

The day after Talal arrived the three of us went out for a walk, taking our two hounds with us for a change. On our return walk Farouk, the remaining saluki, made an abrupt movement and Asad lost his balance and fell -- and he wasn't able to get up. We brought him home in our car which Talal fetched and I started calling doctor after doctor. As often in such crises, it was a holiday and no one was available until very late in the evening when a young Moroccan doctor previously unknown to us arrived at the house. We had placed Asad on a couch downstairs in order to prevent too much movement – I already had a definite feeling that his hip was broken. After a very amateurish and cursory examination the doctor suggested that I rub his hip with some ointment and that in the morning I should call an ambulance to take him down to town for an X-ray.

Early in the morning I telephoned to the clinic to which a surgeon friend belonged and was advised to 'call the fire department!' Finally they gave in to my pleas and brought Asad down to the clinic in their own ambulance. And then the nightmare started . . . .

The X-ray showed that the head of the femur had been broken through and without further ado Asad was placed in a gypsum cast from waist to toe, without even pins being placed to hold the bone together. From the outset I was convinced that this 'treatment' could not possibly be right and I started telephoning again -- this time to our good friend, Dr Abd al-Karim al-Khatib, himself a well-known surgeon with his own private hospital in Rabat. Vainly I tried to reach him, when, about five days later I received a phone call from him. He had come to Tangier to attend a royal wedding, the same wedding to which we had been invited. He had no inkling of what had happened, and when I told him and requested him to see the X-ray, he went immediately to visit Asad in the clinic. He insisted, rightly, that my husband should go by ambulance next morning to the government hospital in Rabat which was very modern and better equipped to handle such a complicated operation. Like the good friend that he was, he made all the necessary arrangements, or what should have been the necessary arrangements, beforehand.

I will not even attempt to describe the period spent in hospital. But he was operated on by a young Moroccan surgeon and a prosthesis was implanted in his hip-bone. About a fortnight later, having received no proper physiotherapy or attention of *any* kind (later I was to learn that he should have been put on his feet only a few days after such an operation), we decided to return home to Tangier -- by ambulance again. There we found an anxious Talal, who had remained to look after things at home -- he would not have been allowed to sleep in the hospital as I had been by special intervention from 'on high'. On arrival Talal immediately told us that he would have to leave for London the next morning, early. It was a pity because never before had Asad needed the presence of his only son as at that time . . . . and I myself would have appreciated it greatly.

During the following year, most of the time on a crutch, Asad began to suffer more and more severe pain in his 'replaced' hip-bone, and finally we decided to take recourse to a specialist in London, who informed us that the head of the prosthesis was a bit small but that it *ought* to 'settle down' in time. But it did not, and we went a second time to London and, through the good offices of a very kind and efficacious doctor, were recommended to one of the top specialists for this kind of operation in England -- and they are the best. But orthopadeic surgeons are never too happy to take on a 'patching-up' operation; finally we persuaded him to take Asad's case, after having consulted with a second surgeon who told us quite coldly that after the operation and if he didn't find an infection when he opened him up Asad would have to walk for the rest of his life on a greatly shortened leg with a dropped shoulder; he actually demonstrated what it would look like. The operation, therefore, was done by the first surgeon of our choice, and in spite of the fact that a lot of soft bone had to be scraped off, the operation was entirely successful. When he was taken to the operation theatre I was told by our London doctor, who had taken the trouble to be present during the operation -- a very complicated one in the best of circumstances -- that it would take about five hours. When the doctor came after only an hour to the room where I was anxiously waiting, he handed me the old prosthesis as a 'souvenir' and informed me that it had taken such a short time for the simple reason that the original -- my souvenir -- had been badly cemented in the first instance and that Asad had been walking for more than a year on a wobbling replacement . . . .

Two days later he was up and walking along the hospital corridor with a very slight limp and, for the first time in an eternity, without pain. At that time he was eighty years old.

During our long period in London -- over two months because we had to wait for the hospital of the surgeon's choice – we saw a lot of our many friends there, as well as Asad's step-brother Martin and his wife, with whom we had almost nothing in common but who were very nice. They had been close friends of Talal and his wife, but didn't exclude me from their warm friendship. Martin was a very successful dental surgeon and his wife Eva was working at that time, I believe, in medical research. Despite the fact that they were Jews by religion and had a deep sympathy for Israel -- mostly sentimental, I suspect, on Martin's part but more strongly on his wife's, who had suffered from the Nazis in Germany. But we managed to keep the subject of Israel, and what they had done and were still doing to the Palestinians, out of our relationship.

Talal and Tanya came up to London to visit his father; he had not written to us in Tangier for more than a year, and he was shocked to learn of his father's condition, but then, he had never inquired about him since the original accident in Tangier, where he had been present...

He had in the meantime been assuring various friends and admirers that his father had been successfully operated on in Rabat and had recovered entirely. But how could he have known that since he had never inquired? He really loved his father, I suppose, but the barrier which he himself had erected between us back in 1952 was impossible to breach, and our relations remained strained to the very end.

IX

I seem to recall that Asad's first visit to Sarawak -- part of Malaysia -- took place between these two operations. One day, from out of the blue, he received an invitation from the then Chief Minister of Sarawak, Tun Datuk Abd ar-Rahman bin Yạ'qub,[6] to attend a kind of symposium there, mainly for the benefit of young Muslims, both male and female. Asad was delighted with the informality of these meetings and tremendously drawn to his host, Tun Datuk. This exceptional man had brought his independent Sarawak into the Malaysian Federation and was a main mover in Malaysian political life in general. He was a highly-educated barrister and a fervent Muslim with a very liberal cast of mind. Asad spent hours with him in lively discussion of various Muslim and Islamic problems and found him to be very close to him in his opinions. He brought back to Tangier the deep impression made by this man, as well as of the enthusiasm of his young audiences, especially the women of Sarawak who were taking their rightful place in society under an Islamic guidance, thanks to the efforts of Tun Datuk. And another memory that he brought back from this, his first sojourn, in Sarawak was of his almost daily meals of huge prawns, which were considered 'poor people's food' in fortunate Sarawak.

Some time later we were visited in Tangier by Tun Datuk, his first wife Norah, and several of their many grandchildren. When we met them at the airport -- with a suite of about twenty people, some family, some friends -- we were horrified when an over-zealous custom's inspector, ignoring Norah's diplomatic passport, opened up a paper bag containing roasted chestnuts which she was carrying -- she happened to *like* roasted chestnuts, a seemingly harmless foible -- and investigated the lot. He must have suspected drugs -- 'carrying coals to Newcastle'... ? And Tun Datuk, when we protested, only quietly remarked, 'The man is only doing his duty.'

Subsequently we both were to visit Sarawak on the occasion of the anniversary of the accession of Sarawak to the Malaysian Federation, as well as the marriage of one of Norah and Tun Datuk's many daughters. We were, of course, two among many guests, but everyone was made to feel that he or she was 'special'. There were many events during this visit -- official receptions and celebrations of various kinds - but the most memorable one was of the wedding itself, where double the number of guests appeared at the Governor's residence (Tun Datuk had since become Governor of Sarawak, with his nephew taking his place as Chief Minister), and all were received and fed with great hospitality -- it must have been a major feat of logistics! And the wedding ceremony itself, with only special guests' participation, was a most fascinating event -- Muslim, of course, but with strong Hindu cultural undertones.

The Prime Minister of Malaysia, Dr Muhathir Muhammad,[7] and his wife came over from Kuala Lumpur for the accession celebrations and we were invited to visit Kuala Lumpur on our return journey.

In Sarawak we were given a special treat by Tun Datuk. On his earlier visit Asad had been taken by helicopter into the dense jungle to visit a settlement of *dayak* long-houses, built over high stilts for obvious reasons, and he wanted me to have the same experience. So Tun Datuk very generously put a helicopter at our disposal and, after flying low over the exuberant and rather frightening jungle, we were landed at a small clearing. The *dayaks,* the indigenous population of Sarawak and the rest of Borneo, are mostly Muslim or Christian now. This particular group were, I believe, Christians, although it was hard to tell. They were very friendly and self-contained, of course, for they were already used to occasional visits by 'privileged' foreigners. Tun Datuk himself is the descendant of *dayaks* who had become Muslims some generations back. He is a small, fine-boned, aristocratic-looking man of middle age; he told us that his father had been a fisherman . . . .

On our return journey we spent several days in Kuala Lumpur, meeting the Prime Minister again, and Asad gave a spontaneous talk on state television, as he had done in Kuching as well. We were royally treated and invited to return at any time we wanted to. But unfortunately this was not to be . . . .

It was during this period that we began seriously to consider leaving our beloved Tangier. The lively international atmosphere had declined in the last few years and a kind of xenophobia — always an unpleasant aspect of former colonial countries -- had begun to be evident with the events in the Spanish Sahara and the ensuing Green March. Although we were in no way involved emotionally, it was sad to witness this subtle change in the normally tolerant and friendly Moroccans. And this became exacerbated by the later events in Iran and the beginning of what Asad always insisted was mistermed 'Islamic fundamentalism'. To my mind it should be called 'Islamic *puritanism'*. The events in Iran really had nothing to do with the rest of the Muslim world, which was mainly *sunni,* but it had an effect on some confused and misguided people in every Muslim country who had a strong emotional attachment to Islam and took this for Islam itself. Unfortunately, instead of trying to return to the early principles and teachings of the Prophet, these misguided people were -- and are -- mostly hearking back only to practices, cultural as well as religious, of a few hundred years earlier – a time of decadence. And so the decadence is perpetuating itself, with unforeseeable results . . . .

Asad had as far back as his early days in India preached and written that the only way for Muslims to be able to live by Islamic Law -- the *shari'ah* -- was to strip it down to its original, very basic essentials, without all the accretions of the many centuries that followed which prevented it from being really workable. These ideas had been presented in 'The Principles of State and Government in Islam' and, years later, in his last book which was to be entitled 'This Law of Ours and Other Essays'.[8] To the end of his days Muhammad Asad remained convinced that only this could revive a truly Islamic attitude among the Muslims and lead them to their destiny.

X

During the early part of 1983 Asad and I went several times to visit Portugal, with a view to a possible shift, and were very much taken both by the country and its people. We found the Portuguese an open race, or races, the only truly non- racist people in Europe -- probably as a result of having lived among and married many peoples in the Far East, in Africa, in Brazil. And life in Portugal was inexpensive still, and relatively free from the narrowness and bureaucracy that pressed upon you in the rest of Western Europe. Eventually we found a beautiful country-house not far from Lisbon and Tun Datuk bridged its purchase because we had not yet been able to sell our house in Tangier. He never accepted repayment!

Shortly before we were to depart for Portugal, very late one night the telephone suddenly sounded. It was the Pakistani Ambassador in London calling on behalf of the President of Pakistan, Zia ul-Haqq, who had for some time been trying to locate Asad's whereabouts. He invited him to come immediately to Islamabad.[9] Asad's spontaneous answer was negative, but after some persuasion by me he agreed to go, even at such short notice and on the eve of a major shift. When he arrived at Islamabad, the new capital of Pakistan which he had not yet seen, he was received at the plane with great honour and escorted to the villa of the President. There, and on many other subsequent occasions, Asad got to know that exceptional leader of Pakistan who, like Liaquat Ali Khan before him, was to die by assassination (in this case, sabotage) before his mission, almost a *sacred* mission on the part of General Zia, was accomplished.

During his stay in Islamabad, there was a series of meetings with various Muslim scholars in order to prepare a kind of programme for the President for the future. Asad agreed with some, and -- as usual -- disagreed with others, which he found retrograde. On one point he was firm and insistent: that Muslim women should have exactly the same rights in the political sphere as had men, to the extent of becoming Prime Minister. Not long afterwards -- unfortunately over the body of

President Zia ul-Haqq -- Benazir Bhutto[10] was to, probably unknowingly, benefit by this advice of Muhammad Asad: she became the first female leader in the Muslim world. She was 'pushed' out of office, of course -- as is usual in Pakistan with someone outstanding -- but she set a precedent that will have its eventual consequences, and so her role was an historical one.

Asad met with his surviving friends in Islamabad and Lahore and at the request of the President made several radio and television appearances, as always spontaneous. On his return home we were besieged by letters from literally hundreds of admirers in Pakistan, offering him land, a house, everything, and demanding to know 'Why Portugal and not Pakistan?' But the answer is to be found in the earlier chapters of my husband's memoirs in Part One. The poor, benighted Pakistanis did not know how much they needed a man like Muhammad Asad -- there was no other -- in their midst, and so they lost him. What a Foreign Minister he would have made, or even Prime Minister -- but, then, he didn't belong to one of the many races to which the other Pakistani people belonged. He was unique.

Soon after his return we began the big packing for our major shift. In retrospect, although we were subsequently to be very happy in Portugal -- I, in particular, found it nearly perfect and to this day find myself totally 'at home' in Lisbon, my favourite city in all the world; although, as I said, we were very comfortable in Portugal, this departure from our home of the past nineteen years was a great mistake. Even then I remember thinking, 'Is this trip necessary?' Asad was already eighty-three years old and, for all his adaptability and reasonably sound constitution, he had safely reached a great age, an age in which it is not advisable to pull up roots and put down new ones . . . .

Towards the end of October we did pull up our roots and left in two cars for Portugal -- one containing a driver by Asad's side and Farouk, our remaining saluki -- the other the driver, myself and our beautiful young Afghan, Shimshir. And the latter, out of some instinct for survival perhaps, didn't want to leave the Villa Asadiyya and the life that he had always been used to . . . .

We were seen off at the port -- we had to take the ferry across to Algeciras -- by our best and oldest and closest friend in Morocco, Muhammad Mashish al-Alami, a well-known lawyer, accompanied by two of his and our mutual friends. The only others to see us off were a Moroccan Jewish couple – Mr. and Mrs. Salvador Azagury. We had in common with them all one thing: friendship.

Endnotes

1 Ahmad Zaki Yamani (1930-); completed his education from Cairo, New York and Harvard Universities; Legal Advisor to Council of Ministers (1958-60); Minister of State (1960-62); Minister of Petroleum and Mineral Affairs (1962); Director, Arabian American Oil Company (1962).

2 Sir Abdullah Gannun was the head of the league of Moroccan 'ulema.

In 1974, Abd al-Salām Yasin wrote a *risalah* to King Hasan II (Eng. tr. *Islam, or, the Deluge: An Open Epistle to the King of Morocco*). Hasan II was outraged by Yasin's epistle and asked Abdallah Gannun, how he should respond to it. Gannun told the king that Yasin should be put in a psychiatric hospital, since only a lunatic could address the king as Yasin had.

3 Habib Chati (1916- ?), Tunisian diplomatist and politician.

4 *Arabia* owed much to Muhammad Salahuddin, an Egyptian who made this magazine a vehicle for promoting Asad and his works. After some years this journal was closed.

5 *The Message of the Qur'an.* Dar al-Andalus, Gibraltar, 1980. This publishing house was established by Asad in 1978 and afterwards all his books were published from here, even after his death (1992); for two dissertations on this translation see Ashraf Sulaiman: *Assessment of Muhammad Asad's "Translation of the Qur'an"*. M.A. Thesis, University of Durham, South Africa, 1987; Abdul Majeed Khan: *A Critical Study of Muhammad Asad's* The Message of the Qur'an." Ph. D. Thesis Department of Islamic Studies, Aligarh, 2005.

6 Tun Datuk Abd ar-Rahman bin Yaqub; All Malaysian Muslim Welfare Association (PERKM) was founded in 1960 by the first prime minister of the newly independent nation, Tunku Abdur Rahman as a religious and social welfare organization; minister-president and general secretary of the organization of Muslim Conference.

cf. *Schulze*, p. 272. *EI*[2], VI (1991), pp. 240-243.

7 Dr. Mahathir Mohamed became prime minister in 1981 and strived hard in uplifting his country.

See D.K. Mauzy and R.S. Milne: "The Mahathir administration in Malaysia: Discipline through Islam" (in: *Pacific Affairs*, Winter 1983-1984, pp. 617-648).

8 *This Law of Ours and other Essays.* Dar al-Gibraltar 1987; Asad's last book consisting of his articles.

Asad's longest stay in any city of the world was in Tangier (Morocco). During these nineteen years, he and sometimes his wife regularly corresponded with his close friend of Pakistan, Muhammad Husain Babri (Lahore). In these letters, many new aspects of his life and scholarly studies come to light.

cf. Asad's letters to Babri, 13 Sept. 1959, Geneva; 10 Sept. 1970, Tangier; another letter from Tangier (undated); 28 Feb. 1983, Tangier; Pola's letters to Babri, 9 Feb. 1962, Geneva; 11 Oct. 1962, Geneva; 15 Sept. 1964, Tangier; 20

Feb. 1966, Tangier; 26 Feb. 1967, Tangier; 8 Sept. 1976, Tangier; also Asad's letter to Muhammad Sadiq Quraishi, 2 May 1983, Tangier.

9 General Muhammad Zia ul-Haq established a Commission under the chairmanship of Maulana Zafar Ahmad Ansari (1908-1991), aimed at submitting the proposals for having the Islamic conduct of State in the country. Muhammad Asad was appointed the advisor of this Commission and officially invited to come to Pakistan as a state guest. This was his last visit of Pakistan but the first one of Islamabad. During his sojourn in the capital (July, August 1983) he met Zia al-Haq and other members of the Commission and expressed boldly his own views about the nominated and unelected Advisory Council (*Majlis-i Shoora*).

See for detail Zafar Ahmad Ansari (ed.): *Report of Ansari Commission* (in Urdu)... Islamabad 1983; Islamic Ideological Council: *Constitutional Proposals for an Islamic State* (in Urdu). Islamabad 1983; Zia Shahid in: *Nawa-i Waqt* (Lahore), 31 July 1983; Muhammad Sadiq Quraishi in: ibid., 13 and 27 August 1982, 29 October 1982, 25 March 1983, 26 August 1983.

10 Benazir Bhutto (1953-2008), daughter of Zulfiqar Ali Bhutto (d. 1979), founder of Pakistan Peoples' Party (PPP) and the prime minister of Pakistan (1971-1977); appointed prime minister of Pakistan twice.

* * * * *

الصحفي الرحالة والمفكر الإسلامي والسياسي

محمد أسد

هبة الإسلام لأوروبا

د. عبد الرحمن الشبيلي

بمناسبة الندوة التي نظمها - عن محمد أسد -
مركز الملك فيصل للبحوث والدراسات الإسلامية والسفارة النمساوية بالرياض
جمادى الأولى ١٤٣٢ هـ - أبريل ٢٠١١ م

Dr. Abdulrahman Alshobaily's Arabic book "Muhammad Asad: Gift of Islam to Europe" (Riyadh, 2011)

XVI
PORTUGAL
(1983-86)

I

On our arrival in Portugal we quickly settled down to having the house repainted, putting things in order and meeting several of the friends whom we had already made in Lisbon. Very soon we came to know the Moroccan Ambassador, Moulay Salamah bin Zaydan, and his very attractive and active wife Fatima. Both of them were first cousins of King Hassan and nobody could have better represented that country than this pair, who personified the very best in Moroccan life. Their charming villa on the outskirts of Lisbon – Restelo, where most of the ambassadors resided -- peopled by two lively young daughters and a pair of enormous white Pyrenean dogs, soon became a second home to us. Whenever we happened to be in town, we could always just 'drop in' on them and were always assured of a genuinely warm welcome. On coming to Portugal Asad had been supposed to present two letters of introduction from the President of Pakistan and the Foreign Minister to the President of Portugal and *his* Foreign Minister. But he was never able to present them; it soon became clear and obvious that the government at that time, under President Ramalho Eanes -- himself a would-be 'strong man' -- had a great prejudice against Zia ul-Haqq. Later, with the arrival of a Pakistani Ambassador to Lisbon, relations improved, but by that time Asad couldn't have cared less whether he was 'received' by the Portuguese President or not. But the new Ambassador was a great personal asset to us. Birjis Hasan Khan, a career diplomat of the first rank, and his wife Kausar quickly became friends of ours and added an extra dimension to our life. And through 'our' two Ambassadors -- that of Morocco and that of Pakistan – we came to know many other diplomatic representatives of the Muslim countries -- notably the Ambassadors of Egypt and Iraq and their attractive wives, all liberal and cultured people. And we met also the representative of the Palestine Liberation Organization[1] and his wife. All these people were wonderful and we always enjoyed both the open, Arab hospitality of their houses and the elegant formal receptions usually held in their spacious gardens. After the social desert in Tangier, I flourished in this lively and very informal social life.

Thus, we had achieved something we had lost in Tangier – extremely pleasant social relations with a superior kind of people, as well as a comfortable, innerly satisfying life in the open country, a combination that suited us both.

Our house was a gem, somewhat large for two people but very pleasant and easy to run. After so many years of tiled floors, we luxuriated in the wooden parquet floors of Portugal. We had central heating, but there were also beautiful fireplaces in the three main reception rooms, and they really *worked* because the house had been built by an Englishman. Besides, things *do* work in Portugal, quite the opposite of Spain, where the people consider themselves 'more developed' than the Portuguese -- in what way I have never been able to learn -- and actually look down their noses at them.

The house was very Portuguese on the outside, a dark 'dusty pink' with white doors, shutters and window-trim-but the interior was quite English in its 'style' and comforts. It was certainly the most beautiful house that I had ever lived in, although not designed specifically to our needs as was the house which we had designed and built for ourselves in Tangier. The garden was vast -- eleven thousand square metres – and all of it was surrounded by walls, with wrought-iron gates at the two main entrances and the long, broad driveways paved with the small, square stone-blocks so characteristic of Portugal, beautiful Portugal. The garden was not as romantic and boisterous as that of the Villa Asadiyya in Tangier, but I immediately started making additions and improvements, and as always the first trees to be planted were cypresses. There were two enormous 'weeping-willow' trees on the slope to the meadow where the swimming pool lay, its walls adorned by the huge Portuguese picture tiles in blue and white. It was my dream house and always will remain so. It was called Casa Caravela (caravel) and we had no reason for changing its very appropriate name: seen from the distance, sitting on top of a hill, it almost resembled a ship in full sail.

It was only a short drive to the nearest small town, Belas, which adjoined the former hunting grounds of bygone Portuguese monarchs --

it was actually medieval and crumbling into ruins, for it had been abandoned long ago. The next, larger town of Queluz was not much farther away. Queluz had been – as had Sintra -- one of the summer residences of the kings of Portugal and the beautiful pink and white baroque palace built by one of its queens later became the guest house for visiting heads of state and it was also used for various official receptions from time to time. And beautiful, lively, nostalgic Lisbon was only seventeen kilometres away . . . .

Of our few neighbours on the adjoining estates we only came to know well the owners of the largest property outside of Belas – Quinta Fonteneira. The owners, the Vilas Boas family, were the leading local gentry: a large, happy family comprising the owner, his lively wife and I forget how many young sons. The two mothers-in-law, both widows, lived in separate apartments of the vast, rambling palace, and there were several annexes as well. It was the most beautiful private house that I have ever seen, and the atmosphere in that house was among the simplest and gayest that I have ever experienced anywhere. The entire family were serious, practising Catholics who took to their hearts two Muslim neighbours and even invited us to their Christmas celebrations, which were really huge family gatherings. If all the Portuguese aristocracy in former times had been anything like *this* family – this clan – the Portuguese monarchy could never have fallen . . . . We were never to forget their open-hearted friendship and easy hospitality, as well as their tolerance of and respect for people of another faith.

II

Four years had already passed since the completion and publication of 'The Message of the Qur'an', and Asad had not yet settled down to work, what with his several operations, our journeys and our shift to Portugal. I had been trying to persuade him to write a second volume of memoirs, starting with the period when he left Arabia for India, the year 1932. But he was still deeply absorbed in his meditations about the Qur'an and proposed to start making notes for a book which was actually intended to be entitled 'Meditations on the Qur'an'[2] which would bring out new aspects of the Holy Book, further deepening the commentary which he had already written -- in short, a commentary on his own commentary. Although he made some notes to this end, he never really got down to writing it and, indeed, it would probably have become an endless task, just as his translation of the Qur'an had almost been. When he had first anticipated the translation of the Qur'an, he had thought two to three years would complete that task; all in all, it took about *seventeen* years.

But I did finally persuade him to put together in book form some of his earlier writings and lectures from his Indian and Pakistani years. The principal essay was entitled 'This Law of Ours' and contained his main ideas about the codification of the basic, clear-cut Law of Islam, the *shari'ah.*

During the first Ramadhan after our departure from Morocco we were invited to Saudi Arabia by Shaikh Zaki Yamani. His Ramadhan celebrations were famous for their warmth and hospitality. The first weeks were spent in Hada, on the outskirts of the summer capital of Taif, where the King and many members of the royal family passed part of their summers. Shaikh Zaki's house, surrounded by a fruit orchard, was large and rambling and yet somehow 'cosy', a real *family* home. Apart from the many guests, there was Zaki's children from both marriages, *their* children, relatives from both his and Tammam's families, and friends, friends and more friends. At the end of the long day's fast everyone would gather in a partially-enclosed salon facing the garden to break their fast with tea and many kinds of dates, to be followed later by a large buffet dinner of every kind of food imaginable, and fruits and desserts . . . . Afterwards some of the guests would sit down together to relax in the cool of the evening and a smaller group would often stay on until before dawn for the last meal before fasting began again. Between these sumptuous repasts the prayers would be performed in company, the men in one group and the women in another. Shaikh Zaki, at the time of breaking the fast at sunset, would hand to my husband a small vial of ginseng to drink -- a charming, special attention which was deeply touching. It is impossible to describe the atmosphere of those Ramadhan gatherings, a combination of gaiety and spiritually rarely to be found elsewhere.

On this first Ramadhan visit, Shaikh Zaki's beautiful Najdi wife, Tammam, was pregnant with their son Ahmad and about the middle of the month she had to leave abruptly for Switzerland for her eventual confinement. But she disappeared in such a discreet manner that one didn't fully realize it until a few days later; she didn't want to break up the festivities.

In the second half of Ramadhan we drove down to Mecca just before dawn, driven by Shaikh Zaki himself, to pay our visit to the *haram* and to say our prayers there and to make the circumambulation around the Ka'ba and afterwards the running to and fro between the two hillocks in memory of Hajar, the wife of the Prophet Abraham, and the spiritual mother of the Arab race. Asad suffered on this occasion because he had to be carried on a litter because of his hipbone . . . .

And later we went with Shaikh Zaki to Medina to pass the last days of Ramadhan in the vicinity of the Prophet's Mosque and to say our prayers near the burial place of Muhammad, the Last Prophet.

During these Ramadhan visits, three years in a row, Asad met many old friends in the house of Shaikh Zaki and called on King Fahd and Amir Abdullah, the Crown Prince, during their stay in Mecca. And once again we met Amir Nawwaf, now happily married and accompanied by his little son, who was possessed of a beauty that I had never before seen in a boy. And one time we were invited to dinner in Taif by King Faysal's son Turki and met there the great King's widow, the Lady 'Iffat, as well as other members of the immediate family, including several of Prince Turki's beautiful sisters and their husbands. There we were made to feel completely 'at home', the dinner being very delicious but entirely informal. And the widow of the great King -- his Life-partner for over forty years – reminisced together with Asad about the early years of their Saudi Arabia -- she married the then Amir Faysal in the early Thirties. She related to us a little about how she had come to Saudi Arabia in the first place from her native Turkey. She had been destined to be the wife of either King Abd al-Aziz or his son Faysal, and didn't learn which it was to be until she had actually arrived. It was the great good fortune of Faysal that his father had chosen not to marry her. Her influence over her husband during the long years of their extremely happy and close marriage was enormous. And the fruit of that marriage – their children -- show with their lives the results of that felicitous partnership. She, like her husband, is a great woman . . . .

And there was the time that Shaikh Zaki asked us to meet him in Geneva, where he was attending an OPEC conference. Of course he was very busy -- for he was the life and soul of OPEC and it was really his creation -- but in the evenings, when his strenuous meetings were over, he was able to join Tammam and ourselves for a relaxing dinner in one or another of the fabulous restaurants in Geneva. And he and his wife truly understood good food.

After a few days Zaki suddenly announced that he would be returning to Riyadh; would we like to accompany him? I pointed out that since it was February, all my clothing was geared to the harsh Geneva winter, and he replied, 'Don't worry about that.' In the evening Tammam's secretary knocked on our hotel room door -- we always stayed at the Intercontinental when we were Zaki's guests with car and driver at our permanent disposal -- and she delivered to me *three* pairs of suitable, and of course expensive and elegant, shoes perhaps selected by Tammam. Later when we reached Riyadh I was supplied amply with appropriate clothing for that hot, as well as conservative, place.

On arrival at Riyadh airport -- one of the most beautiful in the world -- we discovered that we had totally forgotten to request Saudi visas (we subconsciously considered that country our home) but between Zaki's important position and Asad's solid links with the royal family, visas were quickly obtained and we were able to leave for Shaikh Zaki's house.

During this visit Asad met again many old Najdi friends – of course many had disappeared in the course of so many years – and, most interesting of all, he was able to see what had transpired physically in Riyadh since the Twenties and Thirties when it had been his home. What we saw was very attractive, although naturally Riyadh had changed enormously; but the new buildings were in excellent taste, better than those in Medina, and the old royal palace of King Abd al-Aziz had been preserved for posterity. Trees and flowering bushes had been planted along the modern roads and there were gardens everywhere -- a visible refutal of the arrogant claim of the Israelis that only *they* could 'make the desert bloom'. We made it a point to visit the many large farms around Riyadh, and to see with our eyes what had been achieved by a proper application of science. But the occupiers of Palestine -- the Jews -- had achieved this with American and other Western money, while the Saudis had done it with their own . . . . And they had transformed Riyadh, with its mud-brick houses (abode) into a flourishing modern city without losing its character -- it was a real Arabian city.

We spent all our days in the always exhilarating company of Tammam and Zaki and went out occasionally by ourselves outside of Riyadh, for Asad wanted me to get the 'feel' of the old Arabia and the desert. Most importantly we visited Daraiyyah,[3] the cradle of the Wahhabi movement, passing on the way abandoned mud-brick castles and other evocative remnants of a century or more of beduin culture. I came to love Riyadh, as Asad had done so many years before,[4] and I was never expected to cover my face although, in deference to custom, I covered my head and body with a light black-silk *abaya,* which I find a beautiful, feminine and graceful dress. I never had 'problems' in Saudi Arabia . . . .

But the fondest memory of all was of the day when Shaikh

Zaki's wonderful eldest son Hani came up from Jidda. During one of our times together, he asked Asad if he wouldn't speak to his father about getting on with his formal engagement to Leila, the stunning blonde daughter of Ahmad Abd al-Wahhab, at that time still Chief of Protocol to King Fahd, as he had been for years with King Faysal -- he was primarily Faysal's man -- and King Khalid. Asad had known Ahmad Abd al-Wahhab for a long time. He was -- and is -- a great Arab gentleman and was a perfect Chief of Protocol with his excellent manners and great discretion.

In the evening Shaikh Zaki suddenly announced -- his announcements, although always thought out beforehand, usually came suddenly -- that we were 'going out' for dinner. He drove us, together with Tammam, to the home of Ahmad Abd al-Wahhab, informing us on the way that we would be witnesses to Hani's official engagement with the daughter of his old friend. We were greeted at the door by our host, as was his wont, and introduced to his lovely Damascene wife and their two daughters, the elder of which was to be affianced to Hani. She was a beautiful girl, well-educated and the product of the best 'finishing schools', but not vain. She was a bit shy and had impeccable manners, and we saw at once that Hani had made a perfect choice, both in his bride and his in-laws, who were, as I have said before, old and valued friends of Shaikh Zaki. We had dinner together, just the family, and the wife of Ahmad Abd al-Wahhab offered us the most sumptuous of Syrian fare, and afterwards, with the arrival of the 'official' witness, a well-known religious figure, 'it was written' that Hani and Leila would be partners for life. It made us happy to have been witnesses at this beautiful and modest celebration . . . .

III

All these visits to Saudi Arabia, plus the one to attend the wedding of Hani, gave us enormous pleasure, and we were treated by Zaki and his family as we had never been treated before -- or after. But in one sense they had an unsettling effect on Asad; they made him long to be closer physically to these dear friends, who had become *our* family in effect, and he became restless. And in the end it was to culminate in our leaving my beloved Portugal, and to upset our lives in a hundred unexpected ways.

Zaki Yamani was always prepared to help us in any and every way -- for he really wanted Muhammad Asad to have stability and comfort in his old age -- but he never tried to influence us in our decisions, which was right and correct. First Asad considered going back to Switzerland, or at least to the Lake of Geneva, where Zaki had a wonderful estate on the French side of the lake. But when we looked about for a house nearby, we found that anything to our taste was far too expensive and we did not want to burden that generous man in such a way. So, after almost two months spent in exploring the possibility of making our home there, by the Lake of Geneva where we had had such a positive, creative life so many years before, we abandoned the idea and returned home to Portugal and our two hounds.

But then, shortly afterwards, Asad received a letter from his old friend, Shaikh Abdallah Balkhair, who had recently bought an apartment in Marbella on the Costa del Sol and was very pleased with life there. We paid him a brief visit in summer and Asad immediately began to contemplate moving to the Costa del Sol -- a place that had never attracted either of us -primarily to be in physical contact with the Saudi Arabian friends who spent the hot summer months on the congenial – to them -- Spanish coast. We found a 'possible' -- barely possible house outside of Marbella -- nothing to compare with our residences in either Tangier or Portugal -- and decided to put my Casa Caravela up for sale. Unfortunately, we found a buyer fairly soon, and so 'the die was cast' . . .

A few months before our departure from Portugal our Afghan hound Shimshir suddenly fell ill and died overnight, probably as a result of poisoning. We buried him in his and our garden, and in a month's time he was joined by our saluki Farouk, the elder of the two, who suffered a heart attack in front of the veterinary clinic to which we were bringing him for his yearly inoculations. He was already unconscious when we brought him home and in the morning he was dead.

I cannot describe the loneliness and utter desolation of my last days and weeks in Portugal; somehow I felt in my very bones that we were making a major mistake -- and so it proved to be. We took leave of our two ambassadorial friends and their wives and our good neighbours in Belas, the Vilas Boas, with great sadness. I, for one, felt as if a heavy weight had been placed on my heart, and on the last day of packing Asad nearly collapsed with exhaustion. Although we had excellent professional packers -- and they are particularly good in Portugal -- much *had* to be done by ourselves personally, and a man of eighty-six should not have undertaken such a drastic move, and I should not have let him. But the restlessness that had characterized his youthful years, so long before my time, had returned in his late ones, and he could be very stubborn. Perhaps he was already anticipating an eventual 'homecoming of the heart' to the Arabia which he had left so many years ago but had never *really* left. I do not know . . . .

Endnotes

1 Palestine Liberation Organization (PLO), the recognized representative of the Palestian people, was established in 1964 in Jerusalem. Its first leader, the lawyer Ahmad Shuqayri, was a close ally of Egyptian president Nāsir. In 1969, Fatah's leader, Yasir Arafat, took over the organization.

cf. Helena Cobban: *The Palestinian Liberation Organization: People, Power and Politics.* Cambridge 1984.

2 In the list of Asad's books (in print), *Meditations...* is also included but not yet published.

3 Dir'iyyah (near Riyadh), the once great capital of the first Saudi state and the centre of an empire that flourished between 1745 and 1818. The city, which dominated the peninsula and its holy places, was sacked by the Egyptians under Ibrahim Pasha in 1818.

4 Muhammad Asad visited Riyadh (April 1930) and wrote three articles, based on his personal experiences. See for detail:

(i) Arabische Reise (Arabian Journey). Ankunft in Riadh (Arrival in Riyadh). (in: *Neue Zürcher Zeitung* (Zürich), 20 April 1930)

(ii) Bilder aus Riadh (Pictures from Riyadh). I. Das Herz Arabiens (Heart of the Arabs).
(in: Ibid., 8 June 1930)

(iii) Bilder aus Riadh. II. Der König (the King).
(in: Ibid., 6 July 1930)

* * * * *

محمد أسد ـ ليوبولد فايس

(رحلاته إلى العالم العربي)

ترجمة من اللغة الألمانية

إلى اللغة العربية

ترجمة الرسالة العلمية للأستاذ جونتر فيندهاجر

المقدمة لنيل شهادة الدكتوراه إلى معهد الثقافة وعلوم الاجتماع.

بجامعة فيينا مايو ٢٠٠٥م

وزارة التعليم العالي

٢٠١١م

Arabic Translation of Günter Windhager's German book "Muhammad Asad (Journey to the Arab World)", Riyadh 2011.

XVII
THE END OF THE ROAD
(1987-92)

I

When we arrived in Marbella, having left behind our two beloved hounds buried in the garden of Casa Caravela, it was the end of summer, but our friends the Balkhairs were still in residence. They invited us to dinner at their spacious apartment -- many times -- and were helpful to us in many ways. But when they had gone the winter in Marbella was a very lonely one; we had few acquaintances there and no friends. We hardly unpacked our belongings which had come overland from Portugal and had been opened -- against the normal 'rules' – in the customs in Malaga. We were later to find that many valuable belongings had been stolen there, and we had to pay customs dues -- also against the 'rules'. This was a good beginning to our new life in Spain -- or, rather, the Costa del Sol, which hasn't been Spain for many years. Now we were loath to unpack our beautiful carpets, antique furniture and objects d'art because I sensed that this would never be a real home to us.

In spite of its many advantages and attractions to people from all over the world, the Costa did not suit me. The climate was not much different from that of Tangier, but the two worlds were a thousand miles apart, although separated from one another only by the narrow Straits of Gibraltar. And so we decided to 'cut our losses', sell the house in Marbella and put our belongings in storage pending a 'wise' decision. We considered returning to Tangier, where Villa Asadiyya had not yet been sold, but finally decided that there was no going back -- a mistake in retrospect -- and we even inquired from a friend whether the house in Portugal which I had loved so much might not again be up for sale. And it *had* been, and had been bought by a new buyer only a few weeks earlier, and so it was not to be. Then we considered moving to a luxury flat in Gibraltar, then wisely dropped the idea and went to England to explore the possibilities of our living there. It was a very trying period for both of us -- in different ways. In spite of having so many real friends in England -- mostly, of course, in London -- after a few months of searching we gave up the idea of settling there as well.

Country houses -- which I would have preferred -- were either too remote or too expensive, and so were flats in London with their poky rooms. The climate was forbidding after so many years on the Mediterranean, etc., etc., etc. . . . . And Asad listened to the advice of too many people, all friends, all well-meaning, but all with different ideas as to how life should be lived. In the past we had always arrived at our *own* decisions, by ourselves alone and with certainty, and they were usually right ones -- the right ones for *us* . . . .

And so we returned to Spain and looked about for another house, this time in the Mijas area. We found one eventually, the usual 'Andalucian style' villa built by or for foreigners, in an 'urbanization' outside of Mijas. We took our lovely belongings out of storage and moved in about the middle of December 1987. We brought out from England the beautiful black Afghan hound -- called Shaytan -which our lady friends at Oxford had so generously presented to us as a gift from their last contemplated mating of their exceptional Afghans -and we proposed to be happy.

It is very difficult to put one's finger on the exact reasons, but we both still felt that we did not *belong* in the place which we had somewhat fatalistically chosen for ourselves, or which fate had chosen for us. We were blessed by helpful neighbours across the road and several new acquaintances, but we couldn't really settle down. We made the acquaintance of a young Spanish couple, both doctors who had become Muslims, and very good ones. Rahima and Yahya Molina visited us often, with their small children in tow, taking the great trouble to drive the long distance from Malaga, where they were then living. When summer arrived we met several more Saudi Arabian visitors and the Saudi Consul-General in Malaga, Bashir al-Kurdi, came to us often and was very kind to us in innumerable ways -- as he still is to me. But the life we were leading was empty of content, hostile to our natures. To this day I cannot entirely understand it or explain it, but it was so . . . .

II

In the summer of 1988 we received a visitor from Germany, a well-known journalist named Karl Günter Simon. He proposed to have a long interview with Asad at the request of the 'Frankfurter Allgemeine Zeitung', the successor of Asad's original newspaper of pre-Nazi times, the 'Frankfurter Zeitung' . Although he had become tired of giving interviews long ago, Asad was attracted by the idea of doing it for this *particular* newspaper. Mr Simon stayed in a hotel in Mijas and visited us several days in a row. He, too, found it somehow strange and unsettling that Muhammad Asad of Arabian fame was living in what he described so rightly in his interview as 'a house like so many thousands of others' on the Costa del Sol.[1] There was nothing badly wrong with the house as such, or the area in which it was located, overlooking Fuengirola and the sea with rolling mountains on all three sides of us. But we didn't 'belong' there as we had belonged in Switzerland, in Morocco and my Portugal; it was somehow alien to us, although the people were civilized and reasonably nice. But they were mostly prosperous, cold-blooded Scandinavians, who lived in Spain only to warm their old or middle-aged bones -- not at all *our* kind of people . . . .

The interview which appeared in November -- the interview which I had predicted to Hans Günter Simon would be Muhammad Asad's *last* newspaper interview -- caught his spirit very well and was accompanied by some extraordinary photographs of him, almost the last ever to be taken. And in it there was one of Shaytan as well, sitting near my husband -- for all our dogs loved him almost as much as they loved me, who was their slave. It is the only likeness that I have of my poor Shaytan.

In June of the same year we suddenly received a large envelope containing two letters from President Zia ul-Haqq -one rather formally addressed to Asad and the other much more warmly to me. In both letters he invited us to come to Pakistan with a view to returning there for good. I had very much liked life in Pakistan in the brief year that I had been there so many years ago -- in fact I liked it better than my husband did -- and we both still had a number of friends there. And since Asad so admired, and was admired by, Zia ul-Haqq himself, we unanimously decided to accept these invitations and to go there in the near future for the purpose of finding a suitable house. By the time we had accepted, Zia ul-Haqq had been killed in an airplane 'accident' over Pakistan and our fate took another sudden turn. Somehow, after Zia's death, neither of us was enthusiastic about the prospect of returning, although the invitation was automatically taken up by President Zia's successor -1 do not even remember his name; he was certainly not another Zia, or I would have.

Some months later Asad was invited by Amir Salman, a younger full-brother of King Fahd, to lunch at his beautiful but fairly modest -- for a Saudi prince -- villa in Marbella. Asad was much impressed by this true son of Ibn Saud. He had a very good appearance, elegantly dressed, modest and dignified in his bearing, and was quite clearly very, very intelligent. And after a few weeks he called on us at our house, accompanied by one of his sons and a number of Saudi Arabian dignitaries, including Shaikh Abdallah Balkhair. During the ensuing conversation and, I believe, having knowledge of our aborted decision to return to Pakistan, Prince Salman suggested that we settle in Jidda, where he would present us with a house and, if Asad so desired, a Saudi Arabian passport -- almost impossible to obtain on demand -- as well. Was this to be Muhammad Asad's final 'home-coming of the heart' at long last . . . ?

Shortly after the departure of Prince Salman, Asad received a phone-call from Amir Faysal bin Fahd, the son of the King, inviting him to an informal lunch with him -- the Saudi princes are always informal and 'easy' in their entertaining. The photographs of the two taken together at that time are the very last photographs ever to be taken of my husband. He was in appropriate company.

III

That same autumn Shaytan, who had arrived so healthy and so young, fell seriously ill. He proved to be suffering from an inflammation of the pancreas, caused probably by meat which had been purchased locally in Mijas. He was put on pills and a severe diet -- at such an age! -- and lost a lot of weight. Then, when it appeared that he *might* be improving, a blood test revealed that he had contracted the dreaded disease *leishmaniosis* or, as it is popularly called, 'the Mediterranean disease' which had killed so many dogs in our area. This disease is incurable and although in the early stages it can be controlled by more or less permanent daily injections, the dog gets progressively worse as time goes on until nothing can be done. We lost Shaytan towards the end of February; he was not quite two years old.

About a month later lightning struck. Asad had symptoms which caused us to consult a doctor and we learned that he had cancer of the bladder. He was immediately operated on in a clinic near Torremolinos, where no further treatment was even suggested. As always in time of trouble Asad turned to Shaikh Zaki, who immediately asked for the X-rays and all particulars from the clinic and had them sent to the Massachusetts General Hospital in my native Boston, where he proposed to send Asad for further, serious treatment. On my birthday, April 12th, we flew from Malaga to New York, to spend a day or two together with Talal and his wife before going on to the hospital in Boston. Talal had been advised of our arrival beforehand, and we were met by him and his wife at the airport in New York. Talal was deeply distressed and he came closer to me then than he ever had before, or after. Of course he really did love his father and the prospect of what might lie ahead made him very unhappy.

Shaikh Zaki had made all the arrangements in Boston beforehand. A suite in the most luxurious hotel overlooking the Public Gardens and the Boston Common -- where I had spent so many days of my youth -- was put at our disposal for as long as would be necessary, and an appointment had already been made for consultation with a famous, but very unpleasant, specialist at the Massachusetts General Hospital. On examination he coldly confirmed the worst: the cancer was spreading and another operation would be necessary, immediately. He gave Asad a 'fifty-fifty' chance of recovery. The operation was made and followed by a course of many months of chemotherapy alternating with radiation treatment.

And so Asad was in and out of hospital from April to November. He bore the after-treatment amazingly well, although to me it was not really amazing because he had always been very courageous, quite stoical. He never complained. He truly possessed that quality -- that great virtue -called *sabr* in the Qur'an -- the 'patience in adversity' so strongly praised. Zaki telephoned to both of us daily and in July came to pay us a brief visit. He behaved to my husband as if he were his own father, and nothing was too much for him. And during these long months we received telephone calls from various other friends -- there was none like Zaki -- from all over the world.

Early in September Asad was examined in the scanner and pronounced 'cured'; he had only one more session of radiation treatment when lightning struck again. Getting out of the taxi that took us to the hospital, Asad leaned on the window at the driver's side in order to pay him the fare. As he was fumbling in his wallet for change for a tip and before I could reach him, the driver impatiently revved up the car and knocked him to the ground. Asad was unable to get up and I knew that another hip-bone had been broken. When we got him into the hospital I insisted that he should have an X-ray taken before being treated by radiation, and they reluctantly did so. The resulting picture showed a crack right across the head of the femur. I had become quite an expert on hip-bones by this time . . . .

But they insisted on completing the last radiation treatment, which involved Asad's being lifted onto a high table, which certainly could have done him no good. Afterwards he was placed in a wheel-chair -- a sight which cut me to the heart — and it was suggested that he be examined by a scanner at the hospital. Apparently there was a waiting-list in the hospital, one of the best in the world! The resultant delay proved fatal, for by the time it was made -- five days later -- the bone had clearly broken through. There was no remedy except an operation like the ones that he had twice undergone over ten years earlier in Rabat and London.

The operation was undertaken by one of the best orthopaedic surgeons in Boston, and was successful. But, of course, still another operation didn't do his heart, already weakened, any good.

Several days after the operation it was suggested that Asad should go for physiotherapy to the Spaulding Rehabilitation Hospital, where again the many doctor friends of Shaikh Zaki made all the necessary arrangements. After a month there, Asad was prepared to return to the hotel and then back 'home' to Spain. Shaikh Zaki was scheduled to come for his annual lectures at Harvard Law School and so we waited until his arrival. This time his wife accompanied him, as she almost invariably did, and Zaki gave a big dinner party in the private dining-room of our hotel for a few of his many friends in Boston -- some of them judges, some lawyers, others doctors and one delightful Jesuit priest, Dr. Gavin, a great lover of Arabia who was in charge of the Semitic Museum at Harvard, and he was accompanied by his very elderly but still beautiful mother. Shaikh Zaki Yamani has many friends everywhere, because he himself is such a friend to so many, many people. And never had anyone cared more for Asad -- except myself -- than did that wonderful man, whose warmth and generosity of heart can never be properly described -- by me or anyone else.

We returned 'home' via New York in order to see Talal and Tanya at the airport -- although it was inconvenient to us -- to spend a few hours with them. Talal had, of course, come up to Boston three times to visit his father and was often in contact directly with him by telephone -- he had nothing to say to me, not ever. Talal and Tanya saw us to the plane; we little realized, any of us, that this would be the last time that Talal and his father -- 'Abu Talal' as he and his wife and previously his mother -- had always called him. And that was exactly what he was to Talal: 'Abu Talal' . . . .

IV

On our return to Spain we stayed for some months in a luxurious hotel-cum-clinic in Marbella, as usual arranged and insisted on by dear Zaki. He wanted us to recuperate from the strains of the past nine months before facing the harsh reality of daily life in our not-too-comfortable house near Mijas. In our absence our correspondence had piled up and it was very difficult, in fact impossible, to get things completely sorted out. This I only accomplished in the months after my husband's death.

We tried to pick up the pieces of our broken life, but it was very difficult. And the ensuing two years were empty of any real content, except mutual suffering, except that we were at least together.

V

In the summer of 1990 we had a surprise visit -- he always came by surprise and without previous announcement -- by Zaki and Tammam. They had come in their yacht to Malaga, mainly to see us, and we were invited to lunch by a good friend of Shaikh Zaki's who lived in Fuengirola, not very far from Mijas. I was unfortunately unwell that day and so Asad had to go without me, a very exceptional occurrence because we were almost always together. On his return Asad was accompanied by Zaki and Tammam, Tammam's sweet mother and all five of their young, beautifully-behaved children, whom we knew so well. In his brief visit I tried to convey to Zaki how grateful we were to him and his family, which was like our own family -- the only one that we had -- but no words are ever adequate. That was the last time we were to see dear Zaki before Asad's death.

At almost the same period we received an invitation to lunch from Prince Salman, who had just arrived in Marbella. But a few days later the war broke out in the Persian Gulf and both Prince Salman and Shaikh Zaki suddenly left the country -- separately, of course -- and our meeting with that exceptional prince had to be cancelled.

The following year passed uneventfully for us, and I could see that Asad was becoming more and more withdrawn from life -- and from me, which was painful beyond belief. About the beginning of February he began to spend more and more time resting in bed -- a rare thing for him because somehow he had always had the will and energy to live a normal, reasonably active life. And he lost interest in current events, books, everything -- even me. I persuaded him to walk about the house, with my assistance in case he should fall, and I tried, very hard, to make him take a little interest in life, in me, but I felt him gradually slipping away. I requested a local Danish doctor to examine him and he suggested a course of several very up-to-date bio-chemical medicines to pick up his strength and regain his waning appetite. When I took him aside and demanded to know what to expect, the doctor remarked that he could go on like that until he was a hundred years old, it was hard to tell . . . .

And then, abruptly, he went down and within two days he was dead. It was on the evening of February 20th and I had just fed him a little, but it was hard to persuade him to swallow his food or to take his medicines. I decided to call the doctor the same evening, although it was late. Giving him some water, I bent over to kiss him on the lips and felt his weak response; but when I returned immediately from the kitchen, he was gone . . . .

How to describe the nightmare that followed? Our Danish neighbours helped me to reach the doctor -- it was about eleven o'clock by now -- and at my request they contacted Talal on the telephone to let him know what had happened. Talal had been telephoning his father regularly, usually once a week, since our return to Spain, and on the last occasion, talked to me because it was hard for Asad to go to the telephone. He suggested that he would try to take time off in March to visit his father.

That same night I telephoned to Bashir al-Kurdi, the Saudi Arabian Consul-General, but he was away in Sweden. His driver and my good friend, a very intelligent young Indonesian named Abd ar-Rahim bin Sodikin, immediately insisted on coming to the house, and he stayed with me for several hours, although it was very late, trying to give me the comfort of another human presence. I spent the night alone, with the lights on, with the remains of my husband- and even that was better than being without him . . . .

Late that night Bashir al-Kurdi telephoned from Stockholm and asked me if my husband -- my late husband by now -had left any specific wishes about his burial. I replied that the only thing that he would have insisted on -- and I with him -was to be buried in a Muslim graveyard, in the Muslim way. Later Abd ar-Rahim, who by them had been my closest friend in Spain and who remains so to this day -- a very valuable friend -- was to tell me that some months back, while driving Asad on some errand in Marbella, he had said to him that he hoped to be able to die in his beloved Arabia -- his 'homecoming of the heart' -- but he never told *me* this, probably to avoid making me suffer.

Early in the morning the *imam* of the King Abd al-Aziz Mosque in Marbella came to the house, accompanied by some people from the Saudi Consulate -- and of course my faithful Abd ar-Rahim, to wash and prepare Asad's body for burial. It was a very hard thing to witness -- something that had never happened to me before. But I had Abd ar-Rahim with me and that helped. Then they took him away -- it was a Friday -- for the funeral prayers in the beautiful little mosque in Marbella named for Asad's great and beloved friend, King Abd al-Aziz al-Saud. It was really very appropriate . . . .

On Saturday afternoon Asad's only son, Talal, arrived -- he had taken the first available plane from New York via London -- and went straight to the hotel in Mijas. I had hoped that at this point in our strange but long relationship we could have helped to comfort one another ... but it was not to be. In the morning of Sunday we drove together, with my dear friend Abd ar-Rahim competently at the wheel and feeling his moral support beside me, to Granada. A handful of acquaintances and some people from the Saudi Consulate joined us there. We buried my husband of forty long years in the tiny Muslim graveyard opposite the Alhambra hill which had been set aside by the supposedly 'fanatically Catholic' General Franco for the burial of his Moroccan comrades and their families. It was a beautiful but for me desolate place and there was snow on the surrounding hills. We buried him in a shallow grave by the side of that of the infant daughter of our Spanish-Muslim doctor friends Yahya and Rahima Molina -- an infant barely twenty days old and a man of almost ninety-two; it seemed somehow fitting and to me somehow comforting; I don't exactly know why.

The only people present at the modest burial of this truly great man who really knew and loved him were Talal and myself, and Abd ar-Rahim, my Indonesian friend, who had always treated him with such respect and gentle affection, and Doctor Yahya, the father of the dead infant buried by my husband's side.

VI

When the Saudi Arabian Consul-General returned from Sweden Asad had already been buried. I later was to learn that his wife had been operated for a brain tumour in Sweden – thus his absence. But he had given instructions to his staff to do everything in their power to assist me in my distress, and they were all extremely kind and helpful, although I never saw them later. They simply were impervious to the fact that I was entirely alone -- without family or friends by my side – and that I would have welcomed a brief visit, even a short telephone call, from them. But it did occur to them to go in a small delegation to the airport to meet Talal, whom they had never met before, and to visit him in his hotel, and to send him off quite ceremoniously at his departure from the airport of Malaga. I wonder if this is the usual widow's lot in the Arab world after her husband's -- a famous man's -- death. I will never know and if I should, it wouldn't matter to me now. But I always had Abd ar-Rahim to talk to on the telephone, because by the nature of his job as chauffeur and man of all trades to the Consul-General and his Saudi Arabian friends in Marbella, it was impossible for him to visit me at my house. But I knew that he was always there . . . .

What particularly saddened me was that Zaki had been unable to come from Jidda to attend the funeral. On learning of Asad's illness only a few days before by his friend in Fuengirola, Zaki had wanted to come to us immediately and it would have been wonderful to have had him, of all people, at my side. When he telephoned me from Jidda Asad was already dead. He and his wife Tammam both talked to me on the telephone and tried to give me what little comfort anyone can do in this situation. Zaki could hardly speak and it was obvious that he would be unable to come for the funeral. But I felt his presence at the side of the grave -- because Zaki had been the best friend -- much, much more than a friend -- that either Asad or I had ever had.

On learning the news from the Consul-General, Prince Salman telephoned on at least three separate occasions to inquire about my welfare -- so different from all the other Saudis; but he is not only a prince but a great man. It was very considerate of him; he also insisted that he personally be responsible for all the costs of my husband's very modest funeral. The Saudi Arabian royal family have always looked after their own ... and Asad had always loved the descendants of the great Abd al-Aziz ibn Saud, the royal friend of his youth. Thus, his physical 'home-coming of the heart' was never to take place, -- but then, a part of him had *always* remained in Arabia; I knew it so well.

Later, some people were to complain that my husband's body had not been sent for burial in Mecca or Medina -- and I could only respond with the saying of the Prophet, which Asad had so often quoted to me in the past: 'No one knows where his bones will lie' . . . .

And that was the end of the road -- a long and adventuresome road -- for Muhammad Asad: the little graveyard in Granada, by the side of his fellow-Muslims.

VII

In attempting to sum up the personality, character and temperament of the extraordinary -- *literally* out of the ordinary -man who had been my companion for almost forty years, and with as little emotion and as much objectivity as is humanly possible, I would state that he was a passionate, sensual person with enormous self-control (self-knowledge?) and an almost austere, seemingly remote bearing and outer comportment. He was passionate in his love for me until the very end, but avoided any demonstration of it in public, and often even in private. He was incapable of demonstrating, by touch, this feeling for me -- which I so often longed for -- but he showed in innumerable little ways his great consideration for my feelings and my well-being. He hated to see me doing housework, and even in the 'hardest' of times financially, he always managed to have a woman in the house to help me -that is, until we settled in Spain, where it has become so difficult to obtain the kind of help I needed.

He loved animals, especially hounds and horses, deeply, and they felt it and responded with their love. He loved his friends -- and he had many -- but we were unfortunate in that most of our friends -- for his friends invariably became mine -were scattered all over the world. With few exceptions, these friends were all Muslims, but he loved them not because of any imaginary 'Islamic solidarity' but because he had so much more in common with them than with non-Muslims.

He deeply loved his son Talal -- albeit 'in spite of everything'. But he was never, at least in his time with me, able to really communicate with this strange son as he had wanted to do so very much, and which I had wanted for him. Talal himself is a very reserved and complex personality, also incapable of showing in his outward comportment the deep love which he *must* have felt in return. It was sad and, as I was fully aware of it, I tried to explain to Talal that his father had always loved him very much, but that, by his very nature, was unable to put it through to him, which gave Talal the false feeling of 'remoteness'. It simply wasn't so.

As for his relations with me, he was never remote, neither in the interior or exterior sense of the word. He was warm and tender and considerate beyond description. In short, he loved me with all the feeling of which he was capable, which was very much. At the end I was the only true subject -- not object -- of his love, the only one who nearly 'possessed' him -- for no human being can ever 'possess' another.

He loved to be surrounded by beautiful objects -- but he could easily live without them. He loved my physical attributes -- but as I grew older by his side and less beautiful than when he had met me as a very young woman, I never was less beautiful in *his* eyes. It was one to him; he loved *me* . . . .

In the physical sense, he was very imposing. He was tall and straight as a ramrod when I first met him, although at the end, as a result of a convoluted spine and two hip-bone replacements, he was almost bent double -- but only towards the very end.

He looked magnificent in clothes, with his broad, straight, angular shoulders. He had beautiful legs. He never shaved off his beard; we made a pact at the time of our marriage that he would never remove his beard and I would never cut off my long hair; we maintained that pact. As I have said, he looked magnificent when 'dressed', but preferred to go about in sports jacket and worn cordoroy slacks. Most of his lovely, tailor-made suits were given away by me, almost unused, to a good friend of ours after his death. An Arab acquaintance of ours told me not long ago that he had 'known' Muhammad Asad in Medina when he, the acquaintance, was still a child. He still remembered seeing Muhammad Asad striding through the streets of his favourite city -- the favourite of our Prophet as well -- in his sandals, dressed in the most elegant Arab dress that he had ever seen. He loved Arab dress and looked right in it -- but he never wore it 'for show' outside of Arabia itself, as was the case of Lawrence[2] and others -- some of them genuine converts to Islam, but always prone to display what my husband rightly termed 'fancy dress'. There was nothing of the actor in him; he was always his modest self.

During the last few days of his life, I asked him two questions, I don't know why. Perhaps I had an unadmitted premonition that his death was very near. One of these questions was -- Who were the women in your life whom you have truly loved? And he answered immediately -- without a second's hesitation -- 'You and Elsa' (his first wife, who died in Mecca in 1927), and is buried there.[3]

The second question sums up this man's personality. I asked him if he had ever done anything of which he was later ashamed. And he replied, also immediately, 'Yes, once.' And then he explained to me that in the early 1920s, several years before he finally realized that he was already a Muslim and finally embraced Islam formally, he had been travelling with Elsa and her son Ahmad in Iran when he suddenly felt a longing to be entirely alone -- alone with himself and God -and had been 'tempted' to leave her with some friends and to travel alone in order to experience being fully, utterly, by himself -- without companionship, alone with the Absolute that he had always craved. But then, he told me, he thought that it would be cruel and selfish to exclude her from his life -even temporarily -- and had decided against it. He never told Elsa, but she, being so perceptive and loving him so deeply, *must* have sensed a withdrawal of sorts. And this was the event, if one can call it that, which he felt 'ashamed' of almost seventy years later! I am happy to say, to *know,* that he had never experienced that desire to be alone with me; we were always together, even to the end . . . .

He loved Pakistan, *his* conception of Pakistan, even when it turned its back on him, and he never felt resentment at the treatment he had received from it. He remained a citizen -- the first citizen of Pakistan -- until the end, although he had been strongly tempted to accept the generous, spontaneous gesture of Amir Salman to have Saudi citizenship and passport -which would have made his life and his travels so much easier.

His love for Arabia was different because, unlike Pakistan which was an affair of the head, his love for Arabia was truly one of the heart (I was sometimes almost jealous of Arabia, if you can be jealous of a place, a people and an atmosphere). He loved the immense, austere deserts of Arabia, he loved its people, especially the beduin and the people of his beloved Najd. He loved the royal family of Saudi Arabia-the physical descendants of Ibn Saud -- in spite of the occasional lapses or shortcomings of some of its members -- but who is perfect?

He was absolutely without vanity or arrogance. I was astonished when, once in London -- it was in the early Eighties – a bold and seemingly intelligent young Pakistani woman confronted him with the statement, 'You are arrogant!' He was not. He was modest beyond description, but he was equally certain of his *own* certainties. When he reached a conclusion and expressed it, he was ever-ready to listen to the counter arguments of others, but was never shaken by them because he never reached an intellectual conclusion without deep thought and when he was convinced that he was right, he never hesitated to defend his ideas, no matter what the cost in human esteem or in financial benefits. He was modest – but never self-effacing -- in his behaviour. He was, in short, *good*-intensely, quietly good . . . .

He was rarely jealous in his love for me, but when he was, it was terrible. He very seldom lost his temper, but when he did, it was equally terrible, because it took him a long time to get over it -- quite the opposite of myself, who can 'fly off the handle' but immediately get over it. In our rare arguments, it was always *I* who had to apologize and thus break the unbearable ice, even when I was convinced that I was in the right, which was not always the case but often. He was, in short, a perfect husband, if such a thing exists. He was certainly the perfect companion for me for almost forty years.

I do realize that in setting down these random observations, realizations and reminiscences, I am breaking all the rules of literary composition, but it is the *only* way in which I can attempt to get across to the many friends who loved him and to his innumerable admirers in every part of our Muslim world, what this great man was *really* like. Of course, I do realize, also, that some of these reminiscences are intensely personal -- even intimate -- but since he is dead, it cannot hurt his deep sense of propriety. And there can be nothing of impropriety in describing that wonderful personality, at once so complex and so essentially simple.

He was all that I have described, and so much more. For example, he was never interested in money as such, nor in accumulating it, and it was only after the publication of his unequalled translation of and commentary on the Holy Qur'an that he began to accumulate some money, but not by his own intention or effort; it was a *baraka* from God, through the instrumentality of our greatest friend, Shaikh Zaki Yamani, that this came about and left me a relatively wealthy widow upon his death -- wealthy in memories and financially. He himself did not know how to 'handle' or what to do with money when it finally came to him after so many years of relative poverty; he spent it on *me,* but never with extravagance.

He had been born, on his father's side, to a family of scholars; his grandfather had been an eminent rabbi in Rumania,[4] and was famed for his broadness of mind and his tolerance of and friendship for people of other faiths -- his closest friend had been a Catholic priest. His ancestors, on his father's side and almost certainly on his mother's as well, were almost certainly of Turkic origin, descendants of those Khazars about whom Arthur Koestler[5] has written so well in 'The Thirteenth Tribe'. In his old age, I observed, his eyes became distinctly slanted upwards and the high, beautiful cheekbones -- Tolstoy-like -- more pronounced; it made him even more handsome, in his unconventional way, at least in my eyes. He never quite lost his German accent in English – although he wrote it exquisitely, possessing a vocabulary far richer than my own, to whom the English language is native. In his earlier years he had a slight Indian accent, but that disappeared in the time I knew him, to be replaced by German syntax in his very old age. All this I found quite fascinating, as was everything about him.

He loved rich food, but was normally abstemious. When he rarely 'broke the rules', he liked to indulge in his favourite dish, lobsters or crayfish smothered in mayonnaise, and he loved, nay craved, highly-spiced Indian sauces and much fat, what I used to teasingly describe as grease -- for I have a horror of fatty dishes. He loved to eat creamy desserts, and of course chocolate, but rarely indulged in them. When we were undergoing our ordeal in Boston at the time of his cancer treatment, as I have mentioned earlier our beloved Shaikh Zaki insisted on our keeping the suite of rooms at the Four Seasons Hotel overlooking the park. But realizing how costly this was, we almost daily ate a frugal breakfast, little or no lunch, and in the evening -- in our room -- we ate hamburgers -day after day until they were practically coming out of our ears, when we switched to club sandwiches. I, together with him, did not want to impose on Zaki's boundless generosity. Zaki himself would have been horrified -- and will be upon reading this -- had he known, because he stressed that he wanted Asad to 'eat well' -- but it was the correct thing to do and we had no regrets -- so please forgive us, dear Zaki . . . .

He hated to borrow money, when he had none, and never 'begged' from his many immensely wealthy friends. But when he received spontaneous gifts from them, for himself, or for me or for his work, which came to the same thing -- he accepted them without any false pride. He realized what was 'due' to him, even though he never demanded it. Although King Ibn Saud was immensely generous to him, when he was still a relatively poor king, Asad left Arabia a poor man; he could just as easily, without effort or dishonesty, become a multi-millionaire, as most of the people around Ibn Saud and the royal family *did* become. King Faysal -- perhaps as an unconscious reaction to his father's open-handedness -- was not like his father, at least not to my husband, but Asad did not hold this against him. Only once in his life did he ask Faysal to assist him financially. That was when we had almost completed our house in Tangier and had entirely run out of funds. We had a small debt to a bank in Tangier and were quite unable to repay it ourselves. Asad finally wrote to King Faysal and, explaining its purpose, requested from him the enormous sum of five thousand pounds sterling! It was immediately granted, of course, but in the meantime there had been a severe, sudden devaluation of the pound sterling. But, of course, Asad never mentioned this to King Faysal. What he actually received was half of what he had requested -- and needed badly; but somehow or other we managed to raise the rest.

Most of the sons of Ibn Saud are very generous, almost to a fault. Both the present king, Fahd, and his younger full-brother Salman, were generous to him -- to us -- in the last years of his life. As I have not yet met King Fahd, I cannot write about him from first-hand knowledge, but I do know that Asad greatly admired his liberality. Soon upon his accession to the throne on his brother Khalid's death, Fahd gave a speech in Bahrain which impressed us both deeply because it revealed a truly liberal, 'modern' mind, in the best sense of the word. Unfortunately this speech went more or less unperceived by his countrymen -- or his subjects -- and even by the rest of the Muslim world. If he has not been able so far to change things in Arabia as much as he would have liked, he is doing everything possible -- always taking into account the innate conservatism of his people; and in this he is right because you cannot, and should not, 'force' things. A wise king has not only to lead, but also, in a sense, *to follow* his people; and, to my mind, Saudi Arabia is on a good way.

As for Amir Salman, I cannot say more than that he is a great gentleman in the full sense of the word, somewhat like his brother Faysal, but more generous. I believe that he will make an excellent ruler, when his time comes. And the Crown Prince, Abdullah, is also a good man; although I have not met him personally, I have gathered this not only from my husband himself but from many other Saudis as well.

Asad was kind and intensely tender towards animals. He told me once about a Turcoman horse that used to follow him about, without reins, in the streets of Iranian villages, and even tried once to enter the house into which Asad had entered. I can well understand this love which the horse felt for him. His tenderness towards our five hounds -- over so many years of our life together -- cannot be described; but they knew it. Towards 'humanity' at large he felt nothing; towards his *ummah* -- the Muslim community -- everything. To me, his wife, again, everything; towards his son and his real friends, very, very much.

I have been a very fortunate woman, having experienced a love and comportment towards me that few women have experienced. I realize it fully now that he is gone; and the memory keeps me warm and sustains me in my immense loneliness -- for I will always be lonely. How fortunate I have been; how good God has been to me by bestowing upon me the life-companionship of Muhammad Asad!

How lonely was his funeral in Granada; how simple his grave. He was buried by people who, although Muslims, did not have the slightest realization of the greatness, the uniqueness, of the man whose remains they were interring. Only I, and perhaps his son, realized this. And they were a community of so-called *sufis* whom he did not admire or respect, although Asad acknowledged that they were Muslims. Ten years or so in Granada, they had refused his request for assistance in finding a house in Albaicin, recommending him to visit one of their 'shaikhs' in Tangier to 'study Islam'(!) before contemplating taking up residence in Granada -- as if they owned the place. It was a truly insulting letter; he never answered it; he only laughed and decided that Granada was no longer for us . . . .

After his death several of his intimates of earlier years wrote to me, telling me this and that about Muhammad Asad. What they did not know was that *I* already knew all these little things, and much more, about his past, even about his very distant past, long before my birth. He shared his every thought with me, every memory, and thus I am privileged to be able not only to complete his memoirs but also to see to it that the film that will be made of his life -- or part of it because the whole would take many films to convey -- will be as genuine as possible, not only with regard to his appearance and personality, but also respecting the Arabian background of his youth, when most of the beduin were ragged and not all that clean (how could they have been?) and the real Arabs dressed rather differently -- and much more beautifully -- than in later years. I have not only his descriptions in my head but also a unique collection of photographs of that period by my husband.

The most beautiful and most famous photograph ever taken of King Abd al-Aziz was that by my husband, who had the monarch sitting down, turned his head this way and that and adjusted his *kuffiya* to his liking until he was satisfied -- and thus caught on film something of the outer and inner beauty of that great, indescribable personage. The eyes are thoughtful, the face -- in profile -- grave and strong, the mouth sensual , as a man's mouth should be. I am proud to possess the original of this wonderful photograph which has graced the reception room of every house that we have ever inhabited together and still adorns my walls, now that I am alone. I almost feel that I myself have known that beautiful, fantastic man who, as Asad has said so often, was 'larger than life' . . ., Abd al-Aziz ibn Saud was truly gigantic, not only in size -- in height -- but also in character; he was matchless, unique, unrepeatable; it is no wonder that his sons revere his memory and jealously guard it from unfair criticism.

VIII

I can find no better ending for this, the story of the long and fruitful and essentially very happy life of Muhammad Asad than the following passage of 'The Road to Mecca'; it is the core of his life-story:

> 'My arms are crossed under my neck and I am looking into this Arabian night which curves over me, black and starry. A shooting star flies in a tremendous arc, and there another, and yet another: arcs of light piercing the darkness . . . .
>
> How could it be otherwise? Ever since I came to Arabia I have lived like an Arab, worn only Arab dress, spoken only Arabic, dreamed my dreams in Arabic; Arabian customs and imageries have almost imperceptibly shaped my thoughts; I have not been hampered by the many mental reservations which usually make it impossible for a foreigner- be he ever so well versed in the manners and the language of the country -- to find a true approach to the feelings of its people and to make their world his own.
>
> And suddenly I have to laugh aloud with the laughter of happiness and freedom -- so loud that Zayd looks up in astonishment and my dromedary turns its head towards me with a slow, faintly supercilious movement: for now I see how simple and straight, in spite of all its length, my road has been -- my road from a world which I did not possess to a world truly my own.
>
> My coming to this land: was it not, in truth, a home-coming? Home-coming of the heart that has espied its old home backward over a curve of thousands of years and now recognizes this sky, my sky, with painful rejoicing? For this Arabian sky -- so much darker, higher, more festive with its stars than any other sky -- vaulted over the long-trek of my ancestors, those wandering herds-men-warriors, when, thousands of years ago, they set out in the power of their morning, obsessed by greed for land and booty, towards the

fertile country of Chaldea and an unknown future: that small beduin tribe of Hebrews, forefathers of that man who was to be born in Ur of the Chaldees.

That man, Abraham, did not really belong in Ur. His was but one among many Arabian tribes which at one time or another had wound their way from the hungry deserts of the Peninsula towards the northern dreamlands that were said to be flowing with milk and honey -the settled lands of the Fertile Crescent, Syria and Mesopotamia. Sometimes such tribes succeeded in overcoming the settlers they found there and established themselves as rulers in their place, gradually intermingling with the vanquished people and evolving, together with them, into a new nation -- like the Assyrians and Babylonians, who erected their kingdoms on the ruins of the earlier Sumerian civilization, or the Chaldeans, who grew to power in Babylon, or the Amorites, who later came to be known as Canaanites in Palestine and as nomads were too weak to vanquish those who had arrived earlier and were absorbed by them; or, alternatively, the settlers pushed the nomads back into the desert, forcing them to find other pastures and perhaps other lands to conquer. The clan of Abraham -- whose original name, according to the Book of Genesis, was *Ab-Ram,* which in ancient Arabic means 'He of the High Desire' -- was evidently one of the weaker tribes; the Biblical story of their sojourn at Ur on the fringe of the desert relates to the time when they found that they could not win for themselves new homes in the land of the Twin Rivers and were about to move northwest along the Euphrates towards Harran and thence to Syria.

'He of the High Desire', that early ancestor of mine whom God had driven towards unknown spaces and so to a discovery of his own self, would have well understood why I am here -- for he also had to wander through many lands before he was allowed to strike root. To his awe-commanding experience my puny perplexity would have been no riddle. He would have known -- as I know it now -- that the meaning of all my wanderings lay in a hidden desire to meet myself by meeting a world whose approach to the innermost questions of life, to reality itself, was different from all I had been accustomed to in my childhood and youth . . . .'

And in his 'Postscript' to the 1973 edition of 'The Road to Mecca' he wrote the following:

> 'This, then, is the story of my road to Mecca: the story of the home-coming of my heart, as I began to understand it during those distant days in the late summer of 1932, when we rode, rode, two men on two dromedaries, from the confines of Arabia towards the south.'
>
> "Home-coming of the heart": this phrase always echoes in my mind whenever I think of those Arabian years and of the greeting *ahlan wa-sahlan* -- 'welcome home' -- which I so often heard from Arab lips. I heard it in the library of the Great Mosque in Mecca, in the spring of 1927, when I was introduced to Amir Faysal, that princely son of the family which over the years was to become almost a family to me as well. And it was with the same greeting that I was received by his father, the legendary King Ibn Saud, who in time would address me as "my son" . . . .
>
> The words *ahlan wa-sahlan* went on echoing within me as the years rolled by, long after the Arabian years had sunk into the past and disappeared behind the western horizon of the Arabian Sea. By then, the soil of India was under my feet, and the dust of India had replaced the desert-clear air of Arabia: for a dream had called out to me -- a dream that demanded fulfilment and was in the end, despite all its shortcomings, fulfilled by the creation of an Islamic state called Pakistan.
>
> The years which I spent working for and in Pakistan belong to another story, which I may, perhaps, narrate at another time. But these two main streams of my life coalesced once again when I returned to Arabia in 1951, after an absence of more than eighteen years, and looked up once again at the starry Arabian sky on my way from Jidda to Mecca: this time in a fast car flying the Pakistani flag, over a brand-new, macademized highway which covered the countless tracks made by camels and donkeys and sandalled pilgrims over more than a thousand years. I was coming to Saudi Arabia as an emissary of the Government of Pakistan -- and yet, it was a new 'home-coming of the heart . . . .'

Endnotes

1 For the English translation of Simon's interview, see *Gift*, I.

2 Col. T. E. Lawrence (1888-1935), better known as 'Lawrence of Arabia', is famous for the role he played in organizing the revolt of Arabs of the Hejaz against their Ottoman overlords during the First World War (1914-1918).

Lawrence wrote *Seven Pillars of Wisdom* (1926) which he chronicled the constant raiding parties and described what it was to live as a Bedouin in the desert.

His achievements in Arabia were prodigious: his two-month journey over more than one thousand miles of desert and his crossing of the Sinai in a 49-hour camel ride, have become the stuff of legend.

cf. *Travellers in Arabia. British Explorers in Saudi Arabia.* Edited by Eid Al Yahya, London 2006, p. 36.

3 Elsa Schiemann (Islamic name 'Aziza Muhammad") born in Berlin (1878) and died in Mecca (1927); primarily a painter. Asad's first wife and after conversion, she came to Saudi Arabia with her husband. The hot climate of this country was unbearable for her and she died in Mecca. She had only one son, Heinrich Ahmad Schiemann (1916-2002), who was sent back to Germany by his step-father, Asad.

cf. G. Windhager's German book (2002), op. cit., pp. 103-106.

4 Asad's grandfather was Benjamin Weiss (1841-1912). He was Rabbi in Czernowitz (now in Ukraine).

5 Arthur Koestler (1905-1983), British writer and journalist, political refugee and prisoner; his "Darkness at Noon" (1940) is a masterpiece and one of the great political novels of the century.

* * * * *

Günther Windhager

Leopold Weiss alias Muhammad Asad

Von Galizien nach Arabien
1900–1927

böhlauWien

Title page of G. Windhager's German book on Asad (from 1900 to 1927), Vienna 2000

APPENDICES

Neue Zürcher Zeitung

11. Dezember 1932 Blatt 4

Erste Sonntagsausgabe Nr 2329

Gespräch in Indien

After Muhammad Asad's arrival in India (Nov. 1932), his first article sent to Swiss newspaper *Neue Zürcher Zeitung* (Zürich), dated 11 Dec. 1932 (English translation follows)

I

A CONVERSATION IN INDIA

Just before sunset an Indian friend and I sat down on the doorsteps of the royal mosque, which was built by the last powerful ruler of the great Mughals, Aurangzeb, in the 17th century. The mosque towers above the large, silent, wide open courtyard. It is made of pale brown and red stones and wonderfully crowned by three white marble domes. Only a few delicate cream-white ornaments adorn the walls. Four lofty, firmly constructed, austere minarets mark the corners of the square. The whole picture breathes air and architectural deepness, and the rational and sophisticated composition of this sprawling building touched me with its sonorous solemnity. The setting sun sprinkled quivering flecks and agate-coloured streaks of light on the marble dome's tiles, just to let them finally rest on the puce walls.

Suddenly I said: "How they all vanished —"; because I was thinking of Aurangzeb and all the others that were before him, all the great ones who gave India its form and its name. All of them passed by in the course of the centuries. My friend guessed my thoughts and said: "But the Indian nation in its greatness endured them —".

I responded: "This is indeed a thought that torments me since all the months I am staying in India. These people outlived everyone and every thing - but they are a vast and silent nation without a proper form or a history. They are estranged from their destiny and in a passive way chaotic. It seems as if the Indian nation is just a fortuitous conglomerate. Only a very loose connection is tying its different parts together, almost coincidentally, and they only seem connected on grounds of their geographical juxtaposition. It reminds me of a landscape painting which the viewer would frowningly judge as not having "enough air". Their days are passing by without any spiritual rhythm or significance and it is not possible to find a common thread or line in this face of India. There is no meaningful connection."

My friend seemed surprised: "How could you say that You probably did not consider the Indian caste system which is in its convoluted and highly sophisticated structure the strongest connection and form the world has ever seen —".

I answered: "True, but the spirit of the caste system only mirrors the unconscious attempt to overcome and structure the chaos of the Indian existence by establishing an organic system. Therefore, it is a dialectic manifestation confirming the very reality of something it was called to reject on the first hand. An organizational structure in itself is not life, but seeks to overcome life. It seems to be necessary and even natural with regard to the Indian way of life that there is a contradistinction between the strict, even juristic formal caste system and an unrestricted, malleable mythological philosophy. This philosophy or *Weltanschauung* includes all kinds of beliefs, ranging from monotheism to the cult of the phallus. - So much for Hinduism. One should also not forget that Hinduism has already ceased to be the only religious phenomenon of India a long time ago, maybe it never was. Mohammedans constitute about one fourth of the whole population, and by saying this we are not even mentioning the communities that are lesser in number. It was not my intention to exclude the Mohammedans from this point of view: I am talking of the Indian nation as a whole; its chaotic, amorphous way of life is evident to me wherever I look. With respect to other people or nations it is possible to judge their character by paying attention to the details of their everyday lives, their physiognomy, their gestures and their way of dealing with one another. Not so with the Indians. They lack the gentle undertone in their mutual communication which characterizes other communities, harmonizing communication and underlining commonalities of a national character. Any defined mindset and style is completely missing when you look at the Indian nation. I define *style* as something that grows and develops naturally, it harmonizes the mental necessities with their practical implementation in life. In contrast, the term *mindset* describes an ongoing, harmonic, internal reaction to events taking place in the external world, either by an individual or by a group of people. Its most eminent feature is the ability to counter this externally imposed element with a distinctive individual integrity..."

The friend replied: "Now I understand what you are saying. Within the cultural framework of nations the *mindset* would describe an active, whereas *style* – despite its constantly changing nature – would describe the static element of a culture. By denying the Indian nation both you are certainly questioning entire phenomenon that are part of the Indian culture."

Responded I: "This is exactly what I am doing. Could we imagine Indian culture as clearly and distinctive as we would describe the culture of Confucian China? Certainly not. Within the evolution of the Indian nation several cultural spheres can be discerned, and we value them immensely, but there is no unified or homogeneous "all-Indian" sphere. The term "India" is indeed just of fictive nature, it claims to describe a wholeness that exists only as an imaginative notion. Even in a geographical sense India does not constitute a unity, but only an outwardly differentiated plurality. The ocean and towering mountain ranges separate it from the rest of the world, while in its interior free movement is not restricted by any impediments. This is surely a prerequisite for unity, but just imagine the vast extent of this region! It comprises an area as large as Europe without Russia, featuring all sorts of different climate zones from the mountains of the Himalaya, where during winters whole villages are buried in snow, down to the humid jungles of the South and East with their perennial tropical summers. We should not neglect all the other differences and the existence of desert regions with a population of only 2.5 per square kilometer while in the fertile areas of the Southwest, along the coasts of Malabar, Cohin and Travancore the population density could be as high as 1600 inhabitants per square kilometer. How far-reaching are therefore the results of social differences! And we should furthermore not forget how many migrations of peoples flooded the subcontinent, not to speak of wars and social changes, conquerors and invaders coming from all wind directions and various ethnic roots. They never fully amalgamated with one another, forming one coherent entity, but rather locked each other in separate ethnic groups, castes and communities defined by a shared worldview. However, we should not overestimate the role of race, although India seems to be a colourful kaleidoscope in this regard. It could be possible that the shape of the skull or differences of skin colour do not play such a decisive role as we are always inclined to think. Still, it is absolutely essential to unite distinct groups of peoples on grounds of a shared cultural identity if they shall grow together and form a nation. Geographic boundaries alone are not sufficient in defining this identity. Of course, a collective consciousness and memories of collective suffering, such as momentous events that were endured by the whole community and were perceived as having an effect on all different parts of it are facilitating the formation of a national identity. Collective memories help to establish a shared platform of spiritual and material expressions in which it becomes easier for the "I" and the "You" to relate to one another."

My friend spoke again: "So you are saying that the peoples of India are not a nation. Nevertheless, we Indians indeed feel that we are a nation. And the power of this sentiment needs no proof?"

I replied: "My dear friend! You confuse sense with being or existence. From an objective standpoint it is irrelevant whether someone who is eating his meal with me, who is hungry, in his imagination. It only becomes relevant when he actually offers me a real piece of bread. The same applies to the idea of a nation. Objectively speaking, it is irrelevant whether all single parts of a group "feel" that they constitute nation while in fact this is just an imaginary concept and not reality. But as soon as the making of a nation becomes a tangible fact and culminates into the creation of a nation state it influences the fabric of world history and its impact leaves the boundaries of that distinct group behind. For the time being, India's people cannot fall back upon a shared cultural space or a traditional community of fate, and that is the reason why they have no possibility to grow together. Let us for example take a look at the issue of a national language. The 1921 survey showed that 222 languages and dialects exist in India, 20 of them are not related to one another at all - actually, they are as distinct a language as many of the great European languages ..."

"But what about Urdu?", my friend said, interrupting me. "You have to admit that Urdu is clearly all-Indian in its character and it facilitates communication between its various parts perfectly."

I said: "Urdu is not the language of the commoner, it is the language of the élite and with the exception of northern India no one who does not belong to the learned circles is able to understand it. A fanner from Bengal traveling to southern India will probably make the same experience like a farmer from Spain going to Ukraine. They both will have difficulties to converse with each other. Just to stay with this metaphor: in the same sense we cannot speak of a "European Nation" there is also no justification to speak of an Indian nation as if it was reality. We even have to take into account that differences among the European nations are much less significant than among the various communities of India ... In the same way as the pan-European ideology is nothing more but an idle wish, the idea of an Indian nation is just a wish and a dream for now."

The friend replied: "But the developments in India during the last years contradict your theory completely! The Indian rebellion against foreign rule is indeed a national movement, it rests on a clearly discernible national consciousness. This movement left the sphere of "mere emotions" already a long time ago. It was realized by very dispassionate means, that is by action, and not only by feeling. Therefore, the nation who carries this consciousness has the right to be recognised as a substantiality. Or how else could it be possible that someone is conscious of an attitude which he never represented in the first place."

"Again you confuse the terms 'sense' and 'being'", I said to the friend. "Being is primary. Sense or feeling is secondary. A national consciousness is a secondary phenomenon and the movement resting on it only proofs that any feeling or emotion is strong enough to evoke an action. To identify the morphology of this action we have to go back to the roots of its motif and emotional impulse. Regarding the case of the Indian national consciousness this is a simple task. In the way it manifests itself today it is mostly of negative nature. It does not rest on a uniformly national character, but is rather an insurrection of India's peoples against a foreign domination that is perceived as being fully alien. Assuming that the British had settled permanently in India, as did so many conquering nations before them, they would have become nothing but one wave in the vast ocean of the Indian races, and no one would rebel against their reign. However, they are residing here as administrators and regents, having their roots elsewhere. This provokes the sense of being constantly discriminated by a foreign and ethnically different nation. As a result, it generates the illusion of communality among the many heterogeneous communities living on the same soil. With the end of foreign rule this illusion would be deprived of its main reason for existence, and most likely the idea of an Indian nation would disappear. On the contrary, it can be possible that persistent illusions take roots in the life of a nation. Indeed, they can gain the strength to develop this idea from a merely emotional state to the state of 'being', and when this happens the Indian nation, which does not exist today, might one day arise on the far horizon of history."

(in: *Neue Zürcher Zeitung* (Zürich), Sunday 11th December 1932, page 4)

Villa Asadiyya
La Montagne
TANGIER, Morocco

March 19, 1976

My dear Aslam, السلام عليكم ورحمة الله وبركاته

It was with infinite sadness that I received your news of the death of your father and my beloved friend. Although this news was expected for some time, it did not make it less painful. May God grant him all that he so richly deserved through his efforts and his exemplary life, and may He console you and your family for your own irreparable loss. As a matter of fact, I did not write to you for a long time because I was precisely afraid to receive such news as this.

إنا لله وإنا إليه راجعون

The enclosed few lines do not really express - and cannot express - what I felt for him in the course of the forty years of our friendship. I have no doubt, however, that his efforts will be long remembered and appreciated by all Muslims who came into contact with him or heard of him.

Hamida joins me, of course, in my feelings. Al though she did not know him as well as I did, she was always deeply impressed by his shining goodness and sincerity. The world is really a poorer place without him.

May God bless you all. Please keep in contact with us.

Yours as always,

Asad

Muhammad Asad's letter of condolence on Ch. Niaz 'Ali's death (1976)

M. Marmaduke Pickthall

II

MUHAMMAD ASAD'S *ISLAM AT THE CROSSROADS*

Mr. Muhammad Asad (Leopold Weiss) has written a book which is a notable contribution to what we may call the literature of Muslim regeneration, and the fact that he is a European by birth and education, a widely travelled and observant man, makes his achievement the more remarkable. After much study and deliberation he gives in *Islam on the Crossroads* his considered opinion that the safety of the Muslims, and therefore their hope of survival, lies only in complete observance of the *sunnah* of our Prophet. It is by no means a new thesis, being that of orthodoxy, but Mr. Asad's way of proving it on reasonable grounds is new and striking. His book is so full of interesting points that we should like to quote much more extensively than space allows. But some things we must quote in order to give the author his due. He derides the chimerical dream, cherished by some among us, of a Europe converted presently to Islam. He writes :

> "Europe was never farther from Islam than it is today. Its active hostility against our religion may be on the decline; this, however, is not due to an appreciation of the Islamic teachings, but to the growing cultural weakness and disintegration of the Islamic world. The West was once afraid of Islam, and their apprehension forced them to adopt an inimical attitude towards everything that had Islamic colour, even in purely spiritual and social matters. But in a time when Islam has lost most of its importance as a factor opposed to European interests, it is quite natural that with the diminished fear Europe should also lose some of the original intensity of its anti-Islamic feelings. If those feelings have become less

> pronounced and active, it does not entitle us to the conclusion that the West has inwardly come nearer to Islam; it only indicates its growing indifference towards Islam."

Muslims must rely for regeneration solely on their own efforts at revival and reform. Mr. Asad deplores the tendency to adopt an alien civilization.

"The tendency to imitate a foreign civilization is the outcome of a feeling of inferiority. This, and nothing else, is the matter with the Muslims who imitate the Western civilization. They contrast its power and technical skill and brilliant surface with the sad misery of the World of Islam: and they begin to believe that there is no way in our times but the Western way. To blame Islam for our own shortcomings is the fashion of the day. At the best, our so-called intellectuals adopt an apologetic attitude and try to convince themselves and others that Islam can well assimilate the spirit of the Western civilization.

"In order to achieve the regeneration of Islam, the Muslims must, before the adoption of any measures of reform, free themselves entirely from the spirit of apology for their religion. A Muslim must live with his head lifted high."

"Many proposals of reform have been brought forward during the last decades, and many spiritual doctors have tried to devise a patent medicine for the sick body of Islam. But, till now, all was in vain, because all those clever doctors—at least those who get a hearing today—have forgotten to prescribe along with their medicines and tonics and elixirs the natural *diet* on which the early development of the patient was based. This diet, the only one which the body of Islam, sound or sick, can positively accept and assimilate into its organism, is the Sunnah of our Prophet Muhammad (peace and blessings be upon him). The Sunnah is the key to the understanding of the Islamic rise more than thirteen centuries ago, and why should it not be a key to the understanding of our present degeneration? The observance of Sunnah is identical with Islamic existence and progress. The neglect of Sunnah is identical with decomposition and decay of Islam. The Sunnah was the iron framework of the House of Islam; and if you take away the framework out of a building, can you wonder that it breaks down like a house of cards ? This simple truth, almost unanimously accepted by all learned men throughout Islamic history, is—we know it well—most unpopular today for reasons connected with the evergrowing influence of the Western civilization. But it is a truth none the less, and, in fact, the only truth which can save us from the chaos and the shame of our present decay. The word Sunnah is used here in its widest meaning, namely, the example the Prophet has set before us in his actions and sayings.

"The Sunnah is so obviously opposed to the fundamental ideas underlying the Western civilization that those who are fascinated by the latter see no way out of the tangle but to denounce the Sunnah as being not compulsory for Muslims,—because it is 'based on unreliable traditions.' After this summary procedure it becomes easier to twist the teachings of the Quran till they appear to suit the spirit of the Western civilization."

Mr. Muhammad Asad has some very pertinent remarks to make concerning those who lightly question the authenticity of the whole body of Hadith. He points out the error of some "modern" Muslims not more strongly than Professor Krenkow in these pages recently pointed out the error of some European Orientalists, misleaders of the Muslims, in this respect.

"Many modern Muslims profess that they would be ready to follow the Sunnah, but they think they cannot rely upon the body of the Hadis on which it rests. It has become a matter of fashion in our days to deny, in principle, the authenticity of Hadis and, therefore, of the whole structure of the Sunnah. Is there any scientific warrant for this attitude? Is there any scientific justification for the rejection of the Hadis as a dependable source of the Islamic law?

"We should think that the opponents of orthodox thought would be able to bring forward really convincing arguments which would establish, once for all, the unreliability of the traditions ascribed to the Prophet. But this is not the case. In spite of all the efforts which have been employed to challenge the authenticity of the Hadis, those modern critics, both Eastern and Western, have not been able to back their purely temperamental criticism with results of scientific research. It would be rather difficult to do so, as the compilers of the early Hadis-collections, and particularly the Imam Bukhari and Muslim, have done whatever was humanly possible to put the reliability of every Tradition to a very rigorous test— a far more rigorous test than European historians usually apply to any sources of old history."

We think the author exaggerates a little in regarding modern civilization as essentially Satanic, and forgets how large a share Islam can claim in it historically—a larger share, we think, than Christianity can claim in it. Our view is that it represents that part of the Sunnah and the Shari'ah which Muslims have long failed to honour and observe—the part concerning education and material progress—but without the part which Muslims still hold fast, at any rate in theory, the part which regulates the lives and aims of men, and gives religious sanction and control, religious purpose to the progress of mankind as a whole; whence all its menace to the Muslim world and to itself. As Mr. Asad very justly remarks: "Reason knows its limits; but rationalism is preposterous in its claim to encompass the world and all its mysteries within its little individual circle. It hardly even concedes, in religious matters, the possibility of certain things being, temporarily or permanently, beyond the human understanding; but it is, at the same time, illogical enough to concede this possibility to science."

The book is so well written that one forgets that the author is not an Englishman. Very rarely do we find— as in the case of the title,—a wrong preposition or an unfamiliar turn of phrase—"Islam *on* the Crossroads" instead of "*at* the Crossroads." It is the most thoughtful and thought-stimulating work on the means of Islamic revival that has appeared since Prince Sa'id Halim Pasha's famous "Islamlashmaq." We are glad to learn, that it is being translated into Urdu.

(in: *Islamic Culture* (Hyderabad Deccan), October 1934, pp. 665-668)

III

A LIST OF MUHAMMAD ASAD'S ARTICLES in *Neue Zürcher Zeitung* (Zürich), published after his arrival in India (1932-1934)

1. Auf Langer Fahrt (On a long journey),
(6 Nov. 1932)
2. Gespräch in Indien (A conversation in India); Lahore, in September
(11 Dec. 1932)
3. Wer denkt an Kulu? (Who thinks about Kulu?)
(5 Feb. 1933)
4. Zur den Göttern von Kulu. I. (To Kulu's gods)
(12 Feb. 1933)
5. Zu den Göttern von Kulu. II. (To Kulu's gods)
(19 Feb. 1933)
6. Gandhis Fasten. I (Gandhi's fasts).
(4 June 1933)
7. Gandhis Fasten. II (Gandhi's fasts)
(9 June 1933)
8. Politische Probleme Indiens. I: Der rote Faden. (India's political problems. I: (The red threads) Delhi, in June.
(12 July 1933)
9. Politische Probleme Indiens. II: Die Geburt des Verfassungsentwurfs: (India's political problems. II: Origin of constitutional draft). Delhi, end of June.
(20 July 1933)
10. Politische Probleme Indiens. III: Nationalkongress und

Weiβbuch. (India's political problems. III: National Congress and book of wisdom). Delhi, end of June.

(25 July 1933)

11. Die Götter tanzen. (The gods dance). Kulu

(17 Sept. 1933)

12. Tempel und Gottsucher im Himalaya. (Temple and god-seeker in Himalaya).

(24 Sept. 1933)

13. Am Grat der Welt. I: Fahrt nach Kaschmir. (Edge of the world. I: Journey to Kashmir). Lahore, July

(1st Oct. 1933)

14. Am Grat der Welt. II: die Berge wachsen. (Edge of the world. II. The mountains keep watching. II: Talbei Tikes middle of July

(8 Oct. 1933)

15. Am Grat der Welt. III: (Edge of the world).

(15 Oct. 1933)

16. Am Grat der Welt. IV: (Edge of the world).

(22 Oct. 1933)

17. Syrische Reise. (Syrian journey)

(18 Feb. 1934)

18. Aleppo.

(29 July 1934)

19. Wüstenfahrt nach Baghdad. I: (Coastal journey to Baghdad).

(5 August 1934)

20. Wüstenfahrt nach Baghdad. II: (Coastal journey to Baghdad).

(12 August 1934)

21. Wüstenfahrt nach Baghdad. III: (Coastal journey to Baghdad).

(19 August 1934)

22. Die indische Bitternis. (The Indian bitterness). Delhi, early September.

(22 Sept. 1934)

GENERAL INDEX

A

B

C

D

E

K

L

O

P

Q

R

T

U

PHOTOGRAPHS

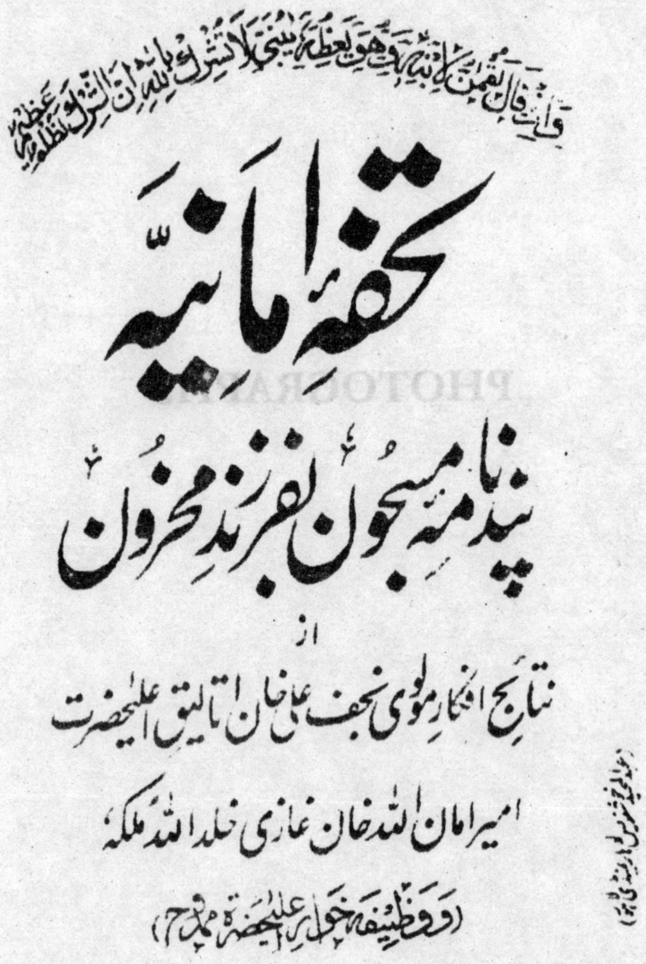

The title-page of "Tuhfa-i Imaniyyah" (in Persian verse), by Najaf Ali Khan, the brother of Dr. Abdul Ghani and teacher of Amanullah Khan, King of Afghanistan

The Kaaba, Mecca

The Mosque of the Prophet at Medina

Pilgrims near Arafat

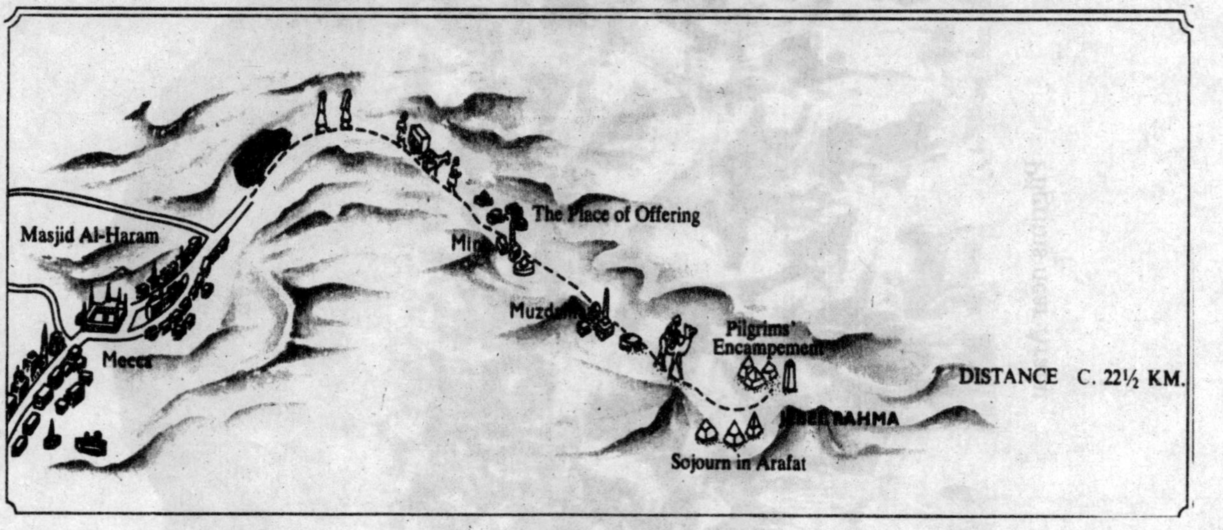

The Hajj Route from Mecca to Arafat

King ‘Abdul ‘Aziz Ibn Sa‘ud

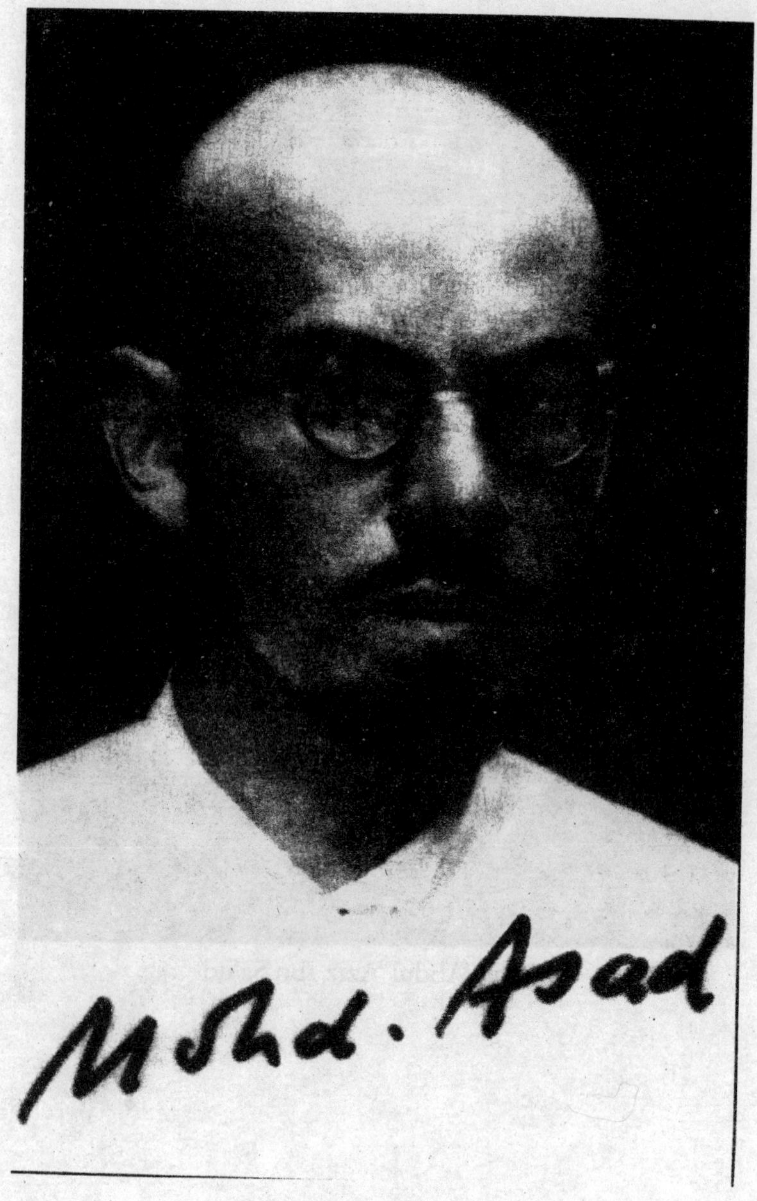

Muhammad Asad (1931)

Dr. Abdul Ghani

Abdul Ghani with Aghus Saleem

Madina Munawwara Bab al-Sham

King Faisal, Muhammad Asad's close friend

Elsa (Aziza) Schiemann (Shiraz, 1924)

Heinrich Ahmed Schiemann, M. Asad's step-son

Munira bint Hussain, M. Asad's Arabian wife with his son, Talal

Jamal ad-Din Afghani (1894)

Muhammad Iqbal

Ch. Niaz Ali (d. 1976)

Department of Islamic Reconstruction, West Punjab, Lahore (1948-49)

Muhammad Asad on Radio Pakistan, Lahore (1948)

Muhammad Asad's speech in Saudi Arabia as an official envoy

Muhammad Asad in UNO (1952)

Muhammad Asad in UNO, as Minister Plenipotentiary (1952)

Muhammad Asad with Zafrullah Khan, Foreign Minister of Pakistan (1952)

Muhammad Asad in a session of UNO (1952)

Muhammad Asad in UNO (1952)

Muhammad Asad in UNO, meeting with other delegates ((1953)

Muhammad Asad's wife, Pola Hamida Asad (1957)

Muhammad Asad, Pola Hamida Asad, Javid Iqbal and others

In Jawharabad (Pakistan) 1957
Sitting: Muhammad Asad, Pola Hamida Asad.
Standing from left: Zeenat Ara, Ch. Niaz Ali, Shawkat Ara, Afzal Khan, Sawlat Ara. (Private Collection, K. M. Azam)

Muhammad Asad (1982)

Muhammad Asad (1984)

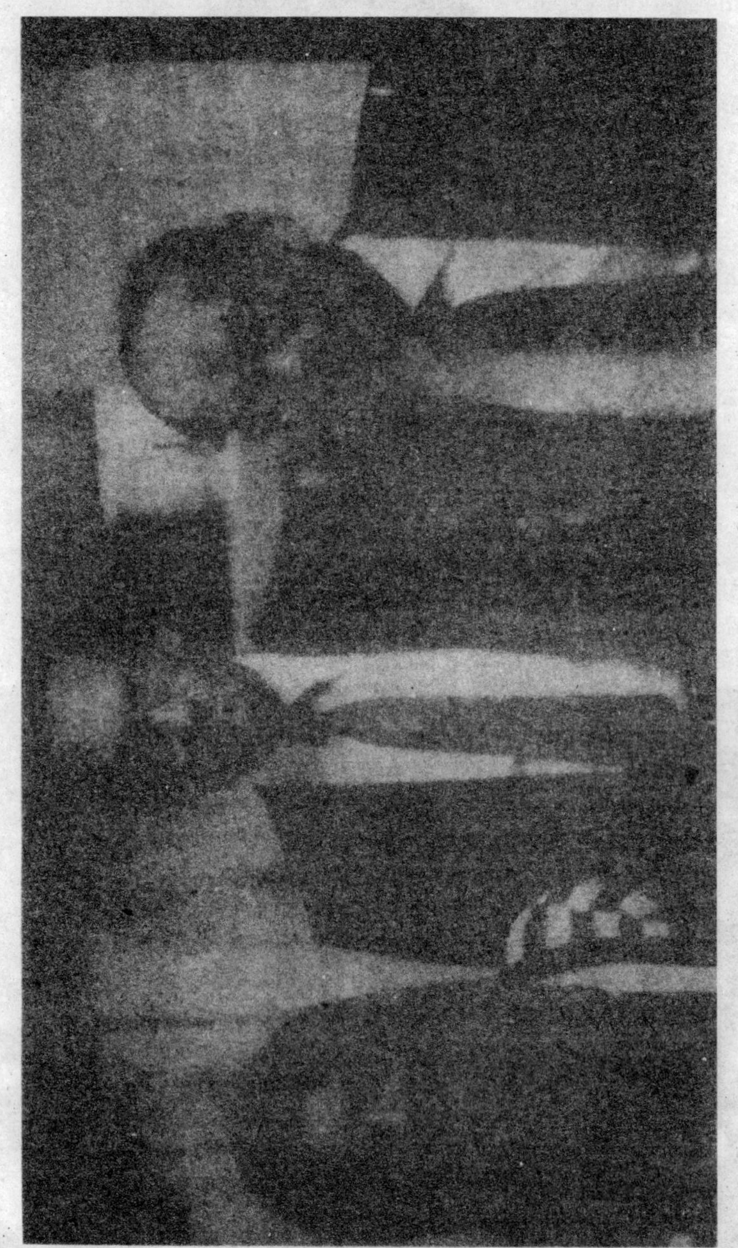

Muhammad Asad, Murad Hofmann and Pola Hamida Asad (1985)

Muhammad Asad (1986)

Muhammad Asad (1988)

Pola Hamida Asad, Muhammad Asad, Khaled Ahmed, Ambassador Birjis Hassan Khan

Muhammad Asad: a few months before his death (1992)

Muhammad Asad's grave (Muslim Cemetery, Granada, Spain)